An Introduction to IMS™

An Introduction to IMS™

Your Complete Guide to IBM's Information Management System

IMS   Information Management Software

Dean Meltz   **Robert Hain**
Rick Long   **Geoff Nicholls**
Mark Harrington

IBM Press
Pearson plc

Upper Saddle River, NJ • Boston • Indianapolis
San Francisco • New York • Toronto • Montreal • London
Munich • Paris • Madrid • Capetown • Sydney • Tokyo
Singapore • Mexico City

ww.phptr.com/ibmpress

The authors and publisher have taken care in the preparation of this book, but make no expressed or implied warranty of any kind and assume no responsibility for errors or omissions. No liability is assumed for incidental or consequential damages in connection with or arising out of the use of the information or programs contained herein.

IBM Press Program Manager: Tara Woodman, Ellice Uffer
IBM Press Consulting Editor: Susan Visser
Cover design: IBM Corporation
Published by Pearson plc
Publishing as IBM Press

Library of Congress Cataloging-in-Publication Data:

An introduction to IMS: your complete guide to IBM's information management system / Dean Meltz ... [et al.].
    p. cm.
 Includes bibliographical references and indexes.
 ISBN 0-13-185671-5 (hardcover : alk. paper)
 1. Management information systems. I. Meltz, Dean. II. Title.

T58.6.I598 2004
658.4'038'011--dc22

2004027560

ISBN 0-13-185671-5

Text printed in the United States on recycled paper at Courier in Westford, Massachusetts.

Second printing, January 2005

CONTENTS _____

CHAPTER 24   Operating IMS   405

CHAPTER 25   IMS System Recovery   439

CHAPTER 26   IBM IMS Tools   443

FIGURES _____

TABLES _____

FOREWORD _____

Welcome to the world of IMS, my world. I have been involved with IMS since 1966. My goal has always been to make IMS as useful as possible. To that end, we in IMS have solicited input from our customers, which we used as requirements for new functions and features to make IMS a more useful product.

Today's IMS has only a superficial resemblance to the product (IMS 360 V1) that we shipped in 1969. An application program that ran on IMS in 1969, however, will still run today, unchanged, on the latest release of IMS. The most important rule for IMS developers all along has been to provide application program compatibility; we should never require a customer to change their application programs in any way to run on a new version of IMS.

I believe a lot of the success IMS has enjoyed is due to our commitment to our customers that their applications will continue to run on all the IMS versions released.

IMS is available as both a transaction manager (IMS TM) and a database manager (IMS DB), which can be used individually or together. IMS DB can be used with other transaction managers, such as IBM's Customer Information Control System (CICS). IMS TM can be used with other database managers, such as DB2 Universal Database for z/OS.

In the mid-1960s, IBM announced and released the System/360, a system that allowed a large number of terminals to be connected to the mainframe. System/360 initiated the start of a revolutionary change in the way data processing was performed in our customers' shops. It was the start of online processing.

In 1966, I was part of a team that was assigned to help a customer connect hundreds of terminals to a single mainframe computer. One of the problems we faced was the complex programming that was required in every application to manage terminals. This was the state-of-the-art in programming design back then. It became obvious to us that requiring each application programmer to provide all the coding necessary to manage the terminals would greatly impede the growth of applications. A different approach was needed.

We came up with a design that defined transactions as the basis for online processing. Transactions in IMS were specified by a transaction code, a character string of length one to eight bytes, and staged for processing on a queue on disk storage. The idea of transactions:

- Enabled the customers to focus the design of their applications on manipulating the data and implementing their business goals.
- Liberated the customers' application developers from having to deal with the complexities of terminal communications.

The user on the terminal would enter the transaction code followed by the required data and send it to IMS. IMS handled all the complexities of managing the terminal and placed the message containing the user data on the appropriate queue. IMS then would schedule the correct application program, which only had to deal with data from the queue.

This design from 1966 is still the basic structure of IMS online systems.

Another major concern was the integrity of message processing and database changes. We journal all events to be sure that all messages that are received are actually processed and that all output messages are actually delivered. We allow the customer to specify that some messages can be designated as non-recoverable (meaning that we do not need to keep track of them). We also provide utility services so our customers can make back up copies of data, which can be combined with copies of data changes (from the journals) to recover data that is lost through hardware failures or other types of failures.

We feel that the growth in IMS usage over the past 35 years provides evidence that our strategies were correct. The integrity and reliability of IMS and its databases are major reasons for its current popularity.

IMS is a growing product. Each new version brings with it a list of new functions and features that have been requested by our customers to make the product more usable. Far from being a dead product, it is a vital and changing product that stays current.

IMS maintains its interfaces for user programs throughout changes to preserve the customer investment in application development. As an example of our support for older applications, I offer the following story that we experienced with one of our early customers:

IMS provides a Language Interface module that is linked with application programs to pass calls into IMS. The first version of this module (in 1968) was not reentrant. We corrected that in 1970 when we provided a reentrant copy of the Language Interface. We assumed that over time, all our customers' application programs would eventually be modified and would then be relinked with the new interface. Meanwhile, we supported both versions of the Language Interface. Finally, in 1973 or 1974, we removed support for the non-reentrant version of the Language Interface. We were immediately notified by a customer that one of their application programs that had not changed since 1969, was failing. We quickly restored support for the non-reentrant module and the customer was able to continue using the old program. To the best of my knowledge, this application program continues to run today exactly as it did in 1969. I am not aware of any other active program offering that has preserved the user interface, like IMS has, through so many versions.

Our original target customer set was manufacturing, but we were careful to keep IMS as general as possible so as not to tailor our system to only that environment. Thanks to this effort, IMS has been successful in many environments such as finance, banking, government, and many others.

We have always encouraged our users to emphasize their applications that run on IMS, rather than focusing on IMS itself. The result has been that many of our customers (as well as our customers' customers) do not know that their work is being performed on IMS. This is one of the reasons this book is important; to help people understand the importance of IMS in today's world of data processing.

—Vern Watts
IBM IMS Distinguished Engineer Emeritus

PREFACE

IBM Information Management System (IMS) is one of the world's premiere software products. Period. IMS is not in the news and is barely mentioned in today's computer science classes, but it has been and, for the foreseeable future, will continue to be, a major, crucial component of the world's software infrastructure.

From its beginnings with NASA, IMS has provided the foundation that enables government agencies and businesses to manage, access, manipulate, and exploit their vast stores of data. As the Information Age evolves and matures, so does IMS.

The purpose of this book is twofold.

- To introduce IMS to those who have not yet heard about it and provide basic education about this cornerstone product.
- To reintroduce IMS to the computer science field in general.

PREREQUISITE KNOWLEDGE

Before reading this book

- You should be able to describe the fundamentals of data processing, including the function of operating systems, access methods, and job control language (JCL). Specifically, you should be familiar with the z/OS operating system or any of its predecessors. The authors of this book assume that most readers are data processing professionals.
- You should also have access to the IMS Version 9 library because there are many references in this book to the IMS Version 9 manuals. These manuals are listed in the Bibliography. You can either read the IMS manuals online or download them from the Library page of the IMS Web site. Go to www.ibm.com/ims and click on the "Library" link in the navigation pane on the left side of the page.

HOW TO SEND YOUR COMMENTS

Your feedback is important in helping us provide the most accurate and highest quality information. If you have any comments about this or any other IMS information, you can take one of the following actions.

- Go to the IMS Library page at www.ibm.com/software/data/ims/library.html and click the Library Feedback link, where you can enter and submit comments.
- Send your comments by e-mail to imspubs@us.ibm.com. Be sure to include the title, the part number of the title, the version of IMS, and, if applicable, the specific location of the text on which you are commenting.

ACKNOWLEDGMENTS

This book would not be possible without the input and efforts of many people. Some of them are listed here. I give my wholehearted thanks to everyone for their participation in and support of this project.

- Rick Long, Mark Harrington, Robert Hain, and Geoff Nicholls (IBM IMS Field Specialists) for the information in the IMS Primer that they developed and was the foundation for this book.
- Kenneth R. Blackman (IBM IMS Field Specialist) for information from his Technical note "IMS Celebrates Thirty Years as an IBM Product."
- Barbara Klein (IBM IMS Brand Manager) and Robert Gilliam (IMS Product Manager) for the use of information from their presentation, "After 36 Years IMS is Still Strategic—for our Customers and for IBM."
- Rolf-Dieter Koch (Sparkassen Informatik System Programmer) and Hannelore Nestinger (IBM IMS IT Specialist) for their guidance and participation in the writing of this book.
- Rich Lewis and Bill Stillwell (IBM Dallas Systems Center) for the use of information from their presentation, "IMS in a Parallel Sysplex®."
- Pete Sadler (IBM IMS IT Specialist) for his extensive review comments.
- The IBM IMS Development and Service organizations for their input, review comments, and answers to questions during the development of this book.
- The IBM Silicon Valley Lab User Technology Management (Tim Hogan, Janet Ikemiya, and Lori Fisher) for recognizing the need for this book and supporting its development.

- The IMS User Technology Department for supporting me in this endeavor with encouraging words, review comments, editorial comments, material from other IMS books, and time, especially Moira M. Lanyi (Technical Editor for IMS) for her in-depth edit.
- Robert Lee (Visual Designer for IMS User Technology) for the wonderful graphics in this book.
- Vern Watts (IBM IMS Distinguished Engineer Emeritus and member of the original IMS Development Team) for his vision, his inspiration for this project, and his words in the Foreword.
- Finally, my wife, Judy Meltz, who unselfishly encouraged and supported me (in spite of the many hours and weekends I worked) in my efforts to bring this book to completion.

—Dean H. Meltz
IMS User Technology

ABOUT THE AUTHORS ___

Dean H. Meltz is team lead for IMS Information Development at IBM's Silicon Valley Lab, in San Jose, California. He has been an IBM technical writer for seventeen years.

Rick Long, IMS systems specialist with IBM's International Technical Support Organization (ITSO), writes about IMS and teaches IMS classes worldwide. He was previously an IMS systems programmer for IBM Global Services, Australia.

Mark Harrington, IMS systems programmer at IBM Global Services, UK, has spent twenty-two years working with IBM mainframes as a developer, application designer, installer, and DBA.

Robert Hain has been an IMS systems programmer for seventeen years. He works for IBM Global Services, Melbourne, Australia, as part of the Telstra Alliance.

Geoff Nicholls, a member of IBM's Worldwide IMS Technical Support Team, works with IMS customers throughout Australia and Asia.

Overview of IMS

CHAPTER 1

IMS:Then and Now

This chapter presents IMS's past and discusses IMS as a strategic part of today's computing environment.

In This Chapter:

- "History of IMS: Beginnings at NASA"
- "Is IMS Still Strategic for Customers and IBM?" on page 4

HISTORY OF IMS: BEGINNINGS AT NASA

IMS has been an important part of world wide computing since its inception.

On May 25, 1961, United States President John F. Kennedy challenged American industry to send an American man to the moon and return him safely to earth. The feat was to be accomplished before the end of the decade, as part of the Apollo program. American Rockwell won the bid to build the spacecraft for the Apollo program and, in 1965, they established a partnership with IBM to fulfill the requirement for an automated system to manage large bills of material for the construction of the spacecraft.

In 1966, 12 members of the IBM team, along with 10 members from American Rockwell and 3 members from Caterpillar Tractor, began to design and develop the system that was called Information Control System and Data Language/Interface (ICS/DL/I). During the design and development process, the IBM team was moved to Los Angeles and increased to 21 members. The IBM team completed and shipped the first release of ICS in 1967.

In April 1968, ICS was installed. The first "READY" message was displayed on an IBM 2740 typewriter terminal at the Rockwell Space Division at NASA in Downey, California, on August 14, 1968.

In 1969, ICS was renamed to Information Management System/360 (IMS/360) and became available to the IT world.

Since 1968, IMS:

- Helped NASA fulfill President Kennedy's dream.
- Started the database management system revolution.
- Continues to evolve to meet and exceed the data processing requirements demanded by today's businesses and governments.

IMS as a Database Management System

The IMS database management system (DBMS) introduced the idea that application code should be separate from the data. The point of separation was the Data Language/Interface (DL/I). IMS controls the access and recovery of the data. Application programs can still access and navigate through the data by using the DL/I standard callable interface.

This separation established a new paradigm for application programming. The application code could now focus on the manipulation of data without the complications and overhead associated with the access and recovery of data. This paradigm virtually eliminated the need for redundant copies of the data. Multiple applications could access and update a single instance of data, thus providing current data for each application. Online access to data also became easier because the application code was separated from data control.

IMS as a Transaction Manager

IBM developed an online component to ICS/DL/I to support data communication access to the databases. The DL/I callable interface was expanded to the online component of the product to enable data communication transparency to the application programs. A message queue function was created to maintain the integrity of data communication messages and to provide for scheduling of the application programs.

The online component to ICS/DL/I ultimately became the Data Communications (DC) function of IMS, which became the IMS Transaction Manager (IMS TM) in IMS Version 4.

IS IMS STILL STRATEGIC FOR CUSTOMERS AND IBM?

IMS joined the mainframe platform officially in 1969. Like the mainframe, IMS has continued to thrive, enjoying its most successful sales year ever in 2003. IMS has successfully reinvented itself many times over those years and its list of state-of-the-art technological innovations is far too lengthy to reproduce here. However, given that there are few, if any, software products still around after all these years, a fair question might be, "Is IMS still strategic?"

The word *strategic* means different things to different people.

For addressing customer needs, the word strategic can be defined by answering the following question:

- Is IMS delivering new functions that fulfill important and essential roles in relation to our customers' goals and objectives?

For addressing IBM's needs, the word strategic can be defined by answering the following questions:

- Is new IMS function consistent with the IBM strategy for the on demand operating environment?
- Is IMS providing sufficient return on IBM's significant investment in IMS to warrant such a strong continued IBM commitment to IMS development?

The following sections consider each of these questions.

IMS Is Strategic for Addressing Customer Needs

Customer acceptance of new IMS versions is the best measure of its strategic value. In 2003, the IMS workload, as measured in the millions of instructions per second (MIPS) capacity of IMS systems, increased 67.9% on our latest versions. At the end of 2003, there was almost three times more work being done on our latest versions, Version 7 and Version 8, than on older versions, Versions 5 and 6, worldwide. Overall, in 2003, MIPS of IMS systems grew almost 20%. By midyear, IMS Version 7 surpassed IMS Version 6 as the most popular version, measured by number of licenses.

Overall, the growth of net new IMS licenses remained positive, fueled largely by expansions required because of mergers and acquisitions among existing customers (in the Americas and Europe) and the selection of IMS for new zSeries® footprints (predominantly by emerging opportunities in Asia). It is noteworthy that customers showed continued confidence in the future of IMS during the years 2001–2003, when much of the rest of the IT industry was showing a downturn and retrenchment.

Who Uses IMS

Over 90% of the top world wide companies in the following industries use IMS to run their daily operations:

- Manufacturing
- Finance
- Banking
- Retailing
- Aerospace
- Communications

- Government
- Insurance
- High technology
- Health care

The following quote is an example of how one analyst[1] views IMS:

> A 35-year-old hierarchical database and transaction processing system is currently growing faster than the world's most popular relational database system. Pretty funny, huh?
>
> Actually, IMS is not forging new ground with innovative marketing or customer-acquisition strategies. It's more the other way around—it's keeping the same old customer base, but the base is growing, a lot. IMS and the mainframes it runs on underpin the vast majority of banks and banking transactions worldwide. And the banking world is growing. China alone may provide more growth in the next few years than the rest of world has in the last decade, and it is certainly not the only Pacific Rim country modernizing its banking system. Combine that kind of geographic growth with advances in online banking in the developed world and it's no wonder mainframes, especially IBM's newer zSeries machines, and IMS are growing. They're the only products capable of keeping up.

IMS is still a viable, even unmatched, platform to implement very large online transaction processing (OLTP) systems and, in combination with Web Application Server technology, it is the foundation for a new generation of Web-based, high-workload applications.

Here are some interesting facts about how IMS is used.

IMS manages a large percentage of the world's corporate data.

- Over 95% of Fortune 1000 companies use IMS.
- IMS manages over 15 million gigabytes of production data.
- $2.5 trillion (in US dollars) per day is transferred through IMS by one customer.

IMS processes over 50 billion transactions per day.

- IMS serves over 200 million users every day.
- IMS processes over 100 million transactions per day for one customer.
- IMS processes over 120 million transactions per day (7 million per hour) for another customer.
- IMS can process 21,000 transactions per second (over 1 billion[2] per day) using IMS data sharing and shared queues.
- A single IMS has processed over 6000 transactions per second over a single TCP/IP connection.

---

1.   Quote taken from abstract of *IMS: Scaling the Wall*, Illuminata, Inc., November 2002. Illuminata is an IT advisory firm (see www.illuminata.com).

2.   1 billion = 10e9.

Related Reading: To learn more about the industries and customers that use IMS, visit the IMS Web site at www.ibm.com/ims, and click "Featured Customer," "IMS Newsletter," or "Overview."

IMS is Strategic for Addressing IBM Needs

IMS's strategic value to IBM can be measured in three areas:

- "IMS Is Strategic in the On Demand Infrastructure"
- "IMS Is Strategic Regarding Continued Investment" on page 8
- "IMS Is Strategic for the Future" on page 8

IMS Is Strategic in the On Demand Infrastructure

IBM defines an on demand enterprise as one whose business processes are integrated end-to-end across the company and with key partners, suppliers, and customers. An on demand enterprise can respond with flexibility and speed to any customer demand, any market opportunity, and any external threat. This need to respond with urgency must be addressed by an on demand infrastructure. This infrastructure is:

Based on open standards. IMS fully supports Java standards for application development and XML for transparent document interchange.

Heterogeneous. IMS applications can be developed on workstations and executed in the host environment. IMS applications and data can be accessed from any platform, including Linux, virtually anywhere on the Internet, through the utilization of the IMS Connect function and the IMS Connector for Java.

Integrated. Integration has always been an IMS priority. IMS ships connectors and tooling with IBM WebSphere® solutions so customers can connect to IMS applications and data utilizing the tools and connectors of their choice.

Scalable. IMS continues to address scalability needs by providing the highest possible availability, performance, and capacity. IMS Version 8 benchmarks show a single system providing 21,000 transactions, including database access, per second. IMS Version 9 continues this performance and offers 24×7 database availability with High Availability Large Database Online Reorganization support.

Enabled with self-managing capabilities. IMS Version 8 and Version 9 address the need to assist technical support staff in being more productive, keep systems continuously available, and do so in an operating environment that is growing more and more complex. IMS Version 8 contains over a dozen new and improved self-managing functions to enhance the productivity and effectiveness of database administrators and systems programmers. These functions and more are available with IMS Version 9.

Reliable. One large IMS customer has operated over 3000 days (and counting) without an outage in a 24×7 environment.

IMS Is Strategic Regarding Continued Investment

The ability of the IMS team to deliver revenue growth to the IBM company is a measure of our success as business managers. Success in this area supports continued investment by IBM in the development of future versions and the growth of resources devoted to that effort. In 2003, IMS enjoyed another record breaking year, surpassing 2002 as the largest revenue producing year in its 35-plus year history. In the first two quarters of 2004, IMS's revenue grew 9% (year to year).

IMS has shown consistent revenue growth each year since adopting the current IMS business model in 2000.

IMS Is Strategic for the Future

The focus for IMS in 2004, and beyond, is striving to remain the strategic choice for:

- The most business-critical applications of our current customers.
- The most business-critical applications of emerging enterprises.

Success in that area and support of the open, integrated, self-managing, on demand operating environment, suggest that IMS will continue as a major factor in the growth strategy of the IBM Corporation, as it has been for the past 36 years.

CHAPTER 2

Overview of the IMS Product

MS consists of three components:

- The Database Manager (IMS DB)
- The Transaction Manager (IMS TM)
- A set of system services that provide common services to IMS DB and IMS TM

Known collectively as IMS DB/DC,[1] the three components create a complete online transaction processing environment that provides continuous availability and data integrity. The functions provided by these components are described in more detail later in this book.

IMS delivers accurate, consistent, timely, and critical information to application programs, which deliver the information to many end users simultaneously.

IMS has been developed to provide an environment for applications that require very high levels of performance, throughput, and availability. IMS uses many of the facilities offered by the operating system and hardware. Currently, IMS runs on z/OS and on zSeries hardware.

IMS TM and IMS DB can be ordered and paid for separately if the functions of one component are not required. The appropriate system services are provided for the component ordered. When IMS DB is ordered by itself, it is called DB control (DBCTL). When IMS TM is ordered by itself, it is called DC control (DCCTL).

---

1. The "DC" in DB/DC is a left-over acronym from when the Transaction Manager was called the Data Communications function of IMS.

IMS is developed so that each new release of IMS is upwardly compatible, meaning that applications that were written for a previous release of IMS will run without modification (in most cases) with a new release. In this way, IMS protects the investment that our customers have made in their applications.

To accommodate the changing requirements of IT systems, many new features have been added to IMS over the years. In many instances, older features have been wholly or partially superseded by the newer features that provide better functionality.

Application programs that are written to use IMS functions can be written in a number of programming languages: Assembler, C/C++, COBOL, Java, Pascal, PL/I, and REXX. These applications access IMS resources by calling a number of standard IMS functions through standard application programming interfaces (APIs):

- DL/I
- Java database connectivity (JDBC)

In This Chapter:

- "IMS Database Manager"
- "IMS Transaction Manager" on page 12
- "IMS System Services" on page 13
- "IMS Documentation" on page 13
- "Hardware and Software Requirements for IMS" on page 13

IMS DATABASE MANAGER

IMS DB is a DBMS that helps you organize business data with both program and device independence.

Hierarchical databases and data manipulation language (DL/I calls) are at the heart of IMS DB. Data within the database is arranged in a tree structure, with data at each level of the hierarchy related to, and in some way dependent upon, data at the higher level of the hierarchy. Figure 2-1 on page 11 shows the hierarchical database model. In a hierarchical database, data is stored within the database only once. The data item is then available to any user who is authorized to use it. Users do not need to have personal copies of the data.

With IMS DB, you can:

- Maintain data integrity. The data in each database is guaranteed to be consistent and guaranteed to remain in the database even when IMS DB is not running.
- Define the database structure and the relationships among the database elements.
- Provide a central point of control and access for the IMS data that is processed by IMS applications.

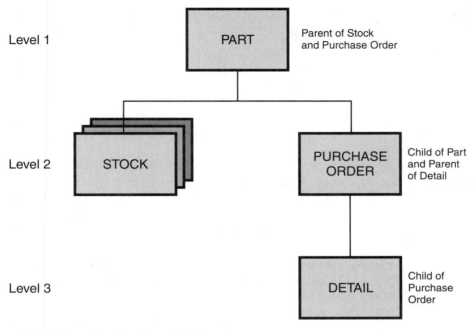

Figure 2-1   Hierarchical Database Model

- Perform queries against the data in the database.
- Perform database transactions (inserts, updates, and deletes) as a single unit of work so that the entire transaction either occurs or does not occur.
- Perform multiple database transactions concurrently with the results of each transaction kept isolated from the others.
- Maintain the databases. IMS DB provides facilities for tuning the databases by reorganizing and restructuring them.

Additionally, IMS DB lets you adapt IMS databases to the requirements of varied applications. Application programs can access common and, therefore, consistent data, thereby reducing the need to maintain the same data in multiple ways in separate files for different applications.

IMS databases are accessed internally using a number of IMS's database organization access methods. The actual database data is stored on disk storage using normal z/OS access methods. See "IMS Hierarchical Access Methods" on page 87 for more information.

IMS DB provides access to these databases from applications running under:

- IMS Transaction Manager
- CICS Transaction Server for OS/390® and z/OS
- z/OS batch jobs
- WebSphere Application Server for z/OS
- DB2 UDB for z/OS stored procedures

Related Reading: For more information about IMS DB, see Part II, "IMS Database Manager," on page 59.

IMS TRANSACTION MANAGER

IMS TM is a message-based transaction processor.

> ## DEFINITIONS:
>
> - A *transaction* is a specific set of input data that triggers the execution of a specific business application program (a process or job). The message that triggers the application program, and the return of any results, is considered one transaction.
>
> - The word *terminal* is used throughout this book to describe devices and controllers. The operator terminals can be keyboard printers, display stations with keyboards, communication terminals, or a mixture of these devices.

IMS TM provides services to:

- Process input messages received from a variety of sources (such as the terminal network, other IMSs, and the Web).
- Process output messages created by application programs.
- Provide an underlying queueing mechanism for handling these messages.
- Provide high-volume, high-performance, high-capacity, low-cost transaction processing for both IMS DB's hierarchical databases and DB2's relational databases.

IMS TM supports many terminal sessions (on a wide variety of terminals and devices) at extremely high transaction volumes. The users of the terminal sessions can be:

- People at terminals or workstations.
- Other application programs, either on the same z/OS system, on other z/OS systems, or on non-z/OS platforms.

When IMS TM is used in conjunction with a database manager, IMS TM extends the facilities of the database manager to the online, real-time environment. IMS TM enables terminals, other devices, and subsystems to enter transactions that initiate application programs, which access IMS DB or DB2 databases and return results.

You can define a variety of online processing options. For example, you can define transactions for high-volume data-entry applications, others for interactive applications, and still others to support predefined queries.

IMS TM also enables you to develop a wide range of high-volume, rapid-response applications, and to geographically disperse your data processing locations while keeping centralized control of your database.

Related Reading: For more information about IMS TM, see Part III, "IMS Transaction Manager," on page 167.

IMS SYSTEM SERVICES

IMS System Services provide the following services to both IMS DB and IMS TM:

- Provide data integrity
- Restart and recover IMS after failures
- Provide security, by controlling access to and modification of IMS resources
- Manage the application programs, by dispatching work, loading application programs, and providing locking services
- Provide diagnostic and performance information
- Provide facilities for operating IMS
- Provide interfaces to other z/OS subsystems that communicate with IMS applications

The IMS System Services are, by:

- Issuing IMS commands
- Running IMS-supplied utility programs
- Running IMS-supplied or user-written exit routines
- Defining the services you want as part of the system definition process

IMS DOCUMENTATION

There are many sources of documentation for IMS (for example, the IMS library, Redbooks, white papers, presentations from technical conferences, and so forth). Some are listed in the "Bibliography" on page 521. For the most up-to-date documentation, always check the Library page of the IMS Web site at www.ibm.com/ims.

HARDWARE AND SOFTWARE REQUIREMENTS FOR IMS

This section briefly describes the hardware and software that is required by IMS Version 9.

Related Reading: For the complete details about the hardware and software requirements and compatibility of IMS releases with versions of the operating system and associated products, see the following release planning guides:

- *IMS Version 7: Release Planning Guide*
- *IMS Version 8: Release Planning Guide*
- *IMS Version 9: Release Planning Guide*

Hardware

IMS Version 9 runs on all IBM processors that are capable of running z/OS System Product Version 1 Release 4 or later. IMS Version 9 can run on either 64-bit processors or 32-bit processors.

For all system libraries and working storage space, any device that is supported by the operating system is allowed.

For IMS database storage, any device that is supported by the operating system is allowed within the capabilities and restrictions of Basic Sequential Access Method (BSAM), Queued Sequential Access Method (QSAM), Overflow Sequential Access Method (OSAM), and Virtual Storage Access Method (VSAM).

Details about the DASD storage requirements for the following items are listed in *IMS Version 9: Program Directory for Information Management System Transaction and Database Servers*:

- SMP/E system entries
- SMP/E data sets
- Target libraries
- Distribution libraries
- Install process
- Optional machine-readable material

Software

IMS Version 9 operates in z/OS Version 1 Release 4 (or later) configurations and requires the following minimum version, release, or modification levels:

- z/OS Version 1 Release 4 (5694-A01)
    - DFSMS*
    - SMP/E*
    - JES2*
    - JES3*
    - TSO/E*

> **N O T E** * These items are base elements of the z/OS operating environment that cannot be ordered separately.

— IBM High-Level Assembler Toolkit (5696-234), a separately orderable feature of z/OS
— RACF® (available with the IBM SecureWay® Security Server for z/OS and OS/390 RACF product) or equivalent product, if security is used
— ISPF Version 4 Release 2 (5655-042)
— e-Network Communications Server for z/OS, if IMS Transaction Manager is used
- IRLM Version 2.1 or later (5655-DB2), if data sharing is used

IMS Version 9 also operates in a virtual machine (VM) under the control of z/OS Version 1 Release 4. This environment is intended for use in a program development, testing, and non-XRF production environment.

CICS Subsystems Supported
IMS DB Version 9 can be connected (using the IMS Database Resource Adapter) to the following systems:

- CICS Transaction Server for z/OS Version 2.2 (5697-E93)
- CICS Transaction Server for OS/390 Version 1.3 (5655-147)

IMS TM Version 9 can be connected (using the appropriate TM interface) to the following systems:

- CICS Transaction Server for z/OS Version 2.2 (5697-E93)
- CICS Transaction Server for OS/390 Version 1.3 (5655-147)

DB2 Subsystems Supported
IMS TM Version 9 can be connected to any of the following DB2 products:

- DB2 UDB for z/OS Version 8 (5625-DB2)
- DB2 for z/OS and OS/390 Version 7 (5675-DB2)
- DB2 Universal Database for OS/390 Version 6 (5645-DB2)

Programming Language
IMS Version 9 is written in High Level Assembler Release 2, PL/X, C, C++, and Java JDK Version 1.3.

Programming Languages Supported

You can write IMS applications in the current versions of the following languages:

- ADA
- COBOL for OS/390 & VM
- Enterprise COBOL for z/OS and OS/390
- High Level Assembler for MVS™ & VM & VSE Version 1 Release 4.0
- IBM SDK for z/OS Java 2 Technology Edition, Version 1.3.1
- PL/I for z/OS and OS/390
- TSO/E REXX
- VS Pascal
- WebSphere Studio Site Developer Version 5.0
- z/OS C/C++

> **REQUIREMENT:**   The following languages require the
> IBM Language Environment® for z/OS:
>
> - COBOL for OS/390 & VM
> - PL/I for z/OS and OS/390

CHAPTER 3

Accessing IMS

 n a broad sense, *accessing* IMS means telling IMS to perform work for you.

- You can write application programs that tell IMS what to do.
- You can use existing application programs that tell IMS what to do.

These application programs can run in many different environments. They tell IMS what to do by calling a number of standard IMS functions through standard APIs: DL/I and JDBC.[1]

In This Chapter:

- "Accessing IMS from Application Programs"
- "Accessing IMS from Other Products" on page 22

Related Reading: For information about writing IMS application programs, see Part IV, "IMS Application Development," on page 215.

ACCESSING IMS FROM APPLICATION PROGRAMS

Application programs that directly use the DL/I interface do so by issuing DL/I calls. Application programs that use the JDBC interface do so by issuing standard SQL (structured query language) calls.

---

1. The IMS implementation of JDBC supports a selected subset of the full facilities of the JDBC 2.1 API.

Accessing IMS by Using DL/I Calls

DL/I is a standard interface to IMS functions that has been in place since IMS's inception. Most of the IMS application programs that have been written over the years are still providing the service for which they were designed. As business needs have evolved, these application programs have either evolved or have become a base for new application programs to meet the new business needs. In many cases, the application programs that run today's businesses are not individual programs, but are a number of layers of application programs that work together to implement the businesses' information technology (IT) infrastructure.

To illustrate how IMS business application programs have evolved, Figure 3-1 on page 19 shows a simple, hypothetical IMS application program that accesses a checking account database through DL/I. Assume that this application program was written 20 years ago, was written in COBOL, and was designed to support IBM 3270 (non-programmable) terminals. There are many such application programs that still run as originally written and provide this kind of support for the banking industry.

Figure 3-1 illustrates the following processing models:

- **Traditional processing model:** The objects on the left side of Figure 3-1 represent the traditional processing model that includes the following components:
  - **DL/I:** The interface to the IMS modules that access and manipulate the data in IMS databases.
  - **Checking account application program:** This program performs basic operations on checking account balances (such as queries and updates) and issues DL/I calls that cause IMS to actually query and update the checking account data that resides in the IMS checking account database.
  - **Message Format Service (MFS):** A service provided with IMS TM that separates the terminal device characteristics from the application program. For more information, see "Message Format Service" on page 182.
  - **z/OS Communication Server:** A communications package that is part of the z/OS operating system. In Figure 3-1, IMS is communicating with the Virtual Telecommunications Access Method (VTAM®) function within the z/OS Communication Server.[2]
  - **Communications Controller:** A device (hardware and software) that is part of the telecommunications network.
  - **3270-type terminal:** Before personal computers (PCs) were invented, these terminals provided access to the mainframe computer—a bank teller might use such a terminal. In general, these types of terminals have been replaced with PCs that run 3270-emulation application programs.

---

2.   Although IMS uses the network facilities of VTAM, it can also control devices that use the basic telecommunications access method (BTAM) or the basic sequential access method (BSAM). VTAM is the preferred access method for IMS.

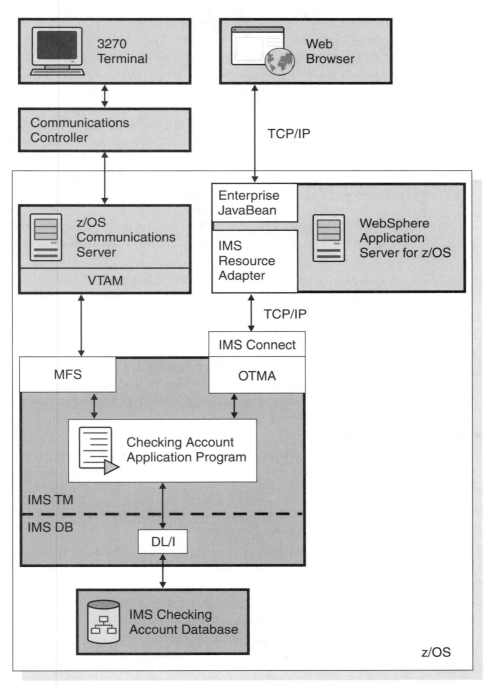

Figure 3-1   Example of a Simple Application That Accesses an IMS Database Through DL/I

- **Updated traditional processing model:** Figure 3-1 on page 19 also shows how the following layers of application programs and protocols have been added to the original application program to enable Web-based personal banking:
    - **OTMA:** Open Transaction Manager Access (OTMA) is an open interface to IMS TM. For more information, see "Open Transaction Manager Access" on page 179.
    - **IMS Connect:** IMS Connect is an optional IMS TM network component that provides high-performance communications for IMS between one or more TCP/IP clients (such as WebSphere Application Server for z/OS) and one or more IMS systems. For more information, see "IMS Connect" on page 187.
    - **WebSphere Application Server for z/OS:** A comprehensive, sophisticated, Java 2 Enterprise Edition (J2EE) and Web services technology-based application platform specifically designed to leverage the qualities of service inherent in the z/OS operating system. For more information about how IMS supports WebSphere Application Server for z/OS, see "WebSphere Application Server for z/OS Applications" on page 317.

      Figure 3-1 on page 19 includes the IMS Resource Adapter, which is delivered with the IMS Connect function and IBM WebSphere Studio Application Developer Integration Edition.
    - **Enterprise JavaBean:** A user-written, object-oriented, distributed, enterprise-level application.
    - **Web Browser:** A client program that initiates requests to a Web server and displays the information that the server returns. The Web browser is the actual end-user interface with which bank customers can manipulate their checking accounts.

Accessing IMS Using JDBC

The IMS Java function provides IMS's implementation of the JDBC API. Application programs that use the JDBC interface to access IMS issue SQL calls and might run on a non-z/OS platform.

The IMS Java function allows you to write Java application programs that access IMS databases and IMS message queues from many different locations:

- Within IMS
- Any environment that supports the JDBC API
- IBM WebSphere Application Server for z/OS
- WebSphere Application Server running on a non-z/OS platform
- IBM Customer Information Control System (CICS) Transaction Server for z/OS
- IBM DB2 Universal Database for z/OS stored procedures

For more information about writing Java applications for IMS, see Chapter 18, "Application Programming in Java" on page 311.

Figure 3-2 illustrates an Enterprise JavaBean (EJB) that can perform work on the IMS checking account database. Notice that in Figure 3-2, IMS does not require an application program to issue DL/I calls.

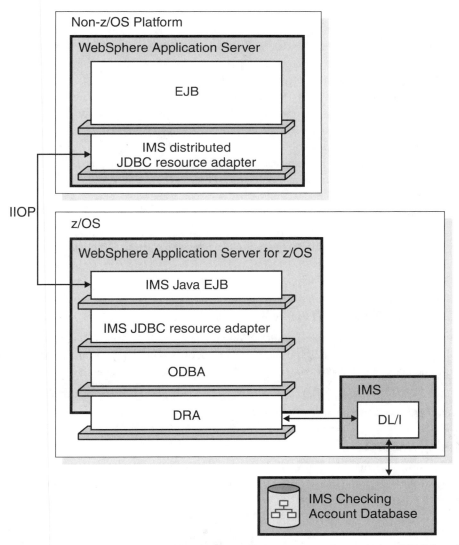

Figure 3-2 Example of an EJB That Accesses an IMS Database Through the JDBC Interface

Figure 3-2 includes the following components:

- **DL/I.**
- **DRA:** The database resource adapter (DRA) is the bridge between ODBA and IMS.
- **ODBA:** Open Database Access (ODBA) is the IMS callable interface for access to IMS DB.
- **IMS JDBC resource adapter:** The IMS JDBC resource adapter that is deployed on the z/OS platform. The IMS JDBC resource adapter is delivered with the IMS Java function.
- **IMS Java EJB:** One of two IMS Java-supplied EJBs is the host-side component that facilitates communication with and passes transaction information to the IMS JDBC resource adapter. These EJBs act as listeners for remote requests.
- **WebSphere Application Server for z/OS.**
- **IIOP:** Internet Inter-ORB Protocol (IIOP) is the protocol that can be used between WebSphere Application Server for z/OS and WebSphere Application Server running on another platform. IIOP allows the servers to exchange data. Data is securely transferred across the Internet using the SSL (Secure Sockets Layer) protocol.
- **IMS distributed JDBC resource adapter:** The resource adapter that is deployed on the non-z/OS platform, which contains a type-3 JDBC driver and is delivered with the IMS Java function.
- **EJB:** The EJB enterprise application that contains your business logic and is deployed on WebSphere Application Server.
- **WebSphere Application Server:** WebSphere Application Server on which the client application runs.
- **non-z/OS platform:** The operating system that hosts WebSphere Application Server.

ACCESSING IMS FROM OTHER PRODUCTS

The scope of this book is not large enough to fully explain all the products and protocols that can access IMS. Instead, some of these products and protocols are briefly mentioned in the following sections to demonstrate that you can access IMS from almost anywhere in the IT world.

Some products are shown in both Figure 3-3 on page 23 and Figure 3-4 on page 25, which indicates that these products can access both IMS DB and IMS TM.

Accessing IMS DB

Figure 3-3 shows the main interfaces to IMS DB (IMS TM, the ODBA interface, and the DRA interface), along with some of the products that use the ODBA and DRA interfaces.

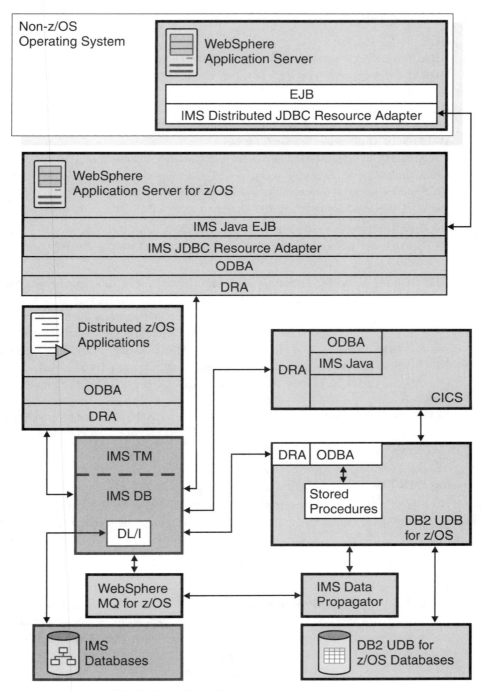

Figure 3-3   Accessing IMS DB from Other Programs

The following components and products are shown in Figure 3-3:

- **DL/I.**
- **DRA:** The DRA comes with IMS DB, but is run where it is used, not within IMS.
- **ODBA:** ODBA comes with IMS DB, but, like the DRA, is run where it is used, not within IMS.
- **Distributed z/OS applications:** Any z/OS application that follows the guidelines and rules associated with the ODBA interface can access IMS.
- **WebSphere Application Server for z/OS.**
- **CICS:** IBM CICS Transaction Server for z/OS, an IBM licensed program that provides online transaction-processing services and management for business applications. CICS can be a transaction manager for either IMS DB or DB2 UDB for z/OS. In Figure 3-3, CICS application programs that need to access IMS DB can do so in two ways:
  - Directly through the DRA by issuing CICS EXEC DL/I calls.
  - Through the DRA using the IMS Java function and issuing the supported SQL calls.
- **DB2 UDB for z/OS:** IBM's premier database manager for relational databases. Stored procedures that run in DB2 UDB for z/OS can access IMS DB through ODBA.
- **IBM WebSphere MQ for z/OS:** A z/OS subsystem that supports the transfer of messages across z/OS address spaces and to other WebSphere MQ products on both IBM and non-IBM platforms. The platforms include AIX®, iSeries™, OS/2®, VSE/ESA™, HP-UX, Solaris, Windows, Compaq NonStop Kernel, Compaq Tru64 UNIX, Compaq OpenVMS (Alpha), and Linux, using the IBM SNA LU 6.2 or TCP/IP communications protocols.
- **IBM IMS DataPropagator™:** Figure 3-3 also shows WebSphere MQ for z/OS working in conjunction with IMS DataPropagator and DB2 UDB for z/OS to replicate IMS data across the DB2 family of databases.

Accessing IMS TM

Figure 3-4 on page 25 shows the main interfaces to IMS TM (the OTMA interface, the IMS Connect function, VTAM, and APPC), along with some of the products and protocols that use these interfaces.

The following components and products are shown in Figure 3-4:

- **DL/I.**
- **Advanced Program-to-Program Communications (APPC):** An implementation of the SNA LU 6.2 protocol that allows interconnected systems to communicate and share the processing of programs. For more information about IMS TM and APPC, see "APPC/IMS and LU 6.2 Devices" on page 185.

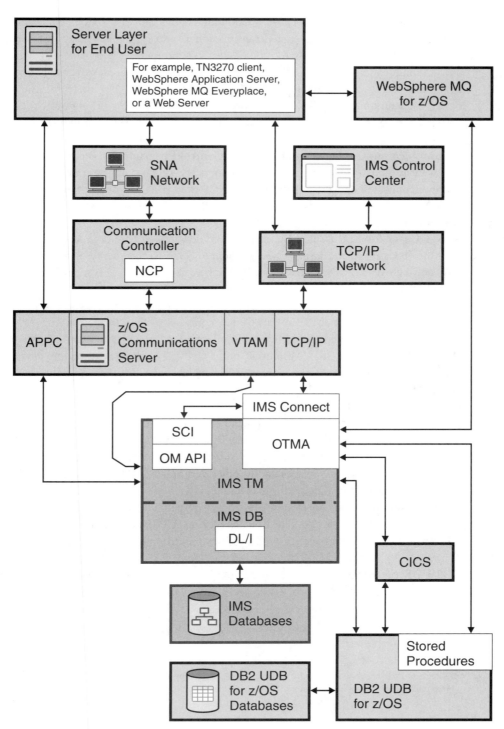

Figure 3-4 Accessing IMS TM from Other Programs

- **z/OS Communications Server:** z/OS Communications Server provides both System Network Architecture (SNA) and Transmission Control Protocol/Internet Protocol (TCP/IP) networking protocols for z/OS. The SNA protocols are provided by Virtual Telecommunications Access Method (VTAM) and include Subarea, Advanced Peer-to-Peer Networking, and High Performance Routing protocols. For more information on z/OS Communications Server SNA protocols or TCP/IP networking protocols for z/OS, see *z/OS V1R4.0 z/OS Communications Server SNA Network Implementation Guide*.

- **Communication Controller and Network Control Program (NCP):** A combination of hardware and software that provides support for single-domain, multiple-domain, and interconnected network capability. The NCP is an IBM licensed program.

- **SNA Network:** Existing (traditional) network that implements the SNA protocols[3] to connect terminals and other devices.

- **Server Layer for End User:** One or more middleware software products that interact with the end user, for example, TN3270 client (TN3270 Telnet server acts as an interface between IP and SNA networks), WebSphere Application Server, or WebSphere MQ Everyplace®.

- **IMS Control Center:** A workstation graphical interface from which you can manage your IMS systems. The IMS Control Center connects to IMS through a TCP/IP network, IMS Connect, and the Structured Call Interface (SCI). For more information about SCI, see Chapter 28, "IMSplexes" on page 495. For more information about the IMS Control Center, see "Operating an IMSplex" on page 499. For more information about IMS Connect, see "IMS Connect" on page 187.

- **OTMA:** An open interface to IMS TM through which a z/OS or TCP/IP application program can send a transaction or command to IMS without using SNA or VTAM. For more information about OTMA, see "Open Transaction Manager Access" on page 179.

- **IBM WebSphere MQ for z/OS:** A z/OS subsystem that supports the transfer of messages across z/OS address spaces and to other WebSphere MQ products on both IBM and non-IBM platforms. The platforms include AIX, iSeries, OS/2, VSE/ESA, HP-UX, Solaris, Windows, Compaq NonStop Kernel, Compaq Tru64 UNIX, Compaq OpenVMS (Alpha), and Linux, using the SNA LU 6.2 or TCP/IP communications protocols.

- **CICS:** In Figure 3-4 on page 25, CICS application programs that need to access IMS TM can do so by using the OTMA callable interface.

- **DB2 UDB for z/OS:** IBM's premier database manager for relational databases. IMS TM can provide transaction processing services for DB2 UDB for z/OS.

---

3. Network access to IMS Transaction Manager was originally provided by IBM's communications systems, which evolved into the System Network Architecture (SNA), as implemented in VTAM.

CHAPTER 4

IMS and z/OS

 his chapter describes how IMS subsystems are implemented on a z/OS system and how IMS uses some of the facilities that are a part of the z/OS operating system.

In This Chapter:

- "How IMS Relates to z/OS"
- "Structure of IMS Subsystems" on page 28
- "Running an IMS System" on page 43
- "Running Multiple IMS Systems" on page 44
- "How IMS Uses z/OS Services" on page 45

How IMS Relates to z/OS

IMS is a large application that runs on z/OS. There is a symbiotic relationship between IMS and z/OS. Both are tailored to provide the most efficient use of the hardware and software components.

IMS runs as a z/OS subsystem and uses several address spaces: one controlling address space, several separate address spaces that provide IMS services, and several address spaces that run IMS application programs. z/OS address spaces are sometimes called *regions*,[1] as in the IMS control region. The term *region* is synonymous with a z/OS address space.

The various components of an IMS system are explained in more detail in "Structure of IMS Subsystems."

---

1. The concept of a region originated in the MVT (Multiprogramming with Variable Number of Tasks) operating system, a precursor to z/OS.

STRUCTURE OF IMS SUBSYSTEMS

This section describes the various types of z/OS address spaces and their interrelationships.

The control region is the core of an IMS subsystem, running in one z/OS address space. Each control region uses many other address spaces that provide additional services to the control region, and in which the IMS application programs run.

Some IMS applications and utilities run in separate, standalone regions, called batch regions. Batch regions are separate from an IMS subsystem and its control region and have no connection with it. For more information, see "IMS Batch Environment" on page 33.

IMS Control Region

The IMS control region is a z/OS address space that can be initiated through a z/OS START command or by submitting job control language (JCL)[2] job.

The IMS control region provides the central point of control for an IMS subsystem. The IMS control region:

- Provides the interface to z/OS for the operation of the IMS subsystem.
- Controls, schedules, and dispatches the application programs that are running in separate regions, called *dependent regions*.
- Provides the interface to the SNA network for IMS TM functions.
- Provides the OTMA interface for access to non-SNA networks.
- Provides the ODBA interface for DB2 UDB for z/OS stored procedures and other z/OS application programs.

The IMS control region also provides all logging, restart, and recovery functions for the IMS subsystems. The terminals, message queues, and logs are all attached to this region. Fast Path (one of the IMS database types) database data sets are also allocated by the IMS control region.

A z/OS type-2 supervisor call (SVC) routine is used for switching control information, message and database data between the control region, all other regions, and back.

Four different types of IMS control regions can be defined using the IMS system definition process. You choose the one you want depending on which IMS functions you want. The four types of IMS control regions support the four IMS environments. These environments are discussed in more detail in "IMS Environments" on page 29.

---

2.   A control language that is used to identify a job to an operating system and to describe the job's requirements.

IMS Environments

Each of the IMS environments is a distinct combination of hardware and programs that supports distinct processing goals. The four IMS environments are:

- DB/DC, which contains all the functionality of both IMS TM and IMS DB (see "IMS DB/DC Environment").
- DBCTL (pronounced DB Control), which contains the functionality of only IMS DB (see "IMS DBCTL Environment" on page 31).
- DCCTL (pronounced DC Control), which contains the functionality of only IMS TM (see "IMS DCCTL Environment" on page 31).
- Batch, which contains the functionality of IMS DB, but is used only for batch jobs (see "IMS Batch Environment" on page 33).

IMS DB/DC Environment

The DB/DC environment has both IMS TM and IMS DB installed and has the functionality of the entire IMS product. The processing goals of the DB/DC environment are to:

- Enable terminal users to retrieve data and modify the database with satisfactory real-time performance. Some typical applications are banking, airline reservations, and sales orders.
- Ensure that retrieved data is current.
- Distribute transaction processing among multiple processors in a communications network.
- Run batch application programs to update databases at certain intervals (for example, process a payroll or produce an inventory report).
- Run database utilities using batch.

As shown in Figure 4-1 on page 30, the DB/DC control region provides access to the:

- Network, which might include a z/OS console, terminals, Web servers, and more.
- IMS message queues for IMS applications running in message processing regions (MPRs) or Java message processing regions.
- IMS libraries.
- IMS logs.
- Fast Path databases.
- DL/I separate address space.
- Database Recovery Control (DBRC) facility region.
- IMS Fast Path (IFP) region.
- Java message processing program (JMP) region.
- Java batch processing program (JBP) region.
- Batch message processing program (BMP) region.

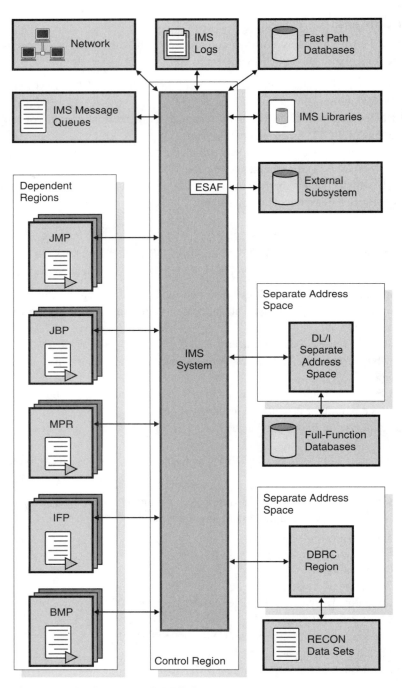

Figure 4-1   Structure of a Sample IMS DB/DC Environment

Related Reading:

- For more information about the address spaces that provide some of the services of the IMS subsystem, see "IMS Separate Address Spaces" on page 36.
- For more information about DBRC, see Chapter 23, "Database Recovery Control (DBRC) Facility" on page 375.
- For more information about the various types of regions for application programs, see "Dependent Regions" on page 36.

IMS DBCTL Environment

The DBCTL environment has only IMS DB installed. The processing goals of the DBCTL environment are to:

- Process network transactions without IMS TM; that is, use IMS DB with a different transaction management subsystem, such as CICS.
- Run batch application programs to update databases at certain intervals (for example, process a payroll or produce an inventory report).
- Run database utilities using batch.

DBCTL can provide IMS database functions to batch message programs (BMP and JMP application programs) connected to the IMS control region, and to application transactions running in CICS regions, as shown in Figure 4-2 on page 32.

When a CICS system connects to IMS using the DRA, each CICS system has a predefined number of connections with IMS. Each of these connections is called a *thread*. Although threads are not jobs from the perspective of IMS, each thread appears to the IMS system to be another IMS dependent region. When a CICS application issues a DL/I call to IMS, the DL/I processing runs in one of these dependent regions.

When a DB/DC environment is providing access to IMS databases for a CICS region, it is referred to in some documentation as providing DBCTL services, though it might, in fact, be a full DB/DC environment and not just a DBCTL environment.

IMS DCCTL Environment

The DCCTL environment is an IMS Transaction Manager subsystem that has no database components. A DCCTL environment is similar to the "DC" component of a DB/DC environment. The primary difference is that a DCCTL control region owns no databases and does not service DL/I database calls. The processing goals of the DCCTL environment are to:

- Process network transactions without IMS DB by using IMS TM with an external database management subsystem, such as DB2 UDB for z/OS.
- Use DBRC to maintain system log information that might be needed to restart IMS.
- Run batch application programs in a TM batch region by using IMS TM to do batch processing with DB2 UDB for z/OS.

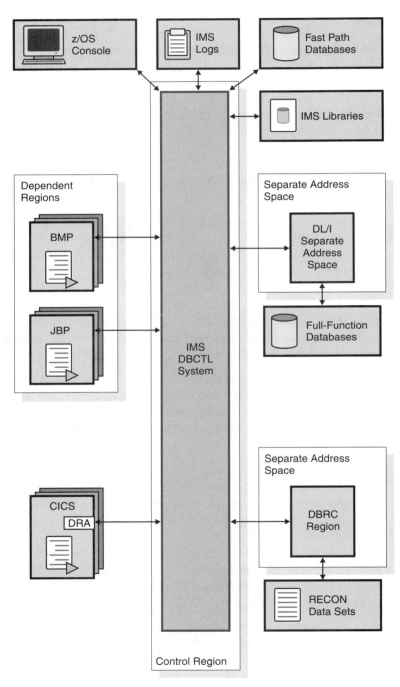

Figure 4-2   Structure of a Sample IMS DBCTL Environment

As shown in Figure 4-3 on page 34, the DCCTL system, in conjunction with the IMS External Subsystem Attach Facility (ESAF), provides a transaction manager facility to external subsystems (for example, DB2 UDB for z/OS). Most IMS customers use a DB/DC environment as a transaction manager front end for DB2 UDB for z/OS.

In a DCCTL environment, transaction processing and terminal management is identical to transaction processing and terminal management in a DB/DC environment.

IMS Batch Environment

The IMS batch environment consists of a batch region (a single address space) where an application program and IMS routines reside. The batch job that runs the batch environment is initiated with JCL, like any operating-system job.

There are two types of IMS batch environments: DB Batch and TM Batch. These environments are discussed in "DB Batch Environment" and in "TM Batch" on page 35.

DB Batch Environment In the DB Batch environment, IMS application programs that use only IMS DB functions can be run in a separate z/OS address space that is not connected to an IMS online control region. These batch applications are typically very long-running jobs that perform large numbers of database accesses, or applications that do not perform synchronization-point processing to commit the work. DB Batch applications can access only full-function databases, which are explained in "Implementation of IMS Databases" on page 62.

Another aspect of a DB Batch environment is that the JCL is submitted through TSO or a job scheduler. However, all of the IMS code used by the application resides in the address space in which the application is running. The job executes an IMS batch region controller that then loads and calls the application. Figure 4-4 on page 35 shows an IMS batch region.

The batch address space opens and reads the IMS database data sets directly.

> **ATTENTION:** If multiple programs, either running under the control of an IMS control region or in other batch regions, need to access databases at the same time, then you must take steps to ensure data integrity. See Chapter 9, "Data Sharing" on page 119 for more information about how the data can be updated by multiple applications in a safe manner.

The batch region controller writes its own separate IMS log. In the event of a program failure, it might be necessary to take manual action (for example, submit jobs to run IMS utilities) to recover the databases to a consistent point. With online dependent application regions, this is done automatically by the IMS control region. You can also use DBRC to track the IMS logs and ensure that correct recovery action is taken in the event of a failure.

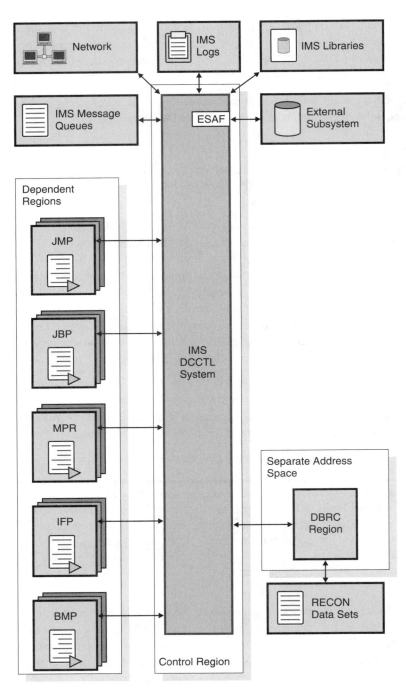

Figure 4-3   Structure of a Sample IMS DCCTL Environment

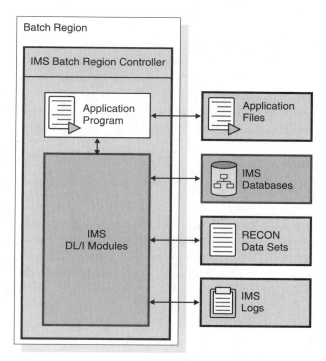

Figure 4-4 Structure of an IMS DB Batch Environment

An application can be written so that it can run in both a batch address space and a BMP address space without change. You can vary the execution environment of the programs between batch and BMP address spaces to lengthen the run time, support the need of other applications to access the data at the same time, or to run your procedures for recovering from application failures.

TM Batch IMS TM supports a batch region for running TM batch application programs. Using TM Batch, you can either take advantage of the IMS Batch Terminal Simulator for z/OS or access an external subsystem through the IMS External Subsystem Attach Facility, ESAF. One example of an external subsystem is DB2 UDB for z/OS.

You can connect DB2 UDB for z/OS in an IMS TM batch environment in one of two ways. You can use the SSM parameter on the TM batch-region execution JCL and specify the actual name of the batch program on the MBR parameter. Alternatively, you can code the DDITV02 DD statement on the batch-region execution JCL and specify the name of the DB2 UDB for z/OS module, DSNMTV01, on the MBR parameter.

TM Batch does not provide DL/I database capabilities.

Related Reading:

- See the *DB2 UDB for z/OS: Application Programming and SQL Guide* for a description of the steps required to allow TM batch programs to issue SQL calls.
- See Chapter 26, "IBM IMS Tools" on page 443 for more information about the IMS Batch Terminal Simulator for z/OS.
- See *IMS Version 9: Installation Volume 2: System Definition and Tailoring* for additional options or requirements of the IMS TM batch environment.

IMS Separate Address Spaces

The IMS control region has separate address spaces that provide some of the IMS subsystem services.

These regions are automatically started by the IMS control region as part of its initialization, and the control region does not complete initialization until these regions have started and connected to the IMS control region. All separate address spaces (except for DBRC) are optional, depending on the IMS features used. For DL/I, separate address space options can be specified at IMS initialization.

DBRC Region

The DBRC region provides all access to the DBRC recovery control (RECON) data sets. The DBRC region also generates batch jobs for DBRC (for example, for archiving the online IMS log). Every IMS control region must have a DBRC region because it is needed, at a minimum, for managing the IMS logs.

DL/I Separate Address Space

The DL/I separate address space (DLISAS) performs most data set access functions for IMS DB (except for the Fast Path DEDB databases). The DLISAS allocates full-function database data sets and also contains some of the control blocks associated with database access and some database buffers.

For a DBCTL environment, the DLISAS is required and always present.

For a DB/DC environment, you have the option of having IMS database accesses performed by the control region or having the DB/DC region start DLISAS. For performance and capacity reasons, use DLISAS.

DLISAS is not present for a DCCTL environment because the Database Manager functions are not present.

Dependent Regions

IMS provides address spaces for the execution of system and application programs that use IMS services. These address spaces are called dependent regions.

The dependent regions are started by the submission of JCL to the operating system. The JCL is submitted as a result of a command issued to the IMS control region, through automation, or by a regular batch job submission.

After the dependent regions are started, the application programs are scheduled and dispatched by the IMS control region. In all cases, the z/OS address space executes an IMS control region program. The application program is then loaded and called by the IMS code.

Up to 999 dependent regions can be connected to one IMS control region, made up of any combination of the following dependent region types:

- Message processing region (MPR)
- IMS Fast Path (IFP) region, processing Fast Path applications or utilities
- Batch message processing (BMP) region, running with or without HSSP (High Speed Sequential Processing)
- Java message processing (JMP) region
- Java batch processing (JBP) region
- DBCTL thread (DBT)

Table 4-1 describes the support for dependent regions by IMS environment type.

Table 4-1 Support for Dependent Region Type by IMS Environment

Application Address Space Type	DCCTL	DBCTL	DB/DC	DB Batch	TM Batch
MPR	Y	N	Y	N	N
IFP	Y	N	Y	N	N
BMP (transaction-oriented)	Y[a]	N	Y	N	N
BMP (batch-oriented)	Y	Y	Y	N	N
JMP	Y	N	Y	N	N
JBP	Y	Y	Y	N	N
Batch	N	N	N	Y	Y
DBT	N	Y	Y	N	N

a. BMP regions attached to a DCCTL control region can access only IMS message queues and DB2 UDB for z/OS databases.

Message Processing Region Message processing regions (MPRs) run applications that process messages that come into IMS TM as input (for example, from terminals or online programs). MPRs can be started by IMS submitting the JCL as a result of an IMS command. The address space does not automatically load an application program but waits until work becomes available.

Priority settings determine which MPR runs the application program. When the IMS determines that an application is to run in a particular MPR, the application program is loaded into that region and receives control. The application processes the message and any further messages for that transaction that are waiting to be processed. Then, depending on options specified on the transaction definition, the application either waits for further input, or another application program is loaded to process a different transaction.

IMS Fast Path Region   An IMS Fast Path (IFP) region runs application programs to process messages for transactions that have been defined as Fast Path transactions.

Fast Path applications are very similar to the applications that run in an MPR. Like MPRs, the IFP regions can be started by the IMS control region submitting the JCL as a result of an IMS command. The difference between MPRs and IFP regions is in the way IMS loads and dispatches the application program and handles the transaction messages. To allow for this different processing, IMS imposes restrictions on the length of the application data that can be processed in an IFP region as a single message.

IMS uses a user-written exit routine (or the IBM-supplied sample) to determine whether a transaction message should be processed in an IFP region and in which IFP region it should be processed. The IMS Fast Path facility that processes messages is called the *expedited message handler* (EMH). The EMH speeds the processing of the messages by having the applications loaded and waiting for input messages, and, if the message is suitable, dispatching it directly in the IFP region, bypassing the IMS message queues.

IFP regions can also be used for other types of work besides running application programs. IFP regions can be used for Fast Path utility programs. For further discussion on using these regions for other types of work, see the *IMS Version 9: Installation Volume 2: System Definition and Tailoring*.

Batch Message Processing Region   Unlike MPR or IFP regions, a BMP region is not usually started by the IMS control region, but is started by submitting a batch job, for example by a user from TSO or by a job scheduler. The batch job then connects to an IMS control region that is defined in the execution parameters.

Two types of applications can run in BMP regions:

- Message-driven BMP applications (also called transaction-oriented BMP applications), which read and process messages from the IMS message queue
- Non-message-driven BMP applications (batch-oriented), which do not process IMS messages

BMP regions have access to the IMS full-function and Fast Path databases, provided that the control region has the Database Manager component installed. BMP regions can also read and write to z/OS sequential files, with integrity, using the IMS GSAM access method (see "GSAM Access Method" on page 107).

BMP regions can also be used for other types of work besides running application programs. BMP regions can be used for jobs that, in the past, were run as batch update programs. The advantage of converting batch jobs to run in BMP regions is that the batch jobs can now run along side of a transaction environment and these BMP applications can be run concurrently instead of sequentially. For a further discussion on using these regions for other types of work, see the *IMS Version 9: Installation Volume 2: System Definition and Tailoring*.

Java Dependent Regions   Two IMS dependent regions provide a Java Virtual Machine (JVM) environment for Java or object-oriented COBOL applications:

Java message processing (JMP) regions

JMP regions are similar to MPR regions, but JMP regions allow the scheduling only of Java or object-oriented COBOL message-processing applications. A JMP application is started when there is a message in the queue for the JMP application and IMS schedules the message to be processed. JMP applications are executed through transaction codes submitted by users at terminals and from other applications. Each transaction code represents a transaction that the JMP application processes. A single application can also be started from multiple transaction codes.

JMP applications are very flexible in how they process transactions and where they send the output. JMP applications send any output messages back to the message queues and process the next message with the same transaction code. The program continues to run until there are no more messages with the same transaction code. JMP applications share the following characteristics:

- They are small.
- They can produce output that is needed immediately.
- They can access IMS or DB2 data in a DB/DC environment and DB2 data in a DCCTL environment.

Java batch processing (JBP) regions

JBP regions run flexible programs that perform batch-type processing online and can access the IMS message queues for output (similar to non-message-driven BMP applications). JBP applications are started by submitting a job with JCL or from TSO. JBP applications are like BMP applications, except that they cannot read input messages from the IMS message queue. Similarly to BMP applications, JBP applications can use symbolic checkpoint and restart calls to restart the application after an abend. JBP applications can access IMS or DB2 data in a DB/DC or DBCTL environment and DB2 data in a DCCTL environment.

Figure 4-5 shows a Java application that is running in a JMP or JBP region. JDBC or IMS Java hierarchical interface calls are passed to the IMS Java layer, which converts them to DL/I calls.

JMP and JBP regions can run applications written in Java, object-oriented COBOL, or a combination of the two.

Related Reading: For more information about writing Java applications for IMS, see Chapter 18, "Application Programming in Java" on page 311 or *IMS Version 9: IMS Java Guide and Reference.*

Common Queue Server Address Space

Common Queue Server (CQS) is a generalized server that manages data objects on a z/OS coupling facility on behalf of multiple clients. CQS is used by IMS shared queues and the Resource Manager address space in the Common Service Layer.

CQS uses the z/OS coupling facility as a repository for data objects. Storage in a coupling facility is divided into distinct objects called *structures*. Authorized programs use structures to implement data sharing and high-speed serialization. The coupling facility stores and arranges the

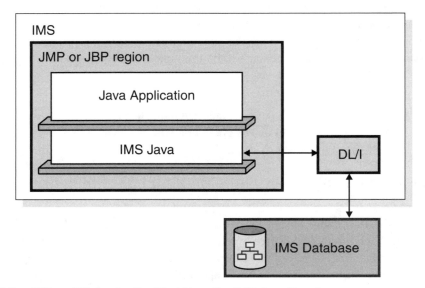

Figure 4-5   JMP or JBP Application That Uses the IMS Java Function

data according to list structures. Queue structures contain collections of data objects that share the same names, known as *queues*. Resource structures contain data objects organized as uniquely named resources.

CQS receives, maintains, and distributes data objects from shared queues on behalf of multiple clients. Each client has its own CQS access the data objects on the coupling facility list structure. IMS is one example of a CQS client that uses CQS to manage both its shared queues and shared resources.

CQS runs in a separate address space that can be started by the client (IMS). The CQS client must run under the same z/OS image where the CQS address space is running.

CQS is used by IMS DCCTL and IMS DB/DC control regions if they are participating in sysplex sharing of IMS message queues or resource structures. IMS DBCTL can also use CQS and a resource if it is using the IMS coordinated online change function.

Clients communicate with CQS using CQS requests that are supported by CQS macro statements. Using these macros, CQS clients can communicate with CQS and manipulate client data on shared coupling facility structures. Figure 4-6 shows the communications and the relationship between clients, CQSs, and the coupling facility.

Related Reading: For complete information about CQS, see *IMS Version 9: Common Queue Server Guide and Reference*.

Common Service Layer
The IMS Common Service Layer (CSL) is a collection of IMS system address spaces that provide the infrastructure needed for systems management tasks.

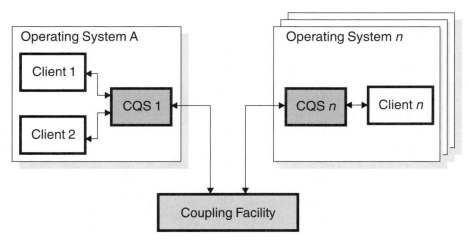

Figure 4-6 Client Systems, CQS, and a Coupling Facility

The IMS CSL reduces the complexity of managing multiple IMS systems by providing you with a single-image perspective in an IMSplex. An IMSplex is one or more IMS subsystems that can work together as a unit. Typically, these subsystems:

- Share either databases or resources or message queues (or any combination)
- Run in a z/OS sysplex environment
- Include an IMS CSL

The CSL address spaces include Operations Manager (OM), Resource Manager (RM), and Structured Call Interface (SCI). They are briefly described in the following sections.

Related Reading: For a further discussion of IMS in a sysplex environment, see:

- Chapter 28, "IMSplexes" on page 495
- *IMS Version 9: Administration Guide: System*

For a detailed discussion of IMS in a sysplex environment, see:

- *IMS in the Parallel Sysplex: Volume I: Reviewing the IMSplex Technology*
- *IMS in the Parallel Sysplex: Volume II: Planning the IMSplex*
- *IMS in the Parallel Sysplex: Volume III: IMSplex Implementation and Operations*

Operations Manager Address Space   The Operations Manager (OM) controls the operations of an IMSplex. OM provides an application programming interface (the OM API) through which commands can be issued and responses received. With a single point of control (SPOC) interface, you can submit commands to OM. The SPOC interfaces include the TSO SPOC, the REXX SPOC API, and the IMS Control Center. You can also write your own application to submit commands.

Related Reading: For a further discussion of OM, see "Operations Manager" on page 497.

Resource Manager Address Space   The Resource Manager (RM) is an IMS address space that manages global resources and IMSplex-wide processes in a sysplex on behalf of RM's clients. IMS is one example of an RM client.

Related Reading: For a further discussion of RM, see "Resource Manager" on page 498.

Structured Call Interface Address Space   The Structured Call Interface (SCI) allows IMSplex members to communicate with one another. The communication between IMSplex members can happen within a single z/OS image or among multiple z/OS images. Individual IMS components do not need to know where the other components reside or what communication interface to use.

Related Reading: For a further discussion of SCI, see "Structured Call Interface" on page 498.

Internal Resource Lock Manager

The internal resource lock manager (IRLM) is delivered as an integral part of IMS, but you do not have to install or use it unless you need to perform block-level or sysplex data sharing. IRLM is also the required lock manager for DB2 UDB for z/OS.

The IRLM address space is started before the IMS control region with the z/OS START command. If the IMS start-up parameters specify IRLM, the IMS control region connects to the IRLM that is specified on startup and does not complete initialization until the connection is successful.

Typically, one IRLM address space runs on each z/OS system to service all IMS subsystems that share the same set of databases. For more information on data sharing in a sysplex environment, see:

- *IMS in the Parallel Sysplex: Volume I: Reviewing the IMSplex Technology*
- *IMS in the Parallel Sysplex: Volume II: Planning the IMSplex*
- *IMS in the Parallel Sysplex: Volume III: IMSplex Implementation and Operations*

> **RECOMMENDATION:** Do not use the same IRLM address space for IMS and DB2 UDB for z/OS because the tuning requirements of IMS and DB2 are different and conflicting. The IRLM code is delivered with both IMS and DB2 UDB for z/OS and interacts closely with both. Therefore, you might want to install the IRLM code for IMS and DB2 UDB for z/OS separately (that is, in separate SMP/E zones) so that you can maintain release and maintenance levels independently. Installing the IRLM code separately can be helpful if you need to install prerequisite maintenance on IRLM for one database product because doing so does not affect the use of IRLM by the other product.

RUNNING AN IMS SYSTEM

IBM supplies the procedures to run IMS address spaces. The procedures for each type of region are located in the IMS.PROCLIB data set.

You must modify the procedures in the IMS.PROCLIB data set with the correct data set names for each IMS system. Table 4-2 contains the procedure member names in IMS.PROCLIB, along with the type of region that each member generates.

Table 4-2   IMS Procedure Members and the Region Type They Generate

Procedure Member Name	Region Type
DBC	DBCTL control region
DBRC	Database Recovery Control region
DCC	DCCTL control region
DFSJBP	Java batch processing (JBP) region
DFSJMP	Java message processing (JMP) region
DFSMPR	Message processing region (MPR)
DLIBATCH	DB batch region
DLISAS	DL/I separate address space
DXRJPROC	Internal resource lock manager (IRLM) region
FPUTIL	Fast Path utility region
IMS	DB/DC control region
IMSBATCH	IMS batch message processing region (BMP)
IMSFP	IMS Fast Path (IFP) region
IMSRDR	IMS JCL reader region

Related Reading: For details of these and other procedures supplied in IMS.PROCLIB, see the "Procedures" chapter in *IMS Version 9: Installation Volume 2: System Definition and Tailoring*.

RUNNING MULTIPLE IMS SYSTEMS

You can run multiple IMS systems on a single z/OS image or on multiple z/OS images. One instance of an IMS system (a control region and all its associated dependent regions) is referred to as one IMS system. In many cases, these IMS systems would be production and testing systems. A batch IMS system (for example, DB batch) is also considered one IMS system.

Running Multiple IMS Systems on a Single z/OS Image

The number of IMS subsystems you can run on a single image of z/OS depends on many factors, including the size of each IMS system (the amount of z/OS common service area [CSA] required by each IMS is often one of the most limiting factors in the equation). In most installations, you can run up to four IMS subsystems, although some installations run as many as eight small subsystems concurrently.

Each IMS subsystem should have unique VTAM access method control block (ACB) and IMSID (IMS subsystem identifier to the operating system) names. The dependent regions use the IMSID to connect to the corresponding IMS control region. If the dependent region starts and there is no control region running using that IMSID, the dependent region issues a message to the z/OS system console and then waits for a reply. Each IMS subsystem can have up to 999 dependent regions. However, there are other limiting factors, such as storage limitations due to pool usage.

Running Multiple IMS Systems on Multiple z/OS Images

There are basically three ways to run multiple IMS subsystems on multiple z/OS images:

- **Multiple Systems Coupling (MSC):** MSC supports only IMS-to-IMS connections. For more information about MSC, see "Multiple Systems Coupling (MSC)" on page 183.
- **Inter System Communications (ISC):** ISC is another way to connect multiple IMS subsystems. ISC is more flexible than MSC, in that ISC supports connections to IMS and other z/OS products, such as CICS. For more information about ISC, see "Intersystem Communication (ISC)" on page 184.
- **Parallel Sysplex:** Running multiple IMS subsystems in a Parallel Sysplex environment is a good way to balance workload, build scalability into your systems, and provide maximum availability. For more information on this topic, see "Parallel Sysplex" on page 48, and Chapter 28, "IMSplexes" on page 495.

HOW IMS USES z/OS SERVICES

IMS is designed to make the best use of the features of the z/OS operating system. IMS does so by:

- **Running in multiple address spaces:** IMS subsystems (except for IMS batch applications and utilities) normally consist of a control region address space, separate address spaces for system services, and dependent address spaces for application programs. Running in multiple address spaces provides the following advantages:
  - Maximizes the use of a central processor complex (CPC). Address spaces can be dispatched in parallel.
  - Isolates the application programs from the IMS system code. Doing so reduces outages from application failures.

- **Running multiple tasks in each IMS address space:** IMS, particularly in the control region, creates multiple z/OS subtasks for the various functions to be performed. Doing so allows other IMS subtasks to be dispatched by z/OS while one IMS subtask waits for system services.
- **Using the z/OS cross memory services:** IMS uses z/OS cross memory services to communicate between the various address spaces that make up an IMS system. IMS also uses the z/OS CSA and ECSA to store IMS control blocks that are frequently accessed by the address spaces of that IMS system. Doing so minimizes the overhead of running in multiple address spaces.
- **Using the z/OS subsystem feature:** IMS dynamically registers itself as a z/OS subsystem and uses the z/OS subsystem feature to detect when dependent address spaces fail, thus preventing the cancellation of dependent address spaces through z/OS command entry.
- **Using a z/OS sysplex:** Multiple IMS subsystems can run on the z/OS systems that make up the sysplex and, therefore, can access the same IMS databases and the same message queue. Doing so provides:
  - High availability: z/OS systems and IMS subsystems can be taken in and out of service without interrupting production.
  - High capacity: multiple IMS subsystems can process far greater volumes than individual IMS subsystems can.

Related Reading: For information about data sharing and shared queues in a sysplex environment, see:

- *IMS in the Parallel Sysplex: Volume I: Reviewing the IMSplex Technology*
- *IMS in the Parallel Sysplex: Volume II: Planning the IMSplex*
- *IMS in the Parallel Sysplex: Volume III: IMSplex Implementation and Operations*

Transmission Control Protocol/Internet Protocol (TCP/IP)

IMS provides support for z/OS TCP/IP communications through a function called Open Transaction Manager Access (OTMA). Any TCP/IP application can access IMS by using OTMA. Examples of such TCP/IP applications are:

- IMS Connect (a function within IMS TM) uses the OTMA interface to connect IMS to Web servers
- CICS
- DB2 UDB for z/OS stored procedures
- WebSphere MQ

Related Reading: For information about OTMA and IMS Connect, see:

- "Open Transaction Manager Access" on page 179 and "IMS Connect" on page 187
- *IMS Version 9: Open Transaction Manager Access Guide and Reference*
- *IMS Version 9: IMS Connect Guide and Reference*

Advanced Program-to-Program Communications (APPC)

IMS supports the z/OS CPI-C (Common Programming Interface for Communications) interface, which is based on Logical Unit type 6.2 formats and protocols for program-to-program communication. APPC is an implementation of the LU type 6.2 protocol. IMS's support for APPC is called APPC/IMS.

APPC/IMS enables applications to be distributed throughout an entire network and to communicate with each other regardless of the underlying hardware.

Related Reading: For more information about IMS's support for APPC, see "APPC/IMS and LU 6.2 Devices" on page 185.

Resource Access Control Facility (RACF)

IMS was developed before the introduction of RACF, which is part of the Security Server for z/OS, and other security products. As a result, IMS has its own security mechanisms to control user access to IMS resources, transactions, and databases.

With the introduction of RACF, IMS was enhanced so that it can use RACF (or an equivalent product) to control access to IMS resources. You can use the original IMS security features, the RACF features, or a combination of both.

> **RECOMMENDATION:** Use RACF for security because it provides more flexibility than the IMS security features provide.

Related Reading: For more information about protecting IMS resources, see Chapter 21, "IMS Security" on page 361. For complete information about IMS security, see the security chapter in *IMS Version 9: Administration Guide: System*.

Resource Recovery Services (RRS)

z/OS includes a facility for managing system resource recovery, called resource recovery services (RRS). RRS is the sync-point manager, which coordinates the update and recovery of multiple protected resources. RRS controls how and when protected resources are committed by coordinating with the resource managers (such as IMS) that have registered with RRS.

RRS provides a system resource recovery platform such that applications that run on z/OS can have access to local and distributed resources and have system-coordinated recovery management of these resources. RRS support includes these features and services:

- A sync-point manager to coordinate the two-phase commit process[3]
- Implementation of the SAA® commit and backout callable services for use by application programs
- A mechanism to associate resources with an application instance
- Services for resource manager registration and participation in the two-phase commit process with RRS
- Services to allow resource managers to express interest in an application instance and be informed of commit and backout requests
- Services to enable resource managers to obtain system data to restore their resources to consistent state
- A communications resource manager (called APPC/PC for APPC/Protected Conversations) so that distributed applications can coordinate their recovery with participating local resource managers

Related Reading: For more information about how IMS uses RRS, see *IMS Version 9: Administration Guide: System.*

Parallel Sysplex

A Parallel Sysplex environment in z/OS is a combination of hardware and software components that enable sysplex data sharing. Data sharing means the ability for sysplex member systems and subsystems to store data into, and retrieve data from, a common area of a coupling facility. In short, a Parallel Sysplex can have multiple CPCs and multiple applications (such as IMS) that can directly share the workload.

In a Parallel Sysplex environment, you can run multiple IMS subsystems that share message queues and databases. This sharing enables workload balancing and insulation from individual IMS outages. If one IMS in the sysplex fails or is stopped, others continue to process the workload, so the enterprise is minimally affected.

Related Reading: For more information, see Chapter 27, "Introduction to Parallel Sysplex" on page 467 and Chapter 28, "IMSplexes" on page 495.

---

3.   Two-phase commit processing is a two-step process by which recoverable resources and an external subsystem are committed. During the first step, the database manager subsystems are polled to ensure that they are ready to commit. If all subsystems respond positively, the database manager instructs them to commit.

CHAPTER 5

Setting Up and Running IMS

This chapter provides an overview of the tasks involved in installing, defining, and operating IMS.

In This Chapter:

INSTALLING IMS

The IMS installation task includes the following activities:

- Installing IMS on your z/OS system using the SMP/E installation process.
- Verifying the installation using the IMS Installation Verification Program (IVP) facility.
- Other installation-related activities, such as tailoring your IMS system, customizing your IMS system, and defining resources to IMS.

Most IMS installations involve migrating an existing version of IMS to a newer version rather than installing a new instance of IMS. When an existing installation is migrated, there are migration, coexistence, and maintenance steps and issues to consider as part of the installation process. The migration issues are usually version specific.

Related Reading: For details about installing IMS, verifying the installation, tailoring IMS, and migrating IMS, see:

- *Program Directory for Information Management System Version 9*
- *IMS Version 9: Release Planning Guide*
- *IMS Version 9: Installation Volume 1: Installation Verification*
- *IMS Version 9: Installation Volume 2: System Definition and Tailoring*

For more information about customizing IMS, see Chapter 20, "Customizing IMS," on page 347 and the *IMS Version 9: Customization Guide.*

Installing IMS Using SMP/E

System modification program/extended (SMP/E) is a z/OS tool designed to manage the installation of software products on your z/OS system and to track the modifications that you make to those products. The IMS code is shipped from IBM on cartridges and you use SMP/E to install IMS onto your computer. You can also use SMP/E to perform maintenance to your IMS.

IMS is delivered in multiple function modification identifiers (FMIDs) that need to be installed depending on what functions you want.

Related Reading: For complete information about SMP/E, see *SMP/E V3R1.0 User's Guide.*

IMS Installation Verification Program (IVP)

The Installation Verification Program (IVP) facility supplied by IMS is an ISPF application that verifies the majority of IMS features and functions of a newly installed IMS. The IVP uses a sample IMS system to perform this verification.

The IVP provides guidance for performing a combination of the following jobs and tasks, depending on your environment:

- Allocating data sets
- Defining the characteristics of an IMS system through the process of system definition
- Establishing IMS interfaces to z/OS and VTAM
- Preparing the IMS system
- Performing an initial program load (IPL) of z/OS
- Preparing the IVP system and IMS applications
- Initializing the IVP system and running IMS applications

You must define the IMS system and you must establish the interface between your IMS system and z/OS before you can run IMS.

Related Reading: For complete information about the IMS IVP, see *IMS Version 9: Installation Volume 1: Installation Verification.*

DEFINING AN IMS SYSTEM

Before you can use IMS TM or IMS DB, you must define the elements and functions that make up the IMS system, including:

- Databases
- Application programs
- Terminals
- All optional features of IMS, including the type of control region that is required (DB/DC, DBCTL, DCCTL)
- Security

IMS provides macros and procedures that enable you to define your system. IMS also provides user exits that enable you to customize processing. A user exit is the point in IMS's code at which an exit routine can be given control.

To define an IMS system, you can either customize the sample IMS system that is verified with the IVP (see "IMS Installation Verification Program (IVP)" on page 50), or copy the sample IMS system and customize the copy for your installation.

Related Reading: For more information about the IMS definition process, see Chapter 19, "The IMS System Definition Process," on page 329 and *IMS Version 9: Installation Volume 2: System Definition and Tailoring.* For more information about the IMS user exits, see Chapter 20, "Customizing IMS," on page 347.

Setting up security for the IMS system is also part of the system definition process. IMS has its own built-in security functions and can provide more extensive security through employing user-written exit routines, a security product (such as RACF), or both.

Related Reading: For more information about IMS security, see Chapter 21, "IMS Security," on page 361. For complete information about IMS security, see *IMS Version 9: Administration Guide: System.*

IMS STARTUP

This section describes the types of IMS system starts that can be performed for an IMS system and how to start IMS-associated regions.

Types of IMS System Start

This section describes the more common types of IMS system starts that can be performed. These types of IMS system starts are applicable to both IMS TM and IMS DB.

Cold start

An IMS control region cold start is done the first time you start the system. During a cold start, IMS initializes the message queues, the dynamic log, and the restart data sets.

Normal restart

Normal restart (or warm start) is the restart of IMS after a normal IMS termination. A normal restart preserves the message queues.

Emergency restart

If IMS terminates abnormally, IMS performs an emergency restart with the logs that were active at the time of failure. Emergency restart processing backs out the full-function database changes of incomplete transactions. The output messages inserted into the message queues by these incomplete transactions are deleted.

After back out processing finishes, the input messages are enqueued and the pending output messages are transmitted again. Application programs must be restarted manually. If a BMP or JBP application was active at the time of failure, it must be resubmitted by using z/OS job management. If the JBP or BMP application uses extended restart calls, which are used to restart the application from a checkpoint and not from the beginning, it must be restarted from its last successful checkpoint to avoid missing or inconsistent output.

Automatic restart

With an automatic restart, IMS starts up using either a normal restart or an emergency restart, depending on the status of the previous shutdown.

If the last IMS shutdown was successful, a normal restart will be performed. If the last IMS shutdown was abnormal (from a failure), IMS automatically performs an emergency restart.

For most installations, automatic restart should be the default (specify AUTO=Y in the control region JCL).

Other types of manual restarts

Numerous other types of manual restarts are possible with IMS, each with unique requirements. For detailed information about these other types of restarts, see *IMS Version 9: Operations Guide* and the *IMS Version 9: Command Reference*.

Starting Regions That Are Related to IMS

The following sections describe how the various IMS-related regions are started.

Address Spaces

All address spaces can run either as a started task or as a job. In most cases, the IMS control region and the separate address spaces will run as started tasks. The application dependent regions are run as either jobs or started tasks.

When a control region is started, it issues a z/OS `START` command to start the DLISAS and DBRC regions, as shown in the following example:

```
START xxxxxxxx, PARM=(DLS,imsid)
START xxxxxxxx, PARM=(DRC,imsid)
```

The *xxxxxxxx* fields are the procedure names. These commands will start the DLISAS and DBRC regions, respectively.

Starting Application Dependent Regions

IMS will not automatically start application dependent regions. There are several ways to start these regions.

- The IMS time controlled operations (TCO) can issue `/START REGION` commands. TCO is a time-initiated IMS facility that can generate any valid operator IMS input.
- Some forms of automation programs can issue either IMS or z/OS `START` commands.
- A job scheduling system can submit jobs based on time or the notification of IMS being started. The notification can be in the form of automated messages.

Message Processing Regions

IMS MPR regions are normally started by an IMS start region command, as shown in the following example:

```
/START REGION xxxxxxxx
```

The *xxxxxxxx* field is the member name in a library. The members contain the jobs for the MPR regions. The IMSRDR procedure is used if the MPRs are jobs. The IMSRDR procedure is customized to point to the correct library to find the job JCL. If you run multiple IMS subsystems on a single z/OS system, they normally use a different version of the IMSRDR procedure, with each pointing to different libraries. The procedure name is specified on the IMSCTF macro in the system definition.

Related Reading: For details about the IMSRDR procedure or the IMSCTF macro, see *IMS Version 9: Installation Volume 2: System Definition and Tailoring*.

IMS Fast Path Application Regions

IMS Fast Path (IFP) regions are normally started in a similar fashion as MPR regions and follow the same rules and procedures.

Batch Message Processing Regions

Batch message processing (BMP) regions are almost always started outside of IMS. Most BMP regions are scheduled at appropriate times to meet application requirements. As long as the IMS control region is available, the BMP regions can run. BMP regions can execute even though there are no MPRs running at the time.

Java Non-Message Driven Application Processing Region

This region, which is called a Java batch processing (JBP) region, is similar to a BMP region. The JBP region is started in the same manner as a BMP region. The default job name is IMSJBP.

Java Message-Driven-Application Processing Region

This region, which is called a Java message processing (JMP) region, is similar to an MPR region. The JMP region is started in the same manner as an MPR region. The default job name is IMSJMP.

IMS LOGGING

While IMS is running, it records the event information that is necessary to restart the system if a hardware or software failure occurs. The event information is recorded on an online log data set (OLDS).

When an OLDS is filled, or some other event causes IMS to switch from one OLDS to another, it is archived to the system log data set (SLDS). There is a finite number of OLDS data sets, although this number can be dynamically changed, which are pre-allocated and defined to the IMS control region. The OLDS are reused during the duration of the control region. There can be an infinite number of SLDSs, which are created and allocated as needed.

Related Reading: For more information, see Chapter 22, "IMS Logging," on page 367.

IMS UTILITY PROGRAMS

IMS includes many utility programs to help you run, fine tune, and monitor IMS. These utilities help you:

- Generate and maintain IMS system control blocks
- Make online changes to the IMS system
- Allocate, monitor, and recover the IMS log data sets
- Analyze system performance
- Generate and maintain the Message Format Service (MFS)
- Maintain multiple IMS systems

- Maintain time-controlled operations
- Define, maintain, recover, and reorganize[1] databases
- Make backup copies of databases

Some of the IMS utilities are discussed in the context of performing tasks in the following sections:

- "Overview of the Database Reorganization Process" on page 128
- Chapter 21, "IMS Security," on page 361
- "Archiving an OLDS" on page 370
- "Using IMS System Log Utilities" on page 406
- "Running Recovery-Related Utilities" on page 421

Related Reading: For information about all of the IMS utilities, see:

- *IMS Version 9: Utilities Reference: Database and Transaction Manager*
- *IMS Version 9: Utilities Reference: System*

IMS RECOVERY

There are a number of tools and features available with IMS to help in recovery scenarios. This section describes these tools and features.

Extended Recovery Facility (XRF)

With XRF, you can have an alternate IMS standby system ready to take over within the same site. For more information about XRF, see "Overview of Extended Recovery Facility (XRF)" on page 440.

Remote Site Recovery (RSR)

With RSR, you can recover the complete IMS system (or systems) very quickly at another site when complete site disasters occur. For more information about RSR, see "Overview of Remote Site Recovery (RSR)" on page 440.

Database Recovery Control (DBRC) Facility

DBRC is an integral part of IMS. IMS relies on DBRC to:

- Record and manage information about many items. DBRC keeps this information in a set of VSAM data sets that are collectively called the RECovery CONtrol (RECON) data sets.
- Advise IMS (based on the information in the RECON data sets) about how to proceed for certain IMS actions.

---

1. To *reorganize* a database is to unload and reload a database to optimize physical segment adjacency or to modify the database definition (DBD).

Related Reading: For more information, see Chapter 23, "Database Recovery Control (DBRC) Facility," on page 375.

Fast Database Recovery (FDBR)

FDBR provides a solution to sysplex customers who need quick access to shared database resources that might otherwise be locked by a failed IMS until the failed system is restarted.

In a sysplex data-sharing environment, multiple IMS subsystems can access a single, shared database resource. If one of the IMS subsystems fails while it has a lock on the database, the other IMS subsystems must wait until the failed IMS is restarted and the locks on the resource are released. Because an emergency restart can take a significant amount of time, waiting for a full restart is unacceptable in situations that require continuous availability of database resources.

FDBR creates a separate IMS control region (the Fast Database Recovery region), which monitors an IMS subsystem, detects failure, and recovers any database resources that are locked by the failed IMS, making them available for other IMS subsystems.

Related Reading: For more information about FDBR, see "Fast Database Recovery" on page 471.

IMS Database Recovery Facility for z/OS, V2

One of the IBM IMS tools, IMS Database Recovery Facility for z/OS, allows you to recover multiple database data sets and Fast Path areas in an IMS DBCTL or DB/DC environment simultaneously. IMS Database Recovery Facility for z/OS simplifies the database recovery process by eliminating the need to run separate recovery jobs for each database data set that requires recovery. Recovery using IMS Database Recovery Facility for z/OS reduces the time that broken databases and areas are unavailable by processing input data in parallel and recovering multiple database data sets and areas simultaneously.

Related Reading: For more information about this and other IMS tools, see Chapter 26, "IBM IMS Tools," on page 443.

IMS Shutdown

There are several different ways to shut down IMS, depending on the type of control region that is running (DB/BC, DBCTL, or DCCTL), and whether or not the IMS message queues are required following the next IMS startup.

A common sequence for shutting down the entire online IMS system is:

1. For an IMS DB/DC or DCCTL environment, stop the transactions.
   For an IMS DBCTL environment, disconnect from the coordinator controller (CCTL).
2. Stop the dependent regions.
3. Stop the control region.
4. For an IMS DB/DC or DBCTL environment, you might want to stop the IRLM, but you do not have to stop IRLM in order to stop IMS. Be careful in stopping an IRLM because other IMSs might be using it.
5. For a shared-queues environment, you might want to shut down the Common Queue Server (CQS), but you do not have to stop CQS in order to stop IMS. Be careful in stopping a CQS because other clients might be using it.
6. For an IMSplex environment, shut down the IMS components that participate in the IMSplex, and then shut down the Common Service Layer.

Related Reading: For more information about:

- Shutting down an IMSplex, see "Operating an IMSplex" on page 499.
- Shutting down an IMS, see *IMS Version 9: Operations Guide*.
- The commands involved in shutting down an IMS, see *IMS Version 9: Command Reference*.

IMS Database Manager

CHAPTER 6

Overview of the IMS Database Manager

ou can order and install the IMS Database Manager (IMS DB) with or without the IMS Transaction Manager (IMS TM).

In This Chapter:

- "Functions of the IMS Database Manager"
- "Implementation of IMS Databases" on page 62
- "Storing Data in IMS and DB2 UDB for z/OS" on page 64
- "Storing XML Data in IMS" on page 65

FUNCTIONS OF THE IMS DATABASE MANAGER

A database management system (DBMS) provides facilities for business application transactions or processes to access stored information. The role of a DBMS is to provide the following functions:

- Allow access to the data for multiple users from a single instance of the data.
- Control concurrent access to the data to maintain integrity for all updates.
- Minimize hardware device and operating system access method dependencies.
- Reduce data redundancy by maintaining only one instance of the data.
- Interface with the operating system and manage the physical location of the data. Application programs that access and manipulate the data do not need to know where the data actually resides.

IMS DB provides a central point for the control and access to application data. IMS provides a set of utility programs that provide these functions.

IMPLEMENTATION OF IMS DATABASES

IMS DB supports multiple forms of enterprise databases, so that varied application requirements can be met by exploiting whichever database technology best suits the users' requirements.

The supported IMS database types are:

Full-function databases

> Hierarchic databases that are accessed through Data Language I (DL/I) call language and can be processed by all six types of application programs: IFP, MPP, BMP, JMP, JBP, and batch.

> Full-function databases can be accessed directly by record or sequentially, and by other sequences that are planned for when the database is designed. Most full-function databases are limited in size to 4 GB or 8 GB (depending on the access method) per data set. Data Set Groups, partitioning, or High Availability Large Databases (HALDBs) offer higher capacities.

Fast Path databases

> Two types of databases designed to provide highly available data and fast processing for IMS applications. They can be processed by all types of application programs. The two types of Fast Path databases are:

> **Data entry databases (DEDBs)**

>> A direct-access database that consists of one or more areas, with each area containing both root segments and dependent segments. DEDBs use a data structure that allows them to be used for both hierarchic processing and journaling. The database is accessed by using VSAM's Media Manager.

>> DEDBs are particularly suited for use where large databases or very low processing costs are required, or when particularly high data availability or very high performance is required.

> **Main storage databases (MSDBs)**

>> MSDB functionality has been superseded by the DEDB Virtual Storage Option (VSO), so this book does not describe MSDBs and you should not to use them.

IMS uses a hierarchical model for its database, which is described in more detail in Chapter 7, "Overview of the IMS Hierarchical Database Model," on page 67. The data stored in the IMS databases is organized using a number of internal IMS access methods. Each of these access methods is tailored for certain types of access to the database. The choice of the appropriate access method is discussed in detail in Chapter 8, "Implementing the IMS Hierarchical Database Model," on page 83.

No single database technology is the best option for all applications, even though industry trends might suggest that an organization standardize on only one database type (for example, a relational database). However, limiting your enterprise to only relational databases would preclude the consideration of other technologies that might result in significant savings in processing time or application development costs far in excess, for example, of the small additional cost of introducing DEDBs to your organization.

Compared to IMS DB, DB2 UDB for z/OS provides well for unstructured or unplanned access to data and therefore provides flexibility in the support of future application requirements. However, any IMS database usually has a significantly lower processing cost than a DB2 UDB for z/OS database.

The IMS access methods are the application's view of how the data is stored. IMS actually uses the operating system access methods to physically store data on disk storage. The software access methods that IMS uses are:

- **VSAM (Virtual Storage Access Method):** A z/OS access method.
- **OSAM (Overflow Sequential Access Method):** An IMS data management access method that combines selected characteristics of z/OS BSAM (Basic Sequential Access Method) and BDAM (Basic Direct Access Method).

Full-Function Databases

Full-function databases are designed to support most types of database requirements and can be used in a wide variety of applications. Most IMS applications make use of full-function databases unless there are specific requirements for DEDBs. The major characteristics of full-function databases are:

- Small or large databases
- Access to records through unique or non-unique keys
- Many types of segments (up to 15 levels allowed)
- Records can be stored in key sequence, but this is not required

One function associated with full-function databases is called data set groups. With *data set groups*, you can put some types of segments in a database record in data sets other than the primary data set without destroying the hierarchic sequence of segments in a database record. You might use data set groups to accommodate the differing needs of your applications. By using data set groups, you can give an application program fast access to the segments in which it is interested. The application program simply bypasses the data sets that contain unnecessary segments. You can define up to 10 data set groups for a single full-function database.

The full-function databases that were created in IMS Version 1 through IMS Version 6 were limited in size: the maximum data set size for VSAM is 4 GB and for OSAM is 8 GB. IMS Version 7 introduced High Availability Databases (HALDBs) to address this size limit. HALDB allows full-function databases to grow much larger. A HALDB is a partitioned full-function database. Partitioning a database allows the use of smaller data sets that are easier to manage. Multiple partitions decrease the amount of unavailable data if a partition fails or is taken offline. HALDBs are implemented with OSAM or VSAM, but always with a maximum 4 GB data set size.

HALDB allows the grouping of full-function database records into sets of partitions that are treated as a single database while permitting functions to be performed independently for each partition. Each HALDB partition has the same capacity limit as a non-HALDB database: each partition can consist of up to 10 data sets.

You can increase the amount of data that is stored in a single partition by using data set groups. The logical design of a database applies for the entire HALDB database, not independently for each partition. The choice to use data set groups, which allow the storage of selected segments into separate nominated data sets, is a logical database design decision. Each HALDB partition has the same logical design because each partition has the same architecture for data set groups. By using data set groups in partitions, a large amount of data can be contained in a single partition. HALDBs can contain up to 1001 partitions.

Related Reading: For more information about HALDBs, see "PHDAM and PHIDAM Access Methods" on page 97.

Data Entry Databases (DEDBs)

DEDBs support intensive IMS database requirements, particularly in the banking industry, for:

- Large databases that contain millions of records and extend well beyond the original 4 GB database limits for full-function databases
- Access to each database record by a key field
- Lower processing costs for each database record and update than are required for full-function databases
- The capability to support higher transaction workloads than full-function databases can sustain, while maintaining per-transaction cost advantages
- Improved availability, with reduced requirements for database outage, especially for database maintenance activities such as database reorganizations
- Lower processing costs for particular types of processing, where data is inserted online and retrieved in batches for further processing, and eventually deleted in batches
- The possibility of eliminating transaction-related I/O from database processing

Application programming for DEDBs is little different from that for full-function databases.

Storing Data in IMS and DB2 UDB for z/OS

Some business applications require that the data be kept in both IMS and DB2 UDB for z/OS databases. One such scenario is a high-performance production application that works with the data in an IMS database and a business decision support application that works with the same data in a DB2 UDB for z/OS database. Production applications running in IMS TM can update data that is stored in a DB2 UDB for z/OS database as well as data that is stored in an IMS database. If not performed in a single, logical unit of work, coordinating these updates can be complex.

IBM IMS DataPropagator can automatically propagate data from IMS databases to DB2 UDB for z/OS tables and vice versa.

Related Reading: For more information about the IBM IMS DataPropagator, see Chapter 26, "IBM IMS Tools," on page 443 or go to www.ibm.com/software/data/dpropnr.

Storing XML Data in IMS

IMS is a natural database management system for managing XML documents because XML and IMS databases are both hierarchical. IMS allows you to easily receive and store incoming XML documents as well as compose XML documents from existing, legacy information that is stored in IMS databases. For example, you can:

- Compose XML documents from all types of existing IMS databases. For example you can support business-to-business on demand transactions and intra-organizational sharing of data.
- Receive incoming XML documents and store them in IMS databases. These databases can be legacy databases or new databases.

You can store XML documents intact, decomposed, or in a combination of intact and decomposed. In decomposed storage mode, the incoming document is parsed and element data and attributes are stored in fields as normal IMS data. Decomposed storage is appropriate for data-centric documents. In intact storage, the incoming document, including its tags, is stored directly in the database without IMS being aware of its structure. Intact storage is appropriate for document-centric documents.

Related Reading: For more information about storing and retrieving XML documents in IMS databases, see "XML Storage in IMS Databases" on page 321.

CHAPTER 7

Overview of the IMS Hierarchical Database Model

I MS uses a hierarchical database model as the basic method of storing data. Unlike the relational model used by DB2 UDB for z/OS, which was the result of theoretical work,[1] the hierarchical model was arrived at as a pragmatic way of storing and retrieving data quickly while using as few computer resources as possible.

In the hierarchical model, individual data types are implemented as *segments* in a hierarchical structure. A segment is the smallest amount of data that can be transferred by one IMS operation, is uniquely defined, and something about which you can collect information.

The hierarchical structure is based on the relationship between the segments and the access paths that are required by the applications.

IMS uses the term *database* slightly differently than other DBMSs. In IMS, a database is commonly used to describe the implementation of one *hierarchy*, so that an application would normally access a large number of IMS databases. Compared to the relational model, an IMS segment is approximately equivalent to a table and an IMS database implements the referential integrity rules.

In This Chapter:

---

1. "A Relational Model of Data for Large Shared Data Banks," paper by Dr. E. F. Codd that was published in *Communications of the Association for Computing Machinery*, June, 1970.

IMS Hierarchical Database Basics

A database segment definition defines the fields for a set of segment instances similar to the way a relational table defines columns for a set of rows in a table. In this way, segments relate to relational tables, and fields in a segment relate to columns in a relational table.

The name of an IMS segment becomes the table name in an SQL query.

A fundamental difference between segments in a hierarchical database and tables in a relational database is that, in a hierarchical database, segments are implicitly joined with each other. In a relational database, you explicitly join two tables. A segment instance in a hierarchical database is already joined with its parent segment and its child segments, which are all along the same hierarchical path. In a relational database, this relationship between tables is captured by foreign and primary keys.

Figure 7-1 illustrates a hierarchical database and Figure 7-2 on page 69 illustrates the relational representation of the database shown in Figure 7-1.

The dealership sample database contains five segment types, which are shown in Figure 7-1. The root segment is the Dealer segment. Under the Dealer segment is its child segment, the Model segment. Under the Model segment are its children: the segments Order, Sales, and Stock.

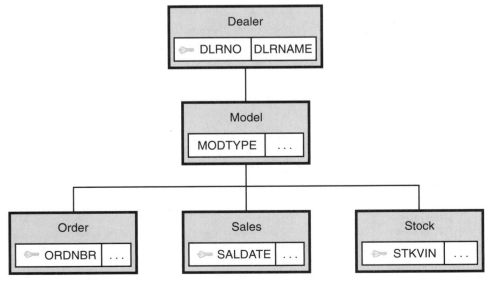

Figure 7-1   Example of a Hierarchical Dealership Database

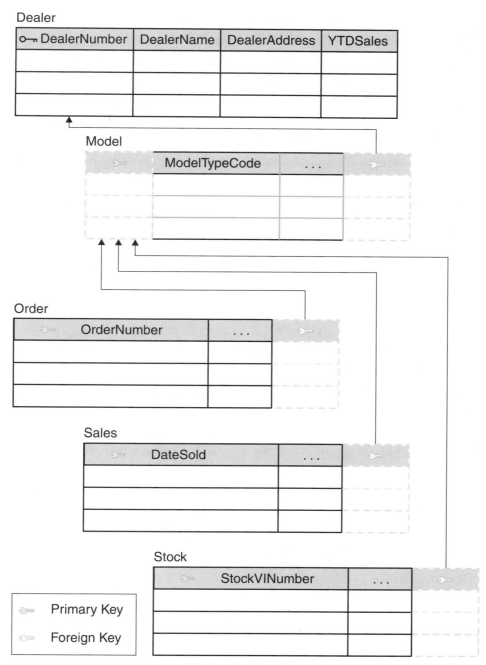

Figure 7-2 Relational Representation of the Dealership Database

The Dealer segment identifies a dealer selling cars, and the segment contains a dealer name and a unique dealer number in the fields DLRNAME and DLRNO.

Dealers carry car types, each of which has a corresponding Model segment. A Model segment contains a type code in the field MODTYPE.

There is an Order segment for each car that is ordered for the dealership. A Stock segment is created for each car that is available for sale in the dealer's inventory. When the car is sold, a Sales segment is created.

Figure 7-2 on page 69 shows a relational representation of the hierarchical dealership database record shown in Figure 7-1 on page 68.

If a segment does not have a unique key, which is similar to a primary key in relational databases, view the corresponding relational table as having a generated primary key added to its column (field) list. An example of a generated primary key is in the Model table (segment) in Figure 7-2. Similar to referential integrity in relational databases, you cannot insert a child segment (Order) into the database without it being a child of a specific parent segment (Model).

Also note that the field (column) names have been renamed. You can rename segments and fields to more meaningful names.

The hierarchical data structure in Figure 7-3 on page 71 describes the data as seen by the application program. It does not represent the physical storage of the data. The physical storage is of no concern to the application program.

The basic building element of a hierarchical data structure is the parent/child relationship between segments of data, illustrated in Figure 7-3.

Each occurrence (or instance) of a parent segment is associated with 0 or more occurrences of a child segment. Each child segment occurrence is associated with one, and only one, occurrence of a parent segment.

Sometimes it is necessary to distinguish between a segment type (the kind of segment) and the segment occurrence (the particular instance of its contents and location).

As shown in Figure 7-3, a parent can have several child segment types. Also, a child segment can, at the same time, be a parent segment; that is, it can have children below it. The segment with no parent segment (the one at the top) is called the *root segment.*

All the parent and child occurrences for a given root segment are grouped together in a database record. The collection of all of the database records with the same root and hierarchical structure (in Figure 7-3, each PART segment with its dependent STOCK, PURCHASE ORDER, and DETAIL segments) is an IMS database (the PART database).

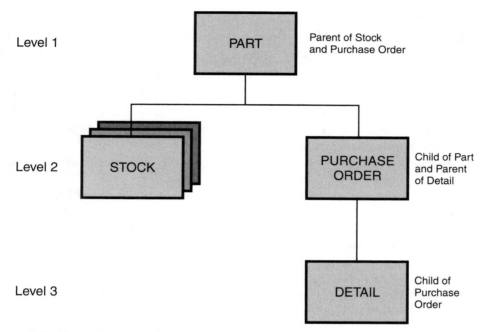

Figure 7-3 Hierarchical Data Structure

For a given database record, only one segment can appear at the first level in the hierarchy, but multiple segments can appear at lower levels in the hierarchy. For example, multiple STOCK and PURCHASE ORDER segments can exist for one PART segment. Since each dependent segment in the hierarchy has only one parent, or immediate superior segment, the hierarchical data structure is sometimes called a tree structure. Each branch of the tree is called a hierarchical path. A hierarchical path to a segment contains all consecutive segments from the top of the structure down to that segment.

Through the concept of program sensitivity, IMS can restrict a program to "seeing" only those segments of information that are relevant to the processing being performed. For example, an inventory program could be written to see only the PART and STOCK segments of the database record shown in Figure 7-3. The program need not be aware of the existence of the PURCHASE ORDER segment.

IMS allows a wide variety of data structures. The maximum number of different segment types is 255 in a single database. A maximum of 15 segment levels can be defined in a hierarchical data structure. There is no restriction on the number of occurrences of each segment type, except as imposed by physical access method limits.

BASIC SEGMENT TYPES

The following list contains a detailed description of the various segment types and their interrelations within a hierarchical data structure. Refer to Figure 7-3 on page 71 and Figure 7-4 while reading these descriptions.

- The segment on top of the structure is the *root segment*. Each root segment normally has a key field that serves as the unique identifier of that root segment, and as such, of that particular database record (for example, the part number). There is only one root segment per database record.
- A *dependent segment* relies on the segments above it in the hierarchy for its full meaning and identification.
- A parent/child relationship exists between a segment and its immediate dependents.
- Different occurrences of a particular segment type under the same parent segment are called *twin segments*.
- Segment occurrences of different types under the same parent are called *sibling segments*.
- A single segment can be a dependent and a child simultaneously. For example, in Figure 7-4, segment DETAIL 211 is a dependent of segment ORDER 21 and of root segment PART 2 and also a child of segment ORDER 21.

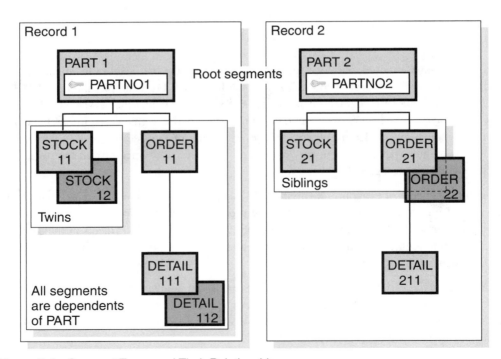

Figure 7-4   Segment Types and Their Relationships

SEQUENCE FIELDS AND ACCESS PATHS

IMS uses *sequence fields* to identify and to provide access to a particular database record and its segments. Each segment normally has one field that is denoted as the sequence field. The sequence fields should be unique in value for each occurrence of a segment type below its parent occurrence. However, not every segment type must have a sequence field defined. The sequence field for the root segment must have a sequence field because it serves as the identification for the database record. Normally, IMS provides a fast, direct access path to the root segment of the database record based on this sequence field. This direct access is extended to lower level segments if the sequence fields of the segments along the hierarchical path are specified too.

N O T E   The sequence field is often referred to as the key field, or simply the key.

In Figure 7-4 on page 72, one access path is through the PART, ORDER, and DETAIL segments. The access path must always start with the root segment. This is the access path that is used by IMS. The application program, however, can directly request a particular Detail segment of a given Order of a given Part in one single DL/I call by specifying a sequence field value for each of the three segment levels.

In addition to the basic hierarchical data structure described so far, IMS provides two additional methods for defining access paths to a database segment.

Logical relationships

> A logical relationship is a user-defined path between two independent segments. Logical relationships allow a logical view to be defined of one or more physical databases. To the application, the logical relationship looks like a single database.

Secondary indexes

> Secondary indexes provide an alternate access path for full-function databases by using a root or dependent segment as the entry location to the database record in one physical database.

Both methods provide different access paths for an application to the physical databases. Logical relationships and secondary indexes are defined to IMS in addition to the definition for the basic hierarchical structure. The logical relationships and secondary indexes are automatically maintained by IMS, transparent to the application.

Use these methods only if there are strong application or performance reasons for doing so, because both involve additional overheads.

Logical Relationships

Through logical relationships, IMS provides a facility to interrelate segments from different hierarchies. In doing so, new hierarchical structures are defined that provide additional access capabilities to the segments involved. These segments can belong to the same database or to different databases. You can define a new database called a *logical database*. This logical database allows presentation of a new hierarchical structure to the application program. Although the connected physical databases could constitute a network data structure, the application data structure still consists of one or more hierarchical data structures.

For example, given the entities and relationships in the two databases illustrated in Figure 7-5, you might decide that, based on the application's most common access paths, the data should be implemented as two physical hierarchical databases: the PART database and the ORDER database. However, there are some reasons why other applications might need to use a relationship between the PART segment and the DETAIL segment. So a logical relationship can be built between PART and DETAIL.

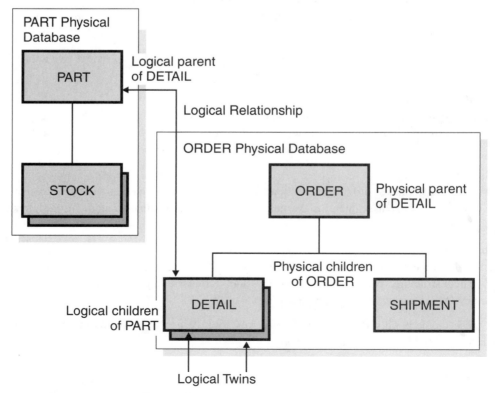

Figure 7-5   Two Logically Related Physical Databases: Part and Order

The basic mechanism used to build a logical relationship is to specify a dependent segment as a logical child by relating it to a second parent, the logical parent.

In Figure 7-5 on page 74, the logical child segment DETAIL exists only once, yet participates in two hierarchical structures. It has a physical parent, ORDER, and logical parent, PART. The data in the logical child segment and in its dependents is called *intersection data* (the intersection of the two hierarchies). For example, intersection data in Figure 7-5 that might be needed by an application could be a value in the DETAIL segment for a part or order quantity.

By defining two additional logical databases, two new logical data structures shown in Figure 7-6 on page 76 can be made available for application program processing, even within one single program.

The DETAIL/PART segment in Figure 7-6 is a *concatenated segment*. It consists of the logical child segment (DETAIL) plus the logical parent segment (PART). The DETAIL/ORDER segment in Figure 7-6 is also a concatenated segment, but it consists of the logical child segment (DETAIL) plus the physical parent segment (ORDER). Logical children with the same logical parent are called *logical twins*. For example, all DETAIL segments for a given PART segment are logical twins. As Figure 7-5 shows, the logical child has two access paths: one via its physical parent, the physical access path, and one via its logical parent, the logical access path. Both access paths are maintained by IMS and can be concurrently available to one program.

You might want to use logical relationships for the following reasons:

- They provide an alternate access path for the application. For example, they allow (depending on pointer choice) an application to have direct access from a segment in one physical database to a lower level segment in another physical database, without the application having to access the second physical database directly and read down through the hierarchy.
- They provide an alternate hierarchical database structure for an application so that different applications, or parts of applications, can have a view of the physical databases that most closely matches that application's view of the data.
- They can make IMS enforce a relationship between two segments in two physically separate databases (that is, IMS preserves referential integrity). You can define the relationship such that a logical parent cannot be deleted if it still has logical children, and a logical child cannot be added it there is no logical parent. For example, referring to Figure 7-6, you could define the relationship such that no order DETAIL could be inserted if there were no corresponding PART, and no PART could be deleted if there were still order DETAIL segments for that part. Any application attempting to make such changes would have the database call rejected by IMS.

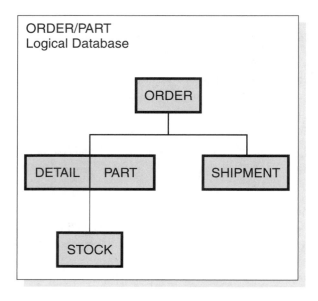

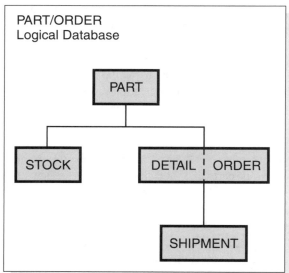

Figure 7-6   Two Logical Databases After Relating the Part and Order Databases

Potential disadvantages in using logical relationships are:

- The performance overhead involved in maintaining the pointers used in the logical relationships. Every time a segment that participates in a logical relationship is updated, the other segment (in another physical database) that participates in the relationship might need to be updated. The additional updating of pointers can result in an appreciable increase in physical I/Os to auxiliary storage.

- When a database needs to be reorganized, except with some very limited pointer choices, all other databases that are logically related must be updated at the same time because the pointers used to maintain the logical relationships rely on the physical position of the segments in that database and the position of the segments can be altered by the reorganization.

Before using logical relationships, carefully weigh the potential performance and administrative overhead against the advantages of using logical relationships. Adding logical relationships and performing the appropriate maintenance increases the overall cost of a database. Therefore, logical relationships are only worthwhile if that additional cost can be justified by other processing benefits.

Related Reading: For more information about implementing logical relationships, see *IMS Version 9: Administration Guide: Database Manager.*

Secondary Index Databases

IMS provides additional access flexibility with secondary index databases. A secondary index represents a different access path (pointers) to any segment in the database other than the path defined by the key field in the root segment. The additional access paths can result in faster retrieval of data.

A secondary index is in its own separate database and must use VSAM as its access method. Because a secondary index is in its own database, it can be processed as a separate database.

There can be 32 secondary indexes for a segment type and a total of 1000 secondary indexes for a single database.

To set up a secondary index, three types of segments must be defined to IMS: a pointer segment, a target segment, and a source segment. After an index is defined, IMS automatically maintains the index if the data on which the index relies changes, even if the program causing that change is not aware of the index. The segments used in a secondary index are illustrated in Figure 7-7 on page 78.

As shown in Figure 7-7:

Pointer segment
> The pointer segment is contained in the secondary index database and is the only type of segment in the secondary index database.

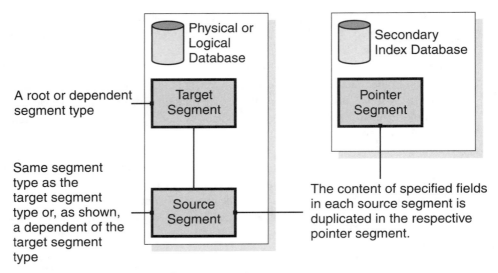

Figure 7-7   Segments Used for Secondary Indexes

Target segment

The index target segment is the segment that becomes initially accessible from the secondary index. The target segment:

- Is the segment that the application program needs to view as a root in a hierarchy.
- Is in the database that is being indexed.
- Is pointed to by the pointer segment.
- Can be at any one of the 15 levels in the database.
- Is accessed directly using the RBA or symbolic pointer stored in the pointer segment.

The database being indexed can be a physical or logical database. Quite often, the target segment is the root segment.

Source segment

The source segment is also in the regular database. The source segment contains the field (or fields) that the pointer segment has as its key field. Data is copied from the source segment and put in the pointer segment's key field. The source and the target segment can be the same segment, or the source segment can be a dependent of the target segment.

The pointer segments are ordered and accessed based on the field contents of the index source segment. In general, there is one index pointer segment for each index source segment, but multiple index pointer segments can point to the same index target segment. The index source and index target segment might be the same, or the index source segment might be a dependent of the index target segment.

The secondary index key (search field) is made up of one to five fields from the index source segment. The search field does not have to be a unique value, but IBM strongly recommends you make it a unique value to avoid the overhead in storing and searching duplicates. There are a number of fields that can be concatenated to the end of the secondary index search field to make it unique:

- A subsequence field, consisting of one to five more fields from the index source segment. This is maintained by IMS but, unlike the search field, cannot be used by an application for a search argument when using the secondary index.
- A system defined field that uniquely defines the index source segment: the /SX variable.
- A system defined field that defines the concatenated key (the concatenation of the key values of all of the segment occurrences in the hierarchical path leading to that segment) of the index source segment: the /CX variable.

Some reasons for using secondary indexes are:

- Quick access, particularly random access by online transactions, by a key other than the primary key of the database.
- Access to the index target segment without having to negotiate the full database hierarchy (particularly useful if the index target segment is not the root segment). This is similar to using logical relationships, but provides a single alternate access path into a single physical database. If this is all that is required, then a secondary index is the better technique to use.
- Ability to process the index database separately. For example, a batch process might need to process only the search fields.
- A quick method of accessing a small subset of the database records by using a sparse index (see "Sparse Indexing with Secondary Indexes" on page 80).

Potential disadvantages in using secondary indexes are:

- The performance overheads in updating the secondary index database every time any of the fields making up the search field in the index source segment is updated or when the index source segment is inserted or deleted.
- The administrative overheads in setting up, monitoring, backing up, and tuning the secondary index database.
- When the database containing the index source segment is reorganized, the secondary index must also be rebuilt because the pointers used to maintain the connection between the source segment and the secondary index database rely on the physical position of the source segment in the database, which can be altered by the reorganization.

As with logical relationships, consider carefully whether the benefits of using a secondary index outweigh the performance and administrative overheads.

Related Reading: For details on implementing secondary indexes, see *IMS Version 9: Administration Guide: Database Manager.*

Sparse Indexing with Secondary Indexes

Another technique that can be used with secondary indexes is sparse indexing. Normally IMS maintains index entries for all occurrences of the secondary index source segment. However, it is possible to cause IMS to suppress index entries for some of the occurrences of the index source segment. You might want to suppress index entries if you were only interested in processing segments that had a non-null value in the field.

As a general rule, only consider this technique if you expect 20% or less of the index source segments to be created. The suppression can be done either by specifying that all bytes in the field should be a specific character (NULLVAL parameter) or by selection with the Secondary Index Maintenance exit routine.

Example of a Secondary Index

Suppose an application needs to retrieve the street address field from the SHIPMENT segment in the ORDER physical database, so that a delivery route can be established. As shown in Figure 7-8 on page 81, an index database can be created with a pointer segment defined for that field (STREET_ADDRESS).

The pointer segment contains a pointer to the ORDER root segment (of the ORDER physical database) and also contains key field information (STREET_ADDRESS) from the SHIPMENT (source) segment.

In Figure 7-8, the secondary index key (the search field) is the STREET_ADDRESS field of the SHIPMENT source segment.

As an example of suppressing index entries (in Figure 7-8), suppose that the ORDER segment had a field set in it to indicate the order could not be fulfilled immediately, but needed to be back ordered. You could define a secondary index including this field, but suppress all entries that did not have this field set, giving rapid access to all back orders.

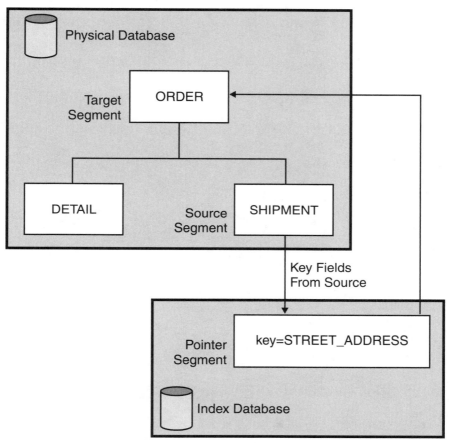

Figure 7-8   A Physical Database and Its Secondary Index Database

8

Implementing the IMS Hierarchical Database Model

C hapter 7, "Overview of the IMS Hierarchical Database Model," on page 67 described the logical model for IMS databases. This chapter describes how the hierarchical database model is physically implemented using IMS DB and z/OS services.

For both IMS DB and IMS TM, application programs interface with IMS through functions provided by the IMS DL/I application programming interface (API). IMS access methods and the operating system access methods are used to physically store the data. See Figure 8-1 on page 84. This chapter addresses only the functions that are relevant to IMS DB.

The individual elements that make up the database, segments, and database records are organized using different IMS access methods. The choice of access method can influence the functionality available to your application, the order in which data is returned to the application, and the performance the application receives from IMS DB.

Underlying the IMS access methods, IMS uses VSAM or OSAM to store the data on DASD and move the data between the DASD and the buffers in the IMS address space, where the data is manipulated.

The structure of the IMS databases, and a program's access to them, is defined by a set of IMS control blocks:

- The database description block (DDB)
- The program specification block (PSB)
- The application control block (ACB)

These control blocks are coded as sets of source statements that are then generated into control blocks for use by IMS DB and the application.

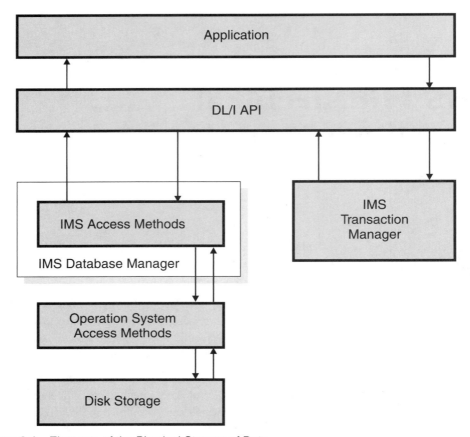

Figure 8-1   Elements of the Physical Storage of Data

In This Chapter:

SEGMENTS, RECORDS, AND POINTERS

As described in Chapter 7, "Overview of the IMS Hierarchical Database Model," on page 67, a segment represents one entity or grouping of related fields. In IMS, unlike DB2 or many other DBMSs, you do not have to define all of the fields to IMS. You must only define the segment as being long enough to contain all the application data to be stored. The only fields you must define to IMS are those that you need to use to identify and search for segments. Specifying non-search fields is optional.

In addition to the application data, each segment contains control information that is used by IMS. The control information is placed at the beginning of the segment in a *segment prefix*. Figure 8-2 shows the layout of a segment with the prefix and application data portions. The prefix is automatically maintained by IMS and is not accessible to the application. The control information in the prefix consists of various flags, descriptive fields (segment type code and delete byte), and pointers to implement the hierarchical structure and access paths. The contents of the prefix will vary, depending on the IMS access method and options chosen when the database is defined.

Prefix					Data
Sement Type Code	Delete Byte	RBA Pointer	RBA Pointer	RBA Pointer	Application Data

Figure 8-2   Layout of a Typical Segment

The RBA pointers in Figure 8-2 consist of the relative offset (number of bytes) of the segment being pointed at, from the start of the data set being used to store the data. This is the relative byte address (RBA). For example, a root segment would contain pointer fields in the prefix for, at a minimum, all of the dependent segment types under the root. IMS will automatically define the minimum set of pointers to maintain the hierarchical structure. The database designer can also specify additional predefined types of pointers, in addition to those necessary for the minimum hierarchical structure. This pointer selection can influence the performance of applications using the databases. Figure 8-3 on page 86 shows database segments with their pointers: physical twin forward (PTF), physical twin backward (PTB), and physical child forward (PCF).

Physical Segment Design

When designing segments, the physical parameters are important. The following list discusses the details of these physical parameters.

- **Segment length:** IMS uses the segment length as it is defined in the DBD to store each segment. If you leave free space at the end of the segment for future use, that space is physically held space on DASD unless you compress the segment. If the application is likely to have additional segment length requirements later, it might be easier to make use of this free space than to increase the segment length later. Balance the cost of making the change to the databases and programs against the cost of wasted DASD space.

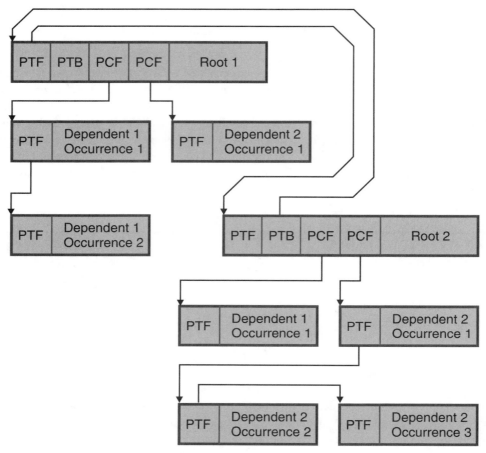

Figure 8-3 Database Segments and Pointers

- **Number of occurrences per segment per parent:** Avoid using long twin chains, which are many occurrences of a particular segment type under one parent. Estimate chain lengths in terms of the number of blocks needed to store each such segment.
- **Location of segments in the hierarchy:** Position the segments that are used together most often with the root segment into one control interval or block. The segments are initially physically stored in hierarchical sequence, so the most frequently used segments should be on the left of the structure (low segment codes).
- **Average database record size:** The average database record is calculated by the total bytes of all segments under the root segment. Although they might have almost the same number of bytes, small segments with more twins result in better performance and space usage than larger segments with fewer twins.

IMS HIERARCHICAL ACCESS METHODS

You can use different IMS access methods to organize and store data segments and records. Choose an access method after you carefully analyze the access requirements of the applications, for example, the functionality available to the application, the order in which segments are returned to the application, and database performance considerations. Some access methods provide a better solution to your business needs than others.

For optimal processing cost, the order for selecting a database type should be:

1. DEDB, unless logical relationships, secondary indexing, or true batch access is required.
2. HDAM, possibly with a sequential randomizer (if key sequence access is needed frequently) or use a secondary index for such access. If you want high availability, PHDAM might be a better choice.
3. HIDAM, if high rates of sequential access are required but no sequential randomizer can be designed. If you want high availability, PHIDAM might be a better choice.

In general, you can change access methods (VSAM or OSAM) during reorganization without affecting application programs. Choose the access method carefully because the access method is one of the most critical performance factors. You might not be able to change database types (HIDAM, HDAM, HISAM) during reorganization without affecting the application.

Table 8-1 describes the most commonly used IMS database organizations.

Table 8-1 Database Organizations

Database Type	Organization
HDAM	Hierarchical Direct Access Method
PHDAM	Partitioned Hierarchical Direct Access Method
HIDAM	Hierarchical Indexed Direct Access Method
PHIDAM	Partitioned Hierarchical Indexed Direct Access Method
HISAM	Hierarchical Indexed Sequential Access Method
SHISAM	Simple Hierarchical Indexed Sequential Access Method
GSAM	Generalized Sequential Access Method
DEDB	Data Entry Database

Related Reading: All the types of the IMS database organizations are described in *IMS Version 9: Administration Guide: Database Manager.*

The three most common IMS access methods are:

- **Hierarchical Direct (HD):** Consisting of the HDAM and HIDAM access methods. These methods are described in "HDAM Access Method" on page 89, and "HIDAM Access Method" on page 94.

  HDAM and HIDAM databases have many similarities. HD databases can be partitioned using either the HALDB Partition Definition utility (%DFSHALDB) or DBRC commands. After you partition an HDAM database, it becomes a partitioned hierarchical direct access method (PHDAM) database. After you partition a HIDAM database, it becomes a partitioned hierarchical indexed direct access method (PHIDAM) database. PHDAM and PHIDAM databases are generically referred to as High Availability Large Databases (HALDBs).

  For information about HALDBs, see "PHDAM and PHIDAM Access Methods" on page 97.

- **Hierarchical Sequential (HS):** Consisting of the HSAM and HISAM access methods. HS access methods are less used today because the HD access methods have a number of advantages. See "HSAM and HISAM Access Methods" on page 108 for a short description of these access methods.

  There are also simple variations of HSAM and HISAM: simple HSAM (SHSAM) and simple HISAM (SHISAM). These are described briefly in "HSAM and HISAM Access Methods" on page 108.

- **Data Entry Database (DEDB):** DEDBs have characteristics that make them suitable for high performance and high availability applications. However, some functions available to DEDBs (such as subset pointers and FLD calls) are not available to full-function databases, so the application must be specifically designed and written to implement something similar. DEDBs are described in "Fast Path DEDBs" on page 101.

The HD and HS databases are full-function databases, and DEDB databases are referred to as Fast Path databases.

In addition to the three most common access methods, there are two more IMS access methods that provide additional functionality:

- **Index Databases:** These are used to physically implement secondary indexes and primary indexes for HIDAM and PHIDAM databases. For more information, see "Index Databases" on page 101.

- **Generalized Sequential Access Method (GSAM):** GSAM is used to extend the restart and recovery facilities of IMS DB to non-IMS sequential files that are processed by IMS batch programs and BMP applications. These files can also be accessed directly by using z/OS access methods. For more information, see "GSAM Access Method" on page 107.

> **E X C E P T I O N S:** Most types of application regions can access the majority of the database organization types. The exceptions are:
> - **GSAM:** GSAM databases cannot be accessed from MPR, JMP, or CICS regions.
> - **DEDB:** DEDBs cannot be accessed from true batch (DB batch) regions.

HDAM Access Method

An HDAM database normally consists of one VSAM entry-sequenced data set (ESDS) or OSAM data set. The information in this section is illustrated in Figure 8-4 on page 90.

To access the data in an HDAM database, IMS uses a *randomizing module*, which computes the address for the root segment of a record in the database. This address consists of the relative number of a VSAM control interval (CI) or OSAM block within the data set and the number of a root anchor point (RAP) within that CI or block. Root anchor points are located at the beginning of each CI or block and are used for the chaining of root segments that randomize to that CI or block. All chaining of segments is done using a 4-byte address. This 4-byte address, the relative-byte address (RBA), is the byte that the segment starts at relative to the start of the data set.

IMS supplies a general randomizing module, DFSHDC40, which is suitable for most applications. The *IMS Version 9: Customization Guide* describes this module and also provides details about how to modify this module or develop your own randomizing routines.

In an HDAM database, the VSAM ESDS or OSAM data set is divided into two areas:

- **The root addressable area:** The first number of CIs or blocks in the data set. You define the root addressable area in your database definition (DBD).
- **The overflow area:** The remaining portion of the data set. The overflow area is not explicitly defined, but is the remaining space in the data set after you allocate space for the root addressable area.

IMS uses the root addressable area as the primary storage area for segments in each database record. IMS always attempts to put new and updated segments in the root addressable area. The overflow area is used when IMS is unable to find enough space for a segment that is inserted in the root addressable area.

IMS uses a number of techniques to distribute free space within the root addressable area to allow future segments to be inserted in the most desirable block. Because database records vary in length, you can use the *bytes* parameter in the RMNAME= keyword (in the DBD) to control the amount of space used for each database record in the root addressable area. The *bytes* parameter limits the number of segments of a database record that can be consecutively inserted into the root addressable area. Note that this limitation only applies if the segments in the record are

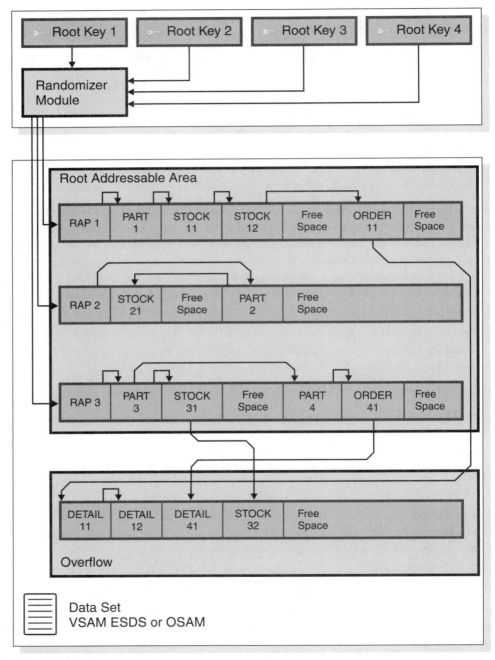

Figure 8-4   Physical Layout of Records in an HDAM Database Data Set

inserted at the same time. When consecutively inserting a root and its dependents, each segment is stored in the root addressable area until the next segment to be stored causes the total space used to exceed the specified number of bytes. Consecutive inserts are inserts to one database record without an intervening call to process a segment in a different database record.

The total space used for a segment is the combined lengths of the prefix and data portions of the segment. When exceeded, that segment and all remaining segments in the database record are stored in the overflow area. It should be noted that the value of the *bytes* parameter controls only segments that are consecutively inserted in one database record.

When you load HDAM databases initially, you can specify that a percentage of the space in each block should be left for subsequent segments to be inserted. This free space allows subsequent segments to be inserted close to the database record they belong to. This free space percentage is specified on the DBD. You can also specify in the DBD that a percentage of blocks in the data set are left empty, but you should not do this with HDAM databases because doing so will result in IMS randomizing segments to a free block, and then placing them in another block. This would result in additional I/O (the block they randomize to, plus the block they are in) each time the segment is retrieved. Analyze the potential growth of the database to determine a percentage amount for this free space.

When IMS inserts segments, it uses the HD space search algorithm to determine which CI or block to put the segment in. By doing so, IMS attempts to minimize physical I/Os while accessing segments in a database record by placing the segment in a CI or block as physically close as possible to other segments in the database record.

Related Reading: For more information about the HD space search algorithm, see the chapter "Designing Full-Function Databases" in *IMS Version 9: Administration Guide: Database Manager.*

In addition to organizing the application data segments in an HDAM database, IMS also manages the free space in the data set. As segments are inserted and deleted, areas in the CI or blocks become free (in addition to the free space defined when the database is initially loaded). IMS space management allows this free space to be reused for subsequent segment insertion.

To enable IMS to quickly determine which CI or blocks have space available, IMS maintains a table (a bitmap) that indicates which CI or blocks have a large enough area of contiguous free space to contain the largest segment type in the database. Note that if a database has segment types with widely varying segment sizes, even if the CI or block has room for the smaller segment types, it is marked as having no free space if it cannot contain the largest segment type. The bitmap consists of one bit for each CI or block, which is set on (1) if space is available in the CI or block or set off (0) if space is not available. The bitmap is in the first (OSAM) or second (VSAM) CI or block of the data set and occupies the whole of that CI or block. Figure 8-5 illustrates the HDAM database free space management.

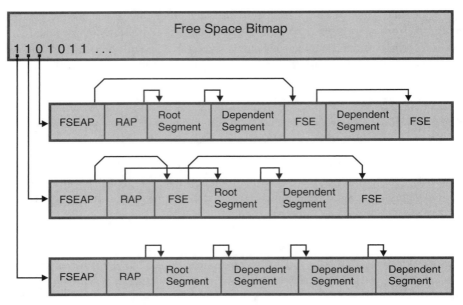

Figure 8-5   HDAM Database Free Space Management

Within the CI or block itself, IMS maintains a chain of pointers to the areas of free space. These are anchored off a Free Space Element Anchor Point (FSEAP). The FSEAP contains the offset, in bytes, from the start of the CI or block to the first Free Space Element (FSE), if free space exists. Each area of free space that is greater than 8 bytes contains an FSE containing the length of the free space, together with the offset from the start of the CI or block to the next FSE.

All management of free space and application segments in the data sets is done automatically by IMS and is transparent to the application. You need to be aware of how IMS manages free space only because of the performance and space usage implications.

Related Reading: See "Choosing a Database Type" in *IMS Version 9: Administration Guide: Database Manager* for a full description of the HDAM internal organization.

Advantages and Disadvantages of the HDAM Access Method
The principle advantages of the HDAM access method are:

- Fast random access to the root segments, via the randomizing module
- Fast direct access (no index accesses) with few I/O operations
- Quick access to segments in a database record, as IMS attempts to store them in the same, or physically near the, CI or block

- Automatic reuse of space after segment deletions
- Can have non-unique root segment keys

The principle disadvantages of the HDAM access method are:

- You cannot access the root segments sequentially, unless you create a randomizing module that randomizes into key sequence, or incur the overhead of creating and maintaining a secondary index.
- An HDAM database is slower to load than a HIDAM database, unless you sort the segments into randomizer sequence (for example, by writing user exit routines for the z/OS DFSORT™ utility that call the randomizing module or by using the Physical Sequence Sort for Reload utility that is available with the IMS High Performance Load for OS/390, V1.1 tool from IBM).
- If the database exceeds the space in the root addressable area, it will extend into overflow. After it is in overflow, the performance of the access to these segments can decrease drastically.
- To increase the space of the database, you must run the Database Description Generation (DBDGEN) utility to increase the number of blocks in the root addressable area and run the Application Control Blocks Maintenance (ACBGEN) utility to rebuild the online ACBs for use in the online system. This will require that you take the database offline (making it unavailable) to complete and coordinate the change. For more information about running the DBDGEN and ACBGEN utilities, see "Generating IMS Control Blocks" on page 233.
- Poor performance is possible if too many keys randomize to the same anchor point.

When to Choose HDAM

Consider using HDAM first because it is recognized as the most efficient storage organization of the IMS HD databases. First, examine the level of access required to the database. If there are no requirements to process a large section of the database in key sequence, you should choose HDAM. If sequential access of the root keys is required, the process can retrieve the data in physical sequence and sort the output.

In many cases, the disadvantages for HDAM do not apply or can be circumvented. Weigh the effort necessary to circumvent the disadvantages against the savings in terms of main storage and CPU usage. There is no doubt, however, that an application with only HDAM databases is the most compact one. Some possible solutions for the HDAM disadvantages are:

- Use the IMS general randomizing module, DFSHDC40, which can be used for any key range
- If heavy sequential processing is required and you cannot design a randomizing module that maintains key sequence, you can use the following sort techniques:

— If the program is non-input driven, as is the case with many report-generating programs, simple get-next processing retrieves (or extracts) all the database records in physical sequential order. If these segments are written to an output file by the program (called an *extract* file), the extract file might contain as much data as is in the original database. You can sort the extract file, which arranges the data into the order that is required for the report. Because in many instances only certain selected segments are needed for the report, you can also filter the data in the extract file, which can result in a fairly small final output file. The report-generating file can now quickly produce the report because only the pertinent data needs to be processed and it is in the correct order.

If the program retrieves the database records through a physically sequential path, you can save significant amounts of time compared to accessing the database in some sort of key sequence, which usually needs to randomly access the blocks in the database and reaccess the blocks several times over the duration of the program. The savings, in elapse time, can be up to 300%.

— If input transactions exist that would normally be sorted in root key sequence, they can be sorted using a DFSORT E61 user exit routine that passes each root key to the randomizing module for address calculation and then sorts on the generated addresses plus the root key instead of on the root key itself.

• A secondary index could be built with the root key as the index search argument. Weigh the cost of building the secondary index against the cost of sorting the root keys. The secondary index provides full, generic key search capability, however. Do not use a secondary index on the root segment to process the whole database because doing so involves many more I/O operations than is required to process the database in physical sequence.

HIDAM Access Method

A HIDAM database on DASD is comprised of two physical databases that are normally referred to collectively as a HIDAM database. Figure 8-6 on page 95 illustrates these two databases. When you define each of the databases through the database description (DBD), one is defined as the HIDAM primary index database and the other is defined as the main HIDAM database. In this section, the term "HIDAM database" refers to the main HIDAM database that you define through the DBD.

A HIDAM database is similar to an HDAM database. The main difference is in the way root segments are accessed. In HIDAM, there is no randomizing module, and normally that are no RAPs. Instead, the HIDAM primary index database takes the place of the randomizing module in providing access to the root segments. The HIDAM primary index is a VSAM key-sequenced

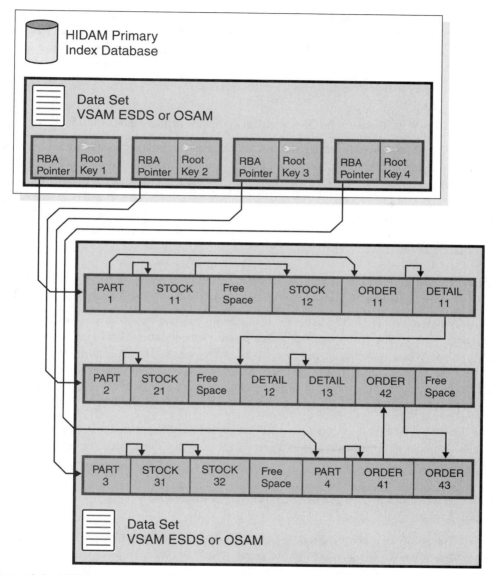

Figure 8-6   HIDAM Database in Physical Storage

data set (KSDS) that contains one record for each root segment, keyed on the root key. This record also contains the pointer (RBA) to the root segment in the main HIDAM database.

The HIDAM primary index database is used to locate the database records stored in a HIDAM database. When a HIDAM database is defined through the DBD, a unique sequence field must be defined for the root segment type. The value of this sequence field is used by IMS to create an index segment for each root segment (record in the KSDS). This segment in the HIDAM primary index database contains, in its prefix, a pointer to the root segment in the main HIDAM database.

The main HIDAM database can be OSAM or ESDS, but the primary index must be KSDS.

When the HIDAM database is initially loaded, the database records are loaded into the data set in root key sequence. If root anchor points are not specified, reading the database in root key sequence will also read through the database in the physical sequence that the records are stored in on DASD. If you are processing the databases in key sequence and regularly inserting segments and new database records, you should specify sufficient free space when the database is initially loaded so that the new segments and records can be physically inserted adjacent to other records in the key sequence.

Related Reading: See the chapter on "Choosing a Database Type" in *IMS Version 9: Administration Guide: Database Manager* for a full description of the HIDAM internal organization.

Free space in the main HIDAM database is managed in the same way as in an HDAM database. IMS keeps track of the free space using free space elements queued off free space element anchor points. When segments are inserted, the HD free space search algorithm is used to locate space for the segment. The HIDAM primary index database is processed as a normal VSAM KSDS. Consequently, a high level of insert or delete activity results in CI or CA splits, which might require the index to be reorganized.

When the HIDAM database is initially loaded, free space can be specified as a percentage of the total CIs or blocks to be left free, and as a percentage of each CI or block to be left free. This is specified on the DBD.

Advantages and Disadvantages of the HIDAM Access Method
The principle advantages of the HIDAM access method are:

- The ability to process the root segments and database records in root key sequence.
- Quick access to segments in a database record, as IMS attempts to store them in the same, or physically near the, CI or block.
- Automatic reuse of space after segment deletions.
- The ability to reorganize the HIDAM primary index database in isolation from the main HIDAM database.

The principle disadvantages of the HIDAM access method are:

- The HIDAM access method has a longer access path, compared to HDAM, when reading root segments randomly by key. There is at least one additional I/O operation to get the HIDAM primary index record before reading the block containing the root segment (excluding any buffering considerations).
- Extra DASD space for the HIDAM primary index.
- If there is frequent segment insert or delete activity, the HIDAM primary database requires periodic reorganization to get all database records back to their root key sequence in physical storage.

When to Choose HIDAM

HIDAM is the most common type of database organization. HIDAM has the same advantages of space usage as HDAM, but also keeps the root keys available in sequence. These days, with the speed of DASD, the extra read of the primary index database can be incurred without much overhead by specifying specific buffer pools for the primary index database to use, thus reducing the actual I/O to use the index pointer segments.

Choose HIDAM only if you need to regularly process the database in root segment key sequence. If you also need fast random access to roots from online systems, look at alternatives for the sequential access, such as unload and sort or secondary indexes.

HIDAM does not need to be monitored as closely as HDAM.

PHDAM and PHIDAM Access Methods

PHDAM databases are partitioned HDAM databases, and PHIDAM databases are partitioned HIDAM databases. PHDAM and PHIDAM databases are two of the HALDB-type databases. Figure 8-7 on page 98 illustrates a logical view of an HDAM database and a PHDAM database.

HDAM and HIDAM databases are limited in size because segments of the same type must be in the same data set and the maximum data set size is limited to 4 GB for VSAM and 8 GB for OSAM. HALDBs allows IMS databases to grow much larger. Partitioning a database allows the use of smaller elements that are easier to manage. Multiple partitions decrease the amount of unavailable data if a partition fails or is taken offline.

Each partition must have an *indirect list data set* (ILDS). The ILDS is a VSAM KSDS and is the repository for *indirect pointers* (called *self-healing pointers*). These pointers eliminate the need to update logical relationships or secondary index pointers after a reorganization. An ILDS contains *indirect list entries* (ILEs), which are composed of keys and data. The data parts of ILEs contain direct pointers to the target segments.

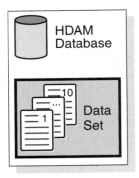

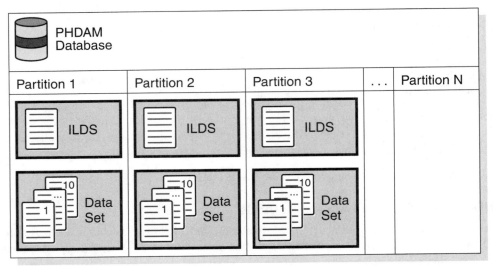

Figure 8-7   Logical View of an HDAM Database and a PHDAM Database

Like the other HD databases, PHDAM and PHIDAM databases are stored on direct-access devices in either a VSAM ESDS or an OSAM data set. The storage organization in HDAM and HIDAM or PHDAM and PHIDAM is basically the same. Their primary difference is in the way their root segments are accessed:

HDAM or PHDAM databases

>   Each root segment's storage location is found using a randomizing module. The randomizing module examines the root's key to determine the address of a pointer to the root segment.

HIDAM or PHIDAM databases

Each root segment's storage location is found by searching an index (called the primary index).

For HIDAM databases, the primary index is a database that IMS loads and maintains. For PHIDAM databases, the primary index is a data set that is in the partition it serves.

The advantage of using the randomizing module versus the primary index for finding the root segment is that the I/O operations required to search an index are eliminated.

Figure 8-8 on page 100 illustrates a logical view of a HIDAM and a PHIDAM database.

Related Reading: For more information about HALDBs, see *IMS Version 9: Administration Guide: Database Manager* and the IBM Redbook, *The Complete IMS HALDB Guide All You Need to Know to Manage HALDBs.*

HALDB Partition Names

Each HALDB partition name is 1 to 7 bytes in length and must be unique among the database names, DEDB names, area names, and partition names that are contained in one RECON data set. The HALDB partition names are used to represent specific partitions and are used interchangeably with database names in commands.

HALDB Data Definition Names

IMS constructs the data definition names (ddnames) for each partition by adding a 1-byte suffix to the partition name for the data sets in that partition. The suffix:

- For the first ddname is A.
- For the second ddname is B.
- For the third ddname is C, and so forth up to J (for the last data set).
- For the primary index of a partition is X.
- For the indirect list data set (ILDS) is L.

For a partitioned secondary index (PSINDEX, see "Index Databases" on page 101) database, there is only one data set per partition, so only one ddname with a suffix of A is required.

The ddname suffix naming convention described in the previous paragraph is extended to M through V and Y when a HALDB is reorganized online.

Related Reading: For more information about reorganizing all types of databases, see Chapter 10, "The Database Reorganization Process," on page 123.

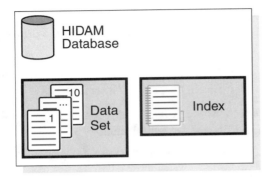

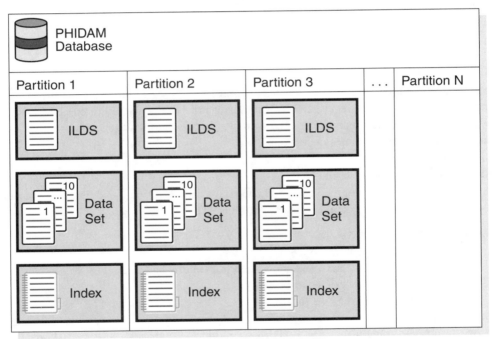

Figure 8-8   A Logical View of a HIDAM and a PHIDAM

When to Choose PHDAM or PHIDAM

The reasons for choosing PHDAM or PHIDAM are the same as described in "When to Choose HDAM" on page 93 and "When to Choose HIDAM" on page 97. The differences are the size of the data store and some administrative considerations.

You might not need to change any of your application programs when you migrate HDAM or HIDAM databases to HALDBs, but there might be exceptions. Exceptions include the initial loading of logically related databases and the processing of secondary indexes as databases.

You might also want to change applications to take advantage of some HALDB capabilities. These capabilities include processing partitions in parallel, processing individual partitions, and handling unavailable partitions.

Index Databases

Index databases are used to implement secondary indexes and the primary index of HIDAM and PHIDAM databases. An index database is always associated with another HD database and cannot exist by itself. An index database can, however, be processed separately by an application program.

An index database consists of a single VSAM KSDS. Unlike the VSAM ESDSs used by IMS, which are processed at the block or control interval level, the index database is processed as a normal indexed file. IMS uses the normal VSAM access method macros to process it.

The records in the KSDS contain the fields that make up the key, and a pointer to the target segment. For a secondary index, the pointer can be direct (relative byte address of the target segment) or symbolic (the complete, concatenated key of the target segment). For a HIDAM primary index, the pointer is always direct.

Because the indexes are a normal VSAM KSDS (and relative byte addresses are not used for data in the index database), they can be processed using the normal VSAM Access Method Services (IDCAMS). For example, you could use the z/OS REPRO function to copy the data set and remove CI or CA splits or resize the data set, without having to perform any other IMS reorganization.

Another type of HALDB is a partitioned secondary Index (PSINDEX) database. A PSINDEX database is the partitioned version of the HD secondary index database discussed in "Secondary Index Databases" on page 77. All the concepts that apply to the HD secondary index databases apply to PSINDEX databases. The only real difference is that PSINDEX pointer segments can point only to target segments that reside in HALDBs.

Fast Path DEDBs

The DEDB implementation of the IMS hierarchical database model is broadly the same as the IMS HDAM access method. However, there are important differences:

- To provide the additional features offered by DEDBs, the implementation of the DEDB access method onto the operating system access method data sets is different (and significantly more complicated) than with HDAM.
- There are restrictions on the facilities available with DEDBs.

The hierarchical structure of a database record within a DEDB is the same as HDAM, except for an additional dependent segment type. Each database record contains one root segment and from 0 to 126 dependent segment types. One of these segment types can, optionally, be a sequential dependent segment type. As with HDAM, a randomizing module is used to provide initial access to the database data sets that contain the DEDB database.

The highest level in the structure used to implement a DEDB is the *area*. A DEDB can consist of from 1 to 2048 areas. Each area is implemented as one VSAM ESDS.

Each DEDB area data set is divided into:

- **A root addressable part:** Contains the VSAM CIs that are addressable by the randomizing module
- **An independent overflow (IOVF) part:** Contains empty CIs that can be used by any unit of work (UOW) in the area.
- **A sequential dependent part:** Optional. Defined only if the DEDB has a sequential dependent segment defined in the hierarchical structure

The root addressable part is further subdivided into units of work (UOWs). These should not be confused with the unit of work that encompasses an application's minimum set of updates to maintain application consistency. The DEDB UOW is similar, however, because it is the smallest unit that some Fast Path utilities (for example, reorganization) work with, and lock, which prevents other transactions from accessing them. Each unit of work consists of from 2 to 32,767 CIs, divided into a base section of 1 or more CIs, and a dependent overflow section consisting of the remaining CIs.

Figure 8-9 on page 103 shows the structure of a DEDB.

N O T E: When a DEDB data set is initialized by the DEDB Initialization utility (DBFUMIN0), additional CIs are created for IMS to use internally, so the DEDB area will physically contain more CIs than are shown in Figure 8-9. These extra CIs were used for the DEDB Direct Reorganization utility (DBFUMDR0), which went out of service with IMS Version 5 and was replaced by the High-Speed DEDB Direct Reorganization Utility (DBFUHDR0). Although IMS does not use the extra CIs, DBFUMIN0 creates them for compatibility purposes.

The randomizing module works in a similar way to an HDAM database. The randomizing module takes the key value of the root segment and performs calculations on it to arrive at a value for a root anchor point. However, for a DEDB this is the root anchor point within the area data set. The randomizing module must also provide the value of the area data set that contains the RAP. Although a sample randomizing module is provided with IMS (DBFHDC44), due to the unique characteristics of DEDBs, you should determine whether you need to code your own.

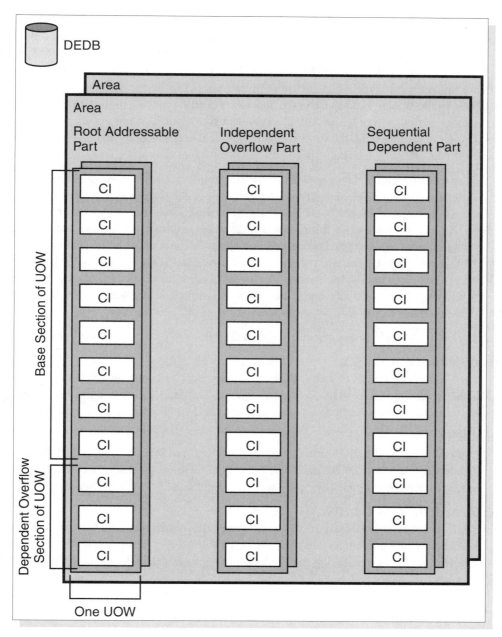

Figure 8-9 Overall Structure of a Fast Path DEDB

The randomizing module produces the value of a root anchor point in the base section of a unit of work. IMS attempts to store all dependent segments of the root (except sequential dependents) in the same UOW as the root. If more than one root randomizes to the same RAP, then they are chained off the RAP in key sequence. If there is insufficient space in that base section CI, then root and non-sequential dependent segments are placed in the dependent overflow section of that UOW. If there is no space in the dependent overflow section in the UOW, a CI in the independent overflow part of the DEDB area is allocated to that UOW and the segment is stored there. This CI in the independent overflow part is then used exclusively by that UOW, and is processed with that UOW by the High-Speed DEDB Direct Reorganization utility (DBFUHDR0).

The free space between the data segments in the CIs in the root addressable part and independent overflow part of a DEDB area data set are managed in the same way as in an HDAM data set: a free space element anchor point is at the start of the CI pointing to a chain of free space elements. As with HDAM, space from deleted segments is automatically reused, and the UOW can be reorganized to consolidate fragmented free space (without making the database unavailable). Unlike an HDAM database, there is no free space map. The segments for a database record can be allocated only in the same UOW (or attached segments in dependent overflow) as the root segment. An out of space condition results if insufficient free space is available in the UOW or independent overflow.

You can use the following optional features with a DEDB:

Virtual Storage Option (VSO)

> The VSO stores the CIs of a DEDB in z/OS data spaces and coupling facility cache structures, which eliminates I/O to the DASD system. The data can either be loaded (partially or completely) when the database is opened, or loaded into the dataspace as it is referenced.

Shared VSO

> You can share VSO DEDB areas, which allows multiple IMSs to concurrently read and update the same VSO DEDB area. The three main facilities used are the coupling facility hardware, the coupling facility policy software, and the XES[1] and z/OS services.

Multiple Area Data Sets (MADS)

> You can define DEDB areas so that IMS automatically maintains up to seven copies of each area. These copies can be used as backups if I/O errors occur, can be redefined on a different device without taking the database offline, or can provide parallel I/O access for very busy applications.

---

1.   Cross-system extended services (XES): A set of z/OS services that enable multiple instances of an application or subsystem, running on different systems in a Parallel Sysplex environment, to implement high-performance, high-availability data sharing by using a coupling facility.

Use the DBRC `INIT.ADS` command to define the copies of the area data set (ADS) to the RECON data set. After the MADS are defined in the RECON data set, run the DEDB Initialization utility (DBFUMIN0) to load the data into the copy data set and bring it online.

High Speed Sequential Processing (HSSP)

The HSSP function provided by Fast Path enhances the performance of programs that are processing segments consecutively in a database. With HSSP, IMS issues a single I/O request that reads one UOW at a time, which causes a reduction in the overhead of multiple I/O requests, and stores the CIs in a separate buffer pool. HSSP also issues the read request in advance of the program asking for the data, which provides parallel processing. In this way, the segments in the database are available to the program without any delays to wait for I/O processing. The overall runtime can be significantly reduced, as long as the database is being read consecutively.

Sequential Dependent Segments (SDEPs)

A DEDB database can have one sequential dependent segment (SDEP) type defined in the database record. The SDEP is processed separately from the other dependent segments. Normal application programs can only insert new SDEPs or read existing SDEPs. All other processing of these SDEPs is performed by IBM-supplied utility programs. The SDEPs are stored in the sequential dependent part of the area data set in chronological sequence, and are processed by the IMS utilities, which read or delete them, in the same sequence.

Related Reading:

- For more details about using DEDBs, together with samples of their use, see the IBM Redbook *IMS Fast Path Solutions Guide*.
- The features of DEDBs are completely described in detail in the "Designing Fast Path Databases" chapter of *IMS Version 9: Administration Guide: Database Manager*.
- The utilities used with DEDB are described in *IMS Version 9: Utilities Reference: Database and Transaction Manager*, and the randomizing module and other Fast Path user exits are described in *IMS Version 9: Customization Guide*.

Advantages and Disadvantages of Fast Path DEDBs

Fast Path DEDBs provide advantages when:

- You have very high volumes of data to store. The DEDB can be spread over up to 2048 VSAM ESDS data sets, each with a maximum capacity of 4 GB. However, not all this space is available for application data because some minimal space is needed for IMS and VSAM overhead and free space.
- You have a small to medium database that needs extremely fast access, you could use the DEDB VSO option and have the data held in a z/OS dataspace, which reduces greatly the physical I/O associated with the database.

- You need a database with very high availability. The use of multiple area data sets, the ability to reorganize online, and the high tolerance of DEDBs to I/O errors means that the database can be kept available for extended periods.
- An application needs to record large amounts of data very quickly (for example, to journal the details of online financial transactions) but does not need to update this data except at specified times, then a DEDB with a sequential dependent segment could provide the solution.

The principal disadvantages of Fast Path DEDBs are:

- The Fast Path DEDB access method is more complicated to use than other IMS access methods. Consequently, it requires a higher degree of support both for initial setup and running.
- The person who designs the application must understand the restrictions and special features of DEDBs and design the application accordingly.
- The DEDBs are available only for applications that run against an IMS control region (MPP, IFP, BMP, JMP, and CICS applications). No batch support exists except indirectly by using the IMS-supplied utilities to extract the data.
- Fast Path DEDBs do not support logical relationships or secondary indexes, so these functions must be implemented in the application.

When to Choose DEDB

The art of knowing when to use a DEDB depends on understanding the differences between DEDBs and other database types. The following list describes some reasons and considerations for choosing DEDBs.

Advantages of areas

Most Fast Path commands and utilities operate on an area level, so they do not affect the whole database at once (unlike a full-function database). For example, you can recover one area of a DEDB while the rest of it is in use.

Another reason you might want to use areas is to spread the I/O load across several devices (and several physical paths in the system I/O configuration).

When to use VSO

Use VSO for your most frequently used databases, for those databases where fast access is crucial, and for data that is updated frequently, even if several applications want to update the same field at the same time. These considerations also apply to shared VSO.

When to use MADS

Use MADS to ensure that I/O errors do not affect a database. Normally two copies of each area is sufficient, but you can have up to seven copies if you need them.

Using MADS is costly because you have several copies of the data. There is also a cost at execution time because IMS has to write several copies of the database updates. The transactions using the DEDB do not notice the extra I/O because the output threads handle the I/O operations asynchronously. Use MADS only when you can justify the extra DASD cost.

When to use HSSP

Use HSSP for only those programs that conform to its restrictions because you get better performance.

Consider using the option to let HSSP take an image copy while it is running, which saves the time you would normally use to take an image copy after your program finishes.

When to use SDEPs

You would typically use SDEPs when you want to insert data quickly, but do not need to read it again until later. For example, you might want to use SDEPs to hold audit records describing sensitive actions the user takes. You would not use SDEPs to hold data for a long time.

GSAM Access Method

Generalized sequential access method (GSAM) databases are sequentially organized databases designed to be compatible with z/OS data sets. However, the normal concepts of hierarchical structures do not apply to GSAM because the GSAM database contains only the normal data records, but no IMS information.

The files in a GSAM database can be z/OS sequential files or VSAM ESDSs. Before or after the IMS application processes them, other applications can process them using the normal BSAM, queued sequential access method (QSAM), and VSAM access methods.

When IMS uses the GSAM access method for sequential input and output files, IMS controls the physical access and position of those files. This control is necessary for the repositioning of such files in case of a program restart. When the program uses GSAM at restart time, IMS repositions the GSAM files in synchronization with the database contents in your application program's working storage. To control this, the application program should use the restart (XRST) and checkpoint (CHKP) DL/I calls, which are discussed in "Using Batch Checkpoint/Restart" on page 275. Note that IMS cannot reposition VSAM ESDS files on restart. Other restrictions on restarting are detailed in the chapter "Designing Full-Function Databases" in *IMS Version 9: Administration Guide: Database Manager*.

If you want your program to be restartable, you should use GSAM for its sequential input and output files. There are two reasons you might want to make your program restartable:

- To save time if a program rerun is required after a program or system failure.
- For online usage of the databases.

HSAM and HISAM Access Methods

The two hierarchical sequential (HS) databases, HSAM and HISAM, use the sequential method of accessing data. All database records and segments within each database record are physically adjacent in storage. Unlike HSAM, however, each HISAM database record is indexed, allowing direct access to a database record.

The HSAM and HISAM access methods have now been superseded by the HD access methods. The HD access methods have a number of features that almost always make them a better choice.

The HSAM access method does not allow updates to a database after it is initially loaded, and the database can be read only sequentially. In the past, the HSAM access method was used to process operating system sequential files, but the GSAM access method is now a better choice.

The HISAM access method offers similar functionality to the HIDAM access method, but has poorer internal space management than the HD access methods (that would normally result in more I/O to retrieve data) and, therefore, must be reorganized much more frequently.

A simple HSAM (SHSAM) database is an HSAM database that contains only one type of segment, a root segment. An SHSAM database is a z/OS physical sequential data set. Similarly, a simple HISAM (SHISAM) database is a HISAM database that contains only one type of segment, a root segment. A SHISAM database is a KSDS. Both SHSAM and SHISAM databases can be processed with the native z/OS access methods outside IMS, as well as with DL/I.

Related Reading: For additional details about the HS access methods, see *IMS Version 9: Administration Guide: Database Manager.*

Applications That Are Suitable for HSAM and HISAM

HSAM is one of the original database access methods and has been superseded. It is rarely used today.

HISAM is not an efficient database organization type. You can easily convert HISAM databases to HIDAM. Applications should receive significant performance improvements as a result. The only situation where HISAM might be preferable to HIDAM is when the database is a root-segment-only database.

An example of the inefficiency of HSAM and HISAM is that segments are not completely deleted and free space is not reclaimed after a segment is deleted until the next database reorganization.

OPERATING SYSTEM ACCESS METHODS

IMS uses two operating system access methods to physically store the data on disk storage and move the data between the disk storage and the buffers in the IMS address space:

- **Virtual Storage Access Method (VSAM):** IMS uses two of the available VSAM access methods:
  - Key-sequenced data sets (KSDSs) are used for index and HISAM databases.
  - Entry-sequenced data sets (ESDSs) are used for the primary data sets for HDAM, HIDAM, PHDAM, and PHIDAM databases.

    The data sets are defined using the VSAM Access Method Services (AMS) utility program.

- **Overflow Sequential Access Method (OSAM):** The OSAM access method is unique to IMS, is delivered as part of the IMS product, and consists of a series of channel programs that IMS executes to use the standard operating system channel I/O interface. The OSAM data sets are defined using JCL statements. To the operating system, an OSAM data set is described as a physical sequential data set (DSORG=PS).

For more information about these operating system access methods, see "VSAM Versus OSAM for Data Set Groups" on page 111.

The VSAM and OSAM access methods define two types of data sets:

- **Indexed sequential data sets:** Defined and accessed as VSAM KSDSs, are used to implement primary and secondary index databases. The index databases are processed using the standard record level instructions of VSAM. A catalog listing (VSAM LIST-CAT) shows all current details of the files. VSAM KSDSs are susceptible to the normal performance degradation from CI or CA splits caused by insert and delete activity. VSAM KSDSs can, if necessary, be processed using AMS utilities such as REPRO.
- **Sequential data sets:** Defined and accessed either as VSAM ESDSs or using OSAM. While these data sets appear as sequential data sets to the operating system, IMS accesses them randomly, therefore the data sets do not contain records. IMS always processes them at the CI (VSAM) or block (OSAM) level. The internal structure within each CI or block is arranged as described in "IMS Hierarchical Access Methods" on page 87. Interpreting catalog listings of these files as if they were sequential files can, therefore, be misleading.

In addition to using VSAM or OSAM, most IMS data sets can be managed by Data Facility Storage Management Subsystem (DFSMS). The exception is the data sets that IMS uses for logging. For more information, see "IMS Log Data Sets and Data Facility Storage Management Subsystem (DFSMS)" on page 373.

Data Set Groups

While most physical databases are implemented over a single VSAM ESDS or OSAM data set, IMS allows you to create data set groups to spread an HDAM or HIDAM physical database over up to nine additional data sets.

One of the restrictions associated with data share groups is that the first (primary) data set group that is defined must contain the root segments, and can optionally contain any dependent segment type. The other (or secondary) data set groups can each contain any dependent (non-root) segment type. However, each dependent segment type can be defined in only one data set group. These restrictions, aside from performance implications, are transparent to applications. If the database must be reorganized, then all data sets that make up the physical database must be reorganized at the same time.

You might want to use secondary data set groups for the following reasons:

- To separate little used segments from the main data set and leave more space for frequently used segments. Doing so increases the chance that all regularly accessed segments are in the same block with the root segment, thus enhancing performance. For example, you might have a segment type that has a new occurrence inserted each month, say month-end audit totals. The audit total segment is only rarely accessed after insertion. Placing this segment type in a secondary data set group, while imposing an overhead on the program that inserts it, might improve the performance of all other programs because doing so increases the chance that the segments they access are in the same block as the root segment, and more database records can be packed into one CI or block.
- A database with one very large segment type and a number of other small segment types can result in unusable space because IMS space management regards only a CI or block within a data set as having free space if the CI or block can accommodate the largest segment type stored in that data set. If you put this large segment type in a secondary data set group, the other data set groups are regarded as full only if they cannot contain the second largest segment type.
- Because you can specify different free space parameters on the different data set groups, you can place nonvolatile segment types in a data set group with little free space, to increase packing in a CI or block, and consequently increase the chances of having several segments that a program is retrieving located in the same block. Volatile segment types (that is, segments with frequent insert or delete operations) could be placed in a data set group with a large free space specification, which allows segments to be inserted near related segments.
- For very large databases, you might be approaching the structural limit of the data set access method (4 GB of data for VSAM and 8 GB for OSAM). If you have one or two segment types that occur very frequently, each of these segment types could be placed

in one or more secondary data set groups to provide more space. In this case, OSAM, DEDBs, or HALDBs might work well because the database can be spread over many more data sets.

When you perform space calculations, be aware that, in addition to the overhead for IMS control information (pointers, for example), VSAM data sets also contain a suffix area at the end of the CI that contains VSAM control information. This makes the space available in the CI for IMS data slightly less than the VSAM CI size.

VSAM Versus OSAM for Data Set Groups

The choice between OSAM and VSAM ESDSs for the primary database data sets depends, to some extent, on whether your site already uses VSAM and whether you need to make use of the additional features of OSAM. The choice between VSAM ESDSs and OSAM is not final because you can change a database from one access method to the other by unloading the database, changing and regenerating the DBD, then reloading the database.

Because the OSAM access method is specific to IMS, it is optimized for use by IMS. The reasons you might want to use OSAM include:

- The availability of sequential buffering (SB). With sequential buffering, IMS detects when an application is physically processing data sequentially or consecutively and fetches in advance any blocks it expects the application to request from DASD, so that the blocks are already in the buffers in the IMS address space when the application requests segments in the blocks. Sequential buffering is manually activated for specific IMS databases and programs and can appreciably increase performance for applications that physically process databases sequentially or consecutively. Sequential buffering is similar to the sequential prefetch that is available with some DASD controllers, but has the advantage that the data is fetched into the address space buffer in main memory rather than the DASD controller cache at the other end of the channel.
- The structural limit on the amount of data that IMS can store in a VSAM ESDS is 4 GB of data. OSAM can process a data set up to 8 GB in size.
- Overall, OSAM is regarded as more efficient than VSAM ESDSs because OSAM has a shorter instruction path.

Related Reading: For details about sequential buffering, see the chapter "Designing Full-Function Databases" in *IMS Version 9: Administration Guide: Database Manager.*

IMS CHECKPOINTS

IMS provides facilities to keep the application data stored in databases in a consistent state. This section describes techniques to maintain consistent data from the application's point of view.

The application must use IMS facilities to maintain consistent data. However, the facilities to consistently update the database also ensure that all internal IMS information (pointers, free space elements, and more) are kept consistent, though these activities are transparent to the application program.

An application program might make updates to several IMS databases. If a problem is encountered part of the way through these updates, either because the program fails or application logic dictates that the application cannot continue with the processing, then the application must restore the data in the databases to the state before the updates started.

For example, a program might add a detail to an order in the order database and then needs to update the part database to reduce the quantity of parts available for ordering. If the program updates the order database, but then fails before updating the part database, the order is recorded, but the quantity of parts is still shown as available for ordering in the part database. The update to the order database and the update to the part database make up a single unit of work (UOW). For the application data to be consistent, either all the updates in a unit of work must be written to the database successfully (committed) or none of the updates in the UOW must be committed.

To maintain database consistency, IMS uses the concept of the *application checkpoint*.

Application Program Checkpoints

An application program checkpoint, which applies to the single execution of an application program, is different from an IMS system checkpoint. IMS takes system checkpoints to allow the IMS subsystem to recover from a failure of the complete IMS subsystem. The application program checkpoint indicates to IMS the end of the application's unit of work (UOW) and causes IMS to commit all updates made in that UOW. An application's UOW commences when the application program starts running. By default, IMS takes an application checkpoint and commits all updates when the application terminates normally.

Application program checkpoints have two levels of functionality: basic checkpoints and symbolic checkpoints.

Basic Checkpoints

A *basic checkpoint* is when you explicitly request a checkpoint by issuing a CHKP call, which also tells IMS that the application program is starting another UOW. If an application program terminates abnormally, then all database changes are backed out to the last commit point (the start of program if application checkpoints are not being used, or last CHKP call if application checkpoints are used). The application can also manually back out all updates within the current UOW by using the ROLB, ROLL, or ROLS calls. The difference between the calls relates to action taken by the IMS TM, if applicable, and whether the application regains control after the call.

Related Reading: For complete descriptions of the CHKP, ROLB, ROLL, and ROLS functions, see "Maintaining Database Integrity" in the "Recovering Databases and Maintaining Database Integrity" chapter of *IMS Version 9: Application Programming: Database Manager.*

For long-running batch and BMP application programs, you should issue explicit CHKP calls at regular intervals. As the programs read database records, details of these database records (internal IMS addresses) are stored by the IMS subsystem until the application reaches a commit point (the application issues a CHKP or terminates). IMS stores the details to prevent other application programs from updating the same database records while the application is working with them. These details are stored in an internal buffer in the IMS address space. If the application does not issue checkpoints at regular intervals, the following problems can occur:

- The IMS address space has insufficient storage to contain all the buffers needed to contain the update details, which results in the application program being terminated.
- If the application fails, or issues a ROLL, ROLB, or ROLS call, IMS must back out all the updates performed by the application. If the application has been running for a long time without issuing CHKP calls, the application might take the same amount of time to back out all the updates as it took to apply them. If you correct the problem and restart the program, it will take the same time again to reprocess the updates.
- With BMP applications, other applications that process the databases that are managed by the same IMS control region might be prevented from accessing these database records. Other applications that are being used by online users might experience severe response-time problems as a result of the BMP application's failure to issue regular CHKP calls. For batch jobs, you might encounter similar problems if block-level data sharing is used. Also, the IMS ENQ/DEQ block supply might become exhausted, which results in a U0775 abend of *all* of the application programs that are running at the time of the abend.

Long-running programs should issue CHKP or SYNC calls based on the number of database calls made. As a rule of thumb, initially issue batch CHKP calls for every 500 database calls. You do not want to issue CHKP calls too frequently because overhead is involved in writing all the updates and the application repositioning itself in all the IMS databases after the CHKP call. Except for DEDBs with PROCOPT=P, IMS loses the position in the databases after a CHKP call, so where such positioning is important to the application logic, a CHKP call must be followed up with a GU call to the last record retrieved in databases.

SYNC calls perform the same synchronization functions as basic CHKP calls but avoid issuing a message to the IMS master terminal for every sync point and, in doing so, flooding the terminal with messages. All online programs must always restart from the last successful sync point, so the CHKP ID issued by a CHKP call is of no value.

Obviously you cannot CHKP more frequently than the number of calls in one UOW. IBM recommends you code the program so it can be easily changed because you might need to tune the checkpoint frequency. It is best to code a CHKP call in the program as a variable, possibly as an input parameter at run time.

Symbolic Checkpoints

For applications that run in batch and BMP address spaces, extended checkpoint functionality is available by using *symbolic checkpoints*. Symbolic checkpoints provide the following additional facilities that enable application programs that run in batch or BMP address spaces to be restarted:

- The XRST call is made at the start of the program and indicates to IMS that the application is using symbolic checkpoints. If this is the first time the application has run, IMS continues processing. If this iteration of the application program is a result of a restart, IMS performs some additional steps that are described later in this list.
- The CHKP call is extended to allow the application to pass up to seven areas of program storage to IMS. These areas are saved by IMS and returned to the program if it is restarted. These areas can be used to store variables (such as accumulated totals or parameters) that the application might need to resume processing.
- Each CHKP call is identified by an ID that is generated by the application program. This ID is displayed in an IMS message output to the operating system log when the checkpoint is successfully completed. IBM recommends that you make each of these IDs unique. Nothing in IMS enforces this practice.
- If the program fails, it can be restarted (after you correct the problem) from either the last successful checkpoint (for true batch jobs only) or any previous successful checkpoint in that run. IMS will reposition the databases (including non-VSAM sequential files that are accessed as GSAM) to the position when the checkpoint was taken. When the XRST call is made on restart, the program receives the ID of the checkpoint it is restarting from, together with any user areas passed to IMS when that CHKP call was issued.

Related Reading: See the "Maintaining Database Integrity" chapter in *IMS Version 9: Application Programming: Database Manager* for the details about symbolic checkpointing.

LOCKING DATA

Previous sections in this chapter described different aspects of a single application program accessing and updating a single IMS database. This section describes how IMS manages multiple applications that need to access and update a single database concurrently.

IMS uses locks to isolate the database changes made by concurrently executing programs to maintain database integrity.

Locking prevents situations in the following example from occurring:

1. Application A reads a record. While application A is processing the record (waiting for a user to respond at a terminal), application B reads the same record.
2. While application B is processing the record, application A reaches a commit point and updates the record.
3. The user of application B now responds, and application B reaches a commit point and updates the record, thus overwriting the update to the record made by application A.

The mechanism to preserve data integrity is to lock or enqueue[2] the database segments or records until the application finishes processing them successfully and reaches the end of a unit of work. This section discusses how IMS ensures that application data is updated consistently; however, IMS also uses locking to keep internal information in the databases (such as pointers) consistent.

One problem that can occur from this enqueueing of database segments is a deadlock between two application programs. For example:

1. Application A reads database record 1.
2. While application A is processing other data, application B reads database record 2, then tries to read database record 1, and is suspended waiting for it because record 1 is enqueued by application A.
3. Application A now attempts to read database record 2, and is suspended because record 2 is enqueued by application B.
4. Both applications are now suspended, waiting for a record that is enqueued by the other: a deadlock.

IMS detects the deadlock, abnormally terminates (abends) the application that has done the least work, and backs out that application's updates to the last commit point.

The mechanism IMS uses to detect the deadlock depends on the method of data sharing being used (see "Methods of Sharing Data" on page 116). IMS either directly detects the deadlock from the details enqueued or detects the deadlock by a predefined timeout value; that is, IMS can terminate a task after a parameter-specified period of waiting for a database record.

---

2.   The term *enqueue* means that when an application program is granted update access to the data, IMS records and maintains the update events in enqueue/dequeue tables defined in the control program storage. These tables consist of 24-byte entries in a z/OS system. As application programs reach synchronization points, the table entries are freed, the storage can be reused, and other applications can now update the data.

DB2 and Deadlocks

If an application is accessing DB2 UDB for z/OS tables, DB2 UDB for z/OS also detects deadlocks by timeouts and instructs IMS to abend the program. The abend code that IMS issues for the application is the same code that IMS would issue for an IMS database deadlock. IMS cannot detect a deadlock between two applications where the two different resources that the applications are trying to get are managed by two separate resource managers. This situation is most common with CICS applications that access IMS databases. For example:

1. CICS task A reads and enqueues a database record.
2. CICS task B then issues a CICS READ UPDATE call for a CICS resource (for example, to access a transient data queue).
3. CICS task B then attempts to read the database record held by task A, and is suspended waiting for it.
4. CICS task A then attempts to read the resource held by task B and is suspended.

A deadlock now exists between tasks A and B, but neither IMS nor CICS is aware of the problem because both can see only the half of the deadlock they are managing. Unless IMS is using one of the data sharing techniques that times out applications that wait for the database, or CICS is set up to abend tasks after a very short time suspended, this deadlock must be resolved manually.

The person who designs an application that uses IMS databases must be aware of the potential problems with database deadlocks, and design the application to avoid them. If the application also locks resources managed by another product, the application designer also must be aware of the potential for a deadlock developing between the IMS database records and the resources managed by the other product. Unfortunately, deadlocks often occur only when the application processes very large volumes because these types of applications often require very precise timing. These large-volume deadlocks might not be detected during testing because, typically, the testing is done with small volumes.

Methods of Sharing Data

IMS supports three methods of sharing data between a number of application tasks:

Program Isolation (PI)

Program Isolation can be used when all applications access the IMS databases via a single IMS control region. IMS maintains tables of all database records enqueued by the tasks in buffers in the control region address space. PI provides the lowest level of granularity for the locking and the minimum chance of a deadlock occurring. Deadlocks are resolved by IMS checking the tables of database records that are enqueued to ensure that no deadlock exists, and abending one of the tasks if one does exist.

Block-level data sharing

Block-level data sharing allows any IMS control region or batch address space running on a z/OS system to share access to the same databases. Block-level data sharing uses a separate feature, the internal resource lock manager (IRLM), which is delivered with IMS, but needs to be separately installed. The IRLM runs in its own address space in the z/OS system and maintains tables of the locks in this address space. With block-level data sharing, IMS locks the databases for the application at the block level. This locking is at a higher level than with Program Isolation (that is, all database records in a block are locked). Because of this coarser level of locking, there is an increased risk of deadlocks and contention between tasks for database records.

Deadlocks are resolved by a timeout limit specified to the IRLM. If the disk storage that the databases are on is shared between two z/OS systems, the databases can be shared between IMS applications running on the two z/OS images, by running an IRLM address space on each of the two z/OS images. The IRLMs communicate using VTAM but maintain lock tables in each IRLM address space. The IRLM is also used as the lock manager for DB2 UDB for z/OS. Because of the different tuning requirements, you should use separate IRLM address spaces for DB2 UDB for z/OS and IMS.

Sysplex data sharing

When a number of z/OS systems are connected together in a sysplex, with databases on DASD that is shared by the sysplex, IMS control regions and batch jobs can run on any of these z/OS images and share access to the databases. To enable sysplex data sharing, an IRLM address space (running IRLM Version 2 or later) must run on each z/OS image that the IMS address spaces are running on. The IRLMs perform the locking at block level, as with block-level data sharing. However, instead of holding details of the locks in the IRLM address space, the lock tables are stored in shared structures in the sysplex coupling facility.

Related Reading: For more information about data sharing, see:

- Chapter 9, "Data Sharing," on page 119.
- Chapter 27, "Introduction to Parallel Sysplex," on page 467.
- The chapter "Administering a Data Sharing Environment" in *IMS Version 9: Administration Guide: System.*

CHAPTER 9

Data Sharing

An IMS system includes a set of databases that are potentially available to all the declared application programs. Access to an individual database is a characteristic that you define in a program's PSB. Data sharing support makes it possible for application programs in separate IMSs to have concurrent access to the same set of databases. IMSs use lock management to ensure that database changes at the segment level that originate from one program are fully committed before other programs can access that segment's data.

IMS systems can share data in a sysplex environment and in a non-sysplex environment.

- *Sysplex data sharing* is data sharing between IMS systems on multiple z/OS images. A coupling facility is used by IRLM to control access to databases.

    Related Reading: For more information about IMS and running in a sysplex environment, see Chapter 27, "Introduction to Parallel Sysplex," on page 467.

- *Non-sysplex data sharing* is data sharing between IMS systems on a single z/OS image. A coupling facility can be used, but is not required.

With data sharing, two levels of control are possible (controlled through DBRC):

- With *database-level sharing*, an entire database is locked while an application program updates it. Locking prevents concurrent database access and scheduling of application programs that might jeopardize database integrity.
- With *block-level sharing*, you use a global block-locking scheme to maintain database integrity during concurrent access of a database. The blocks are locked instead of the entire database. Multiple application programs can update a database at the same time if they are updating different blocks.

Differences exist in support for data sharing configurations. Generally, a complete database is regarded as a data resource. When invoked within an IMS online system, or as a batch IMS system, the data resource must be available for an individual application program to process. The resource is not available if, for example, a data resource is either used exclusively by one IMS, is flagged as needing recovery, or backup procedures are in process.

For DEDBs, the data resource is further divided; each individual area is considered a unit of data resource. Throughout this chapter, a "database" is equivalent to a DEDB area unless otherwise noted.

Here are some of the restrictions that apply to data sharing:

- Only IMS online systems can share DEDBs.
- MSDBs and GSAM databases cannot participate in data sharing. Convert MSDBs to VSO DEDBs.

Related Reading:

- For more information about the concepts of IMS data sharing, see *IMS Version 9: Administration Guide: System*.
- For information about operating an IMS data sharing environment, see *IMS Version 9: Operations Guide*.

In This Chapter:

- "How Applications Share Data"
- "DBRC and Data Sharing" on page 121

HOW APPLICATIONS SHARE DATA

To understand data sharing, you must understand how applications and IMSs share data.

The processing options for an application program are declared in the PSB and express the intent of the program regarding data access and alteration. The processing options are specified with the PROCOPT keyword as part of the group of statements that make up the program communication block (PCB) for a particular database access. The PCB declaration implies a processing intent.

If the application program is to insert, delete, replace, or perform a combination of these actions, the application program is said to have *update access*. An online program that has exclusive access, specified as PROCOPT=E, is interpreted as having update access.

Programs that need access to a database but do not update the data can do so in two ways. They can access the data with the assurance that any pending changes have been committed by the program that instigated the change; this is termed *read access* (PROCOPT=G). Alternatively, programs can read uncommitted data, if the program does not specify protection of data status. This is termed *read-only access* (PROCOPT=GO).

Related Reading:

- For more information about PSBs and PCBs, see "IMS Control Blocks" on page 230.
- For more information about PROCOPT values, see "The Database PCB" on page 231.

DBRC AND DATA SHARING

Concurrent access to databases by systems in one or more operating systems is controlled with a common (shared) Database Recovery Control (DBRC) facility RECON data set. IMSs perform an automatic sign-on to DBRC, and this action ensures that DBRC knows which IMSs and utilities are currently participating in shared access. Subsequently, a system's eligibility to be authorized for access to a database depends on the declared degree of sharing permitted and other status indicators in the RECON data set.

To maintain data integrity, status indicators in the RECON data set control concurrent access and recovery actions for the databases. This common RECON data set is required in a data sharing IMSplex[1] because a given database must have a database management block (DMB) number that uniquely identifies it to all the sharing subsystems. The DMB number that DBRC records in its RECON data set is related to the order in which databases are registered to DBRC. Using multiple RECON data sets can result in the same DMB number existing in each RECON data set for different databases, which in turn can result in damage to databases.

Databases that are to take part in data sharing must be registered in the RECON data set. Each registered database has a current status that reflects whether it can take part in sharing and the scope of the sharing. The concept of scope combines several ideas:

- The type of access: read or update
- Whether more than one access can occur within the database simultaneously
- Whether an IMS that needs access is in the same or a different z/OS image

Related Reading: For more information about DBRC, see Chapter 23, "Database Recovery Control (DBRC) Facility," on page 375.

---

1. For an overview of IMSplexes, see Chapter 28 "IMSplexes," on page 495.

CHAPTER 10

The Database Reorganization Process

This chapter provides an overview of the database reorganization tasks that an IMS Database Administrator performs.

Specifically, this chapter:

- Introduces the requirements for and the process of IMS database reorganization.
- Describes the available IMS utilities for reorganizing HD databases.
- Describes how to use the utilities for particular situations, including which utility must be run to reorganize an HD database with and without logical relationships or secondary indexes.
- Includes a short discussion about initially loading databases with logical relationships and secondary indexes, because doing so also requires the reorganization utilities to build the logical relationships and secondary indexes.
- Discusses reorganizing HALDBs, which have a simpler and shortened reorganization process than do the other full-function databases. As of IMS Version 9, you can reorganize HALDB databases without taking them offline.

Related Reading:

- For more information about reorganizing HALDBs, see "Reorganizing HALDBs" on page 128.
- For a complete discussion on the topic of database reorganization, see *IMS Version 9: Administration Guide: Database Manager.*

In This Chapter:

- "Purpose of Database Reorganization"
- "When to Reorganize Databases"
- "Overview of the Database Reorganization Process" on page 128

PURPOSE OF DATABASE REORGANIZATION

Database reorganization is the process of changing how the data in the database is organized to improve performance. There are two types of database reorganization: *physical reorganization* (to optimize the physical storage of the database) and *restructuring* (to alter the database structure).

The most common reasons to reorganize a database are:

- To reclaim and consolidate free space that has become fragmented due to repeated insertion and deletion of segments.
- To optimize the physical storage of the database segments for maximum performance (get dependent segments that are in distant blocks, which increases physical I/O, back in the same block as the parent or root), a situation that is normally the result of high update activity on the database.
- To alter the structure of the database, change the size of the database data sets, alter the HDAM root addressable area, and add or delete segment types.

The solution to the first two reasons is reorganization. The solution to the last reason is restructuring.

The need for reorganization is always due to change (for example, setting up a new database, amending the structure of the database as application requirements change, or as a result of update activity against the database). If you do not update a database, then after you have it in an optimum state for performance, there is no further need to reorganize it.

Reorganizing and restructuring the databases is only part of the process of tuning and monitoring access to IMS databases. You can also tune IMS DB itself and the applications that access the databases. These topics and more are covered in more detail in:

- *IMS Version 9: Administration Guide: Database Manager.*
- The IBM Redbook *IMS Version 7 Performance Monitoring and Tuning Update.*

WHEN TO REORGANIZE DATABASES

There are no fixed rules about when to reorganize. There are two approaches to deciding when to reorganize, *reactive* and *proactive*, and you will probably do a mixture of both.

When you initially install the application and set up the databases, a lot of the reorganization will be done reactively, as performance and space problems manifest themselves. As you develop a history of the behavior of the application and the databases, the scheduling of reorganization should become more proactive.

Reactive Reorganizing

Reactive scheduling of reorganization is normally a result of perceived problems with the performance of the application, or problems with shortage of free space in the database.

Where there are perceived application performance problems, closely monitor what the application is doing. The initial items to examine are the average and maximum online response times and the batch run times. Are they excessive for the amount of work the application is doing? The IBM Redbook *IMS Version 7 Performance Monitoring and Tuning Update* describes monitoring and investigating performance of IMS applications, and subsystems in great detail.

Only after you have gone through the procedures detailed in the IBM Redbook *IMS Version 7 Performance Monitoring and Tuning Update* and identified potential problems with the databases should you start to look at reorganizing the database. Do not look only at the total time that the application program takes for database processing, but also look at the amount of database calls the application is processing. For example, if an online application is taking 10 seconds for database processing, but is reading 100–150 database segments, then there might be little room for database tuning. However, you might want to look more closely at why, and whether, the application really needs to read all these segments. The solution to performance problems is normally an interactive process involving the database administrator, application developers, and the operating system support organization, because all three control areas that affect performance.

When you encounter problems due to shortage of space in database data sets, there is little you can do but schedule a database reorganization to increase the database size. However, you should then acquire an understanding of the data growth rate. Consult with the application developers to gain this understanding. Also, a history of the volume of the application data stored in the database over time will help you determine the potential growth rate of the data. Questions to ask are whether growth will continue at the current rate or at a different rate, and whether this data all needs to be online. Remember that there are finite architectural limits to the size of the databases that vary depending on the IMS and operating system access methods.

Proactive Reorganization

The proactive approach to scheduling database reorganization relies on regular monitoring of the databases. For more information, see "Monitoring the Database" on page 126. In addition to monitoring the databases, you should maintain a history of the monitoring information you collect, so that you can analyze this information for trends and schedule database reorganization and restructuring before any problems occur.

When you decide to make a change to a database, implement only one change at a time, if possible, and then monitor application performance before and after the change so that you can see what effect this one change had.

The main things you do when you look at the monitoring data are to try to minimize the physical I/O for each database access and optimize the free space available in the database so it is not excessive, but is sufficient for normal update access on the databases.

The physical I/O from the disk storage into the buffers in the IMS subsystem is the major component of the elapsed time for database access. You want to minimize this elapsed time by:

- Making the best use of buffers in the IMS subsystem; the more requests for database access you satisfy from the buffers, the fewer physical I/Os are necessary. This is covered in the IBM Redbook *IMS Version 7 Performance Monitoring and Tuning Update*.
- Minimizing the number of physical I/Os when a segment must be retrieved from disk. For example, try to place as many dependents as possible in the same block or CI as the parent, ensuring HDAM root segments are in the same block or CI as the RAP. Moving segments is where database reorganization and restructuring is used.

Monitoring the Database

Monitor your databases in order to determine when they need to be reorganized.

Database monitoring falls into two categories: monitoring program and subsystem access to the databases, and monitoring the structure, space usage, and pointer chains in the actual database data sets.

The principle tools provided by IMS that are used to monitor database access are:

- The IMS Monitor (an integral part of the control program in the DB/DC environment), used to gather details of buffer usage and database calls over a specified time period in an IMS subsystem. It gathers information for all dispatch events and places the information (in the form of IMS Monitor records) on a sequential data set. Use the IMSMON DD statement in the IMS control region JCL to specify the IMS Monitor data set. IMS adds data to this data set when you activate the IMS Monitor using the /TRACE command. The IMS MTO can start and stop the Monitor to obtain snapshots of the system at any time.
- The //DFSSTAT DD statement, used in batch JCL to provide a summary of buffer usage and database calls. Because very little overhead is involved in including this statement (the details printed to the DD at region termination are accumulated by the IMS region controller whether they are output or not), it is normally worthwhile putting the //DFSSTAT DD statement in all batch jobs.
- The DB Monitor (run on a batch job), used to collect performance data during the execution of an IMS DB batch system. The DB Monitor can be active during the entire execution of an IMS batch job, or you can stop and restart it from the system console.

Because overhead is involved in running the DB Monitor, you would normally turn it on only when you are investigating specific problems.

Related Reading: There are a number of products available to let you monitor the databases and the data sets in which they are stored. For more information about these products, see Chapter 26, "IBM IMS Tools," on page 443. For information about monitoring program access to the database, see the IBM Redbook *IMS Version 7 Performance Monitoring and Tuning Update.*

Sample Reorganization Guidelines

Although there are no fixed guidelines for when to reorganize an IMS database, the following guidelines were used successfully with a medium-sized commercial application using IMS HD databases stored in VSAM files. You might want to use these guidelines as a starting point for scheduling database reorganization and, when you have monitored the effects of the reorganization, adjust these parameters accordingly.

HD Databases in General

- Database performance has deteriorated. This can happen either because segments in a database record are stored across too many CIs or blocks, or because you are running out of free space in your database.
- There is too much physical I/O to DASD.
- The database structure has changed. For example, you should reorganize a HALDB partition after changing its boundaries or high key.
- The HDAM or PHDAM randomizer has changed.
- The HALDB Partitions Selection exit routine has changed.
- Fewer than 50% of database records have all segments making up the record (root and dependents) in the same block or CI.
- Limit your free space to less than 20%. You might want to increase this limit if you have volatile data or infrequent windows of time for reorganization.

HDAM Databases Only

- Reorganize the database if calculation of the root addressable area showed it needed to be larger, then restructure at same time. Put fewer than 75% of root segments in the root addressable area. Recalculate the root addressable area (as described in Chapter 8, "Implementing the IMS Hierarchical Database Model," on page 83).
- Fewer than 50% of root anchor points (RAPs) point to root segments in the same block or CI. That is, the RAP points to a root that has been placed in another block or CI because there is no room in this block or CI. This placement causes two I/Os, one to the RAP block, and one to the block that the root is in, instead of one I/O.

VSAM or OSAM File

Allocate the database with secondary extents. This will allow the data sets to expand as the volume of data increases.

VSAM KSDS

- When your VSAM KSDS (index) has control area (CA) splits or more than 15 CI splits.
- When your VSAM KSDS (index) has less than 20% free space (because IMS manages free space in VSAM ESDS, this applies only to a KSDS).

DEDBs

Reorganize DEDBs when there are lots of database segments in the independent overflow (IOVF) portion of the DEDB area.

OVERVIEW OF THE DATABASE REORGANIZATION PROCESS

The database reorganization process can vary from being very simple to very complex, depending on the databases involved. If the databases involved do not have IMS logical relationships or secondary indexes, then the process is very simple. When logical relationships and secondary indexes are involved, the process becomes more involved.

IMS supplies utility programs that help you with the reorganization process. They are mentioned in the following sections that discuss the database reorganization process. An overview of when you would use which utility is in "Offline Reorganization Utilities" on page 130.

Most database types must be reorganized while they are offline (unavailable for updates—see "Offline Reorganization" on page 129). DEDBs and IMS Version 9 HALDBs can be reorganized while they are online (available for updates—see "Online Reorganization" on page 144).

Reorganizing HALDBs

Both PHDAM and PHIDAM HALDBs can be reorganized online or offline. A PSINDEX HALDB can only be reorganized offline. Whether you are reorganizing your HALDB online or offline, the reorganization process is different from the reorganization processes used for other full-function databases.

You can reorganize HALDBs online using the HALDB Online Reorganization function (OLR) that is available with IMS Version 9 and later. HALDB OLR maintains the availability of your data during the reorganization process, even in the partition it is actively reorganizing.

Reorganizations of HALDBs with logical relationships and secondary indexes do not require the execution of utilities to update these pointers. Instead, HALDB uses a self-healing pointer process to correct these pointers when they are used.

Related Reading: For more information about reorganizing HALDBs offline, see "Reorganizing HALDBs Offline" on page 142. For more information about reorganizing HALDBs online, see "Reorganizing HALDBs Online" on page 145.

Offline Reorganization

The offline reorganization process, in its simplest form, is to unload the database, delete and redefine the physical data set, and then reload it. If the database is not involved in any logical relationships and does not have any secondary indexes, then that is the complete process. To reorganize HD databases that have both logical relationships and secondary indexes, complete the following steps:

1. Back up the databases (both the data and, if you are changing them, the appropriate control blocks; for example, DBDs) so that you have a fallback point if there are any problems during the reorganization. See Chapter 11, "The Database Recovery Process," on page 151 for more information.
2. Unload the existing database data sets to sequential files using the IMS utilities. The process is discussed in "Database Unload Process" on page 132.
3. Delete the database data sets. If you are making any changes to the definitions of the database data sets, make them now, remembering to save the old definitions as a fallback.
4. Redefine the database data sets.
5. This step is necessary only if you are making any changes to the database structure by altering the DBD.

    Make the changes to the DBD and reassemble it by running the Database Description Generation (DBDGEN) utility. Then run the Application Control Blocks Maintenance utility (ACBGEN) utility with the DBD= parameter to ensure all appropriate control blocks are regenerated. You *must* make sure that all programs and utilities use the new versions of the control blocks if you change the DBD; otherwise, database corruption will result.
6. Run the IMS utilities to reload the database. If you altered the DBD, the reload utility, and any subsequent programs or utilities, should use the new DBD.
7. If the database has secondary indexes or participates in logical relationships, then you must run additional utilities to rebuild these connections. These connections (unless using symbolic pointers) rely on the database segments' relative position in the database, which has been altered by the reorganization. The utilities will determine the new positions and amend the direct pointers in the indexes and logically related databases.

8. If your databases are registered with DBRC (as they should be), then you must take an image copy of the reorganized databases. Taking an image copy provides you with a backup copy of the database and establishes a point of recovery with DBRC (in case of system failure). IMS database forward recovery, using changes recorded in IMS logs, relies on the position of the segments relative to the start of the data set, which is altered by the reorganization. You must take the image copies to establish a new base from which the databases can be rolled forward.

Offline Reorganization Utilities

The IMS-supplied utilities that perform offline database reorganization are completely described in *IMS Version 9: Administration Guide: Database Manager* and *IMS Version 9: Utilities Reference: Database and Transaction Manager*. The following sections briefly describe the database reorganization utilities.

The database reorganization utilities fall into three groups, based on the type of reorganization you plan to perform:

- "Partial Offline Database Reorganization"
- "Offline Database Reorganization Using the Utility Control Facility" on page 131
- "Offline Database Reorganization without Using the Utility Control Facility" on page 131

Partial Offline Database Reorganization   If you are reorganizing an HD database, you can reorganize parts of it instead of the entire database. There are reasons why you might want to reorganize parts of the database:

- Only parts of it need to be reorganized.
- You can minimize the amount of time it takes to do a total reorganization by breaking the total time into smaller pieces.

The IMS utilities that perform a partial reorganization are:

- The Database Surveyor utility (DFSPRSUR), which helps you determine which parts of your database to reorganize.
- The Partial Database Reorganization utility (DFSPRCT1 and DFSPRCT2), which does the actual physical reorganization.

> **N O T E:** The Partial Database Reorganization utility does not apply to HALDBs. Also, the Partial Database Reorganization utility needs a lot of information from the database to perform its functions and is not usually considered to be worthwhile compared with reorganizing the whole database.

Offline Database Reorganization Using the Utility Control Facility   You can reorganize a database using a single program, called the Utility Control Facility (DFSUCF00), or by using various combinations of the utilities. When you use UCF, it acts as a controller, determining which of the various reorganization utilities needs to be run, and then running them. The Utility Control Facility:

- Reduces the number of JCL statements you must create.
- Eliminates the need to sequence the running of the various utilities.
- Allows you to stop, and then later restart, a job.
- Reduces the number of decisions operations people must make.

> **N O T E:**   The only reorganization utilities that cannot be run under the control of the Utility Control Facility are the Database Surveyor utility and the Partial Database Reorganization utility. Also, the Utility Control Facility does not support HALDBs.

Offline Database Reorganization without Using the Utility Control Facility   When you do not use UCF, reorganization of the database is done using a combination of utilities. Which utilities you need to use, and how many, depends on the type of database and whether it uses logical relationships or secondary indexes.

If your database does not use logical relationships or secondary indexes, you simply run the appropriate unload and reload utilities:

- For HISAM databases, the HISAM Reorganization Unload utility and the HISAM Reorganization Reload utility
- For HIDAM index databases (if reorganized separately from the HIDAM database), the HISAM Reorganization Unload utility and the HISAM Reorganization Reload utility or the VSAM REPRO utility
- For SHISAM, HDAM, and HIDAM databases, the HD Reorganization Unload utility and the HD Reorganization Reload utility

If your database uses logical relationships or secondary indexes, you need to run the HD Reorganization Unload and Reload utilities (even if it is a HISAM database). In addition, you must run a variety of other utilities to collect, sort, and restore pointer information from a segment's prefix. Remember, when a database is reorganized, the location of segments changes. If logical relationships or secondary indexes are used, update prefixes to reflect new segment locations. The various utilities involved in updating segment prefixes are:

- Database Prereorganization utility
- Database Scan utility (DFSURGS0)
- Database Prefix Resolution utility
- Database Prefix Update utility

NOTE: The Database Prefix Resolution and Database Prefix Update utilities do not apply to HALDBs.

RECOMMENDATION: Use the DBRC GENJCL command to generate the JCL necessary to run the reorganization utilities. For complete details about the DBRC commands, see *IMS Version 9: Database Recovery Control (DBRC) Guide and Reference.*

Database Unload Process

The unload processing for HD databases is very simple. The HD Reorganization Unload utility (DFSURGU0) unloads the main database and the primary index data set if the database is HIDAM. The output of this utility is a sequential data set, which is input to the HD Reorganization Reload utility (DFSURGL0). If the database is a HIDAM database, then the primary index database must also be present. The HD Reorganization Unload utility can unload only a single database at a time. If there are logically related databases that are to be reorganized at the same time, then the step should be executed once for each database. Figure 10-1 shows a diagram of the inputs and output for the HD Reorganization Unload utility.

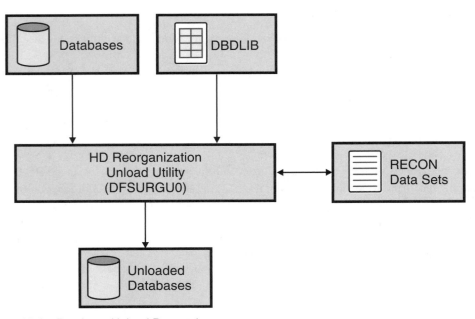

Figure 10-1   Database Unload Processing

Keep the following information in mind when you plan for the database unload process:

- IBM highly recommends that you make an image copy of the database before you attempt to reorganize it.
- The database is allocated by the ddnames in the DBD. Dynamic allocation cannot be used; the database DD statements must be present.
- If a HIDAM database is being unloaded, the primary index database DD statement must also be present.
- The HD Reorganization Unload utility checks with DBRC for database registration. If the database is registered, then the HD Reorganization Unload utility requests RD access authorization. HD Reorganization Unload utility is allowed to authorize the database even if the PROHIBIT AUTH flag is set on.
- If the database is being reorganized to change the structure of the database, then the old DBD definition should be used.
- Regardless of how many database data set groups the database is divided into, there is only one output data set.
- The HD Reorganization Unload utility can unload only one database per job step. To unload multiple databases, you must use multiple job steps.

Defining Databases

After unloading the database and before reloading it, you must define the new database.

If the access method used for the database is VSAM, then an IDCAMS job step is required to delete and redefine the VSAM cluster. The IMS reload utilities will fail if the data sets are not empty. If OSAM is used, specify DISP=OLD in the DD statement to overwrite the data set. If, however, the database is on more than a single DASD volume, IBM highly recommends that you delete the data set and redefine it (using the z/OS program IEFBR14 to preallocate the data sets) to ensure that the correct end-of-file marker is placed.

Database Reload Process

The reload process for HD databases can be more complex than the unload process. If the database does not have any secondary indexes and is not involved in a logical relationship, then the database can simply be reloaded.

If there are no secondary indexes or logical relationships involved, the reloading of the database is the same as the unloading: simply reload the database.

If, however, there are secondary indexes or logical relationships involved, you must run additional utility programs before and after the database is reorganized to rebuild the logical relationships and secondary indexes so that they reflect the new physical positions of the segments in the reorganized database. Until all this processing is complete, the logical relationships and secondary indexes are not usable. If you attempt to use them before completing this process, the applications will fail with IMS abend codes indicating that there are invalid IMS pointers.

The following sections discuss each combination of reload processing required:

- "Reload Only"
- "Reload with Secondary Indexes" on page 135
- "Reload with Logical Relationships" on page 137
- "Reload with Logical Relationships and Secondary Indexes" on page 138

Reload Only   The reload processing for an HD database without any logical relationships or secondary indexes is shown in Figure 10-2.

Keep the following information in mind when you plan for the database reload process:

- The database is allocated by the ddnames in the DBD. Dynamic allocation cannot be used; the database DD statements must be present.
- If a HIDAM database is being reloaded, the primary index database DD statement must also be present.
- The HD Reorganization Reload utility checks with DBRC for database registration. If the database is registered, the HD Reorganization Reload utility requests EX access authorization. The HD Reorganization Reload utility is allowed to authorize the database even if the PROHIBIT AUTH flag is set on.
- If the database is being reorganized to change the structure of the database, the new DBD definition should be used.

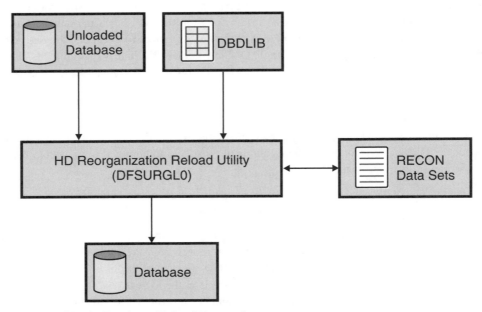

Figure 10-2   Simple Database Reload Processing

- Regardless of how many database data set groups the database is divided into, there is only one input data set.
- The HD Reorganization Reload utility can reload only one database per job step. To reload multiple databases, you must use multiple job steps.
- The DFSURWF1 DD statement can be specified as DUMMY, but it must be present.

Reload with Secondary Indexes   Figure 10-3 on page 136 illustrates the reload process when secondary indexes are involved. The process is as follows:

1. Identify the databases involved in secondary index relationships using the Database Prereorganization utility (DFSURPR0). This utility creates a control file (DFSURCDS) that contains this information. DFSURCDS is then used subsequently by other utilities.
2. The databases are reloaded using the HD Reorganization Reload utility. This utility updates the RECON data set and also generates a work data set (DFSURWF1) that is used as input to the Database Prefix Resolution utility.
3. The Database Prefix Resolution utility is used to extract and sort the RBAs. This utility generates a work data set (DFSURIDX) that contains the unload secondary index segments and is used as input to the HISAM Reorganization Unload utility (DFSURUL0).
4. The HISAM Reorganization Unload utility reads the DFSURIDX data set and creates load files for each secondary index database. The secondary index databases can be empty.
5. The HISAM Reorganization Reload utility (DFSURRL0) reloads the secondary index databases and also updates the RECON data set. The HISAM Reorganization Reload utility can reload all the secondary index databases in one job step.

Considerations to keep in mind:

- The database is allocated by the ddnames in the DBD. Dynamic allocation cannot be used; the database DD statements must be present.
- If a HIDAM database is being reloaded, the primary index database DD statement must also be present.
- The HISAM Reorganization Reload utility checks with DBRC for database registration. If the database is registered, then the utility requests EX access authorization. The HISAM Reorganization Reload utility is allowed to authorize the database even if the PROHIBIT AUTH flag is set on.
- If the database is being reorganized to change the structure of the database, then the new DBD definition should be used.
- Regardless of how many database data set groups the database is divided into, there is only one input data set.
- The HISAM Reorganization Reload utility can reload only one database per job step. To reload multiple databases, you must use multiple job steps.
- The DFSURWF1 DD statement can be specified as DUMMY, but it must be present.

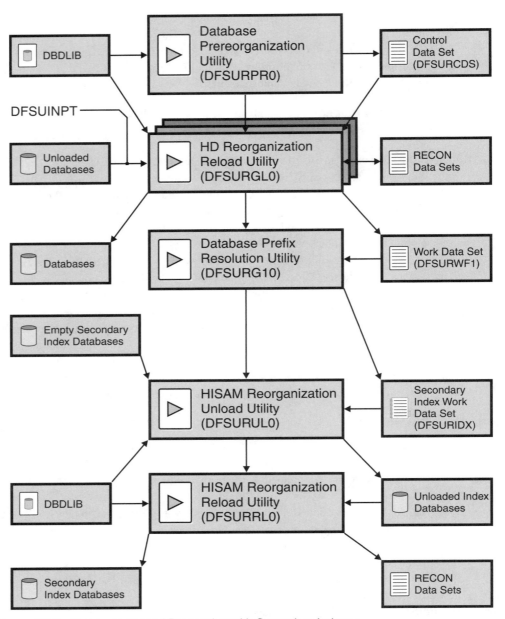

Figure 10-3   Database Reload Processing with Secondary Indexes

Reload with Logical Relationships   Figure 10-4 on page 138 illustrates the reload process when logical relationships are involved. The process is as follows:

1. Identify the databases involved in logical relationships using the Database Prereorganization utility. This utility creates a control file (DFSURCDS) that contains this information. DFSURCDS is then used subsequently by other utilities.

2. The databases are reloaded using the HD Reorganization Reload utility. This utility updates the RECON data set and also generates a work data set (DFSURWF1) that is used as input to the Database Prefix Resolution utility.

   If all the databases that are logically related to each other are being reloaded (and they normally are), use the DBIL option on the control statement. The DBIL option resets all the pointers and logical parent counters. If not, then use the DBR option.

3. The Database Prefix Resolution utility is used to accumulate and sort the information that is in the DFSURWF1 working data set. This utility generates a work data set (DFSURWF3) that contains the sorted prefix information and is used as input to the Database Prefix Update utility (DFSURGP0).

4. The Database Prefix Update utility updates the database segment prefixes. The prefix fields updated by this utility include the logical parent, logical twin, and logical child pointer fields, and the counter fields associated with logical parents. Log output data sets are optionally created if log DD statements are included in the JCL. This log output can be used if a later database recovery is required.

Considerations to keep in mind:

- The database is allocated by the ddnames in the DBD. Dynamic allocation cannot be used; the database DD statements must be present.
- If a HIDAM database is being reloaded, the primary index database DD statement must also be present.
- The HD Reorganization Reload utility checks with DBRC for database registration. If the database is registered then the HD Reorganization Reload utility requests EX access authorization. The HD Reorganization Reload utility is allowed to authorize the database even if the PROHIBIT AUTH flag is set on.
- If the database is being reorganized to change the structure of the database, then the new DBD definition should be used.
- The HD Reorganization Reload utility can reload only one database per job step. To reload multiple databases, use multiple job steps.
- The DFSURWF1 DD statement must be present.
- The Database Prefix Update utility acquires EX access to the databases being updated.
- The IMAGE COPY NEEDED flag is set on (in the RECON data set) by the HD Reorganization Reload utility.

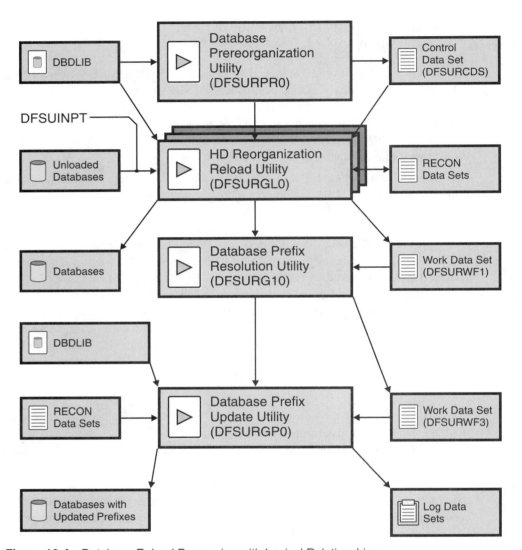

Figure 10-4   Database Reload Processing with Logical Relationships

Reload with Logical Relationships and Secondary Indexes   The reload processing for both secondary indexes and logical relationships is a combination of both the individual reload processes described in "Reload Only" on page 134, "Reload with Secondary Indexes" on page 135, and "Reload with Logical Relationships" on page 137.

Figure 10-5 on page 140 illustrates the database reload process when both secondary indexes and logical relationships are involved. The process is as follows:

1. Identify the databases involved in secondary indexes and logical relationships using the Database Prereorganization utility. This utility creates a control file (DFSURCDS) that contains this information. DFSURCDS is then used subsequently by other utilities.

2. The databases are reloaded using the HD Reorganization Reload utility. This utility updates the RECON data set and also generates a work data set (DFSURWF1) that is used as input to the Database Prefix Resolution utility.

3. The Database Prefix Resolution utility is used to accumulate and sort the information that is in the DFSURWF1 working data set. This utility generates two work data sets:

   • DFSURWF3, which contains the sorted prefix information and is used as input to the Database Prefix Update utility.

   • DFSURIDX, which contains the unload secondary index segments and is used as input to the HISAM Reorganization Unload utility.

4. The Database Prefix Update utility updates the database segment prefixes. The prefix fields updated by this utility include the logical parent, logical twin, and logical child pointer fields, and the counter fields associated with logical parents. Log output data sets are optionally created if log DD statements are included in the JCL. This log output can be used if a later database recovery is required.

5. The HISAM Reorganization Unload utility reads the DFSURIDX data set and creates load files for each secondary index database. The secondary index databases can be empty.

6. The HISAM Reorganization Reload utility reloads the secondary index databases and also updates the RECON data set. The HISAM Reorganization Reload utility can reload all the secondary index databases in one job step.

Considerations to keep in mind:

   • The database is allocated by the ddnames in the DBD. Dynamic allocation cannot be used and the database DD statements must be present.

   • If a HIDAM database is being reloaded, the primary index database DD statement must also be present.

   • The HD Reorganization Reload utility checks with DBRC for database registration. If the database is registered then the HD Reorganization Reload utility requests EX access authorization. The HD Reorganization Reload utility is allowed to authorize the database even if the PROHIBIT AUTH flag is set on.

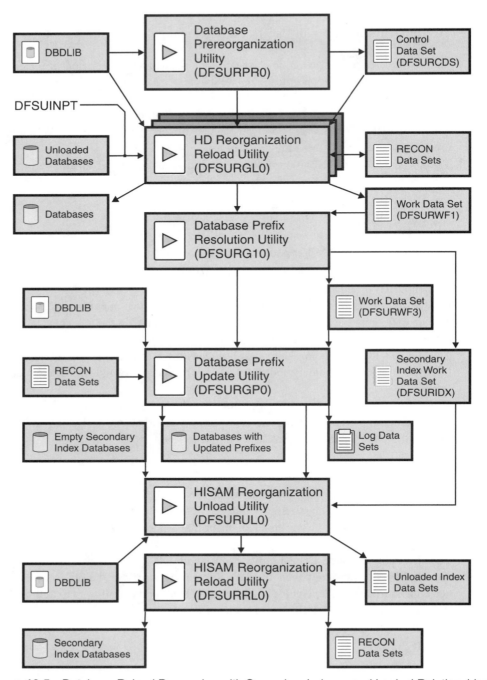

Figure 10-5   Database Reload Processing with Secondary Indexes and Logical Relationships

- If the database is being reorganized to change the structure of the database, use the new DBD definition.
- The HD Reorganization Reload utility can only reload one database per job step. To reload multiple databases use multiple job steps.
- The DFSURWF1 DD statement must be present.
- The Database Prefix Update utility acquires EX access to the databases that are being updated.
- The IMAGE COPY NEEDED flag is set on (in the RECON data set) by the HD Reorganization Reload utility.

Reorganizing Fast Path DEDBs Offline

The process for reorganizing a Fast Path DEDB can be appreciably different from reorganizing full-function databases.

If you are reorganizing a DEDB only to reclaim fragmented free space or get the best placement of the segments for performance (that is, the DBD or data set definitions are not being changed), then you can run the High-Speed DEDB Direct Reorganization utility (DBFUHDR0). This utility can be run while the DEDB is either offline or online. In this instance, *offline* means that the DEDB is still up and available, but you have prevented applications from accessing it. The DEDB is still technically online.

Related Reading: For more information about the High-Speed DEDB Direct Reorganization utility (DBFUHDR0), see *IMS Version 9: Utilities Reference: Database and Transaction Manager.*

If you are reorganizing a DEDB to alter the structure, then you need to have your own user-written programs to unload and reload the database data set at the appropriate points, or use the DEDB Unload and Reload utilities from the separately priced IBM IMS High Performance Fast Path Utilities, V2.1 (program number 5655–K94). You must also run the DEDB Initialization utility (DBFUMIN0), provided with the IMS base product, immediately before reloading the database. You do not have to run additional utilities after the database is reloaded because DEDBs do not support secondary indexes or logical relationships.

Related Reading: For more information about:

- The separately priced tools available from IBM, see Chapter 26, "IBM IMS Tools," on page 443.
- The database reorganization process and the steps you must take to alter specific attributes of the structure of a DEDB, see the chapters on monitoring and tuning databases in *IMS Version 9: Administration Guide: Database Manager.*

Reorganizing HALDBs Offline

The offline reorganization processes for a HALDB database and other full-function IMS databases are similar: they both consist of an unload and reload of the database; however, the HALDB reorganization process has advantages over the reorganization process of other full-function databases, such as:

- You can reorganize one HALDB partition at a time, or reorganize multiple partitions in parallel.
- The self-healing pointer process of HALDBs eliminates the need to manually update logical relationships and secondary indexes after reorganizing a HALDB.
- You do not need to include DD statements for HALDB data sets when you reorganize a HALDB. HALDB data sets are dynamically allocated.

An offline reorganization of a HALDB database can be done with one or more parallel processes. These processes unload one or more partitions and reload them. If the database has secondary indexes or logical relationships, additional steps are not required. The amount of time required for a reorganization depends on the sizes of the partitions. Smaller partitions reduce the time. You can reduce your reorganization time by creating more partitions and reorganizing them in parallel.

The basic steps involved in reorganizing a HALDB offline are:

1. Run the HD Reorganization Unload utility to unload the entire database, a range of partitions, or a single partition.
2. Optionally, initialize the partitions by running either of the following utilities:
   - HALDB Partition Data Set Initialization utility (DFSUPNT0)
   - Database Prereorganization utility
3. Run the HD Reorganization Reload utility to reload the database or partitions.
4. Make image copies of all reloaded partition data sets.

Figure 10-6 on page 143 shows the offline processes used to reorganize a HALDB database with logical relationships and secondary indexes. In this case, the partitions are reorganized by parallel processes. Each partition can be unloaded and reloaded in less time than unloading and reloading the entire database. This is much faster than the process for a non-HALDB full-function database. Additionally, no time is required for updating pointers in the logically related database or rebuilding secondary indexes. This further shortens the process.

Reorganizing HALDB Partitioned Secondary Index Databases   You might need to reorganize your partitioned secondary index (PSINDEX) database. Because the reorganization of HALDBs does not require the recreation of their secondary indexes, a PSINDEX database can become disorganized as entries are added to it over time.

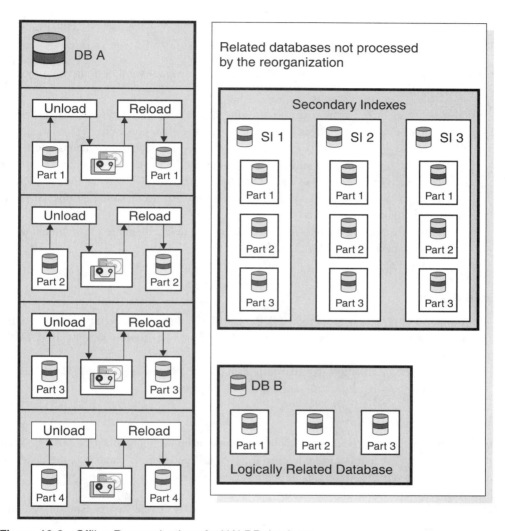

Figure 10-6 Offline Reorganization of a HALDB database

The HD Reorganization Unload utility and the HD Reorganization Reload utility can be used to reorganize PSINDEX databases. The restrictions and recommendations for reorganizing other HALDB databases also apply to PSINDEX databases with one exception: HALDB secondary indexes have no ILDSs. The HD Reorganization Reload utility control statements should not be used with secondary indexes.

The steps for reorganizing a PSINDEX database are the same as those for reorganizing other types of HALDBs offline.

Options for Offline Reorganization of HALDBs   You have several options when reorganizing a HALDB database:

- You can reorganize any number of partitions. If you need to reorganize only one partition, you can unload and reload it without processing other partitions.
- You can reorganize partitions in parallel or you can reorganize the database with one process. The degree of parallelism is determined by the number of reorganization jobs you run. Each job can process one or multiple partitions. To increase the parallelism you can increase the number of reorganization jobs and decrease the number of partitions each job processes.
- You can reuse existing database data sets or you can delete them after they are unloaded and allocate new data sets for the reload.
- You can add partitions, delete partitions, or change partition boundaries.

Related Reading:

- For more information about reorganizing HALDBs offline or changing partition definitions (including partition boundaries), see *IMS Version 9: Administration Guide: Database Manager*.
- For complete information about the utilities mentioned in this section, see *IMS Version 9: Utilities Reference: Database and Transaction Manager*.

Online Reorganization

With offline reorganization, the database is unavailable during the reorganization process. With online reorganization, which is available only for HALDB and DEDB databases, the database remains available for updates during the reorganization process.

Related Reading: For complete information about HALDB Online Reorganization, see *IMS Version 9: Administration Guide: Database Manager*.

Reorganizing Fast Path DEDBs Online

As mentioned in "Reorganizing Fast Path DEDBs Offline" on page 141, if you are only reorganizing to reclaim fragmented free space or to get the best placement of the segments for performance (that is, the DBD or data set definitions are not being changed), or both, you can run the High-Speed DEDB Direct Reorganization utility while the DEDB is online.

Related Reading: For more information about the High-Speed DEDB Direct Reorganization utility, see *IMS Version 9: Utilities Reference: Database and Transaction Manager*.

Reorganizing HALDBs Online

Prior to IMS Version 9, you had to ensure that HALDB partitions were offline before you could perform database reorganization for them. IMS Version 9 introduced an integrated HALDB Online Reorganization function that allows HALDB partitions to remain online and available for IMS application programs during a database reorganization.

An online reorganization of PHDAM or PHIDAM HALDB partitions runs non-disruptively, allowing concurrent IMS updates, including updates by data sharing IMS systems. The online reorganization is non-disruptive because IMS copies small amounts of data from the partition's original data sets (the input data sets) to separate output data sets. IMS tracks which data has been copied so that IMS applications can automatically retrieve or update data from the correct set of data sets.

When you reorganize either PHDAM or PHIDAM HALDB partitions online, the online reorganization process requires additional data sets to hold the reorganized data. The additional data sets are equal in number to the data sets being reorganized, excluding the ILDS.

In a PHDAM database, online reorganization increases the maximum number of data sets associated with a partition to twenty-one. In a PHIDAM database, which includes a primary index, online reorganization increases the maximum number of data sets associated with a partition to twenty-three. In either case, online reorganization needs only as many new data sets as the data sets that exist in the partition at the time the reorganization process begins.

Each additional data set requires an additional ddname. To distinguish between the ddnames for the data sets that are being reorganized and the ddnames for the data sets into which online reorganization moves the reorganized data, HALDB online reorganization extends the HALDB naming convention to include the suffixes M through V for the ddnames of the primary data sets and the suffix Y for the ddname for the additional primary index. The suffixes M through V and Y correspond in order to the standard HALDB ddname suffixes A through J and X.

The initial load or offline reorganization reload of a HALDB partition always uses the A-through-J (and X) data sets. Until the first time that you reorganize a HALDB partition online, only the A-through-J (and X) data sets are used.

There are three phases of online reorganization for a HALDB partition:

- The initialization phase, during which IMS prepares the output data sets and updates the RECON data sets.
- The copying phase, during which IMS performs the actual reorganization by copying the data from the input data sets to the output data sets.
- The termination phase, during which IMS closes the input data sets and updates the RECON data sets.

The Initialization Phase for HALDB Online Reorganization   You start the online reorganization of a HALDB partition using the INITIATE OLREORG command. See the *IMS Version 9: Command Reference* for more information about this command.

During the initialization phase, IMS updates the RECON data sets to establish the ownership of the online reorganization by the IMS subsystem that is performing the online reorganization. This ownership means that no other IMS subsystem can perform a reorganization of the HALDB partition until the current online reorganization is complete or until ownership is transferred to another IMS subsystem. IMS adds the M-through-V (and Y) DBDSs to the RECON data sets if those DBDS records do not already exist. IMS also adds the M-through-V (and Y) DBDSs to any existing change accumulation groups and DBDS groups that include the corresponding A-through-J (and X) DBDSs.

> **DEFINITION:**
>
> Change accumulation is the process of creating a compacted version of one or more IMS log data sets by eliminating records not related to recovery, and by merging multiple changes to a single segment into a single change. For more information about change accumulation, see "Database Change Accumulation Utility" on page 158.

Before online reorganization begins for a HALDB partition, there is a single set of *active* data sets for the HALDB partition. These active data sets are the input data sets for the copying phase. There might also be a set of *inactive* data sets from a prior online reorganization that is not used by IMS application programs.

During the initialization phase, IMS evaluates each of the inactive data sets to ensure that it meets the requirements for output data sets. If any of the output data sets does not exist, IMS creates it automatically during this phase.

At the end of the initialization phase, IMS considers the original active set of data sets as the input set and the inactive data sets as the output set. This use of the input and output sets of data sets is represented by the *cursor-active* status for the partition, which is recorded in online reorganization records in the RECON data sets. A listing of the partition's database record in the RECON data sets shows OLREORG CURSOR ACTIVE=YES. A listing of the partition also shows that both sets of DBDSs are active; the first set of DBDSs listed is for the input data set, and the second set of DBDSs is for the output data set, for example, DBDS ACTIVE=A-J and M-V. While the partition is in the cursor-active status, both sets of data sets must be available for the partition to be processed by any application.

The Copying Phase for HALDB Online Reorganization   During the copying phase, the HALDB partition is comprised of the A-through-J (and X) data sets and the M-through-V (and Y) data sets. During this phase, both sets of data sets must be available in order for IMS applications to access the partition.

While IMS reorganizes a HALDB partition online, IMS applications can make database updates to the partition. Some of the database updates are made to the input data sets, while others are made to the output data sets, depending on which data is updated by the application. Which data sets are updated is transparent to the application program. Figure 10-7 illustrates the relationship between the input and output data sets at a point during the online reorganization.

Figure 10-7 shows two sets of database data sets for a HALDB partition, the input data sets that have not been reorganized and the output data sets that have been (at least partially) reorganized. The figure shows the reorganization as progressing from left to right, from the input data sets above to the output data sets below. The data sets in the figure are divided into four areas:

1. An area within the input data sets that represents the data that has been copied to the output data sets. This area reflects the old data organization (prior to the reorganization) and is not used again by IMS applications until the data sets are reused as the output data sets for a later online reorganization.
2. An area within the output data sets that represents the data that has been copied from the input data sets. This data in this area has been reorganized and can be used by IMS applications during the reorganization.

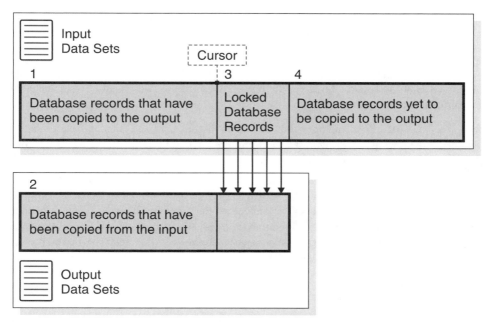

Figure 10-7   The Relationship between Input Data Sets and Output Data Sets during the Online Reorganization of a HALDB Partition

3. An area within both the input and output data sets that represents data that is locked and in the process of being copied and reorganized from the input data sets to the output data sets. This area of locked records is called a *unit of reorganization*. From a recovery point of view, this unit of reorganization is equivalent to a unit of recovery.

   While IMS processes the current unit of reorganization, IMS applications that access any of the locked data records must wait until IMS completes the reorganization for those records. After the copying and reorganization completes for the unit of reorganization, IMS commits the changes and unlocks the records, thus making them available again for IMS applications.

4. An area within the input data sets that represents the data that has not yet been copied to the output data sets. This data has also not yet been reorganized and can be used by IMS applications during the reorganization.

As the online reorganization progresses, IMS uses a type of pointer called a *cursor* to mark the end point of those database records that have already been copied from the input data sets to the output data sets. As the reorganization and copying proceeds, this cursor moves forward through the partition, from left to right in the figure.

When an IMS application program accesses data from a HALDB partition that is being reorganized online, IMS retrieves the data record:

- From the output data sets if the database record is located at or before the cursor.
- From the input data sets if the database record is located after the cursor.

If the data record happens to fall within the unit of reorganization, IMS retries the data access after the records are unlocked. An application program does not receive an error status code for data within a unit of reorganization.

To allow recovery of either an input data set or an output data set, all database changes are logged during the online reorganization, including the database records that are copied from the input data set to the output data sets.

The Termination Phase for HALDB Online Reorganization   The online reorganization of a HALDB partition terminates after the end of the copying phase, or when IMS encounters an error condition during the reorganization. You can also stop the online reorganization of a HALDB partition using the `TERMINATE OLREORG` command. See *IMS Version 9: Command Reference* for more information about this command.

After the copying phase is complete for a HALDB partition, the output data sets become the *active* data sets, and the input data sets become the *inactive* data sets. The active data sets are used for all data access by IMS application programs. The inactive data sets are not used by application programs, but can be reused for a subsequent online reorganization. Unless you perform an initial load or a batch reorganization reload for the partition, successive online reorganizations for the partition alternate between these two sets of data sets.

IMS updates the partition's database record in the RECON data sets to reset the cursor-active status for the partition to reflect that there is now just one set of data sets. A listing of this record from the RECON data sets shows OLREORG CURSOR ACTIVE=NO and the ACTIVE DBDS field shows the active (newly reorganized) data sets. IMS also updates the online reorganization records in the RECON data sets with the timestamp when the reorganization completed.

If you specified the DEL keyword for the INITIATE OLREORG command (or the UPDATE OLREORG command), IMS deletes the inactive data sets after resetting the cursor-active status for the partition. Before deleting the inactive data sets, IMS notifies all sharing IMS subsystems (including batch jobs) that the online reorganization is complete and is recorded in the RECON data sets. The IMS subsystem that is performing the online reorganization waits until it receives an acknowledgement from each of these sharing subsystems that they have closed and deallocated the now-inactive data sets, and then it deletes these data sets. However, if the acknowledgements are not received within 4.5 minutes, the owning subsystem will attempt to delete the inactive data sets anyway. Without the acknowledgements, the deletion attempt is likely to fail.

Finally, at the end of the termination phase, IMS updates the RECON data sets to reset the ownership of the online reorganization so that no IMS subsystem has ownership. This resetting of ownership means that any IMS subsystem can perform a subsequent reorganization of the HALDB.

If online reorganization of a HALDB partition terminates prior to completion, either because of an error or because you issued the TERMINATE OLREORG command, you need to restart the online reorganization or you need to perform an offline reorganization for the partition.

Figure 10-8 on page 150 shows the normal processing steps of a successful online reorganization of a HALDB partition. The columns represent the flow of control through the phases of the online reorganization, from the user to IMS, and the status of the data sets as the processing events occur.

Related Reading: For more information about reorganizing HALDBs online, see *IMS Version 9: Administration Guide: Database Manager.*

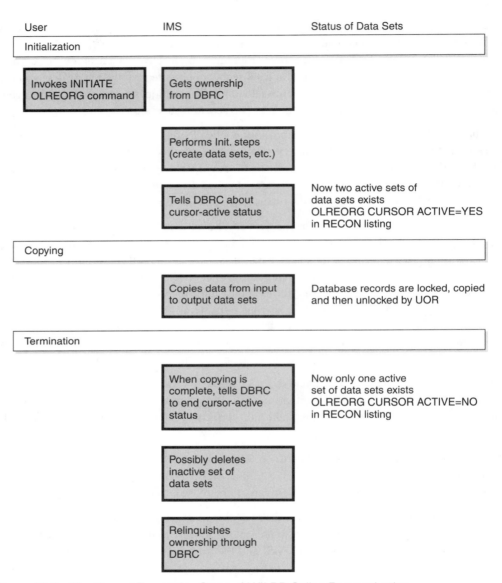

Figure 10-8   The Normal Processing Steps of HALDB Online Reorganization

11

The Database Recovery Process

T he following sections provide a general overview of IMS database backup and recovery concepts and describes the processes involved.

In This Chapter:

- "Determining When Recovery Is Needed"
- "Overview of the Database Recovery Process" on page 152
- "IMS Backup and Recovery Utilities" on page 153

DETERMINING WHEN RECOVERY IS NEEDED

Database recovery is normally performed only when there has been a failure of some sort. Most of the time recovery is done as a result of a system, hardware, or application failure. However, you can also use recovery procedures to return a database to a previous point in time, and to recover from application logic failures.

In general, a database might need to be recovered under the following circumstances:

- A DB batch update job fails after making at least one database update.
- A failure occurs on a physical DASD device.
- A failure occurs in a database recovery utility.
- A failure of a dynamic backout or a run of the Batch Backout utility (DFSBBO00) has occurred.
- An IMS online system failure and emergency restart has not been completed.

OVERVIEW OF THE DATABASE RECOVERY PROCESS

Database recovery, in its simplest form, is the restoration of a database after its partial destruction due to some failure.

> **N OT E:** The term *database recovery process* is slightly misleading because the unit of granularity for recovery is the data set: usually only a single failed data set needs to be recovered. HALDBs and DEDBs take advantage of this characteristic by allowing continued access to the rest of the database while individual partitions or areas are recovered.

In order to facilitate this process, some forward planning needs to be done.

Periodically, a copy of the data in the database is saved. This copy is normally referred to as a *backup copy* or *image copy*. These image copies can reside on DASD or cartridges. Though this process can be done anytime, it is normally done when there is no other database activity. Image copies are complete copies of the database. There are other strategies for taking a database backup, but they will not be discussed in this book.

In addition to taking an image copy of the databases, you can log and save all changes made to the data in the database, at least until the next image copy. These changes are contained in data sets called *log data sets*. This provides a complete recovery environment so that no data is lost in the event of a system or application failure.

The recovery process for IMS databases can include these three basic steps, although the details of the process can vary with the type of database to be recovered:

1. Restore the database to the most current image copy.
2. Use the log data sets (or change accumulation data sets) to restore changes made to the database since the image copy was made.
3. Back out any incomplete changes.

Figure 11-1 illustrates a simple database recovery.

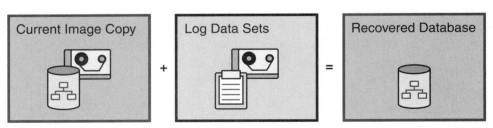

Figure 11-1   IMS Database Recovery Process

As mentioned earlier in this book, DBRC can be used to help ensure that there is always a recovery process available. Using DBRC to control database backup and recovery is not mandatory but is *highly recommended.*

Related Reading: For more information about DBRC, see Chapter 23, "Database Recovery Control (DBRC) Facility," on page 375.

The following sections discuss other aspects of the recovery process:

- "Online Programs and Recovery"
- "DB Batch Update Programs and Recovery"

Online Programs and Recovery

IMS online transactions use dynamic backout to undo updates done in any incomplete unit of work. Online programs that abend are automatically backed out by the online system using the log records. In addition, if the system fails while an application program is active, any updates made by that program are automatically backed out when the system is restarted.

If the program was a BMP program, the updates are automatically backed out to its most recent checkpoint. Because of this automatic backout, the recovery of individual databases is not needed.

At IMS restart time, if the emergency restart cannot complete the backout for any individual transactions, then the databases affected by those updates are stopped, and DBRC is requested to set the recovery needed flag to ensure that a correct recovery is completed before the database is opened for more updates. In the case of dynamic backout failure, a batch backout or database recovery must be performed, depending on the reason for the backout failure.

DB Batch Update Programs and Recovery

DB batch update programs can make use of dynamic backout as do BMP programs, provided the following JCL changes are made:

- The BKO=Y parameter is set in the EXEC statement
- A DASD log data set is provided in the IEFRDER DD statement
- A ROLB call is issued in the program code for non-system abends

The dynamic backout backs out the updates to the last checkpoint found on the log data set.

IMS BACKUP AND RECOVERY UTILITIES

IMS provides the following utilities for recovering a database:

"Database Image Copy Utility" on page 154
    The Database Image Copy utility creates image copies of databases.

"Database Image Copy 2 Utility" on page 157

> The Database Image Copy 2 utility takes image copies of IMS databases by using the concurrent copy function of the Data Facility Storage Management Subsystem (DFSMS).

"Online Database Image Copy Utility" on page 157

> The Online Database Image Copy utility creates an as-is image copy of the database while it is being updated by the online system.

"Database Change Accumulation Utility" on page 158

> The Database Change Accumulation utility accumulates database changes from DL/I log tapes since the last complete image copy.

Log Archive Utility

> The Log Archive utility (DFSUARC0) produces an SLDS from a filled OLDS or a batch IMS SLDS. The utility runs as a z/OS batch job, and multiple log archive utility jobs can execute concurrently. For more information about the Log Archive utility, see "Archiving an OLDS" on page 370.

"Database Recovery Utility" on page 161

> The Database Recovery utility restores the database, using a prior database image copy and the accumulated changes from DL/I log tapes.

"Batch Backout Utility" on page 163

> The Batch Backout utility removes changes made to databases by a specific application program.

Another utility program, the Log Recovery utility (DFSULTR0), produces a usable log data set in the event of an operating system or hardware failure, thus enabling use of the log by the four principal programs of the recovery system.

For those databases that consist of multiple data sets, recovery is done by individual data set. To recover a complete database composed of multiple data sets, database recovery must be performed for each of its component data sets.

Figure 11-2 on page 155 illustrates the relationship between the backup and recovery utilities.

Database Image Copy Utility

The Database Image Copy utility (DFSUDMP0) creates a copy of each data set within the database. This copy is not an exact duplicate of the database data set, but it can be used to recover the database data set. The set of output data sets from the Database Image Copy utility is called an image copy. Each data set in the image copy is a sequential data set and can be only used as input to the Database Recovery utility (DFSURDB0). The Database Image Copy utility does not use DL/I to process the database, but uses track I/O instead. There is no internal checking to determine if all the IMS internal pointers are correct. There are tools available to run as part of

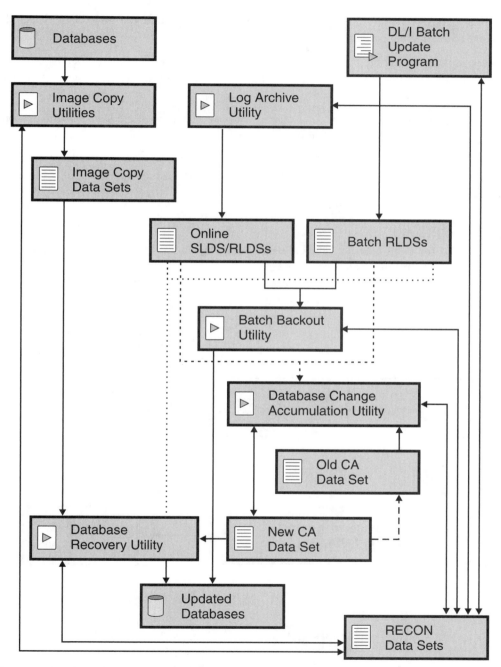

Figure 11-2 Overview of the Recovery Utilities

the image copy process to do this checking. IBM recommends that you periodically check the validity of the internal pointers.

There can be no changes to the DBD when this database is recovered using the Database Recovery utility. In order to make changes to the DBD, a database reorganization is needed to implement those changes.

Multiple databases and data sets can be copied with one execution of the Database Image Copy utility. All data sets of a database should be copied at the same time: when there is no intervening database processing.

The IMS Database Recovery Control (DBRC) facility can be used to generate the JCL to run the Database Image Copy utility, if required.

Related Reading:

- For more information about DBRC, see Chapter 23, "Database Recovery Control (DBRC) Facility," on page 375.
- For more information about the Database Image Copy utility, see *IMS Version 9: Utilities Reference: Database and Transaction Manager.*

A flow diagram of the Database Image Copy utility is shown in Figure 11-3.

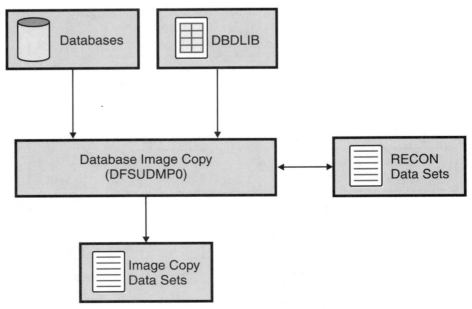

Figure 11-3   Inputs to and Outputs from the Database Image Copy Utility

Database Image Copy 2 Utility

The Database Image Copy 2 utility (DFSUDMT0) is very similar to the Database Image Copy utility (DFSUDMP0). The Database Image Copy 2 utility has several advantages, however, in that it can take image copies with databases being unavailable for a very short time.

The IMS Database Image Copy 2 utility (DFSUDMT0) calls the concurrent copy function of the Data Facility Storage Management Subsystem (DFSMS) to make consistent image copies (that is, with no updates occurring while the utility is making the copy) or concurrent image copies (called *fuzzy* image copies) of an IMS database data set. Database Image Copy utility (DFSUDMP0) cannot make concurrent image copies.

The concurrent copy function of DFSMS is a hardware and software solution that allows you to back up a database or any collection of data at a point in time and with minimum down time for the database. The database is unavailable only long enough for DFSMS to initialize a concurrent copy session for the data, which is a very small fraction of the time that the complete backup takes.

Related Reading: For more information about DFSMS, see *DFSMS V1R5 DFSMSdss Storage Administration Guide*, or *DFSMS V1R5 DFSMSdss Storage Administration Reference*.

The Database Image Copy 2 utility differs from the Database Image Copy utility in the following ways:

- The data sets to be copied must reside on a subsystem that supports DFSMS concurrent copy. The Database Image Copy 2 utility requires that the databases be registered to DBRC. For fuzzy KSDS copies, the database define cluster must specify BWO(TYPIMS) and the KSDS data sets must be managed by SMS.
- An image copy created by the Database Image Copy 2 utility is in DFSMS dump format, rather than standard batch image copy format. The copy is registered with DBRC as an SMSNOCIC or SMSCIC image copy, depending on the parameters specified when the image copy was taken.
- Up to four copies of a data set can be created. Only the primary and secondary (first and second) copies are recorded in the RECON data set.

Related Reading: For more information about the Database Image Copy 2 utility, see *IMS Version 9: Utilities Reference: Database and Transaction Manager*.

A flow diagram of the Database Image Copy 2 utility is shown in Figure 11-4 on page 158.

Online Database Image Copy Utility

The Online Database Image Copy utility (DFSUICP0) creates an as-is image copy of the database while it is being updated by the online system. The Online Database Image Copy utility runs as a BMP program. You can use it only for HISAM, HIDAM, and HDAM databases. If IMS

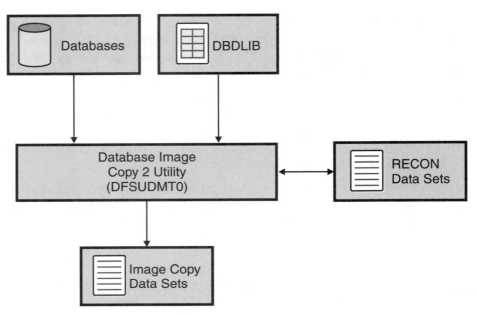

Figure 11-4   Inputs to and Outputs from the Database Image Copy 2 Utility

updates these databases while the utility is running, IMS requires all logs for any subsequent recovery, including the log in use when you started this utility. IMS requires the logs because the image copy is not an image of the database at any particular point in time.

The output from the Online Database Image Copy utility is used as input to the Database Recovery utility.

Related Reading: For more information about the Online Database Image Copy utility, see *IMS Version 9: Utilities Reference: Database and Transaction Manager.*

A flow diagram of the Online Database Image Copy utility is shown in Figure 11-5 on page 159.

Database Change Accumulation Utility

The Database Change Accumulation utility (DFSUCUM0) creates a sequential data set that contains only the database log records from all the log data sets that are necessary for recovery. This *change accumulation log data set* is used by the Database Recovery utility. The accumulation is done by sorting only the required log records in physical record within data set sequence. Change accumulation provides efficient database recovery whenever needed. The number of log data sets that need to be kept is significantly reduced.

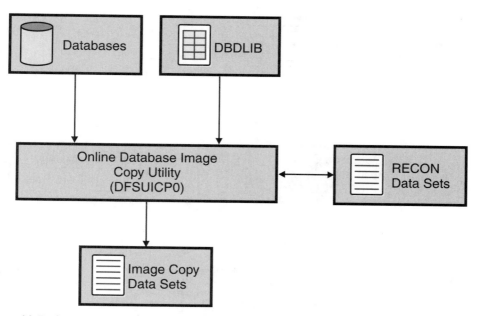

Figure 11-5   Inputs to and Outputs from the Online Database Image Copy Utility

The Database Change Accumulation utility can be run independently of DL/I application programs.

IBM highly recommends that you use DBRC to create the JCL for each execution of the Database Change Accumulation utility. DBRC will ensure that a complete set of log data sets is used to create the change accumulation log data set. The log records must be supplied to the Database Change Accumulation utility in the correct sequence.

Related Reading: For more information about the Database Change Accumulation utility, see *IMS Version 9: Utilities Reference: Database and Transaction Manager.*

A flow diagram of the Database Change Accumulation utility is shown in Figure 11-6 on page 160.

The input to the Database Change Accumulation utility consists of:

- All log data sets created since either the last execution of an image copy utility or the last execution of the Database Change Accumulation utility.

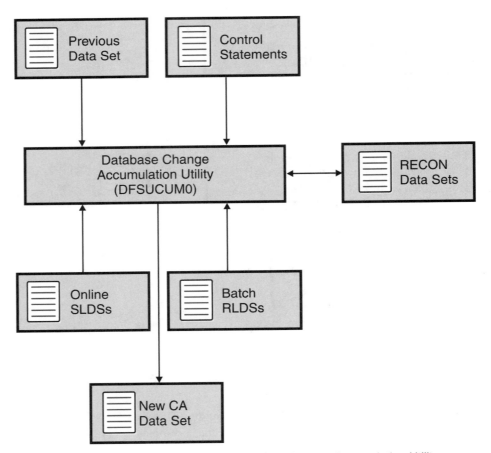

Figure 11-6   Inputs to and Outputs from the Database Change Accumulation Utility

- The old (previously created) change accumulation log data set. This data set would be the output from the last execution of the Database Change Accumulation utility. The first change accumulation run after a new image copy must not include any old change accumulation data set, that is, those created during the previous period.
- Control statements that specify any purge dates and how the database log records are to be processed.

The output from the Database Change Accumulation utility consists of a new change accumulation data set, a sequential data set that contains the combined database records for all database data sets.

Database Recovery Utility

The Database Recovery utility (DFSURDB0) restores a database data set. The Database Recovery utility does not provide a means of recovery from application logic errors: you must ensure the logical integrity of the data in the database.

The process for recovering a HALDB data set that is not being reorganized online is different from recovering a HALDB data set that is being reorganized online. For more information, see "Recovering HALDB Data Sets During Online Reorganization."

Unlike the image copy utilities, the Database Recovery utility recovers one database data set per job step. Thus, to recover multiple data sets for a database, the Database Recovery utility must be run once for each data set.

> **RECOMMENDATION:** Use DBRC to create the JCL for each execution of the Database Recovery utility. DBRC ensures that all the correct inputs are supplied.

You can run the Database Recovery utility in a number of ways, depending on what input is required. Generally, the main input to the Database Recovery utility is the image copy data set. Other input can consist of any log data sets or change accumulation data sets that might be needed. You can run the Database Recovery utility with only the log information as input. In this case, the database that already exists is used as input.

A flow diagram of the Database Recovery utility is shown in Figure 11-7 on page 162.

The input to the Database Recovery utility consists of an image copy data set and, optionally, a change accumulation data set and any log data sets that are not included in the change accumulation data set.

The Database Recovery utility is run in a DL/I batch region and will allocate the database in exclusive mode so that there can be no other database activity at the time.

Recovering HALDB Data Sets During Online Reorganization

After DBRC sets the cursor-active status for the partition in the RECON data sets, and until the copying phase completes and DBRC resets the cursor-active status, you can recover any of the input or output data sets using the Database Recovery utility. To restore the output data sets, the Database Recovery utility uses the database change records (type X'50' log records) and applies them to empty output data sets.

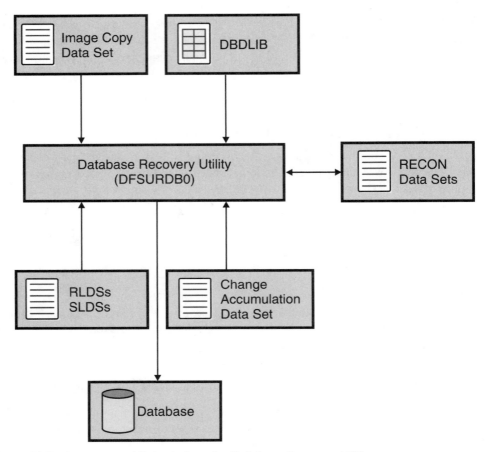

Figure 11-7   Inputs to and Outputs from the Database Recovery Utility

> **RECOMMENDATION:** Make an image copy of the
> output data sets as soon as possible after the online reorganization
> completes. Recovering from this image copy is faster than recovering
> from the database change records that are logged during the online
> reorganization. However, you cannot make an image copy while the
> partition is in cursor-active status.

To recover an output data set before the online reorganization completes, perform the following tasks:

1. Stop the online reorganization by using the TERMINATE OLREORG command. If the online reorganization encountered an abend, it is stopped automatically.

2. Issue the /DBR or the UPDATE DB command for the HALDB partition.

3. Run database change accumulation, as necessary. You can create the JCL by issuing the GENJCL.CA command, or you can run the Database Change Accumulation utility (DFSUCUM0) from your own JCL. The purge time for the change accumulation must be equal to the time of the beginning of the online reorganization to represent restoring from the initial empty state of the data set.

4. Create the output data set to be recovered, either by using a JCL DD statement or by using Access Method Services, as appropriate.

5. Recover the database changes. You can create the JCL by issuing the GENJCL.RECOV command. Alternatively, you can run the Database Recovery utility from your own JCL with the DD statement for DFSUDUMP specified as DUMMY to indicate that there is no image copy from which to restore.

6. Run the Batch Backout utility (DFSBBO00), because you might need to back out uncommitted data.

7. After you have recovered, and possibly backed out, all of the required data sets of the HALDB partition, issue the /STA DB or the UPDATE DB command for the HALDB partition.

8. Issue the INITIATE OLREORG command to resume the online reorganization.

You can also recover an output data set after the online reorganization completes but before an image copy has been made. Follow the same steps as for recovering an output data set before the online reorganization completes, except the steps for stopping and restarting the online reorganization.

In addition, you can recover an output data set from a point other than the beginning of the online reorganization, such as from a full dump of a DASD volume, using existing procedures if the online reorganization is either completed or terminated.

Related Reading: For more information, see "Recovery for HALDB Online Reorganization" in *IMS Version 9: Administration Guide: Database Manager.*

Batch Backout Utility

Batch backout, in its simplest form, is the reading of log data sets to back out all database updates after an abnormal termination. Backout is done by using the *before image data* in the log record to re-update the database segments. Backout has the effect of undoing the previous updates.

> **N O T E:** The Batch Backout utility is needed only for full-function and HALDB databases.

The Batch Backout utility removes changes in the database that were made by a specific failing program. The following limitations apply:

- The log data set of the failing program must be on DASD.
- No other update programs can have been executed against the same database between the time of the failure and the backout.

The Batch Backout utility operates as a normal DL/I batch job and uses the PSB that is used by the program whose changes are to be backed out. All databases updated by the failed program must be available to the Batch Backout utility.

Figure 11-8 illustrates the inputs and outputs for the Batch Backout utility.

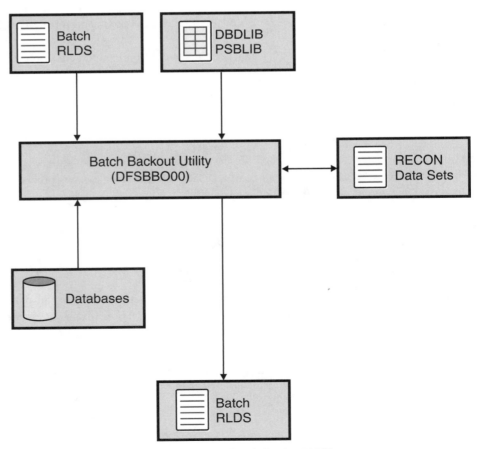

Figure 11-8   Inputs to and Outputs from the Batch Backout Utility

A log data set is created during the backout process. This log data set, preceded by the log data set produced for the failing job, must be included in the next change accumulation run, as any other log data set, and must not be used as input to any subsequent backout attempt.

Usage Notes for the Batch Backout Utility

Keep the following items in mind when using the Batch Backout utility:

- If checkpoint/restart is not used, then the Batch Backout utility always backs out all the database changes of the program. For an overview of checkpoint/restart, see "IMS Checkpoints" on page 111.
- If checkpoint/restart is used (program uses XRST and CHKP-ID calls), then backout will only perform a backout if the specified CHKP-ID is found on the log data set during read forward. If no CHKP-ID is specified, then the last one on the log data set is used (the first one encountered during read backward).
- If, when using checkpoint/restart, you want to be able to completely back out a job (steps), you must issue a CHKP call immediately after the XRST call, that is, before any real database activity. The CHKP-ID of this call can then be used for a full backout operation.
- To run batch backout for a DB batch that had completed successfully, the DBRC=C parameter must be added to the EXEC PARM keyword if online backout failed, but only to the prior checkpoint.

IMS Transaction Manager

CHAPTER 12

Overview of the IMS Transaction Manager

IMS Transaction Manager (IMS TM) performs online transaction processing, which, in its simplest form, comprises the following steps:

1. Receiving a request for work to be done. The request is entered at a remote terminal and is usually made up of a transaction code, which identifies to IMS the type of work to be done, and data, which is used in performing the work.
2. Initiating and controlling a specific program that uses the data in the request to complete the work that the remote operator requested, and to prepare data for the remote operator in response to the request for work (for example, an acknowledgment of work done or an answer to a query).
3. Transmitting the data prepared by the program back to the terminal that originally requested the work.

IMS TM also provides solutions for cooperative processing, distributed database processing, and continuous operation, such as:

- Providing a high-performance transaction processing environment for database management systems, such as IMS Database Manager (IMS DB) and DB2 UDB for z/OS.
- Enhancing system management.
- Simplifying network administration.
- Managing and securing the IMS TM terminal network.
- Routing messages from terminal to terminal, from application to application, and between application programs and terminals.

- Queuing input and output messages, and scheduling transactions by associating programs with the messages.
- Participating in distributive processing scenarios where other programs, such as IBM WebSphere Studio Application Developer Integration Edition, need to access IMS.

> **DEFINITION:**
>
> A *logical unit* is an addressable resource that can be an application program, a terminal, or a subsystem, such as CICS. A logical unit can also be a component of a general-purpose terminal system that consists of a programmable controller and its attached operator terminals, printers, and auxiliary control units.

Terminals or logical units can also be thought of as ports or windows through which a business gives a user access to the network and its functions. In times past, the port was a physical device (for example, a 3270 terminal—not an emulation program). Today, the port is more likely to be an application program that implements an installation's business rules.

In This Chapter:

- "IMS TM Control Region"
- "IMS TM Messages" on page 171
- "IMS Transaction Flow" on page 173
- "IMS TM Network Overview" on page 175
- "The Data Communication Control (DCCTL) Environment" on page 189
- "Operating an IMS Network" on page 190

IMS TM Control Region

The IMS TM control region is a z/OS address space that can be initiated through a z/OS START command or by submitting JCL. The terminals, databases, message queues, and logs are all attached to this control region. A z/OS type-2 supervisor call routine is used to control IMS access to z/OS resources.

The IMS TM control region normally runs as a system task and uses z/OS access methods for terminal and database access.

After the IMS TM control region is started, it starts the system dependent regions, DLISAS and DBRC. Then you can start the MPR and BMP regions through the use of:

- IMS jobs
- Job submission
- Automated operator commands

IMS TM MESSAGES

A message, in the most general sense, is a sequence of transmitted symbols. The network inputs and outputs to IMS TM take the form of messages (plus control information) that are input to or output from IMS and the physical terminals, or application programs on the network (referred to as destinations).

Each unit of input to or output from IMS TM is called a *transmission*. A transmission can consist of a single message or multiple messages and the control information that is associated with those messages.

In general, IMS processes these messages asynchronously, which means that IMS does not always send a reply immediately, or ever, when it receives a message, and that unsolicited messages might also be sent from IMS. However, APPC/IMS and OTMA also support synchronous protocols, which means IMS always sends a reply when it receives a message.

There are three types of messages:

- Transactions. The data in these messages is passed to IMS application programs for processing.
- Messages to go to another logical destination (for example, network terminals).
- Commands for IMS to process.

If IMS is not able to process an input message immediately, or cannot send an output message immediately, the message is stored on a message queue that is external to the IMS system. IMS does not normally delete the message from the message queue until it has received confirmation that an application has processed the input message or that the output message has reached its destination.

Multiple and Single Segment Messages

A message can have one or more segments. A segment is defined by an end-of-segment (EOS) symbol, a message is defined by an end-of-message (EOM) symbol, and a transmission is defined by an end-of-data (EOD) symbol. Table 12-1 shows the valid combinations of the conditions represented by the EOS, EOM, and EOD symbols.

Table 12-1   Valid Combinations of the EOS, EOM, and EOD Symbols

Condition	Represents
EOS	End of segment
EOM	End of segment / end of message
EOD	End of segment / end of message / end of data

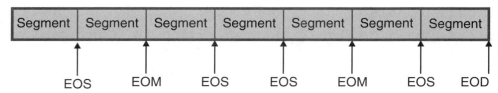

Figure 12-1   Transmission, Message, and Segment Relationships

The relationships between transmission, message, and segment are shown in Figure 12-1.

The character values or conditions that represent the end of segment and the end of the message, or both, depend on the terminal type.

For 3270 terminals, the physical terminal input is always a single segment message and transmission, but MFS can edit this into multiple IMS message segments. The EOS, EOM, and EOD conditions are all set after the Enter function key or the program function key is pressed and the data is transmitted.

On the output side, a message can be divided into multiple segments. Also, an application program can send different messages to different terminals, for example, a message to a printer terminal and a message to the display terminal. Each segment requires a separate insert call by the application program.

The format of a message segment, as presented to or received from an application program, is shown in Figure 12-2, and shows the following fields:

LL

Total length of the segment in bytes, including the LL and ZZ fields.

ZZ

IMS system field

Data

Application data, including the transaction code

LL	ZZ	Data
2 bytes	2 bytes	n bytes

Figure 12-2   Format of a Message Segment

IMS TRANSACTION FLOW

The general flow of an input message is from a terminal or user to the MPP, and the general flow of the output reply message is from the MPP to the terminal or user. This flow is illustrated in Figure 12-3 on page 174. This figure describes a general flow of the message through the system, not a complete detailed description.

A further description of Figure 12-3 follows:

1. The input data from the terminal is read by the data communication modules. After editing by MFS, if appropriate, and verifying that the user is allowed to execute this transaction, this input data is put in the IMS message queue. The messages in the queue are sequenced by destination, which could be either transaction code (TRAN) or logical terminal (LTERM). For input messages, this destination is TRAN.

2. The scheduling modules determine which MPR is available to process this transaction, based on a number of system and user-specified considerations, and then retrieves the message from the IMS message queues, and starts the processing of a transaction in the MPR.

3. Upon request from an MPR, the DL/I modules pass a message or database segment to or from the MPR.

> **N O T E:** In z/OS, the DL/I modules, control blocks, and pools reside in the common storage area (CSA or ECSA) and the control region is not used for most database processing. The exception is Fast Path DEDB processing.

4. After the MPP has finished processing, the message output from the MPP is also put into the IMS message queues, in this case, queued against the logical terminal (LTERM).

5. The communication modules retrieve the message from the message queues, and send it to the output terminal. MFS is used to edit the screen and printer output (if appropriate).

6. All changes to the message queues and the databases are recorded on the logs. In addition, checkpoints for system (emergency) restart and statistical information are logged.

> **N O T E S:** a. The physical logging modules run as a separate task and use z/OS ESTAE for maximum integrity.
>
> b. The checkpoint identification and log data set information are recorded in the restart and RECON data sets.

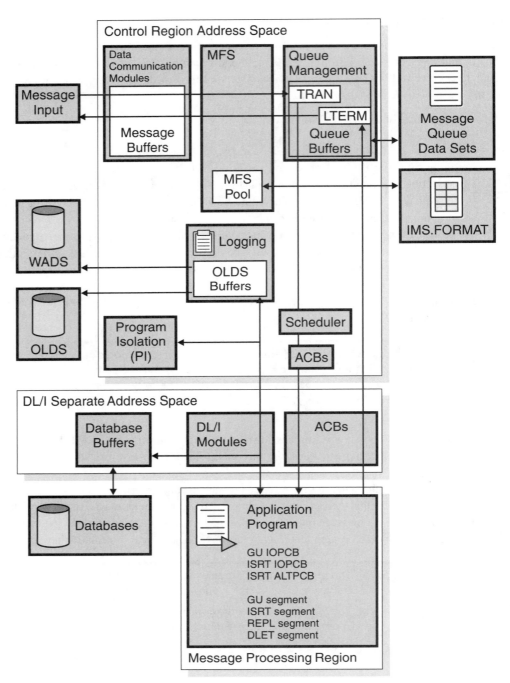

Figure 12-3   The IMS Control Region, Its Control, and Data (Message) Flow

7. Program isolation (PI) locking assures database integrity when two or more MPPs update the same database. The system also backs out database changes made by failing programs by maintaining a short-term, dynamic log of the old database element images. IRLM is an optional replacement for PI locking. IRLM is required, however, if IMS is participating in data sharing.

Related Reading: For more information about IMS TM transaction flow, see Chapter 13, "How IMS TM Processes Input," on page 195.

IMS TM NETWORK OVERVIEW

IMS TM provides the necessary support for an advanced telecommunications network. Planning for an IMS network requires an understanding of each component and of its relationship to the others.

IMS TM interacts with:

- The IBM Systems Network Architecture (SNA), which brings together multiple products in a unified design. SNA formally defines the functional responsibilities of the network components.

  IMS TM supports SNA as currently implemented by the Communication Server for z/OS, which includes the functions of Virtual Telecommunications Access Method (VTAM). VTAM controls the physical transmission of data in the network, directing data to IMS from various logical units and from IMS to the appropriate logical units. IMS TM interacts directly with VTAM.

- Applications that use the z/OS APPC protocol.
- Networks that use TCP/IP. Access using TCP/IP is achieved by way of an additional address space, which is the IMS Connect function of IMS TM. IMS Connect must be configured to use the Open Transaction Manager Access (OTMA) protocol of IMS TM.

  Related Reading: For more information about:

  — OTMA, see "Open Transaction Manager Access" on page 179, or the *IMS Version 9: Open Transaction Manager Access Guide and Reference*.
  — IMS Connect, see "IMS Connect" on page 187, or *IMS Version 9: IMS Connect Guide and Reference*.
  — The options available for accessing IMS using TCP/IP, see Chapter 27, "Introduction to Parallel Sysplex," on page 467.

A network consisting of IMS and programmable logical units enables users to distribute functions throughout network components. This distribution of function can:

- Reduce processing requirements that are placed on the central processor (also referred to as the *host*).
- Reduce the impact on the rest of the network when one component encounters a problem.

DEFINITIONS:

- When a logical unit wants to communicate with IMS, the logical unit requests a connection with IMS. When IMS accepts the request, a logical connection is established between the logical unit and IMS. This logical connection is called a *session*.

- A *programmable logical unit (LU)* is an input or output device that is in session with IMS. Application programs in remote logical units can be designed to control more than one terminal.

Figure 12-4 illustrates the components of a sample communications network system. The arrows in Figure 12-4 indicate communications that occur between components. Figure 12-4 shows the following components:

- IMS and its application programs
- VTAM
- Tivoli NetView® for z/OS
- z/OS operating system (including APPC/MVS, if APPC/IMS is used)
- IBM 37x5 Communications Controller and Network Control Program (NCP)
- Terminal (or logical unit)

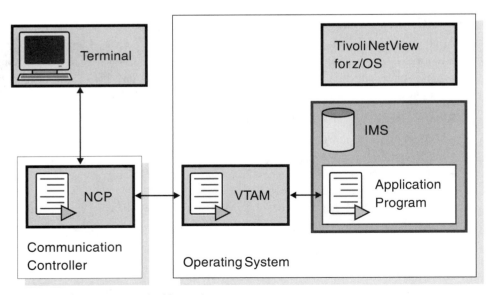

Figure 12-4   Components of a Network

The following lists summarize how each of the components in Figure 12-4 participates in the network:

IMS

- Checks transaction security.
- Schedules the proper application program.
- Directs output to the proper terminal or logical unit.
- Provides checkpoint and recovery capabilities.

Application program

- Reads data sent from the terminal or logical unit.
- Reads data from the database.
- Manipulates the data.
- Writes data to the database.
- Writes data to the message queue for the terminal or logical unit.

VTAM

- Connects and disconnects the terminal or logical unit from the network.
- Sends data from the terminal or logical unit to IMS.
- Permits both monitoring and modifying of the network.
- Sends data from IMS to the terminal or logical unit.
- Manages the physical network, with Tivoli NetView for z/OS.

VTAM controls the allocation of network resources, and enables these resources to be shared among VTAM users. To VTAM, IMS is a single VTAM user; VTAM is unaware of the IMS application programs.

IMS application programs use the DL/I callable interface to request IMS services; IMS uses VTAM macros to activate VTAM facilities.

If APPC/IMS is active, VTAM regards it as a separate user.

Related Reading: For more information about VTAM and its use, see *z/OS V1R4.0 z/ OS Communications Server: SNA Network Implementation Guide.*

Communications Controller and NCP

VTAM uses the facilities of NCP, which runs in the 37x5 Communications Controllers. VTAM uses NCP to:

- Control lines and devices that are attached to the controllers.
- Transmit data between the logical unit and the host central processor complex (CPC).
- Perform error recovery.
- Collect statistics about the network.

The Communications Controller:

- Adds line control characters.
- Transmits data.
- Receives data.
- Removes line control characters.
- Checks for transmission errors.
- Controls buffering.

The NCP:

- Sends and receives data from communication lines and adapters.
- Checks for and records errors.

Terminal (or logical unit)

Depending on the system type, each LU can consist of one or more terminals. An application program that controls an LU consisting of more than one terminal or component must be able to direct output to a specific device. Therefore, the application program must be capable of some form of data interrogation in order to make the proper device selection. IMS assists the application program in this process by:

- Allowing LU components to be defined and addressed individually.
- Providing, in the header of each output message, the identification of the component to which the message is directed.

Some of the functions performed by the remote application program include:

- Reading from and writing to associated terminals.
- Editing and verifying the data that is received from a terminal.
- Reading from and writing to disk storage within the remote LU.
- Reading from and writing to the host in which IMS is running.
- Editing and verifying data that is received from the host in which IMS is running.
- Communicating with other network logical units.
- Formatting display and printer devices.
- Operating offline when the host, VTAM, IMS, or NCP is unavailable.

Required IMS TM Network Components

An IMS telecommunications network must include the following components:

- IMS
- VTAM
- Communications hardware, such as control units
- Terminals

Optional IMS TM Network Components

The network can optionally include any of the following components:

- IMS TM services, such as:
    — Open Transaction Manager Access (OTMA)
    — Extended Terminal Option (ETO)
    — Fast Path
    — Message Format Service (MFS)
    — Multiple Systems Coupling (MSC)
    — Intersystem Communication (ISC)
    — APPC
- IMS Connect function
- Common Queue Server (CQS) and a z/OS coupling facility with any of the following structures:
    — Shared-queues structures
    — Resource structures
- Common Service Layer (CSL), including:
    — Operations Manager (OM)
    — Resource Manager (RM)
    — Structured Call Interface (SCI)
- VTAM generic resource groups

Related Reading: For more information about:

- IMS Connect, see "IMS Connect" on page 187.
- CQS, see "Common Queue Server" on page 496.
- CSL, see "Common Service Layer" on page 496.
- VTAM generic resources, see "VTAM Generic Resources" on page 476.

IMS TM Services

This section describes several specialized optional Transaction Manager services.

Open Transaction Manager Access OTMA is an open interface to IMS TM customers. With OTMA, a z/OS or TCP/IP application program can send a transaction or command to IMS without using SNA or VTAM. Many programs can connect to IMS TM using OTMA: middleware software, gateway programs, databases, and applications written by IMS users. Each of the programs or applications that communicates with IMS using OTMA is considered an OTMA client.

The OTMA interface is very flexible. An OTMA client, an application program of the client, or both, can use OTMA in many different ways. The execution of some transactions can involve complex "handshaking" between IMS and the client program; some transactions can simply use the basic protocol.

OTMA can be used to process an IMS transaction using one of the following methods:

Commit-then-send (CM0)

IMS processes the transaction and commits the data before sending a response to the OTMA client. Input and output messages are recoverable. The commit-then-send protocol is the traditional IMS asynchronous protocol, which is similar to the APPC asynchronous protocol.

Send-then-commit (CM1)

IMS processes the transaction and sends the response to the OTMA client before committing the data. Input and output messages are non-recoverable. This is the synchronous protocol, similar to APPC synchronous support.

If the application program uses send-then-commit processing, you must also decide which of the three synchronization levels to use:

None

Output is sent and no response from the client is requested. Data is committed if the send is successful. Data is backed out if the send fails.

Confirm

Output is sent and a response from the client is requested. The OTMA client must respond with an acknowledgement signal to IMS Connect that confirms whether or not the output message send was successful or unsuccessful. Data is committed if the send was successful. Data is backed out if the send was not successful.

Syncpt

Output is sent, and a response from the client is requested. Use syncpt to coordinate commit processing through the z/OS Resource Recovery Service (RRS). The OTMA client must respond with a signal that the send was successful or not. Data is committed if the send was successful and an RRS commit is received. Data is backed out if the send was not successful or an RRS abort is received.

An application can decide, for example, that inquiry transactions should use a synchronization level of none (because there are no database updates) and that update transactions should use a synchronization level of confirm.

The OTMA resynchronization interface ensures that no duplicate CM0 input and output messages exist by using a unique recoverable sequence number in every CM0 message. The client can optionally initiate the resynchronization during connection time. IBM WebSphere MQ for z/OS and IMS Connect extensively exploit this OTMA interface. An IBM WebSphere MQ for z/OS application program can send a persistent message to IMS to take advantage of resynchronization. However, sending an IBM WebSphere MQ for z/OS non-persistent CM0 message to IMS bypasses resynchronization.

D E F I N I T I O N S:

Persistent message   A message that survives a restart of the queue manager.

Non-persistent message   A message that does not survive a restart of the queue manager.

Tpipe   A named IMS process management resource. An OTMA client must specify this resource when submitting a transaction to IMS. A Tpipe is analogous to an LTERM.

Use Table 12-2 to determine which OTMA method is appropriate for your application.

Extended Terminal Option (ETO)   IMS Extended Terminal Option (ETO) provides dynamic terminal and local and remote logical terminal (LTERM) support for IMS TM. ETO is a separately priced feature of IMS TM.

Table 12-2   OTMA Methods for Processing Transactions

Type of Processing	Commit-then-send (CM0)	Send-then-commit (CM1)
Conversational transactions	Not supported	Supported
Fast Path transactions	Not supported	Supported
Remote MSC transactions	Supported	Supported
Shared queues	Supported in IMS Version 7 and later	Supported in IMS Version 8 and later
Recoverable output	Supported	Not supported
Synchronized Tpipes	Supported	Not supported
Program-to-program switch	Supported	Supported, but with qualifications.[a]

a.   If a series of programs within one IMS perform program-to-program switches from one program to the next program, all the programs process as send-then-commit (CM1). If more than one program-to-program switch is performed within a single program (to other programs), only one of the program-to-program switches processes as send-then-commit (CM1). The other program-to-program switches process as commit-then-send (CM0). The techniques to mitigate this situation are described in *IMS Version 9: Open Transaction Manager Access Guide and Reference.*

You can add terminal hardware and LTERMs to the IMS without first defining them. ETO gives you the option of eliminating macro statements in the IMS system definition of VTAM terminals and LTERMs. ETO enhances the availability of your IMS by eliminating the need for you to bring the system down in order to add terminals and LTERMs.

ETO also enhances security for the IMS TM user by associating all output with a specific user, instead of with a device. ETO requires the user to sign on.

ETO reduces the IMS system definition time for those systems where the terminal network is defined dynamically.

> **RESTRICTION:**   The Security Maintenance Utility (SMU) does not support ETO. Security for ETO is enforced using RACF or a similar product.

Related Reading: For more information about how ETO can dynamically add terminals and users to an IMS system, see "The Extended Terminal Option (ETO)" on page 338. For complete information about ETO, see *IMS Version 9: Administration Guide: Transaction Manager* and *IMS Version 9: Installation Volume 2: System Definition and Tailoring*.

Fast Path   Fast Path is capable of performing transaction and database processing at high rates. When your system requirements include a high transaction volume, using Fast Path can be advantageous if you do not require all the facilities of full-function processing. Examples of such applications include teller transactions in banking and point-of-sale transactions (inventory update) in retail marketing. Fast Path input and output messages use expedited message handling (EMH) and bypass message queuing and the priority-scheduling process.

Related Reading:

- For more information on the expedited message handler (EMH), see "Scheduling Fast Path Transactions" on page 212.
- For more information on message queuing and message scheduling, see "Message Queuing" on page 198.

Message Format Service   IMS Message Format Service (MFS) is a facility that formats messages to and from:

- Terminals, so that application programs do not have to process device-dependent data in input or output messages. An application program can format messages for different device types using a single set of editing logic, even when device input and output differ from device to device.

- User-written programs in remote controllers and subsystems, so that application programs do not have to be concerned with the transmission-specific characteristics of the remote controller.

Related Reading: For more information on MFS, see Chapter 17, "Editing and Formatting Messages," on page 297.

Connections to Other IMS and CICS Subsystems through MSC and ISC   IMS TM has special protocols for connecting to other IMS systems, such as Multiple Systems Coupling (MSC), and to other CICS and IMS systems, such as Intersystem Communication (ISC), which allows work to be routed to and from the other systems for processing.

The MSC connections can be through the network to other IMS systems on the same or other z/OS systems, by using:

- Channel-to-channel connections to the same or another channel-attached z/OS system.
- Cross memory services to another IMS subsystem on the same z/OS system.
- The VTAM LU 6.1 protocol.

ISC links to other CICS or IMS systems are provided over the network by using the VTAM LU 6.1 protocol.

Multiple Systems Coupling (MSC)   MSC is a service of IMS TM that provides the ability to connect geographically dispersed IMSs. MSC enables programs and operators of one IMS to access programs and operators of the connected IMSs. Communication can occur between two or more (up to 2036) IMSs running on any supported combination of operating systems.

MSC permits you to distribute processing loads and databases. Transactions entered in one IMS system can be passed to another IMS system for processing and the results returned to the initiating terminal. Terminal operators are unaware of these activities; their view of the processing is the same as that presented by interaction with a single system.

MSC supports transaction routing between the participating IMSs by options specified in the IMS system definition process.

DEFINITIONS:
- The IMS system where the transaction is entered by the terminal user is referred to as the *front-end* system.
- The IMS system where the transaction is processed is referred to as the *back-end* system.

The transaction is entered in the front-end system and, based on the options specified in the IMS system definition process, the transaction is sent to the back-end system. When the transaction reaches the back-end system, all standard IMS scheduling techniques apply. After processing, the results are sent back to the front-end system, which then returns the results to the terminal user, who is unaware of this activity.

Intersystem Communication (ISC)   ISC is also a service of IMS TM and, in addition to MSC, provides another way to connect multiple subsystems. ISC is more flexible than MSC because ISC supports the following connections:

- IMS-to-IMS
- IMS-to-CICS
- IMS-to-user-written VTAM program

The transaction routing specification for ISC is contained in the application program, instead of in the IMS system definition as it is for MSC.

ISC links between IMS and CICS use the standard VTAM LU 6.1 protocol that is available within the network. ISC links can use standard VTAM connections or direct connections.

As defined under SNA, ISC is an LU 6.1 session that:

- Connects different subsystems to communicate at the subsystems level.
- Provides distributed transaction processing that permits a terminal user or application in one subsystem to communicate with a terminal or application in a different subsystem and, optionally, to receive a reply. In some cases, the application is user-written; in other cases, the subsystem itself acts as an application.
- Provides distributed services. Therefore, an application in one subsystem can use a service (such as a message queue or database) in a different subsystem.

SNA makes communication possible between unlike subsystems and includes SNA-defined session control protocols, data flow control protocols, and routing parameters.

Comparing the Functions of MSC and ISC   As discussed in "Multiple Systems Coupling (MSC)" on page 183 and "Intersystem Communication (ISC)" on page 184, both MSC and ISC enable a user to:

- Route transactions
- Distribute transaction processing
- Grow beyond the capacity of one IMS system

Both ISC and MSC take advantage of the parallel session support that VTAM provides. Some key differences exist, however. Table 12-3 on page 185 compares the major functions of MSC and ISC.

Table 12-3   Comparing MSC and ISC Functions

Comparative Aspect	MSC Functions	ISC Functions
Connections	IMS systems can connect only to each other. These IMS systems can all reside in one processor, or they can reside in different processors.	Systems connect either like or unlike subsystems, as long as the connected subsystems both implement ISC. You can couple an IMS subsystem to: • Another IMS subsystem • A CICS subsystem • A user-written subsystem
Communication	Message queue to message queue.	Subsystem to subsystem. The subsystems themselves are session partners, supporting logical flows between the applications.
Processing	Processing is transparent to the user. MSC processing appears as if it is occurring in a single system.	Message routing for processing requires involvement by the terminal user or the application to determine the message destination because ISC supports coupling of unlike subsystems. Specified routing parameters can be overridden, modified, or deleted by MFS.
Message routing	MSC routing is performed automatically through system definition parameters or by exit routines (for directed routing). Neither the terminal operator nor any application is concerned with routing.	ISC provides a unique message-switching capability that permits message routing to occur without involvement of a user application.
Distributed conversations	MSC supports the steps of a conversation being distributed over multiple IMS subsystems, transparent to both the source terminal operator and to each conversational step (application).	ISC supports the use of MFS in an IMS subsystem to assist in the routing and formatting of messages between subsystems.
Fast Path Expedited Message Handler (EMH)	MSC does not support the use of the Fast Path EMH.	ISC supports the use of Fast Path EMH between IMS subsystems.

APPC/IMS and LU 6.2 Devices   APPC/IMS is a part of IMS TM that supports the formats and protocols for program-to-program communication. APPC/IMS allows you to use Common Programming Interface Communications (CPI-C) to build CPI application programs. APPC/IMS supports APPC with facilities provided by APPC/MVS.

APPC/VTAM is part of the Communication Server for z/OS and facilitates the implementation of APPC/IMS support. In addition, APPC/MVS works with APPC/VTAM to implement APPC/IMS functions and communication services in a z/OS environment. APPC/IMS takes advantage of this structure and uses APPC/MVS to communicate with LU 6.2 devices. Therefore, all VTAM LU 6.2 devices supported by APPC/MVS can access IMS using LU 6.2 protocols to initiate IMS application programs, or, conversely, be initiated by IMS.

APPC/IMS Application Programming Interfaces   IMS supports implicit and explicit application program interfaces (APIs) for APPC support.

- **Implicit API for APPC:**
  - Supports only a subset of the APPC functions, but enables an APPC incoming message to trigger any standard IMS application that is already defined in the normal manner to IMS, and uses the standard IMS message queue facilities, to schedule the transaction into any appropriate dependent region.
  - Allows the IMS application program to communicate with APPC devices using the same techniques employed with other remote devices.
  - Allows an application program, written by a programmer who has no knowledge of APPC LU 6.2 devices, to:
    - ➤ Be started from an APPC LU 6.2 device
    - ➤ Receive input messages from originating LU 6.2 devices
    - ➤ Send output messages back to originating LU 6.2 devices
    - ➤ Start transaction programs on remote LU 6.2 devices

  The same application program can work with all device types, (LU 6.2 and non-LU 6.2) without new or changed coding.

- **Explicit APPC/IMS Interface:**
  - Supports the complete CPI-C interface. The CPI-C interface is available to any IMS application program. The IMS application program can issue calls to APPC/MVS through this interface. The IMS application program can also use z/OS ATBxxx call services. For information on these call services, see *z/OS MVS Programming: Writing Transaction Programs for APPC/MVS*.
  - Supports the full set of CPI-C command verbs. IMS applications are written specifically to respond only to APPC-triggered transactions. The standard IMS message queues are not used in this case and the IMS control region helps create only the APPC conversation directly between the APPC client and the IMS dependent region to service this request. The IMS control region takes no further part, regardless of how much time the conversation might use while active.

Related Reading: For more information on APPC/IMS, see *IMS Version 9: Administration Guide: Transaction Manager*.

IMS Connect

IMS Connect is an optional IMS TM network component that provides high performance communications for IMS between one or more TCP/IP clients (such as IBM WebSphere Application Server for z/OS) and one or more IMS systems. IMS Connect provides the following features:

- Provides commands to manage the communication environment.
- Assists with workload balancing.
- Reduces design and coding efforts for client applications.
- Offers easy access to IMS applications and operations with advanced security and transactional integrity.

As shown in Figure 12-5, IMS Connect enables TCP/IP or local z/OS clients to exchange messages through the IMS OTMA facility or to exchange commands through the IMS Structured Call Interface (SCI) to the IMS Operations Manager (OM).

IMS Connect runs in a separate address space.

IMS Connect performs router functions between TCP/IP clients, and local option clients on z/OS with datastores (IMSs) and IMSplex resources. Request messages that are received from TCP/IP clients (using TCP/IP connections) or local option clients (using the z/OS Program Call PC) are passed to a datastore through cross-system coupling facility (XCF) sessions. IMS Connect receives response messages from the datastore and then passes them back to the originating TCP/IP or local option clients.

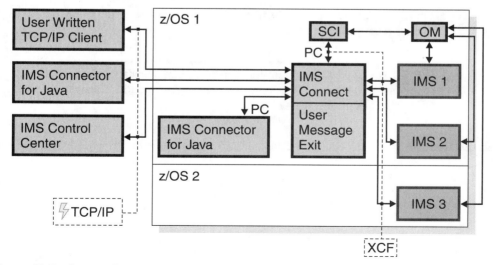

Figure 12-5   System Overview using IMS Connect

IMS Connect supports TCP/IP clients communicating with socket calls, but it can also support any TCP/IP client that communicates with a different input data stream format. User-written message exit routines can execute in the IMS Connect address space to convert customer message format to OTMA message format before IMS Connect sends the message to IMS. The user-written message exit routines can also convert OTMA message format to customer message format before sending a message back to IMS Connect. IMS Connect then sends output to the client.

If the datastore goes down, the status of the datastore is sent to IMS Connect from OTMA through XCF. When the datastore is brought back up and restarted, IMS Connect is notified and automatically reconnects to the datastore. You do not need to manually reconnect to the datastore.

In addition to TCP/IP client communications, IMS Connect also supports local communication through the *local option*, which provides a non-socket (non-TCP/IP) communication protocol for use between IBM WebSphere Application Server for z/OS and IMS Connect in the z/OS environment. Servlets that run in IBM WebSphere Application Server for z/OS and use IMS Connector for Java,[1] can communicate with IMS Connect through the local option.

IMS Connect also supports TCP/IP connections from the DB2 UDB V8.1 Control Center to exchange IMS Control Center commands and responses. A single IMS Connect can support communication between the IMS Control Center and any IMS within the sysplex. For more information about the IMS Control Center, see "Operating an IMSplex" on page 499.

> **REQUIREMENT:** To use local option client communications, both IMS Connect and the IBM WebSphere Application Server for z/OS instance where IMS Connector for Java is running must reside in the same z/OS image.

> **RESTRICTION:** Local option client communications are supported only through IMS Connector for Java and the IMS Connect HWSJAVA0 user message exit.

Related Reading: For the complete details of IMS Connect, see *IMS Version 9: IMS Connect Guide and Reference*.

---

1.   IMS Connect for Java is included in IBM WebSphere Studio Application Developer Integration Edition.

THE DATA COMMUNICATION CONTROL (DCCTL) ENVIRONMENT

The Data Communication Control (DCCTL—pronounced "DC control") environment allows you to use IMS TM independently of IMS DB. DCCTL provides improved system performance in terms of throughput, system availability, and integrity. DCCTL can coexist with IMS TM application programs and installed terminals.

The following scenarios involving DCCTL do not require modifications to your existing environment:

- Application programs that access external database managers can use DCCTL without any modifications. For example, DCCTL can function as a front-end transaction manager for DB2 UDB for z/OS. DB2 UDB for z/OS subsystems do not require modifications in order to run with DCCTL.
- IMS exit routines and IMS application programs that access external subsystem resources in a DCCTL environment do not require modifications.
- Global resource management is the same in a DCCTL environment as it is in a DB/DC environment.

The following procedures might require modifications for a DCCTL environment:

- Operational procedures.
- The general procedure that is produced by the system definition.
- Application programs that contain a mixture of calls that access both external subsystems and IMS databases do require changes. DL/I calls result in a status code of AD.

Your existing system definition procedures support the generation of a DCCTL system. DCCTL executes with a collection of control blocks that identifies your data processing environment. These control blocks describe the system, data communication, and Transaction Manager components.

Using a DCCTL environment system definition, you can generate a TM batch environment. TM batch support allows only DBB and DL/I regions. It does not provide DL/I database capabilities. Using TM batch, you can either take advantage of the IMS Batch Terminal Simulator or access DB2 UDB for z/OS systems.

Related Reading:

- For more information on accessing DB2 UDB for z/OS, see *DB2 for z/OS Application Programming and SQL Guide*.
- For more information about the IMS Batch Terminal Simulator, see Chapter 26, "IBM IMS Tools," on page 443.
- For more information on the DCCTL environment, see *IMS Version 9: Administration Guide: System*.

OPERATING AN IMS NETWORK

Operating a basic IMS network involves:

- Establishing a communication session between a logical unit and IMS
- Sending data between a logical unit and IMS
- Terminating the session between a logical unit and IMS
- Restarting the session after a failure

As in many areas of IMS, the tasks involved in operating an IMS system have evolved over time. Historically, these tasks were performed by a person (called the *master terminal operator*) sitting at a *master terminal* (an important, required device that is defined to IMS as part of the system definition process). Some IMS systems are still operated in this manner. Most IMS customers are automating their operations by documenting their operational procedures and writing automation application programs to implement those procedures. These automation application programs can interact with IMS in the following ways:

- By interrogating the messages sent that IMS sends to the master terminal and then issuing appropriate IMS commands to react to those messages
- By monitoring IMS's operational status and issuing IMS commands to react to that status

"The Master Terminal" describes the tasks performed by the master terminal operator (MTO), which are still applicable today even though these tasks might be automated.

As IMSs are joined together into sharing groups (sharing databases, resources, or message queues), system management becomes more complex. Prior to IMS Version 8, the IMS systems in sharing groups had to be managed individually.

IMS Version 8 introduced system management enhancements so that a single IMS or multiple IMS systems could be monitored and managed from a single point of control. With IMS Version 8 or later, you can issue commands and receive responses from one, many, or all of the IMSs in the group from this single point of control. For more information about these enhancements, see Chapter 28, "IMSplexes," on page 495.

The Master Terminal

The task of the master terminal operator (MTO) is to monitor and manage an individual IMS.

The master terminal operator (MTO) has the following responsibilities:

- Running IMS

  The MTO starts and shuts down dependent regions and manages the system log.

- Knowledge of the ongoing status of the IMS subsystem

  The MTO continuously monitors processing and detects any error situations.

- Control over contents of the system and network

  The MTO can control the network, connect other IMS systems, and perform other pre-arranged tasks.

- Privileged commands

  In addition to routine work, the MTO responds to error conditions, changes the scheduling algorithm, alters passwords, and reconfigures the system as necessary.

Table 12-4 shows the activities usually performed by the MTO and the commands usually reserved for the MTO's use.

The MTO interacts with IMS through the master terminal. The master terminal is the key control point for IMS online operations. When the IMS system is defined, the master terminal must be included, and consists of two components:

- Primary master
- Secondary master

All messages are routed to both the primary and secondary master terminals. Special MFS support is used for the master terminal.

Table 12-4   Master Terminal Operator Activities and Associated IMS Commands

Activity	IMS Command
Activate IMS (cold start)	/NRE CHKPT 0
Start a message region	/START REGION IMSMSG1
Start communications lines	/START LINE ALL
Display message queues, terminal status, transaction status, IMS status, and more	/DISPLAY
Prepare for VTAM communication	/START DC
Initiate static VTAM sessions	/OPNDST NODE ALL
Initiate dynamic VTAM sessions	/OPNDST NODE *nodename*
Send a message to terminals	/BROADCAST
Shut down VTAM terminals and IMS	/CHECKPOINT FREEZE
Restart IMS (warm start)	/NRESTART
Restart IMS after a failure	/ERESTART

The following sections of this chapter discuss the tasks of monitoring and managing an individual IMS using the MTO:

- "The Primary Master"
- "The Secondary Master" on page 193
- "Using the z/OS System Console as the Master Terminal" on page 193
- "MCS/EMCS Console Support" on page 194

The Primary Master

Traditionally, the primary master was a 3270 display terminal of 1920 characters (24 lines by 80 columns). A sample traditional IMS master terminal is shown in Figure 12-6.

```
   03/04/04  14:49:48                                              IMSC
   DFS249 14:43:46 NO INPUT MESSAGE CREATED
 DFS994I COLD START COMPLETED
 DFS0653I PROCECTED CONVERSATION PROCESSING WITH RRS/MVS ENABLED
 DFS2360I 14:29:28 XCF GROUP JOINED SUCCESSFULLY.



-- - - - - - - - - - - - - - - - - - - - - - - - - - - - - - - - - - -



                                                          PASSWORD:

 -
```

Figure 12-6   Sample Traditional Master Terminal Screen

The display screen of the master terminal is divided into four areas. They are the:

Message area

 The message area is for IMS command output (except /DISPLAY and /RDISPLAY), message switch output that uses a message output descriptor name beginning with DFSMO (see "MFS Control Blocks" on page 305), and IMS system messages.

Display area

 The display area is for /DISPLAY and /RDISPLAY command output.

Warning message area

 The warning message area is for the following warning messages:

- MASTER LINES WAITING
- MASTER WAITING
- DISPLAY LINES WAITING
- USER MESSAGE WAITING

To display these messages or lines, press PA1. An IMS password can also be entered in this area after the "PASSWORD" literal.

User input area

The user input area is for operator input.

Program function key 11 or PA2 requests the next output message, and program function key 12 requests the Copy function if it is a remote terminal.

The Secondary Master

Traditionally, the secondary master was a 3270 printer terminal; however, the use of a 3270 printer terminal has been phased out in many sites, who instead define the secondary master as spooled devices to IMS, in effect writing the messages to physical data sets.

By writing the messages to physical data sets, the secondary master can be used as an online log of events within IMS. To accomplish this, add the definitions in Figure 12-7 into the IMS stage 1 system definition. Add these definitions after the COMM macro and before any VTAM terminal definitions.

```
*
    LINEGRP DDNAME=(SPL1,SPL2),UNITYPE=SPOOL
        LINE BUFSIZE=1420
        TERMINAL FEAT=AUTOSCH
    NAME   (SEC,SECONDARY)
```

Figure 12-7   Sample JCL for the Secondary Master Spool

To complete the system definitions, code SPL1 and SPL2 DD statements in the IMS control region JCL. The data sets should be allocated with the following DCB information:

```
DCB=(RECFM=VB,LRECL=1404,BLKSIZE=1414)
```

Using the z/OS System Console as the Master Terminal

IMS always has a communications path with the z/OS *system console*[2] and uses the write-to-operator (WTO) and write-to-operator-with-reply (WTOR) facilities for this purpose. Whenever the IMS control region is active, there is an outstanding message requesting reply on the z/OS system console that can be used to enter commands for the control region. All functions available to the IMS master terminal are available to the system console. The system console and master terminal can be used concurrently to control the system. Usually, however, the system

---

2.   System console: The main operating system display station, usually equipped with a keyboard and display screen, that is used by an operator to control and communicate with a system.

console's primary purpose is as a backup to the master terminal. The system console is defined as IMS line number one by default.

MCS/EMCS Console Support

You can also communicate with IMS using the z/OS MCS/EMCS (multiple console support/extended multiple console support).

Any z/OS console can issue a command directly to IMS, using either a command recognition character (CRC) as defined at IMS startup, or using the 4-character IMS ID to be able to issue commands.

An MCS/EMCS console has the option of using RACF or exit routines for command security. For further details, see Chapter 21, "IMS Security," on page 361.

Operating the Network with APPC/IMS

APPC/IMS supports IMS commands for network operation, but the LU 6.2 device handles normal operations such as session startup, transaction initiation, and error handling that does not require master terminal operator (MTO) intervention.

Initiating a Session with IMS

A session can be initiated by a logical unit, by the VTAM network operator, by the IMS MTO, automatically by VTAM, or by IMS itself. After a logical unit connects to IMS, it remains connected until one of the following actions occurs:

- The logical unit itself requests disconnection.
- The IMS MTO requests disconnection.
- Another VTAM application program requests connection to the terminal.
- IMS, VTAM, NCP, the logical unit, or the entire network is stopped.

After the physical connection between the controller and VTAM is established, an LU-to-LU session is initiated. The LU that is requesting the session informs VTAM that it wants to communicate with IMS. VTAM notifies IMS of the request through the VTAM Logon exit routine. IMS indicates that it will accept the request, and VTAM then logically connects the LU to IMS. A session is required before communication between the LU and IMS can be accomplished. To open a session, all nodes in the communication path (IMS, NCP, line, and station) must be in active status. After a session is established, VTAM directs all data between the logical unit and IMS.

IMS also supports SNA communication links in an Extended Recovery Facility (XRF) complex.

Related Reading: For information on establishing sessions in an XRF environment, see:

- *IMS Version 9: Customization Guide*
- *IMS Version 9: Administration Guide: System*

CHAPTER 13

How IMS TM Processes Input

MS can accept input messages from a variety of sources.

In This Chapter:

- "Input Message Types"
- "Terminal Types" on page 197
- "Input Message Origin" on page 197
- "Terminal Input Destination" on page 197
- "Message Queuing" on page 198
- "Message Scheduling" on page 206
- "Transaction Scheduling" on page 208

See Figure 13-1 on page 196 while reading the sections listed above.

INPUT MESSAGE TYPES

When IMS reads data that has come from the telecommunication access method, IMS first checks the type of input data. Input can consist of three types of messages:

Input transaction message

This message is routed to an application program for processing, with the first 1 to 8 bytes of the message identifying the transaction code.

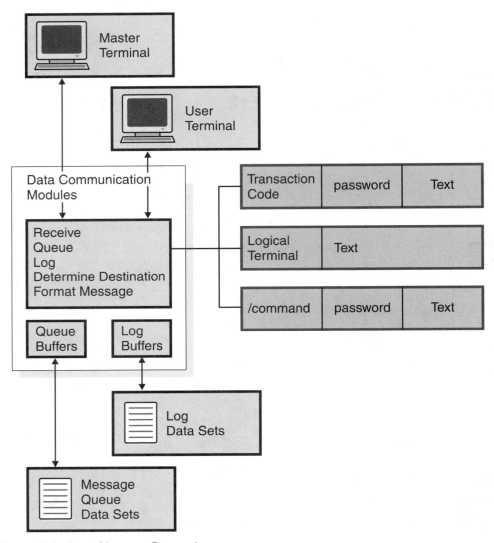

Figure 13-1 Input Message Processing

Message switch

This message is routed to another terminal, with the first 1 to 8 bytes used as the name of the destination logical terminal (LTERM). The LTERM can be a user ID if the Extended Terminal Option (ETO) is used.

Command message

A command message is processed by IMS itself.

TERMINAL TYPES

There are two basic types of terminals that can connect to IMS:

Static

A static terminal is specifically defined in the IMS system definition, and the definition determines the physical terminal name (called the *node name*) and logical terminal name (LTERM) available for use.

Dynamic

A dynamic terminal is not statically defined in the IMS system definition. IMS can create a dynamic terminal definition. This requires either the IMS Extended Terminal Option (ETO), a separately ordered feature of IMS, or other third-party vendor products. Dynamic terminals have not been previously defined to IMS—their definitions are generated by ETO when the user logs on.

If a terminal user attempts to connect to IMS using a terminal that is defined to IMS as static, then the user will use the defined node name and LTERM name combination.

If a terminal user attempts to connect to IMS using a terminal that is not defined to IMS as static, and dynamic terminal support is available, then a dynamic terminal product (such as ETO) is used to determine the LTERM name and whether the name is based on the user's user ID, the node name, or some other value.

If a terminal user attempts to connect to IMS using a terminal that is not defined to IMS as static, and dynamic terminal support is not enabled, then the user is unable to logon to IMS.

INPUT MESSAGE ORIGIN

IMS maintains the name of the terminal or user from which an input message is received. When a message is passed to an application program, this is also made available to that program, via its program communication block (PCB).

This origin is the LTERM name. The LTERM name can be specific to the user, or can be specific to the physical location, depending on how the IMS system is defined.

TERMINAL INPUT DESTINATION

The destination of the terminal input is dependent upon the type of input.

An input command message goes directly to the IMS command processor modules, while a message switch or a transaction is stored on the message queue. When a 3270-based message is received by IMS, the message input is first processed by IMS's Message Format Service (MFS), except when the input is from a previously cleared or unformatted screen. MFS provides an extensive format service for both input and output messages and is discussed in detail in "Message Format Service" on page 298.

When the input message is enqueued to its destination in the message queue, the input process-ing is completed. If more than one LTERM is defined or assigned to a physical terminal, the LTERMs are maintained in a historical chain: the oldest defined or assigned first. Any input from the physical terminal is considered to have originated at the first logical terminal of the chain. If, for some reason (such as security or a stopped LTERM), the first logical terminal is not allowed to enter the message, all logical terminals on the input chain are interrogated in a chain sequence for their ability to enter the message. The first appropriate LTERM found is used as message ori-gin. If no LTERM can be used, the message is rejected with an error message.

MESSAGE QUEUING

All full-function input and output messages in IMS are queued in message queues, as shown in Figure 13-2 on page 199. For Fast Path transactions, see "Fast Path Transactions and Message Queues" on page 200.

IMS uses message queues to enable input processing, output processing, command processing, and application program processing to be performed asynchronously, to a large extent. This means, for example, that the input processing of message A can be performed in parallel with the database processing for message B and the output processing for message C. Messages A, B, and C can be different occurrences of the same or different message types or transaction codes.

Messages in the IMS message queues are stored by destination, priority, and the time of arrival in IMS. A destination can be:

* A message processing program (MPP) or a message-driven Java application (JMP), which is for transaction input. Ordering is by transaction code.
* A logical terminal (LTERM), which is for a message switch, command responses, and output generated by application programs.

For a single instance of IMS, the message queue buffers are maintained in main storage (defined by the MSGQUEUE macro). If the memory-based message queue buffers become full, mes-sages are then stored on the message queue data sets on DASD. The queue blocks in main stor-age and on direct access storage are reusable. IMS stores as many messages as possible in the message queue buffers to minimize the number of I/O operations required during processing.

Message Queue Size and Performance Considerations

Messages in the IMS message queue are primarily held in buffers in main storage. However, when messages are added to the queues faster than IMS can process these messages, the mes-sage queue buffers can fill. In this situation, any new messages are written to the message queue data sets. The performance of these data sets then becomes very important. The data sets should be on a DASD volume with fast response times, and the data sets should be appropriately sized to ensure that there is always space available.

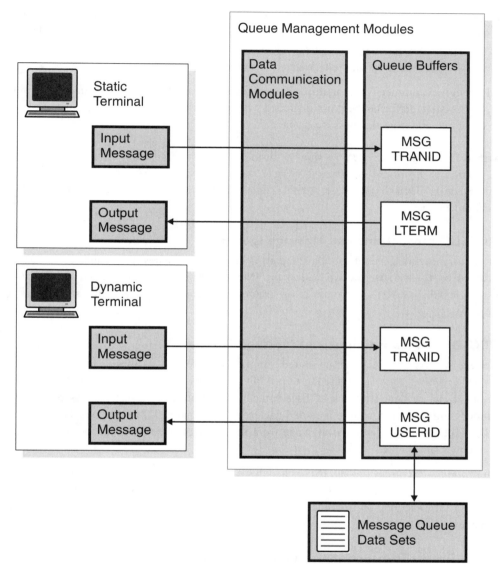

Figure 13-2 Overview of the Message Queuing Process

Multiple Message Queue Data Sets

The IMS Queue Manager supports concurrent I/O operations to its message queue data sets, allowing the IMS message queue to be distributed across multiple physical queue data sets. This enhancement supports the long and short message queue data sets.

The multiple message queue data set function is activated when you supply more than one DD statement per message queue data set. You can supply up to ten DD statements for each queue data set. These DD statements can be allocated on different device types, but LRECL and BLK-SIZE must be the same for all the data sets of a single queue.

IBM strongly recommends that multiple queue data sets be used, so that in an emergency situation, IMS system performance is not degraded while IMS tries to handle a large volume of messages going to and from the message queue data sets.

Related Reading: See *IMS Version 9: Installation Volume 1: Installation Verification* and *IMS Version 9: Installation Volume 2: System Definition and Tailoring* for detailed guidelines about selecting message queue parameters such as block sizes, QPOOL size, and queue data set allocation.

Fast Path Transactions and Message Queues

Fast Path transactions do not use the standard IMS message queues. Fast Path transactions are scheduled by a separate function within the IMS transaction manager, called the Expedited Message Handler (EMH). For more information, see "Scheduling Fast Path Transactions" on page 212.

APPC-Driven Transactions and Message Queues

There are two types of APPC transactions: implicit and explicit. With *implicit* APPC transactions, IMS receives a transaction request via APPC. This transaction is placed onto the IMS message queues in the same way as a 3270-generated transaction. The message is passed to an MPP for processing, and the response is routed back to the originating APPC partner. The MPP uses the DL/I interface to receive the message from the message queue and put the response back onto the message queue.

With *explicit* APPC transactions, IMS schedules a program into an MPR (message processing region). This program uses APPC verbs to communicate with the APPC partner program to process the transaction. The standard IMS messages queues are not used for explicit APPC transactions.

OTMA-Driven Transactions and Message Queues

OTMA allows IMS to receive a message through a different communications protocol (for example, WebSphere MQ, remote procedure calls, and IMS Connect for TCP/IP sockets). The message is received by IMS and is placed into the IMS message queue for processing in the usual manner. The response message is passed back to the originator through OTMA.

Shared Queues

IMS provides the ability for multiple IMS systems in a parallel sysplex environment to share a single set of message queues. This is known as *shared queues* and the messages are held in structures in a coupling facility. All the IMS subsystems in the sysplex share a common set of queues for all non-command messages (that is, input, output, message switch, and Fast Path messages). A message that is placed on a shared queue can be processed by any of several IMS subsystems in the share queues group as long as the IMS has the resources to process the message. Results of these transactions are then returned to the initiating terminal. End users need not be aware of these activities; they view the processing as if they were operating a single system.

Using shared queues is optional and you can continue to process with the non-sysplex message queue buffers and message queue data sets.

Operating in a shared-queues environment allows multiple IMSs in a sysplex environment to share IMS message queues and EMH message queues. The IMSs work together as an IMSplex providing a single-image view of multiple IMSs.

DEFINITIONS:

- A *shared queue* is a collection of messages that are associated by the same queue name. A shared queue is managed by a Common Queue Server (CQS) and can be shared by CQS clients in an IMSplex.

- A *Common Queue Server* receives, maintains, and distributes data objects from a shared queue that resides in a coupling facility list structure for its client.

- A *CQS client* is an IMS DB/DC or DCCTL system that accesses shared queues through its own CQS.

- A *coupling facility* is a special, logical partition that provides high-speed caching, list processing, and locking functions in a sysplex environment.

- A *sysplex environment* is a set of z/OS systems that communicate and cooperate with one another through certain multisystem hardware components and software services in order to process workloads.

- An *IMSplex* is one or more IMS control regions, managers, or servers that work together as a unit. Typically, but not always, IMSs in an IMSplex:
  - Share either databases or resources or message queues (or any combination)
  - Run in an S/390® Parallel Sysplex environment
  - Include an IMS Common Service Layer (CSL)

In general, IMS handles messages in the following manner:

1. IMSs register interest in those queues for which they are able to process messages.
2. When an IMS receives a message and places it on the shared queue, all IMSs that have registered interest in that queue are notified.
3. One IMS retrieves the message and processes it.
4. The IMS that processes the message places a response on the queue.
5. The IMS that submitted the original message is notified that the response message was placed on the queue.
6. The IMS that submitted the original message sends the response message to the originating terminal.

Figure 13-3 shows a basic shared-queues environment.

Benefits of Using Shared Queues
The major benefits of operating in a shared-queues environment are:

Automatic workload balancing
A message that is placed on a shared queue can be processed by any participating IMS that is available to process work.

Incremental growth
You can add new IMSs as workload increases.

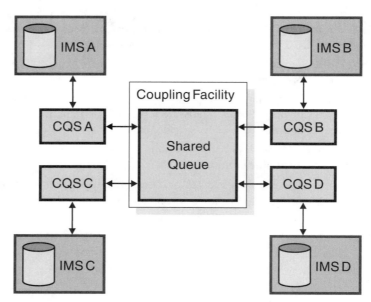

Figure 13-3   Basic Shared-Queues Environment

Increased reliability

If one IMS fails, work that is placed on a shared queue can still be processed by other IMSs.

> **RECOMMENDATIONS:**
> - Enabling shared queues does not require the use of generic resource groups; however, IBM recommends that you use the two functions together.
> - IBM recommends that all data in an IMSplex be shared across the IMSplex.

Related Reading:

- For information on generic resource groups, see "VTAM Generic Resources" on page 476.
- For information on data sharing, see *IMS Version 9: Administration Guide: System.*

Required Components of a Shared-Queues Environment

Although you can operate many different configurations of a shared-queues environment, the required components of shared-queues processing, shown in Figure 13-4 on page 204, include:

Common Queue Server (CQS)

One CQS is required for each client. Each CQS accesses the shared queues, which reside on coupling facility list structures.

CQS client

One or more IMS DB/DC or DCCTL subsystems that can access the shared queues using CQS client requests.

z/OS coupling facility list structures

A type of coupling facility structure that maintains the shared queues.

> **DEFINITIONS:**
> - A *list structure* is an area of storage in a coupling facility that enables multisystem applications in a sysplex environment to share information that is organized as a set of lists or queues. The list structure consists of a set of lists and an optional lock table.
> - CQS maintains list structures in pairs, called *structure pairs*, with a primary list structure and an overflow list structure.
> - The *primary list structure* contains the shared queues.
> - The *overflow list structure*, if defined, contains shared queues that overflow after the primary list structure reaches a predefined threshold.

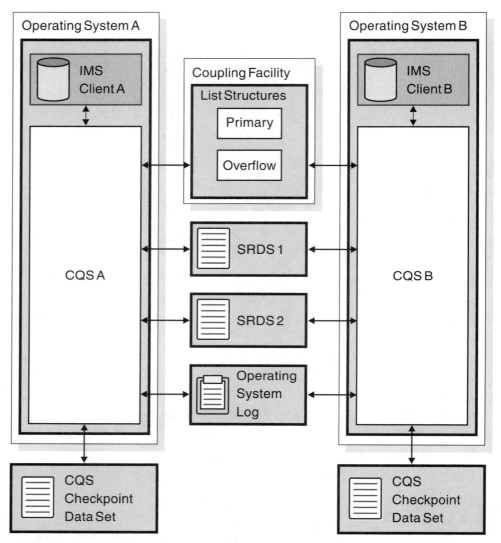

Figure 13-4   Components of a Shared-Queues Environment

z/OS system log

One z/OS system log is used for each structure pair. CQS places recovery information about the work it has processed and about the list structure pair in the z/OS log streams. These log streams are then shared by all CQSs that access the list structure pair.

CQS checkpoint data set

One CQS checkpoint data set is maintained for each structure pair of each CQS. The CQS checkpoint data set contains CQS system checkpoint information.

CQS structure recovery data sets (SRDSs)

CQS maintains two SRDSs for each structure pair so that shared queues on the structures can be recovered. The SRDSs maintain structure checkpoint information for the shared queues.

Related Reading: For more information on CQS requests and other CQS topics, see *IMS Version 9: Common Queue Server Guide and Reference.*

Overview of the Common Queue Server

The Common Queue Server (CQS) is an internal interface by which IMS communicates with shared message queues. You can use IMS commands to initiate CQS requests. The CQS address space is started by the IMS.

CQS performs the following services:

- Notifies registered clients when work exists on the shared queues.
- Provides clients with an interface for accessing shared queues and CQS.
- Writes CQS system checkpoint information to a CQS checkpoint data set.
- Writes structure checkpoint information to an SRDS for recovery of a shared-queues list structure.
- Provides structure recovery and overflow processing for the shared-queues list structure.
- Drives the following CQS client exit routines:
  - The Client CQS Event exit routine notifies the client of system events, such as CQS abnormal termination and CQS restart completion.
  - The Client Structure Event exit routine notifies the client of structure events, such as structure copy, structure recovery, structure overflow, structure checkpoint, and structure resynchronization.
  - The Client Structure Inform exit routine notifies the client when work exists on the shared queues.
- Drives the following CQS user-supplied exit routines:
  - The CQS Queue Overflow user-supplied exit routine allows the exit to approve or reject a queue that CQS selects for overflow.
  - The CQS Initialization/Termination user-supplied exit routine is notified when CQS initializes and when CQS terminates after disconnecting from all structures (under normal termination conditions).

— The CQS Client Connection user-supplied exit routine participates in connecting clients to structures and in disconnecting clients from structures.

— The CQS Structure Statistics user-supplied exit routine gathers structure statistics during CQS system checkpoints.

— The CQS Structure Event user-supplied exit routine tracks structure activity, such as structure checkpoint, structure rebuild, structure overflow, and structure status change. It also tracks when CQS connects to a structure or disconnects from a structure.

• Provides the Log Print utility with sample JCL that enables you to print log records from the z/OS log.

Related Reading:
• For more information on CQS, CQS client routines, and CQS utilities, see *IMS Version 9: Common Queue Server Guide and Reference*.
• For information on IMS commands, see *IMS Version 9: Command Reference*.

MESSAGE SCHEDULING

Scheduling is the loading of the appropriate program into a message processing region. IMS can then pass messages stored on the IMS message queue to this program when it issues the Get Unique (GU) IOPCB call. For more information about application calls, see Chapter 14, "Application Programming Overview," on page 217.

After an input message is available in the message queue, it is eligible for scheduling. Scheduling is the routing of a message in the input queue to its corresponding application program in the message processing region or the Java message processing region.

The linkage between an input message (defined by its transaction code) and an application program (defined by its name) is established at system definition time in the PSB (see Figure 13-5 on page 207). Multiple transaction codes can be linked to a single application program, but only one application program can be linked to a given transaction code.

You can specify the *class* that transaction codes are assigned. This class assignment determines into which message region an application program is loaded. When the IMS message regions are started, they are assigned from one to four message classes. When a message region is assigned more than one class, the scheduling algorithm treats the first class specified as the highest priority class, and each succeeding class is treated as a lower-priority class.

The class in which a transaction code runs is defined in two ways:

• On the APPLCTN macro
• On the MSGTYPE parameter of the TRANSACT macro

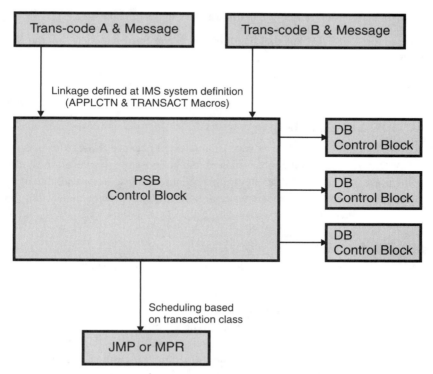

Figure 13-5   Message Scheduling Based on Information in the PSB

If the class is specified on the APPLCTN macro, it need not be defined on the TRANSACT macro. If it is specified on both, then the class on the TRANSACT macro overrides the APPLCTN macro specification. Figure 13-6 illustrates the definition of a transaction.

```
APPLCTN PSB=DFSIVP1,PGMTYPE=TP
    TRANSACT CODE=IVTNO,MODE=SNGL,                          X
        MSGTYPE=(SNGLSEG,NONRESPONSE,1)
APPLCTN PSB=DFSIVP2,PGMTYPE=(TP,1)
    TRANSACT CODE=IVTNO2,MODE=SNGL,                         X
        MSGTYPE=(SNGLSEG,NONRESPONSE)
```

Figure 13-6   Sample APPLCTN Macro Transaction Definition in IMS Stage 1 Input

Note the following about the transaction definitions in Figure 13-6 on page 207:

- Transaction DFSIVP1 has the class defined as the third parameter on the MSGTYPE parameter on the TRANSACT macro.
- Transaction DFSIVP2 has the class defined on the APPLCTN macro.
- Both transactions are assigned to class 1.

TRANSACTION SCHEDULING

The transaction scheduling algorithm is very sophisticated because it needs to make use of all the IMS and system resources in the most efficient manner possible. However, most users do not need to use the power of the scheduling algorithms because the resources available in IMS today (such as the number of message processing regions) are much greater than when these algorithms were designed several decades ago.

Scheduling Conditions

The following conditions must be met for successful transaction scheduling:

- An MPR region must be available. Actually, the termination of a prior transaction running in an MPR region triggers the scheduling process.
- A transaction input message must exist in the queue.
- The transaction and its program are not in a stopped state.
- Enough buffer pool storage is available to load the program specification block (PSB) and the referenced database control blocks, if not already in main storage.
- The database processing intent does not conflict with an already active application program (for instance, if the active program's processing intent is declared as exclusive use). Processing intent is discussed in more detail in "Database Processing Intent" on page 212.

If the first transaction code with a ready input message does not meet all these conditions, the next available input transaction is interrogated. If no message can be scheduled, the scheduling process is stopped until another input message is enqueued. If the scheduling is successful, the IMS routines in the dependent region load the corresponding MPP and pass control to it.

Scheduling in a Dependent Region

The IMS scheduler assigns the application transaction processing to a dependent MPR. The number of MPRs available to an IMS system is 999 dependent regions.

The transactions are assigned to classes. The maximum number of transaction classes is set at system generation time by the MAXCLAS keyword of the IMSCTRL macro.

Class Processing

Each dependent MPR can run up to four transaction classes. The order in which they are speci-fied is a priority sequence, which means that the transaction class named first is the highest and the one named last is the lowest. Each MPR can have a different sequence of the same or differ-ent transaction combinations. The classes are named on the PROC statement of the JCL that runs the MPR. Figure 13-7 shows an example of the MPR PROC statement JCL. The MPR can be run as a job or as a started task.

```
//IVP6TM11 EXEC PROC=DFSMPR,TIME=(1440),
//          AGN=BMP01,            AGN NAME
//          NBA=6,

//          OBA=5,
//          SOUT='*',             SYSOUT CLASS
//          CL1=001,              TRANSACTION CLASS 1
//          CL2=006,              TRANSACTION CLASS 2
//          CL3=013,              TRANSACTION CLASS 3
//          CL4=000,              TRANSACTION CLASS 4
//          TLIM=10,              MPR TERMINATION LIMIT
//          SOD=,                 SPIN-OFF DUMP CLASS
//          IMSID=IMSY,     IMSID OF IMS CONTROL REGION
//          PREINIT=DC,           PROCLIB DFSINTXX MEMBER
//          PWFI=N                PSEUDO=WFI
//*
```

Figure 13-7   Example of MPR PROC Statement

The classes that the MPR runs can be changed while the MPR is running through the /ASSIGN command. When the /ASSIGN command is executed, only those classes specified on the com-mand are available to that MPR. The changes are maintained until the MPR is restarted, at which time the values on the startup JCL are used again. Figure 13-8 illustrates an example of an /ASSIGN CLASS command. Again, the order of classes on the command is the priority sequence of those classes.

```
/ASSIGN CLASS 1 4 6 9 TO REGION 1
```

Figure 13-8   Example of /ASSIGN CLASS Command

You can use the /DISPLAY ACTIVE command to list the classes assigned to an MPR. Figure 13-9 on page 210 shows an example /DISPLAY ACTIVE command and its output.

```
/DIS ACTIVE
     REGID JOBNAME   TYPE TRAN/STEP PROGRAM STATUS          CLASS         IMSY
         1 SJIMSYM1  TP                     WAITING         1, 4, 6, 9 IMSY
         2 SJIMSYM2  TP                     WAITING         2, 3, 5, 1 IMSY
           BATCHREG  BMP  NONE     IMSY
           FPRGN     FP   NONE     IMSY
           DBTRGN    DBT  NONE     IMSY
           SJIMSYDB  DBRC                            IMSY
           SJIMSYDL  DLS     IMSY
     VTAM ACB OPEN          -LOGONS DISABLED   IMSY
     IMSLU=N/A.N/A             APPC STATUS=DISABLED     IMSY
     OTMA GROUP=IMSCGRP    STATUS=ACTIVE        IMSY
     APPLID=SCSIM6YA  GRSNAME=         STATUS=DISABLED    IMSY
     LINE ACTIVE-IN -    1 ACTIV-OUT -    0  IMSY
     NODE ACTIVE-IN -    0 ACTIV-OUT -    0  IMSY
     *99298/155826*      IMSY
```

Figure 13-9   Example of /DISPLAY ACTIVE Command

Note the following points about Figure 13-9:

- There are two MPRs: SJIMSYM1 and SJIMSYM2.
- The MPR named SJIMSYM1 runs classes 1, 4, 6, and 9.
- The MPR named SJIMSYM2 runs classes 2, 3, 5, and 1.
- Class 1 has the highest priority in MPR SJIMSYM1 and the lowest in MPR SJIMSYM2.

When an MPR searches for a transaction to schedule, it uses the following criteria:

1. The highest priority transaction ready in the highest priority class
2. Any other transaction in the highest priority class
3. The highest priority transaction ready in the second highest priority class
4. Any other transaction in the second priority class

This sequence of priorities is used for all the available classes for this MPR.

> **N O T E:** If a transaction has a class for which there are no MPRs currently allowed to run that class, the transaction is not scheduled and remains on the input queue.

Definition Macro Keywords That Affect Transaction Scheduling

The values you assign to a few macro keywords at system definition time can affect how IMS schedules transactions. The following sections describe some of these keywords.

PROCLIM Keyword Processing   IMS tries to increase throughput of the MPR by processing more than one message for the same transaction. This technique makes use of the fact that the program has already been loaded into the MPR's storage, and the PSB and DBD control blocks also have been loaded. The throughput of the number of messages processed by this MPR is increased because some of the overhead involved with reloading the program and control blocks is avoided.

At the completion of the transaction, IMS checks the value specified on the PROCLIM keyword of the TRANSACT macro for this transaction. The PROCLIM keyword specifies the number of messages (count) of this transaction code a program can process in a single scheduling, and the amount of time (in seconds) allowable to process a single transaction (or message). BMP programs are not affected by the PROCLIM keyword.

The MPR processes the number of messages allowed in the first value of this keyword before looking to see what other transactions are available for scheduling, which means the MPR can process more transactions without having to go through the scheduling logic for each transaction.

Parallel Scheduling   A transaction processes in only one MPR at a time unless parallel processing is specified. To allow more than one MPR to schedule a transaction type at a time, code SCHDTYP=PARALLEL on the APPLCTN macro. The SCHDTYP keyword specifies whether (PARALLEL) or not (SERIAL) this application program can be scheduled into more than one MPR or BMP region simultaneously. The default value is SERIAL. For example:

```
APPLCTN PSB=DFSIVP1,PGMTYPE=(TP,1),SCHDTYP=PARALLEL
```

Unless there are application restrictions on processing the message in strict first-in, first-out sequence, parallel scheduling should be applied to all transactions. Parallel scheduling allows IMS to make the best use of IMS resources while providing the best possible response time to individual transactions.

The PARLIM keyword on the TRANSACT macro determines when a transaction is scheduled in another region. The PARLIM keyword specifies the threshold value to be used when SCHDTYP=PARALLEL is specified in the preceding APPLCTN macro instruction. When the number of messages on the queue for a transaction exceeds the value on the PARLIM, another region is used.

Use the MAXRGN keyword to restrict the number of MPRs that can process a transaction at any one time. Do so in order to avoid the situation of all the MPRs being tied up by a single transaction type.

Priority Keyword   The PRTY keyword on the TRANSACT macro sets the priority of a transaction, which indicates how to differentiate one transaction from another if they run in the same transaction class. A transaction of a higher priority is scheduled before a lower priority one. However, an MPR processes a transaction in a higher class (for this MPR, see "Scheduling in a Dependent Region" on page 208 for more details) before a transaction in a lower class regardless of the priority. A transaction priority increases after the number of transactions on the message queue exceeds the value set on the third parameter of the PRTY keyword. The priority will increase up to the value set on the second parameter of the PRTY keyword, which has the effect of trying to avoid a long queue on any single transaction code by giving the transaction code a higher priority.

Database Processing Intent

A factor that significantly influences the scheduling process is the *intent* of an application program toward the databases it uses. Intent is determined by examining the intent that is last associated with the PSB to be scheduled. At initial selection, this process involves bringing the intent list into the control region. The location of the intent list is maintained in the PSB directory. If the analysis of the intent list indicates a conflict in database usage with a currently active program in the dependent region, the scheduling process selects another transaction and tries again.

The database intent of a program at scheduling time is determined by the PROCOPT= parameters in the PCB.

A conflicting situation during scheduling occurs only if a segment type is declared exclusive use (PROCOPT=E) by the program being scheduled and an already active program references the segment in its PSB (any PROCOPT), or vice versa. PROCOPT=E only applies within a single IMS and is not effective in an IMSplex.

Scheduling a BMP or JBP Application

BMP and JBP applications are initiated in a standard z/OS address space via any regular job submission facility, from either:

- TSO and submitting the job
- A job scheduling system

However, during its initialization, the IMS scheduler in the control region is invoked to assure the availability of the database resources for the BMP or JBP application.

Scheduling Fast Path Transactions

Apart from standard IMS transactions, there are two types of Fast Path online transactions:

- "Fast Path Exclusive Transactions" on page 213
- "Fast Path Potential Transactions" on page 213

Fast Path Exclusive Transactions   Fast Path schedules input messages by associating them with a load balancing group. A *load balancing group* (LBG) is a group of Fast Path input messages that are ready for balanced processing by one or more copies of a Fast Path program. One LBG exists for each unique Fast Path message-driven application program.

The messages for each LBG are processed by the same Fast Path program. The EMH controls Fast Path messages by:

- Managing the complete execution of a message on a first-in-first-out basis.
- Retaining the messages that are received in the control program's storage without using auxiliary storage or I/O operations.
- Supporting multiple copies of programs for parallel scheduling.
- Requiring that programs operate in a wait-for-input mode.

Fast Path Potential Transactions   Fast Path potential transactions are a mixture of standard IMS full-function and Fast Path exclusive transactions.

The same transaction code can be used to trigger either a full-function or a Fast Path transaction, with an exit used to determine whether this instance of the transaction will be full-function or Fast Path.

Shared Queues
Scheduling of transactions in a shared-queues environment is similar to those in a non-shared-queues environment. All the checks, however, are across all the IMS systems in the shared-queues environment.

Related Reading: For further information on scheduling shared queues, see:

- *IMS in the Parallel Sysplex: Volume I: Reviewing the IMSplex Technology*
- *IMS in the Parallel Sysplex: Volume II: Planning the IMSplex*
- *IMS in the Parallel Sysplex: Volume III: IMSplex Implementation and Operations*

IMS Application Development

CHAPTER 14

Application Programming Overview

This section explains application program basics for any program that runs in an IMS environment.

IMS programs (online and batch) have a different structure than non-IMS programs (see "Application Program Structure" on page 218). An IMS application program is always called as a subroutine of the IMS region controller and must have a program specification block (PSB) associated with it. The PSB provides an interface from the program to IMS services that the program needs to use. These services can be:

- Sending or receiving messages from online user terminals
- Accessing database records
- Issuing IMS commands
- Issuing IMS service (checkpoint or synchronization) calls

The IMS services available to any program are determined by the IMS environment in which the application is running.

In This Chapter:

JAVA PROGRAMS

The IMS Java function allows you to write Java application programs that access IMS databases from:

- Within IMS
- IBM WebSphere Application Server for z/OS
- WebSphere Application Server that is running on a non-z/OS platform
- IBM CICS Transaction Server for z/OS
- IBM DB2 Universal Database for z/OS stored procedures

Related Reading: IMS Java application support is discussed in Chapter 18, "Application Programming in Java," on page 311 and not covered in this chapter.

APPLICATION PROGRAM STRUCTURE

During initialization, both the application program and its associated PSB are loaded from their respective libraries by the IMS system. The IMS modules interpret and execute database CALL requests issued by the program. These modules can reside in the same or different z/OS address spaces, depending on the environment in which the application program executes.

Application programs that execute in an online transaction environment are executed in a dependent region called the message processing region (MPR) or Fast Path region (IFP). The programs are often called message processing programs (MPPs). The IMS modules that execute online services run in the control region while the full-function database services run in the DL/I separate address space (DLISAS). The association of the application program and the PSB is defined at IMS system generation time through the APPLTN and TRANSACTION macros.

Batch application programs can execute in two different types of regions.

- Application programs that need to make use of message processing services or databases being used by online systems execute in a batch message processing region (BMP).
- Application programs that can execute without messages services execute in a DB batch region.

For both of these types of batch application programs, the association of the application program to the PSB is done on the PARM keyword on the EXEC statement.

Figure 14-1 on page 219 illustrates how the program elements of an application program interface with IMS and are functionally structured. The program elements are:

An ENTRY statement
> The ENTRY statement specifies the PCBs utilized by the program (see "Entry to the Application Program" on page 220).

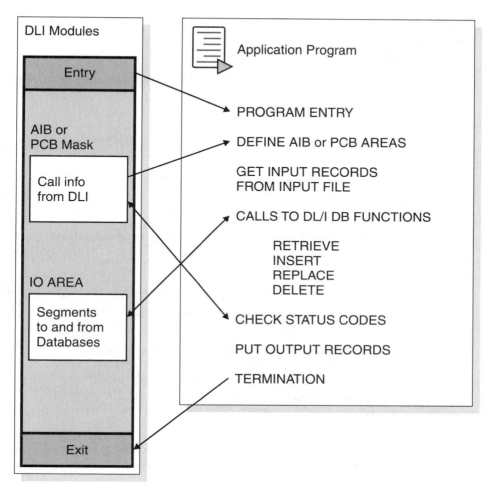

Figure 14-1   Structure of an IMS Application Program

A PCB or AIB

IMS describes the results of each DL/I call using the AIBTDLI interface in the application interface block (AIB) and, when applicable, the program communication block (PCB). See "PCB Mask" on page 223. To find the results of the call using the AIBTDLI interface, your program must use the AIB. If your program references the PCB in the call, it must use that PCB to find the results of the DL/I call.

Your application program can use the PCB address that is returned in the AIB to find the results of the call. To use the PCB, the program defines a mask of the PCB and can then reference the PCB after each call to determine the success or failure of the call. An application program cannot change the fields in a PCB; it can only check the PCB to determine what happened when the call completed.

There are two types of PCBs: a database (DB) PCB and a telecommunication-program (TP) PCB.

An input/output (I/O) area

IMS passes segments to and from the program in the program's I/O area.

Some DL/I calls

The program issues DL/I calls to perform the requested function (see "Calls to IMS" on page 227).

A status code processing section

The program checks the status code for each DL/I call to find out if the call was successful (see "Status Code Processing" on page 228).

A termination statement

The program returns control to IMS when it has finished processing (see "Termination of the Application" on page 229). In a batch program, your program can set the return code and pass it to the next step in the job.

> **RECOMMENDATION:**   If your program does not use the return code in this way, it is a good idea to set it to 0 as a programming convention. Your program can use the return code for this same purpose in BMP programs. MPPs cannot pass return codes.

The PCB mask and I/O area are described in the program's data declaration section. Program entry, calls to IMS processing, and program termination are described in the program's procedural section. Calls to IMS, processing statements, and program termination can reference PCB masks or I/O areas. In addition, IMS can reference these data areas.

The individual program elements mentioned in the previous list are discussed in the following sections.

Entry to the Application Program

As shown in Figure 14-1, IMS passes control to the application program through the entry point. At entry, all the PCBs or AIBs used by the application program are specified. The order of the PCB names in the ENTRY statement must be the same as in the PSB for this application program. The sequence of PCBs in the linkage section or declaration portion of the application program need not be the same as in the ENTRY statement.

IMS passes the PCB pointers to a PL/I program differently than it passes them to an assembler language, C language, COBOL, or Pascal program. In addition, Pascal requires that IMS pass an integer before passing the PCB pointers. IMS uses the LANG keyword or the PSBGEN statement of PSBGEN to determine the type of program to which it is passing control. Therefore, you must be sure that the language specified during PSBGEN is consistent with the language of the program.

Application interfaces that use the AIB structure (AIBTDLI or CEETDLI) use the PCB name rather than the PCB structure and do not require the PCB list to be passed at entry to the application program.

When you code each DL/I call, you must provide the PCB you want to use for that call. For all IMS TM application programs, the list of PCBs the program can access is passed to the program at its entry point.

> **R E S T R I C T I O N:** DB batch programs cannot be passed parameter information using the PARM field from the EXEC statement.

AIB Mask

The AIB is used by your program to communicate with IMS when your application does not have a program communication block (PCB) address or the call function does not use a PCB. The AIB mask enables your program to interpret the control block defined. The AIB structure must be defined in working storage, on a fullword boundary, and initialized according to the order and byte length of the fields as shown in Table 14-1. The notes at the bottom of the table describe the contents of each field.

Table 14-1   AIB Fields

Descriptor	Byte Length	DB/DC	DBCTL	DCCTL	DB Batch	TM Batch
AIB identifier[1]	8	X	X	X	X	X
DFSAIB allocated length[2]	4	X	X	X	X	X
Subfunction code[3]	8	X	X	X	X	X
Resource name[4]	8	X	X	X	X	X
Reserved[5]	16					
Maximum output area length[6]	4	X	X	X	X	X

continues

Table 14-1   AIB Fields (Continued)

Descriptor	Byte Length	DB/DC	DBCTL	DCCTL	DB Batch	TM Batch
Output area length used[7]	4	X	X	X	X	X
Reserved[8]	12					
Return code[9]	4	X	X	X	X	X
Reason code[10]	4	X	X	X	X	X
Error code extension[11]	4	X		X		
Resource address[12]	4	X	X	X	X	X
Reserved[13]	48					

Notes:

1. AIB Identifier (AIBID)

This 8-byte field contains the AIB identifier. You must initialize AIBID in your application program to the value DFSAIBƀƀ. before you issue DL/I calls. This field is required. When the call is completed, the information returned in this field is unchanged.

2. DFSAIB Allocated Length (AIBLEN)

This field contains the actual 4-byte length of the AIB as defined by your program. You must initialize AIBLEN in your application program before you issue DL/I calls. The minimum length required is 128 bytes. When the call is completed, the information returned in this field is unchanged. This field is required.

3. Subfunction Code (AIBSFUNC)

This 8-byte field contains the subfunction code for those calls that use a subfunction. You must initialize AIBSFUNC in your application program before you issue DL/I calls. When the call is completed, the information returned in this field is unchanged.

4. Resource Name (AIBRSNM1)

This 8-byte field contains the name of a resource. The resource varies depending on the call. You must initialize AIBRSNM1 in your application program before you issue DL/I calls. When the call is complete, the information returned in this field is unchanged. This field is required.

For PCB related calls where the AIB is used to pass the PCB name instead of passing the PCB address in the call list, this field contains the PCB name. The PCB name for the I/O PCB is IOPCBƀƀ. The PCB name for other types of PCBs is defined in the PCBNAME= parameter in PSBGEN.

5. Reserved

This 16-byte field is reserved.

6. Maximum Output Area Length (AIBOALEN)

This 4-byte field contains the length of the output area in bytes that was specified in the call list. You must initialize AIBOALEN in your application program for all calls that return data to the output area. When the call is completed, the information returned in this area is unchanged.

7. Used Output Area Length (AIBOAUSE)

This 4-byte field contains the length of the data returned by IMS for all calls that return data to the output area. When the call is completed this field contains the length of the I/O area used for this call.

8. Reserved

This 12-byte field is reserved.

9. Return code (AIBRETRN)

When the call is completed, this 4-byte field contains the return code.

10. Reason Code (AIBREASN)

When the call is completed, this 4-byte field contains the reason code.

11. Error Code Extension (AIBERRXT)

This 4-byte field contains additional error information depending on the return code in AIBRETRN and the reason code in AIBREASN.

12. Resource Address (AIBRSA1)

When the call is completed, this 4-byte field contains call-specific information. For PCB related calls where the AIB is used to pass the PCB name instead of passing the PCB address in the call list, this field returns the PCB address.

13. Reserved

This 48-byte field is reserved.

The application program can use the returned PCB address, when available, to inspect the status code in the PCB and to obtain any other information needed by the application program.

PCB Mask

A mask or skeleton PCB structure is used by the application program to access data from a TP PCB or DB PCB. One PCB is required for each view of a database or online service. The program views a hierarchical data structure by using the DB PCB mask. The program uses a TP PCB to communicate with a terminal or other application program. Figure 14-2 on page 224 shows the structure of a PCB mask and how that structure maps to the database.

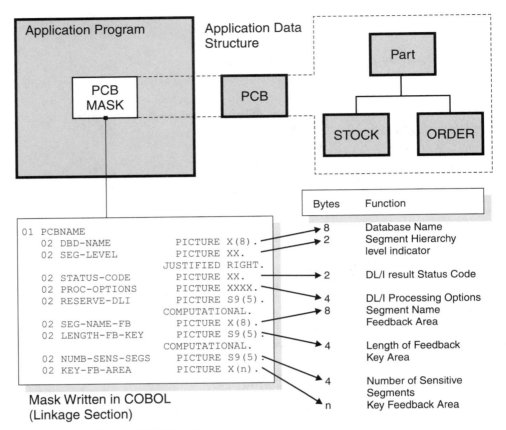

Figure 14-2   Application PCB Structure

One PCB is required for each data structure. An example of a database PCB mask is shown in Figure 14-3 on page 225 and explained in the text that follows the figure. An example of a TP PCB mask is shown in Figure 14-5 on page 227.

Define the PCB mask as an assembler DSECT, a COBOL linkage section entry, or a PL/I-based variable because the PCB does not actually reside in the application program.

The PCB provides specific areas used by IMS to inform the application program of the results of its calls. At execution time, all PCB entries are controlled by IMS. Access to the PCB entries by the application program is for read-only purposes. The PCB masks for a TP PCB and a database PCB are different.

DB PCB Mask

Figure 14-3 shows an example of a program's DB PCB mask, which defines the PCB area used by IMS to return the results of the call.

```
01 PCBNAME.
     02 DBD-NAME           PICTURE X(8).
     02 SEG-LEVEL          PICTURE XX.
     02 STATUS-CODE        PICTURE XX.
     02 PROC-OPTIONS       PICTURE XXXX.
     02 RESERVED-DLI       PICTURE S9(5).
     02 SEG-NAME           PICTURE X(8).
     02 LENGTH-FB-KEY      PICTURE S9(5).
     02 NUMB-SENS-SEGS     PICTURE S9(5).
     02 KEY-FB-AREA        PICTURE X(n).
```

Figure 14-3   Example of a DB PCB Mask in COBOL

The following items comprise a PCB for a hierarchical data structure from a database:

Name of the PCB (PCBNAME)

> The name of the area that refers to the entire structure of PCB fields. The PCB name is used in program statements. This name is not a field in the PCB. It is the 01 level name in the mask shown in Figure 14-3.

Name of the database (DBD-NAME)

> The first field in the PCB, and provides the DBD name from the library of database descriptions associated with a particular database. It contains character data and is eight bytes long.

Segment hierarchy level indicator (SEG-LEVEL)

> IMS uses this area to identify the level number of the last segment encountered that satisfied a level of the call. When a retrieve call is successful, the level number of the retrieved segment is placed here. If the retrieve is unsuccessful, the level number returned is that of the last segment that satisfied the search criteria along the path from the root (the root segment level being '01') to the desired segment. If the call is completely unsatisfied, the level returned is '00'. This field contains character data: it is two bytes long and is a right-justified, numeric value.

DL/I status code (STATUS-CODE)

> A status code that indicates the results of the DL/I call is placed in this field and remains here until another DL/I call uses this PCB. This field contains two bytes of character data. When a successful call is executed, DL/I sets this field to blanks or to an informative status indicator. A complete list of DL/I status codes can be found in *IMS Version 9: Messages and Codes, Volume 1.*

DL/I processing options (PROC-OPTIONS)

This area contains a character code that tells DL/I the processing intent of the program against this database (that is, the kinds of calls that can be used by the program for processing data in this database). This field is four bytes long and is left-justified. It does not change from call to call. It gives the default value coded in the PCB PROCOPT parameter, although this value might be different for each segment. DL/I does not allow the application to change this field, nor any other field in the PCB.

Reserved area for IMS (RESERVED-DLI)

IMS uses this area for its own internal linkage related to an application program. This field is one fullword (four bytes), binary.

Segment name feedback area (SEG-NAME)

When a retrieve call is successful, IMS places the name of the retrieved segment here. If a retrieve is unsuccessful, the name returned is that of the last segment, along the path to the desired segment, that satisfied the search criteria. This field contains eight bytes of character data. This field may be useful in GN calls. If the status code is 'AI' (data management open error), the ddname of the related data set is returned in this area.

Length of key feedback area (LENGTH-FB-KEY)

This area specifies the current active length of the key feedback area. This field is one fullword (four bytes), binary.

Number of sensitive segments (NUMB-SENS-SEGS)

This area specifies the number of segment types in the database to which the application program is sensitive. This would represent a count of the number of segments in the logical data structure viewed through this PCB. This field is one fullword (four bytes), binary.

Key feedback area (KEY-FB-AREA)

IMS places in this area the concatenated key of the last segment encountered that satisfied a level of the call. When a retrieve call is successful, the key of the requested segment and the key field of each segment along the path to the requested segment are concatenated and placed in this area. The key fields are positioned from left to right, beginning with the root segment key and following the hierarchical path. Figure 14-4 on page 227 shows examples of concatenated keys.

When a retrieve call is unsuccessful, the keys of all segments along the path to the requested segment for which the search was successful are placed in this area. Segments without sequence fields are not represented in this area.

RECOMMENDATION: Do not use the key feedback area after a completed unsuccessful call because this area is never cleared and it will contain information from a previous call.

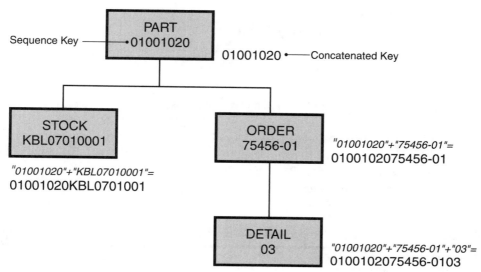

Figure 14-4 Examples of Concatenated Keys

TP PCB Mask

Figure 14-5 shows an example of an online program's PCB mask, which defines the PCB area used by IMS to return the results of the call.

```
01 IOPCB.
      02 LTERM        PICTURE X(8).     Logical Terminal Name
      02 FILLER       PICTURE XX.       Reserved
      02 STATUS-CODE  PICTURE XX.       Status Code
      02 LOCAL-TIME   PICTURE X(8).     Local Date/Time
      02 SEQ-NUMBER   PICTURE X(4).     Input Message Sequence Number
      02 MOD-NAME     PICTURE X(8).     Message output descriptor name
      02 USERID       PICTURE X(8).     USERID
      02 RACF         PICTURE X(8).     RACF Group
      02 TIMESTMP     PICTURE X(12).    12-Byte Timestamp
      02 USER-INDIC   PICTURE X.        Userid Indicator
      02 FILLER       PICTURE X(3).     Reserved
```

Figure 14-5 Example of an Online Application PCB Mask

Calls to IMS

Actual processing of IMS messages, commands, databases, and services is accomplished using a set of input and output functional call requests. A call request is composed of a CALL statement with a parameter list. The parameter list varies, depending on the type of call to be made. The call request consists of the following components:

- A function call
- An AIB identifier or PCB name
- I/O area
- Segment search argument (SSA) (database calls only)

Table 14-2 briefly describes the components of a call request. The call request components for database processing are discussed in more detail in Chapter 15, "Application Programming for the IMS Database Manager," on page 241. The online services and commands call request components are discussed in more detail in Chapter 16, "Application Programming for the IMS Transaction Manager," on page 281.

Table 14-2   IMS Call Request Components

Call Request Component	Description
Function call	Identifies the DL/I function[a] to be performed. This argument is the name of the 4-character field that describes the I/O operation.
AIB name or PCB name	The AIB name specifies the name of the pointer variable that contains the address of the structure that defines the application interface block (AIB) in user-defined storage. For more information on the contents of the AIB, see "AIB Mask" on page 221. The PCB name is the name of the PCB within the PSB that identifies which specific data structure the application program wants to process. The PCB is defined in more detail in "PCB Mask" on page 223.
I/O area	The name of an I/O work area of the application program into which DL/I puts a requested segment, or from which DL/I takes a designed segment. If this is a common area used to process multiple calls, it must be long enough to hold the longest path of segments to be processed.
SSA1...SSAn	The names of the Segment Search Arguments (SSAs), which are optional, depending on the type of call issued. Used only for database calls. The SSA provides information to define the segment to be retrieved or written.

a.   The DL/I functions are completely described in *IMS Version 9: Application Programming: Database Manager* and *IMS Version 9: Application Programming: Transaction Manager*.

Status Code Processing

After each IMS call, a 2-byte status code is returned in the AIB or PCB that is used for that call. There are three categories of status codes:

- The blank status code, which indicates a successful call
- Exceptional conditions and warning status codes, from an application point of view
- Error status codes, specifying an error condition in the application program or IMS

The grouping of status codes in these categories somewhat depends on the installation. It is recommended that you use a standard procedure for status code checking and the handling of error status codes. The first two categories should be handled by the application program after each single call. Figure 14-6 shows an example of a COBOL application program that is testing status codes.

```
CALL 'CBLTDLI' USING ....
IF PCB-STATUS EQ 'GE' PERFORM PRINT-NOT-FOUND.
IF PCB STATUS NE 'bb' PERFORM STATUS-ERROR.
everything okay, proceed...
```

Figure 14-6 Example of a COBOL Application Program Testing Status Codes

Notice that it is more convenient to directly test the regular exceptions inline instead of branching to a status code check routine. In this way, you clearly see the processing of conditions that you want to handle from an application point of view, leaving the real error situations to a central status code error routine.

Termination of the Application

At the end of the processing of the application program, control must be returned to the IMS control program. Table 14-3 shows examples of the termination statements.

Table 14-3 Examples of Termination Statements in Different Languages

Language	Termination Statement
Assembler	RETURN(14,12),RC=0
COBOL	GOBACK.
Java	return;
PL/I	RETURN;

For application programs that are written in C or C++, when there are no more messages for the program to process, the program returns control to IMS by returning from main or by calling exit(). For application programs that are written in Pascal, when there are no more messages for your MPP to process, you return control to IMS by exiting the PASCIMS procedure. You can also code a RETURN statement to leave at another point.

WARNING: Returning to IMS causes storage that was occupied by your program to be released because IMS links to your application program. Therefore, you should close all non-DL/I data sets for COBOL and Assembler before return, to prevent abnormal termination during close processing by z/OS. PL/I automatically causes all files to be closed upon return.

IMS SETUP FOR APPLICATIONS

Before you can run an application program under IMS, you must define and generate the control blocks that are described in the following sections.

IMS Control Blocks

Before executing an application program under IMS, you must describe that program and its use of logical terminals and logical data structures through a program specification block (PSB) generation, using the PSB Generation utility. The PSB contains one PCB for each DL/I database (logical or physical) the application program will access. The PCBs specify which segments the program will use and the kind of access (retrieve, update, insert, delete) for which the program is authorized. The PSBs are maintained in one or more IMS system libraries called a PSBLIB library.

All IMS databases require a database descriptor block (DBD) created to have access to any IMS databases. The details of these control blocks are described in "Generating IMS Control Blocks" on page 233. The DBD is assembled into a system library called a DBDLIB.

The IMS system needs to combine and expand the PSB and DBD control blocks into an internal format called application control blocks (ACBs). The Application Control Blocks Maintenance utility is used to create the ACBs.

For a DB batch environment, the ACB blocks are either built dynamically at step initialization time (as specified in the DLIBATCH procedure) or the ACB blocks are built by running the Application Control Blocks Maintenance utility (as specified in the DBBBATCH procedure). In an online environment, the ACB blocks need to be created before an application can be scheduled and run. The Application Control Blocks Maintenance utility is run offline and the resulting control blocks are placed in an ACB library (IMS.ACBLIB).

The IMS system needs to access these control blocks (DBDs and PSBs) in order to define the application's use of the various IMS resources required. The environment in which the application program is executed determines how IMS accesses those control blocks. See Figure 14-9 on page 234 for an overview of the processing.

The Transaction Processing (TP) PCB

Besides the default TP PCB (also known as the I/O PCB), which does not require a PCB statement in a PSB generation, additional TP PCBs (sometimes called alternate PCBs) can be coded. These TP PCBs are used to insert output messages to:

- LTERMs other than the LTERM that originated the input message. A typical use of an alternate PCB is to send output to a 3270 printer terminal.
- A non-conversational transaction.
- Another USERID.

Figure 14-7 is an example of a TP PCB.

```
01 TPPCB.
      02 LTERM       PICTURE X(8).    Logical Terminal Name
      02 FILLER      PICTURE XX.      Reserved
      02 STATUS-CODE PICTURE XX.      Status Code
```

Figure 14-7 Sample TP PCB

The destination of the output LTERM can be set in two ways:

- During a PSB generation by specifying the LTERM or TRANNAME in an alternate PCB.
- Dynamically by the MPP during execution, by using a change call against a modifiable alternate PCB.

The method used depends on the PCB statement.

The PCB Statement This is the only statement required to generate an alternate PCB (multiple occurrences are allowed). Its format is:

```
PCB TYPE=TP,LTERM=name,MODIFY=YES
```

Table 14-4 describes the possible keywords.

The Database PCB

The DB PCB for a BMP program or MPP can be simple or complex. The DB PCB has two more processing intent options than the TP PCB. These additional processing intent options can be specified with the PROCOPT= keyword of the PCB or the SENSEG statement or both.

Table 14-4   TP PCB Keywords

Keyword	Description
TYPE=TP	Required for all alternate PCBs.
LTERM=*name*	Specifies that this PCB is pointing at a known LTERM defined in the IMS system. The name is optional.
MODIFY=YES	If MODIFY is specified, the LTERM name can be changed by a change call within the application program. **Note:** If MODIFY=YES is specified, the MPP must specify a valid alternate output LTERM with a change call before inserting any message using this PCB.

Figure 14-8 is an example of a simple DB PCB:

```
PCB TYPE=DB,                                      X
DBDNAME=EXCEPTA,                                  X
PROCOPT=A,                                        X
KEYLEN=24                                         X
SENSEG NAME=QB01,                                 X
PARENT=0
```

Figure 14-8   Example of a Simple DB PCB

In Figure 14-8:

TYPE=DB

Required for all DB PCBs.

DBDNAME=*name*

The database that this PCB is pointing to.

PROCOPT=

Application processing intent options.

You can use five options of the PROCOPT parameter (in the DATABASE macro) to indicate to IMS whether your program can read segments in the hierarchy, or whether it can also update segments. From most restrictive to least restrictive, these options are:

G   Your program can read segments.

R   Your program can read and replace segments.

I   Your program can insert segments.

D   Your program can read and delete segments.

A   Your program needs all the processing options. It is equivalent to specifying G, R, I, and D.

Related Reading: There are more processing options than are listed here. For more information about all the processing options, see *IMS Version 9: Application Programming: Design Guide*.

KEYLENGTH=

The length of the concatenated keys for this database.

SENSEG

The SENSEG statement is used in a DB PCB statement to define a hierarchically related set of data segments.

Related Reading: For more information about generating these control blocks, see *IMS Version 9: Utilities Reference: System*.

Generating IMS Control Blocks

In addition to database PCBs, a PSB for MPPs or BMP programs contains one or more TP PCBs.

The order of the PCBs in the PSB must be:

1. Data communication PCBs
2. Database PCBs
3. GSAM PCBs (not allowed for MPPs)

One TP PCB (an I/O PCB) is always automatically included by IMS at the beginning of each PSB of an MPP or BMP program. This default TP PSB is used to insert output messages back to the originating LTERM or USERID and can also be used for system service calls such as CHKP.

Generating PSBs

The PSBGEN statement is basically the same as a DB PCB statement. The only real differences are that the IOEROPN= parameter must be omitted and the COMPAT=YES parameter is ignored.

Generating ACBs

Before PSBs and DBDs can be used by the control region, they must be expanded to an internal control block format. This expansion is done by the Application Control Blocks Maintenance (ACBGEN) utility. The expanded control blocks are maintained in the IMS.ACBLIB library. This is a standard z/OS partitioned data set.

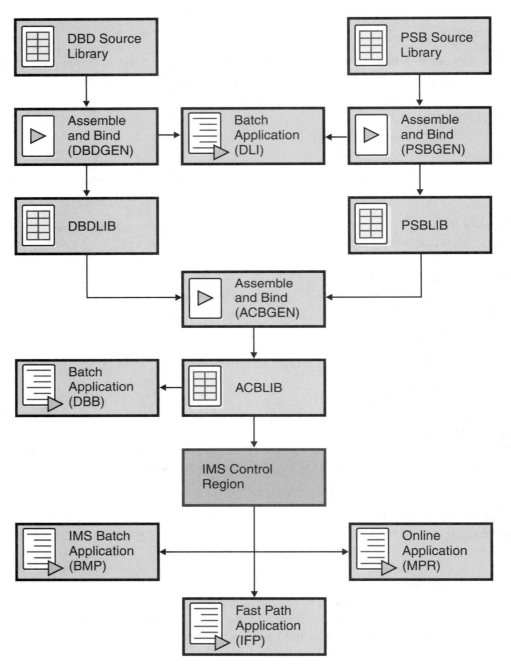

Figure 14-9   IMS Control Block Generation and Usage

An ACBGEN procedure is placed in IMS.PROCLIB during IMS system definition.

> **N O T E:** Multiple BUILD statements can be coded for both DBDs and PSBs and, if IMS.ACBLIB is already populated, the order does not matter. If IMS.ACBLIB is not populated, specify the DBDs first. Better yet, specify only PSBs (not DBDs) and let the ACBGEN utility find and use the correct DBDs. If you want to completely populate IMS.ACBLIB from a PSBLIB and a DBDLIB, use just the single statement BUILD PSB=ALL. The ACBGEN utility knows what to do with the DBDs.

IMS APPLICATION PROGRAMMING INTERFACES

IMS provides a standard set of functions to allow applications to access and manipulate data managed by IMS DB. These functions also allow applications to access and process messages managed by IMS TM and to perform certain system functions.

Calls to these standard functions can be made in a number of ways:

- A language-specific call interface. There is a language-specific call interface for each programming language in which IMS applications can be written.
- A language-independent call interface for applications written in any language that supports IBM's Language Environment for z/OS.
- The application interface block (AIB) call interface.
- For CICS applications that access IMS databases, the application can use the CICS command level interface to provide IMS DB support.
- REXX EXECs can invoke IMS functions by using the IMS Adapter for REXX.

IMS APPLICATION CALLS

The following list describes some of the calls that IMS application programs can use.

get unique (GU)

The GU (get unique) call retrieves a specific segment or path of segments from a database. At the same time, the GU call establishes a position in a database from which additional segments can be processed in a forward direction.

get next (GN)

The GN (get next) call retrieves the next segment or path of segments from the database. The get next call normally moves forward in the hierarchy of a database from the current position, but can be modified to start at an earlier position than the current position in the database through a command code. However, its normal function is to move forward from a given segment to the next required segment in a database.

get hold unique (GHU) and get hold next (GHN)

GHU (get hold unique) and GHN (get hold next) calls indicate the intent of the user to issue a subsequent delete or replace call. A GHU or GHN call must be issued to retrieve the segment before issuing a delete or replace call.

insert (ISRT)

The ISRT (insert) call inserts a segment or a path of segments into a database. It is used to initially load segments in databases and to add segments in existing databases.

To control where occurrences of a segment type are inserted into a database, the user normally defines a unique sequence field in each segment. When a unique sequence field is defined in a root segment type, the sequence field of each occurrence of the root segment type must contain a unique value (except for HDAM and PHDAM). When defined for a dependent segment type, the sequence field of each occurrence under a given physical parent usually contains a unique value. If no sequence field is defined, a new occurrence is inserted after the last existing one.

delete (DLET)

The DLET (delete) call deletes a segment from a database. When a segment is deleted from a DL/I database, its dependents, if any, are also deleted.

replace (REPL)

The REPL (replace) call replaces the data in the data portion of a segment or path of segments in a database. Sequence fields cannot be changed with a replace call.

system service calls

In addition to the calls described previously, which are used to manipulate the data, there are a number of system service calls provided to allow the application to make use of other facilities provided by IMS. These system service calls are described in Table 14-5 on page 237 and Table 14-6 on page 238.

DEFINITION:

Current position is where IMS starts its search for the segments that you specify in the calls. Before you issue the first call to the database, the current position is the place immediately before the first root segment occurrence in the database. This means that if you issue an unqualified GN call, IMS retrieves the first root segment occurrence. It is the next segment occurrence in the hierarchy that is defined by the DB PCB that you referenced.

ACCESSING DB2 FOR Z/OS USING A RESOURCE TRANSLATION TABLE

The resource translation table (RTT) maps IMS application control block names to DB2 for z/OS plan names. When an IMS transaction accesses DB2 for z/OS, the plan name used is, by default, the IMS application control block name. The control block name is the same as the PSB name that is specified in the APPLCTN macro. For more information about the APPLCTN macro, see "IMS System Definition Macros" on page 335.

The RTT is assembled in a CSECT with the name that is the same as the label of the first macro in the table. This CSECT must then be placed in an APF authorized library in the IMS.SDFS-RESL concatenation of the IMS control region. The RTT is pointed to in the PROCLIB member that defines the DB2 attachment. If the RTT parameter is null, the RTT is not used.

It is possible to set up an RTT that translates an IMS application control block name to a different DB2 plan name. Setting up such a table is described in the DB2 for z/OS (not IMS) documentation. See "Defining DB2 plans for IMS applications (optional)" in *DB2 Universal Database for z/OS Installation Guide* for details on how to generate a resource translation table.

The reassembled table is picked up the next time IMS is stopped or started or after a stop (/STO SUBSYS xxxx) and restart (/STA SUBSYS xxxx) of the DB2 connection.

IMS SYSTEM SERVICE CALLS

Table 14-5 and Table 14-6 on page 238:

- Contain summaries of most of the IMS system service calls that application programs can use.
- Indicate where these system service calls can be used.

Related Reading: For complete information about the IMS system service calls, see:

- *IMS Version 9: Application Programming: Database Manager*
- *IMS Version 9: Application Programming: Transaction Manager*

Table 14-5 Summary of IMS DB Application System Service Calls

Function Code	Meaning and Use
APSB	Allocate PSB; allocates a PSB for an ODBA application program
CHKP (Basic)	Basic checkpoint; prepares for recovery
CHKP (Symbolic)	Symbolic checkpoint; prepares for recovery
GMSG	Get message; retrieves a message from the AO exit routine

continues

Table 14-5   Summary of IMS DB Application System Service Calls (Continued)

Function Code	Meaning and Use
ICMD	Issue command; issues an IMS command and retrieves the first command response segment
INIT	Initialize; application receives data availability and deadlock occurrence status codes
INQY	Inquiry; returns information and status codes about I/O or alternate PCB destination type, location, and session status
LOGb[a]	Log; writes a message to the system log
PCBb[a]	Specifies and schedules another PCB
RCMD	Retrieve command; retrieves the second and subsequent command response segments resulting from an ICMD call
ROLB	Roll back; eliminates database updates
ROLL	Roll; eliminates database updates; abend
ROLS	Roll back to SETS; backs out database changes to SETS points
SETS	Set synchronization point; establishes as many as nine intermediate sync (backout) points
SETU	SET unconditional
SYNC	Synchronization; releases locked resources
TERM	Terminate; releases a PSB so another can be scheduled; commits database changes
XRST	Extended restart; works with symbolic checkpoint to restart application program

a.   b indicates a blank. All calls must be four characters.

Table 14-6   Summary of IMS TM System Service Calls

Function Code	Meaning and Use
APSB	Allocate PSB; allocates a PSB for use in CPI-C driven application programs
CHKP (Basic)	Basic checkpoint; for recovery purposes
CHKP (Symbolic)	Symbolic checkpoint; for recovery purposes
DPSB	Deallocate PSB; frees a PSB in use by a CPI-C driven application program
GMSG	Get message; retrieves a message from the AO exit routine
ICMD	Issue command; issues an IMS command and retrieves the first command response segment
INIT	Initialize; application receives data availability status codes

Table 14-6 Summary of IMS TM System Service Calls (Continued)

Function Code	Meaning and Use
INQY	Inquiry; retrieves information about output destinations, session status, execution environment, and the PCB address
LOGƀ[a]	Log; writes a message to the system log
RCMD	Retrieve command; retrieves the second and subsequent command response segments resulting from an ICMD call
ROLB	Rollback; backs out messages sent by the application program
ROLL	Roll; backs out output messages and terminates the conversation
ROLS	Roll back to SETS; returns message queue positions to sync points set by the SETS or SETU call
SETS	Set synchronization point; sets intermediate sync (backout) points
SETU	SET unconditional; sets intermediate sync (backout) points
SYNC	Synchronization; requests commit point processing
XRST	Restart; works with symbolic CHKP to restart application program failure

a.   ƀ indicates a blank. All calls must be four characters in length.

TESTING IMS APPLICATIONS

DFSDDLT0 is an IMS application program test tool that issues calls to IMS based on control statement information. You can use it to verify and debug DL/I calls independently of application programs. You can run DFSDDLT0 using any PSB, including those that use an IMS-supported language. You can also use DFSDDLT0 as a general-purpose database utility program.

The functions that DFSDDLT0 provides include:

- Issuing any valid DL/I call against any database using:
  - Any segment search argument (SSA) or PCB, or both
  - Any SSA or AIB, or both
- Comparing the results of a call to expected results. This includes the contents of selected PCB fields, the data returned in the I/O area, or both.
- Printing the control statements, the results of calls, and the results of comparisons only when the output is useful, such as after an unequal compare.
- Dumping DL/I control blocks, the I/O buffer pool, or the entire batch region.
- Punching selected control statements into an output file to create new test data sets. This simplifies the construction of new test cases.

- Merging multiple input data sets into a single input data set using a SYSIN2 DD statement in the JCL. You can specify the final order of the merged statements in columns 73 to 80 of the DFSDDLT0 control statements.
- Sending messages to the z/OS system console (with or without a reply).
- Repeating each call up to 9,999 times.

Related Reading: For more information about the DFSDDLT0 interface, see *IMS Version 9: Application Programming: Transaction Manager* or *IMS Version 9: Application Programming: Database Manager.*

CHAPTER **15**

Application Programming for the IMS Database Manager

 pplication programs can interact with IMS DB in two ways:

- Traditional applications can use the DL/I database call interface.
- Java applications can use the IMS Java function's implementation of JDBC or the IMS Java hierarchical interface, which is a set of Java classes that you can use in Java that are similar to DL/I calls.

This chapter discusses the DL/I database call interface. See Chapter 18, "Application Programming in Java," on page 311 for information about how Java applications call IMS.

In This Chapter:

INTRODUCTION TO DATABASE PROCESSING

In general, database processing is transaction oriented. Even batch jobs should be pseudo-transactional to allow for checkpointing. An application program accesses one or more database records for each transaction it processes. There are two basic types of DL/I application programs:

- Direct access programs
- Sequential access programs

A *direct access program* accesses, for every input transaction, segments in one or more database records. These accesses are based on database record and segment identification. This identification is essentially derived from the transaction input and is normally the root-key value and additional (key) field values of dependent segments. For more complex transactions, segments can be accessed in several DL/I databases concurrently.

A *sequential access program* accesses sequentially selected segments of all of a consecutive subset of a particular database. The sequence is usually determined by the key of the root segment. A sequential access program can also access other databases, but those accesses are direct, unless the root keys of both databases are the same.

A DL/I application program normally processes only particular segments of the DL/I databases. The portion that a given program processes is called an *application data structure*. This application data structure is defined in the program specification block (PSB). An application data structure always consists of one or more hierarchical data structures, each of which is derived from a DL/I physical or logical database.

At execution time, each application program uses one PSB and it is usually a different PSB than those used by other application programs.

Application Programming Interfaces to IMS

During initialization, both the application program and its associated PSB are loaded from their respective libraries by the IMS system The DL/I modules, which reside together with the application program in one region, interpret and execute database call requests issued by the program.

Calls to DL/I

A call request is composed of a CALL statement with an argument list. The argument list specifies the processing function to be performed, the hierarchic path to the segment to be accessed, and the segment occurrence of that segment. One segment can be operated upon with a single DL/I call. However, a single call never returns more than one occurrence of one segment type.

The arguments contained within any DL/I call request are defined in "Calls to IMS" on page 227. The following code is a sample basic CALL statement for COBOL:

```
CALL 'CBLTDLI' USING function,PCB-name,I/O Area, SSA1,...SSAn.
```

Table 15-1 describes some of the components of the CALL statement: the basic DL/I call functions to request DL/I database services.

Table 15-1 Basic DL/I Call Function and Descriptions

Database Service Request	DL/I Call Function
GET UNIQUE	'GUƀƀ'[a]
GET NEXT	'GNƀƀ'[a]
GET HOLD UNIQUE	'GHUƀ'[a]
GET HOLD NEXT	'GHNƀ'[a]
INSERT	'ISRT'
DELETE	'DLET'
REPLACE	'REPL'

a.   ƀ indicates a blank. Each call function is always four characters.

The DL/I calls listed in Table 15-1 fall into four segment access categories. Table 15-2 describes these categories.

Table 15-2 Segment Access Categories

Segment Access Category	DL/I Call Function
Retrieve a segment	'GUƀƀ',[a] 'GNƀƀ', 'GHUƀ', 'GHNƀ'
Replace (update) a segment	'REPL'
Delete a segment	'DLET'
Insert (add) a segment	'ISRT'

a.   ƀ indicates a blank. Each call function is always four characters.

In addition to the database calls listed in Table 15-1 and Table 15-2, there are also system service calls. System service calls are used to request system services such as checkpoints and restarts. All the calls in Table 15-1 and Table 15-2 are discussed in detail in the following sections.

Segment Search Arguments (SSAs)

For each segment accessed in a hierarchical path, one segment search argument (SSA) can be provided. The purpose of the SSA is to identify by segment name and, optionally, by field value the segment to be accessed.

The basic function of the SSA permits the application program to apply three different kinds of logic to a call:

- Narrow the field of search to a particular segment type, or to a particular segment occurrence.
- Request that either one segment or a path of segments be processed.
- Alter DL/I's position in the database for a subsequent call.

SSA names represent the fourth (fifth for PL/I) through last arguments (SSA1 through SSAn) in the call statement. There can be zero or one SSA per level, and, because DL/I permits a maximum of 15 levels per database, a call can contain from zero to 15 SSA names. In the code examples in this section, an SSA consists of one, two, or three of the following elements:

- **Segment name:** The segment name must be eight bytes long, left-justified with trailing blanks required. The segment name is the name of the segment as defined in a physical or logical DBD that is referenced in the PCB for an application program.
- **Command codes:** The command codes are optional and provide functional variations to be applied to the call for that segment type. An asterisk (*) following the segment name indicates the presence of one or more command codes. A blank or a left parenthesis is the ending delimiter for command codes. A blank is used when no qualification statement exists. For more information, see "Calls with Command Codes" on page 255.
- **Qualification statement:** The presence of a qualification statement is indicated by a left parenthesis following the segment name or, if present, command codes. The qualification statement consists of a field name, a relational operator, and a comparative value. The qualification statement consists of the following elements:
  - **Start of qualification statement character:** A left parenthesis indicates the beginning of a qualification statement. If the SSA is unqualified, the eight-byte segment name or, if used, the command codes should be followed by a blank.
  - **Field name:** The field name is the name of a field that appears in the description of the specified segment type in the DBD. The name is up to eight characters long, left-justified with trailing blanks as required. The named field can be either the key field or any data field within a segment. The field name is used for searching the database and must have been defined in the physical DBD.
  - **Relational operator:** The relational operator is a set of two characters which express the manner in which the contents of the field, referred to by the field name, are to be tested against the comparative value. See Table 15-3 on page 245 for a list of the possible values for the relational operator.
  - **Comparative value:** The comparative value is the value against which the content of the field, referred to by the field name, is tested. The length of the comparative value field must be equal to the length of the named field in the segment of the

Table 15-3   Relational Operator Values[a]

Operator	Meaning
'ƀ'= or 'EQ'	Must be equal to
'>=' or 'GE'	Must be greater than or equal to
'<=' or 'LE'	Must be less than or equal to
'ƀ>' or 'GT'	Must be greater than
'ƀ<' or 'LT'	Must be less than
'<>' or 'NE'	Must be not equal to

a.   ƀ represents a blank character.

database. That is, the length includes leading or trailing blanks (for alphanumeric fields) or zeros (usually needed for numeric fields) as required. DL/I performs a collating sequence comparison, not an arithmetic comparison.

— **End of qualification statement character:** A right parenthesis indicates the end of the qualification statement.

Qualification of SSAs

Just as calls are qualified by the presence of an SSA, SSAs are categorized as either qualified or unqualified, depending on the presence or absence of a qualification statement. Command codes can be included in or omitted from either qualified or unqualified SSAs.

In its simplest form, an SSA is unqualified and consists only of the name of a specific segment type as defined in the DBD. In this simple form, the SSA provides DL/I with enough information to define the segment type required by the call. In the following example, the last character is a blank, which indicates the SSA is unqualified:

```
SEGNAMEƀƀ
```

Qualified SSAs, which are optional, contain a qualification statement composed of three parts:

- A field name that is defined in the DBD
- A relational operator
- A comparative value

DL/I uses the information in the qualification statement to test the value of the segment's key or data fields within the database, and thus to determine whether the segment meets the user's specifications. Using this approach, DL/I performs the database segment searching. The program need process only those segments that precisely meet some logical criteria. For example:

```
SEGNAMEƀ(fieldxxx>=value)
```

The qualification statement test is terminated either when the test is satisfied by an occurrence of the segment type, or when DL/I determines that the request cannot be satisfied.

Command Codes in SSAs

Both unqualified and qualified SSAs can contain one or more optional command codes which specify functional variations applicable to the call function or the segment qualification. For more information about command codes, see "Calls with Command Codes" on page 255.

General Characteristics of SSAs

General characteristics of segment search arguments:

- An SSA can consist of the segment name only (unqualified). It can optionally also include one or more command codes and a qualification statement.
- SSAs following the first SSA must proceed down the hierarchical path. Not all SSAs in the hierarchical path need to be specified because there might be missing levels in the path. However, IBM strongly recommends that you always include SSAs for every segment level.

Examples of SSAs are given with the sample calls at each DL/I call discussion in "Processing a Single Database Record."

PROCESSING A SINGLE DATABASE RECORD

This section describes how to process a single database record. A database record comprises a root segment and all of its physically dependent child segments.

DL/I calls are introduced in the following sections, and all the samples in those sections are in the standard format shown in Figure 15-1 on page 247.

Each call example contains three sections:

1. The first section presents the essential elements of working storage as needed for the call.
2. The second part, the processing section, contains the call itself. Note that the PCB-NAME parameter should be the selected PCB defined in the linkage section. Some examples have additional processing function descriptions before or after the call, in order to show the call in its correct context.
3. The third section contains the status codes and their interpretation, which can be expected after the call.

   The last category of status code, labeled "other: error situation", would normally be handled by a status code error routine. For more information, see "Status Code Processing" on page 228.

```
77  GU-FUNC                PICTURE XXXX VALUE 'GUbb'


01  SSA001-GU-SE1PART.
    02  SSA001-BEGIN  PICTURE ...
    02  ...
    02  ...


01  IOAREA                 PICTURE X(256).
-----------------------------------------------------------------------
CALL 'CBLTDLI' USING GU-FUNC,PCB-NAME,IOAREA,SSA001-GU-SE1PART.
-----------------------------------------------------------------------
STATUS CODES:
-------------
    bb:    succesfull call
    --:    exceptional but correct condition
 other:    error condition
```

Figure 15-1   Sample Call Format

The samples in each of the following sections are presented in COBOL format. The coding of a call in PL/I is described in "PL/I Programming Considerations" on page 263. For information about coding DL/I applications in other languages, see *IMS Version 9: Application Programming: Database Manager*.

DL/I Positioning

To satisfy a call, DL/I relies on two sources of segment identification:

- The established position in the database, as set by the previous call against the PCB.
- The segment search arguments, as provided with the call.

The database position is the knowledge of DL/I of the location of the last segment retrieved and all segments above it in the hierarchy. This database position is maintained by DL/I as an extension of, and reflected in, the PCB. When an application program has multiple PCBs for a single database, these positions are maintained independently. For each PCB, the position is represented by the concatenated key of the hierarchical path from the root segment down to the lowest- level segment accessed. It also includes the positions of non-keyed segments.

If no current position exists in the database, then the assumed current position is the start of the database, which is the first physical database record in the database. With HDAM, PHDAM, and DEDB, the first physical database record in the database is not necessarily the root segment with the lowest key value.

Retrieving Segments

You can retrieve a segment in two basic ways:

- Retrieve a specific segment by using a GU type call
- Retrieve the next segment in the hierarchy by using a GN type call

If you know the specific key value of the segment you want to retrieve, then the GU call allows you to retrieve only the required segment. If you do not know the key value or do not care, then the GN call retrieves the next available segment that meets your requirements.

Get Unique (GU) Call

The basic get unique (GU) call, function code GUƀƀ, normally retrieves one segment in a hierarchical path. The segment that is retrieved is identified by an SSA for each level in the hierarchical path down to and including the requested segment. Each SSA should contain at least the segment name. The SSA for the root segment should provide the root key value. For information about how to retrieve more than one segment in the path, see "D Command Code" on page 255.

Figure 15-2 shows an example of the get unique call.

```
77   GU-FUNC                PICTURE XXXX VALUE 'GUƀƀ'

01   SSA001-GU-SE1PART.
     02   SSA001-BEGIN       PICTURE x(19)  VALUE 'SE1PARTƀ(FE1PGPNRƀ='.
     02   SSA001-FE1PGPNR   PICTURE X(8).
     02   SS1001-END        PICTURE X       VALUE ')'.


01   IOAREA                 PICTURE X(256).
--------------------------------------------------------------------------
MOVE PART-NUMBER TO SSA001-FE1PGPNR.
CALL 'CBLTDLI' USING GU-FUNC,PCB-NAME,IOAREA,SSA001-GU-SE1PART.
--------------------------------------------------------------------------
STATUS CODES:
-------------
     ƀƀ:     succesfull call
     GE:     exceptional but correct condition
  other:     error condition
```

Figure 15-2   Basic Get Unique Call

The main use of the GU call is to position the application to a database record and obtain a path to the segments. Typically, the GU call is used only once for each database record you want to access. Additional segments within the database record are then retrieved by means of get next calls. You can also use the GU call to retrieve a dependent segment, by adding additional SSAs to the call.

For example, if you add a second SSA that specifies the stock location, you would retrieve a STOCK segment below the identified part. If the SSA did not provide a stock location number, this would be the first STOCK segment for this part.

Get Next (GN) Calls

The get next (GN) call, function code 'GNbb', retrieves the next segment in the hierarchy as defined in the PCB. To determine this next segment, DL/I relies on the previously established position.

Get next calls can be unqualified or qualified, as described in the next two sections.

Unqualified Get Next Calls   Figure 15-3 shows a get next call with no SSAs that, if repeated, returns the segments in the database in hierarchical sequence. Only those segments to which the program is defined as sensitive to in its PCB are returned.

```
77  GN-FUNC              PICTURE XXXX VALUE 'GNbb'


01  IOAREA               PICTURE X(256).
---------------------------------------------------------------------

CALL 'CBLTDLI' USING GN-FUNC,PCB-NAME,IOAREA.

---------------------------------------------------------------------
STATUS CODES:
-------------
     bb:    if previous call retrieved a PART, then a STOCK segment will be
            be retrieved
     GK:    a segment is returned in IOAREA, but it is a different type
            at the SAME level, for instance, a PURCHASE ORDER segment
            after the last STOCK segment.
     GA:    segment returned is IOAREA, but it is of a higher level than
            the last one, that is, a new PART segment
     GB:    possible end of database reached, no segment returned
  other:    error condition
```

Figure 15-3   Unqualified Get Next Call

If the unqualified get next call in Figure 15-3 is issued after the get unique call in Figure 15-2 on page 248, then the unqualified get next call retrieves the first STOCK segment for this part (if one exists). Subsequent calls retrieve all other STOCK, PURCHASE ORDER, and DESCRIP-TION segments for this part. After all the segments for this part are retrieved, the next part is retrieved along with its dependent segments, until the end of the database is reached. Special status codes are returned whenever a different segment type at the same level or a higher level is returned. No special status code is returned when a different segment at a lower level is returned. You can check for reaching a lower-level segment type in the segment level indicator in the PCB. Remember, only those segments to which the program is defined as sensitive to in its PCB are available to you.

Although the unqualified GN call illustrated in Figure 15-3 on page 249 might be efficient, especially for report programs, you should use a qualified GN call whenever possible.

Qualified Get Next Calls   A qualified GN call should at least identify the segment you want to retrieve. If you identify the segment in the qualified GN call, you achieve greater flexibility to make database structure changes in the future. Figure 15-4 shows an example of a qualified GN call. If you supply only the segment name in the SSA, then you retrieve all segments of that type from all the database records with subsequent get next calls.

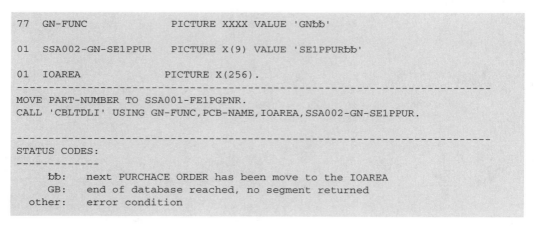

```
77   GN-FUNC              PICTURE XXXX VALUE 'GNƀƀ'

01   SSA002-GN-SE1PPUR    PICTURE X(9) VALUE 'SE1PPURƀƀ'

01   IOAREA               PICTURE X(256).
----------------------------------------------------------------------
MOVE PART-NUMBER TO SSA001-FE1PGPNR.
CALL 'CBLTDLI' USING GN-FUNC,PCB-NAME,IOAREA,SSA002-GN-SE1PPUR.


----------------------------------------------------------------------
STATUS CODES:
-------------
      ƀƀ:    next PURCHACE ORDER has been move to the IOAREA
      GB:    end of database reached, no segment returned
   other:    error condition
```

Figure 15-4   Qualified Get Next Call

Repeating the GN call in Figure 15-4 results in retrieving all subsequent PURCHASE ORDER segments of the database, until the end of the database is reached. To limit the retrieval to a specific part, you can add a fully qualified SSA for the PART segment. The fully qualified SSA for the PART segment would be the same SSA used in Figure 15-2 on page 248.

Figure 15-5 on page 251 shows an example of a qualified get next call with a qualified SSA.

```
77   GN-FUNC                 PICTURE XXXX VALUE 'GNƀƀ'

01   SSA001-GU-SE1PART.
     02   SSA001-BEGIN        PICTURE x(19)  VALUE 'SE1PARTƀ(FE1PGPNRƀ='.
     02   SSA001-FE1PGPNR PICTURE X(8).
     02   SS1001-END          PICTURE X       VALUE ')'.

01   SSA002-GN-SE1PPUR       PICTURE X(9)   VALUE 'SE1PPURƀ'.
01   IOAREA                  PICTURE X(256).
------------------------------------------------------------------------

CALL 'CBLTDLI' USING GN-FUNC,PCB-NAME,IOAREA,SSA001-GU-SE1PART
                     SSA002-GN-SE1PPUR.
------------------------------------------------------------------------

STATUS CODES:
-------------
     ƀƀ:   next PURCHASE ORDER segment is in IOAREA
     GE:   segment not found; no more purchase orders for this part,
           or part number in SSA001 does not exist
   other:  error condition
```

Figure 15-5   Qualified Get Next Call with Qualified SSA

> **R E C O M M E N D A T I O N:**   Primarily use fully qualified get
> next calls because they always clearly identify the hierarchical path
> and the segment you want to retrieve.

Get Hold Calls

To change the contents of a segment in a database through a replace or delete call, the program must first obtain the segment. The program then changes the segment's contents and requests DL/I to replace the segment in the database or to delete it from the database.

Programs use a get hold call to obtain the segment. Get hold calls are similar to get unique and get next calls, except the letter H immediately follows the letter G in the code (for example, GHU, GHN). The get hold calls work exactly as the corresponding get calls for the user. For DL/I, the get hold calls indicate a possible subsequent replace or delete call.

After DL/I provides the requested segment to the user, one or more fields, but not the sequence field, in the segment can be changed.

After the user has changed the segment contents, your program can call DL/I to return the segment to, or delete it from, the database. If, after issuing a get hold call, the program determines that it is not necessary to change or delete the retrieved segment, the program can proceed with other processing, and the hold is released by the next DL/I call against the same PCB.

Updating Segments

Segments can be updated by application programs and returned to DL/I to be restored in the database with the replace call, function code REPL. Two conditions must be met to successfully update a segment:

- The segment must first be retrieved with a get hold call (GHU or GHN). No intervening calls can reference the same PCB.
- The sequence field of the segment cannot be changed. You can change the sequence field of the segment only by using combinations of delete and insert calls for the segment and all its dependents.

Figure 15-6 shows an example of a combination of a GHU call and a REPL call. Notice that the replace call must not specify an SSA for the segment to be replaced. If, after retrieving a segment with a get hold call, the program decides not to update the segment, it need not issue a replace call. Instead, the program can proceed as if it were a normal get call without the hold.

```
77  GHU-FUNC            PICTURE XXXX VALUE 'GHUb'.
77  REPL-FUNC           PICTURE XXXX VALUE 'REPL'.

01  SSA001-GU-SE1PART.
    02  SSA001-BEGIN    PICTURE x(19) VALUE 'SE1PARTb(FE1PGPNRb='.
    02  SSA001-FE1PGPNR PICTURE X(8).
    02  SS1001-END      PICTURE X     VALUE ')'.
01  SSA002-GN-SE1PPUR   PICTURE X(9)  VALUE 'SE1PPURbb'.
01  IOAREA              PICTURE X(256).
--------------------------------------------------------------------
MOVE PART-NUMBER TO SSA001-FE1PGPNR.
CALL 'CBLTDLI' USING GHU-FUNC,PCB-NAME,IOAREA,SSA001-GU-SE1PART
             SSA002-GN-SE1PPUR.
   the retrieved PURCHASE ORDER segment can now be changed by the program
   in the IOAREA.
CALL 'CBLTDLI' USING REPL-FUNC,PCB-NAME,IOAREA.
--------------------------------------------------------------------
STATUS CODES:
-------------
    bb:   segment is replaced with contents in the IOAREA
  other:  error condition
```

Figure 15-6   Sample Combination of a Get Hold Unique Call and a Replace Call

Use the get hold call whenever there is a reasonable chance (5% or greater) that you will change the segment. The difference in performance between the get call and the get hold call is small.

Deleting Segments

To delete an occurrence of a segment from a database, the segment must first be obtained by issuing a get hold call (GHU, GHN). After the segment is acquired, you can issue a delete call (DLET).

If DL/I calls that use the same PCB attempt to intervene between the get hold call and the delete call, the delete call is rejected. Often a program might want to process a segment prior to deleting it. This sequence of processing is permitted as long as the processing does not involve a DL/I call that refers to the same database PCB used for the get hold or delete calls. However, other PCBs can be referred to between the get hold and delete calls.

When the user issues a call that has the function DLET, DL/I is advised that a segment is to be deleted. The deletion of a parent deletes all the segment occurrences beneath that parent, whether or not the application program is sensitive to those segments. If the segment being deleted is a root segment, that whole database record is deleted. The segment to be deleted must still be in the IOAREA of the delete call (with which no SSA is used), and its sequence field must not have been changed. Figure 15-7 shows an example of a delete call.

```
77   GHU-FUNC             PICTURE XXXX VALUE 'GHUƀ'.
77   DLET-FUNC            PICTURE XXXX VALUE 'DLET'.

01   SSA001-GU-SE1PART.
     02   SSA001-BEGIN    PICTURE X(19)  VALUE 'SE1PARTƀ(FE1PGPNRƀ='.
     02   SSA001-FE1PGPNR PICTURE X(8).
     02   SS1001-END      PICTURE X      VALUE ')'.
01   SSA002-GN-SE1PPUR    PICTURE X(9)   VALUE 'SE1PPURƀƀ'.
01   IOAREA              PICTURE X(256).
---------------------------------------------------------------------
MOVE PART-NUMBER TO SSA001-FE1PGPNR.
CALL 'CBLTDLI' USING GHU-FUNC,PCB-NAME,IOAREA,SSA001-GU-SE1PART
             SSA002-GN-SE1PPUR.

   the retrieved PURCHASE ORDER segment can now be processed by the
   program in the IOAREA.

CALL 'CBLTDLI' USING DLET-FUNC,PCB-NAME,IOAREA.
---------------------------------------------------------------------
STATUS CODES:
-------------
     ƀƀ:    requested purchase order segment is deleted from the database;
            all its dependents, if any, are deleted also.
  other:    error condition
```

Figure 15-7   Sample Combination of a Get Hold Unique Call and a Delete Call

Inserting Segments

The insert (ISRT) call adds new segment occurrences to a database.

The insert call is used for two distinct purposes:

- To load the segments during creation of a database
- To add new occurrences of an existing segment type into an established database

The processing options field in the PCB indicates whether the database is being added to or loaded. The format of the insert call is identical for either use.

When loading or inserting a segment, the last SSA must specify only the name of the segment that is being inserted. The SSA should specify only the segment name, not the sequence field. Thus, an unqualified SSA is always required.

Up to a level to be inserted, the SSA evaluation and positioning for an insert call is exactly the same as for a GU call. For the level to be inserted, the value of the sequence field in the segment in the user I/O area establishes the insert position. If no sequence field is defined, then the segment is inserted at the end of the physical twin chain. If multiple non-unique keys are allowed, then the segment is inserted after existing segments with the same key value.

Figure 15-8 shows an example of an insert call. The status codes in this example are applicable only to non-initial load inserts. The status codes at initial load time are discussed in "Loading Databases" on page 269.

```
77   ISRT-FUNC             PICTURE XXXX VALUE 'ISRT'.

01   SSA001-GU-SE1PART.
     02   SSA001-BEGIN    PICTURE x(19) VALUE 'SE1PARTb(FE1PGPNRb='.
     02   SSA001-FE1PGPNR PICTURE X(8).
     02   SS1001-END      PICTURE X     VALUE ')'.
01   SSA002-GN-SE1PPUR    PICTURE X(9)  VALUE 'SE1PPURbb'.
01   IOAREA               PICTURE X(256).
-----------------------------------------------------------------------
MOVE PART-NUMBER TO SSA001-FE1PGPNR.
MOVE PURCHASE-ORDER TO IOAREA.
CALL 'CBLTDLI' USING ISRT-FUNC,PCB-NAME,IOAREA,SSA001-GU-SE1PART
              SSA002-GN-SE1PPUR.
-----------------------------------------------------------------------
STATUS CODES:
------------
     bb:   new PURCHASE ORDER segment is inserted in database
     II:   segment to insert already exists in database
     GE:   segment not found; the requested part number (that is, a
           parent of the segment to be inserted) is not in the database
  other:   error condition
```

Figure 15-8   Basic Insert Call

You need not check the existence of a segment in the database with a preceding retrieve call. DL/I does that at insert time, and notifies you with an II or GE status code. Checking previous existence is only relevant if the segment has no sequence field.

Calls with Command Codes

Both unqualified SSAs and qualified SSAs can contain one or more optional command codes that specify functional variations applicable to either the call function or the segment qualification. Command codes in an SSA are always prefixed by an asterisk (*), which immediately follows the 8-byte segment name. Figure 15-9 illustrates an SSA with command codes D and P.

```
01   SSA001-GU-SE1PART.
     02   SSA001-BEGIN     PICTURE x(19)  VALUE 'SE1PART*ḅDP(FE1PGPNRḅ='.
     02   SSA001-FE1PGPNR  PICTURE X(8).
     02   SS1001-END       PICTURE X      VALUE ')'.
```

Figure 15-9   Example of an SSA with D and P Command Codes

D Command Code

The D command code is the most widely used command code. The D command code tells DL/I to issue path calls. A *path call* enables a hierarchical path of segments to be inserted or retrieved with one call. The meaning of the D command code is as follows:

- For retrieval calls, multiple segments in a hierarchical path are moved to the I/O area with a single call. The first through the last segment retrieved are concatenated in the user's I/O area. Intermediate SSAs might be present with or without the D command code. If without the D command code, these segments are not moved to the user's I/O area. The segment named in the PCB segment name feedback area is the lowest-level segment retrieved, or the last level satisfied in the call in the case of a not-found condition. Higher-level segments that are associated with SSAs that have the D command code are placed in the user's I/O area even in the not-found case. The D is not necessary for the last SSA in the call because the segment that satisfies the last level is always moved to the user's I/O area.

  Except for DEDBs, a processing option of P must be specified in the PSBGEN for any segment type for which a command code D will be used.

- For insert calls, the D command code designates the first segment type in the path to be inserted. The SSAs for lower-level segments in the path need not have the D command code set. The D command code is propagated to all specified lower-level segments.

Figure 15-10 on page 256 shows an example of a path call.

```
77  GU-FUNC              PICTURE XXXX VALUE 'GUbb'.

01  SSA004-GU-SE1PART.
    02  SSA004-BEGIN    PICTURE x(21) VALUE 'SE1PART*bD(FE1PGPNRb='.
    02  SSA004-FE1PGPNR PICTURE X(8).
    02  SS1004-END      PICTURE X     VALUE ')'.
01  SSA005-GN-SE1PGDSC  PICTURE X(9)  VALUE 'SE1PGDSCb'.

01  IOAREA              PICTURE X(256).
-------------------------------------------------------------------

CALL 'CBLTDLI' USING GU-FUNC,PCB-NAME,IOAREA,SSA004-GU-SE1PART
               SSA004-GN-SE1PGDSC.

-------------------------------------------------------------------
STATUS CODES:
-------------
    bb:    both segments (PART and DESCRIPTION) have been placed in IOAREA
    GE:    segment not found; PART segment may be retrieved in IOAREA;
           check segment name and level indicator in PCB.
  other:   error condition
```

Figure 15-10 Sample Path Retrieve Call

Figure 15-10 shows a common usage of the path call. Although the retrieve call does not know if the requested part has a separate DESCRIPTION segment (SE1PGDSC), it is retrieved at almost no additional cost, if one exists.

P Command Code
The P command code establishes parentage of present level.

> **DEFINITION:**
>
> *Parentage* is a term that describes:
> - How the search for a segment on a GNP call is limited to the dependents of the lowest-level segment most recently accessed by a successful GU or GN call.
> - The direct lineage in a hierarchy of segments. For a given segment, the parent is the segment one level higher than this segment in the hierarchy.

Parentage determines the end of the search, and is in effect only following a successful GU or GN call.

Ordinarily, IMS sets parentage at the level of the lowest segment that is accessed during a call. To set parentage at a higher level, use the P command code in a GU, GN, or GNP call.

For example, in the following hierarchy:

segment_A

segment_B

segment_C

segment_D

segment_E

If a GU call was issued for segment D, the parentage would be set at D so that a GNP call would return segment E. If the GU call was issued for segment D and the P command code was in the SSA for segment B, a GNP call would return segment C.

F Command Code

The F command code allows you to back up to the first occurrence of a segment under its parent. The F command code has meaning only for a get next call. A get unique call always starts with the first occurrence. Command code F is disregarded for the root segment.

L Command Code

The L command code allows you to retrieve the last occurrence of a segment under its parent. This command code should be used whenever applicable.

N Command Code

When a replace call follows a path retrieve call, DL/I assumes that all segments previously retrieved with the path call are being replaced. If any of the segments have not been changed, and therefore need not be replaced, the N command code can be set at those levels, which tells DL/I not to replace the segment at this level of the path. The status codes returned are the same as for a replace call.

Hyphen (-) Command Code

The hyphen is a null command code, whose purpose is to enable you to reserve one or more positions in a SSA in which a program can store command codes, if they are needed during program execution. Using the hyphen command code simplifies the maintenance of SSAs.

Figure 15-11 shows the null command code being used to reserve a position for two command codes.

```
GU    PATIENT**--(PATNObbb=b07755)
      ILLNESS*(ILLDATEb=19930303)
      TREATMNT
```

Figure 15-11   Example of a Hyphen (-) Command Code

Database Positioning After DL/I Calls

Database position is used by DL/I to satisfy the next call against a PCB. The segment level, segment name, and the key feedback areas of the PCB are used to present the database position to the application program.

These basic rules apply to database positioning after DL/I calls:

- If a get call is completely satisfied, current position in the database is reflected in the PCB key feedback area.
- A replace call does not change current position in the database.
- Database position after a successful insert call is immediately after the inserted segment.
- Database position after return of an II status code is immediately prior to the duplicate segment. This positioning allows the duplicate segment to be retrieved with a get next call.
- Database position after a successful delete call is immediately after all dependents of the deleted segment. If no dependents existed, database position is immediately after the deleted segment.
- Database position is unchanged by an unsuccessful delete call.
- After a partially unsuccessful retrieve call, the PCB reflects the lowest-level segment that satisfies the call. The segment name or the key feedback length should be used to determine the length of the relevant data in the key feedback area. Contents of the key feedback area beyond the length value must not be used, as the feedback area is never cleared out after previous calls. If the level-one (root) SSA cannot be satisfied, the segment name is cleared to blank, and the level and key feedback length are set to zero.

When you consider the current position in the database, remember that DL/I must first establish a starting position to be used in satisfying the call. This starting position is the current position in the database for get next calls, and is a unique position normally established by the root SSA for get unique calls.

The following are clarifications of current position in the database for special situations:

- If no current position exists in the database, the assumed current position is the start of the database.
- If the end of the database is encountered, the assumed current position to be used by the next call is the start of the database.
- If a get unique call is unsatisfied at the root level, the current position is such that the next segment retrieved is the first root segment with a key value higher than the key value of the unsuccessful call, except when the end of the database is reached or, for HDAM, where the next segment retrieved is the next segment in physical sequence.

You can always reestablish your database positioning with a get unique call that specifies all the segment key values in the hierarchical path. It is recommended that you use a get unique call after each not found condition.

Using Multiple PCBs for One Database

Use different PCBs whenever there is a need to maintain two or more independent positions in one database. Using different PCBs avoids the need to issue additional get unique calls to switch forward and backward from one database record or hierarchical path to another. There are no restrictions as to the call functions available in these multiple PCBs. However, to avoid position confusion in the application program, you should not apply changes by using two PCBs to the same hierarchical path. Limit the updates to one PCB unless this causes additional calls.

System Service Calls

In addition to call functions that manipulate database segments, DL/I provides special system service calls. The most common system service calls are:

Statistics (STAT)

STAT obtains various statistics from DL/I.

Checkpoint (CHPK)

CHPK informs DL/I that a checkpoint was taken during a previous execution of the program and the application program can be restarted at this point. The current position is maintained in GSAM databases. For all other databases, you must reposition the program after each checkpoint call with a get unique call.

Restart (XRST)

XRST requests that DL/I restore checkpointed user areas and reposition GSAM databases for sequential processing if a checkpoint ID for restarting has been supplied by the call or in the JCL.

The XRST and CHKP calls are discussed in more detail in "Using Batch Checkpoint/Restart" on page 275.

Processing GSAM Databases

All access to GSAM databases is done through DL/I calls. DL/I checks to determine whether a user request is for a GSAM database. If the request is for a GSAM database, control is passed to GSAM, which is resident in the user region. If the request is not for a GSAM database, control is passed to DL/I, and standard hierarchical processing results.

The format of the CALL statement to access a GSAM database is:

```
CALL 'CBLTDLI' USING call-func,pcb-name,ioarea.
```

call-func

    The name of the field that contains the call function. The function options are:

    OPEN Open the GSAM database

    CLSE Close the GSAM database

    GN   Get the next sequential record

    ISRT   Insert a new logical record (at the end of the database only)

    The open and close calls are optional calls. Use them to explicitly initiate or terminate database operations. The database is opened automatically by the issuance of the first processing call used, and automatically closed at "end-of-data" or at program termination.

    You cannot randomly add records to GSAM data sets. However, you can extend the data set by opening in the load mode, with DISP=MOD, and using the insert call.

pcb-name

    The name of the GSAM PCB.

ioarea

    The name of the I/O area for get next and insert calls.

Table 15-4 contains the status codes that are associated with processing GSAM databases.

Table 15-4 Status Codes Associated with Processing GSAM Databases

Status Code	Meaning
bb	Successful call, proceed
GL	End of input data (get next calls only)
other	error situation

Record Formats

Records can be fixed length or variable length, blocked or unblocked. Records must not have a sequence key. The record in the IOAREA includes a halfword record length for variable-length records.

The use of GSAM data sets in a checkpoint/restart environment is discussed further in "Using Batch Checkpoint/Restart" on page 275.

COBOL AND PL/I PROGRAMMING CONSIDERATIONS

This section discusses programming considerations that are unique to the COBOL and PL/I programming languages.

The basic programming considerations for Java are discussed in Chapter 18, "Application Programming in Java," on page 311.

COBOL Programming Considerations

A few considerations apply when you are coding DL/I programs in COBOL. In the text that follows Figure 15-12, the numbers between parentheses map to the line numbers in Figure 15-12. Specific parameter values and formats are described throughout the rest of this chapter.

```
ID
  DIVISION.                                                         000001
                                                                    000002
ENVIRONMENT DIVISION.                                               000003
                                                                    000004
DATA DIVISION.                                                      000005
WORKING-STORAGE SECTION.                                            000006
77         GU-FUNC            PIC XXXX    VALUE    'GUbb'.           000007
77         GN-FUNC            PIC XXXX    VALUE    'GNbb'.           000008
77         ERROPT            PIC XXXX    VALUE    '1bbb'.            000009
77         DERRID            PIC X(8)     VALUE     'DERROR01'.      000010
01         IOAREA            PIC X(256) VALUE SPACES.               000011
01         SSA001-GU-SE1PART.                                       000012
           02 SSA001-BEGIN      PIC X(19) VALUE 'SE1PARTb(FE1PGPNRb='.  000013
           02 SSA001-FE1PGPNR   PIC X(8).                           000014
           02 SSA001-END        PIC X       VALUE ')'.              000015
                                                                    000016
LINKAGE SECTION.                                                    000017
01         D1PC.                                                    000018
           02   D1PCDBN  PIC X(8).                                  000019
           02   D1PCLEVL PIC 99.                                    000020
```

continues

Figure 15-12   Example of a COBOL Batch Program

```
          02    D1PCSTAT PIC XX.                                    000021
          02    D1PCPROC PIC XXXX.                                  000022
          02    D1PCRESV PIC S9(5) COMP.                            000023
          02    D1PCSEGN PIC X(8).                                  000024
          02    D1PCKFBL PIC S9(5) COMP.                            000025
          02    D1PCNSSG PIC S9(5) COMP.                            000026
          02    D1PCKFBA PIC X(20).                                 000027
                                                                    000028
PROCEDURE DIVISION.                                                 000029
  ENTRY 'DLITCBL' USING D1PC.                                       000030
    :                                                               000031
    :                                                               000032
  CALL 'CBLTDLI' USING GU-FUNC, D1PC, IOAREA,                       000033
      SSA001-GU-SE1PART.                                            000034
    :                                                               000035
  CALL 'CBLTDLI' USING GN-FUNC, D1PC, IOAREA.                       000036
  IF D1PCSTAT NOT = 'bb',                                           000037
     CALL 'ERRRTN' USING D1PC, DERRID, IOAREA, ERROPT.              000038
     MOVE +4 TO RETURN-CODE.                                        000039
    :                                                               000040
  CALL DFSOAST USING D1PC.                                          000041
    :                                                               000043
    :                                                               000044
  GOBACK.                                                           000045
```

Figure 15-12   Example of a COBOL Batch Program (Continued)

In Figure 15-12:

- The DL/I function codes (line 7), IOAREA (line 11), and segment search arguments (line 12) should be defined in the working-storage section of the data division. Typically, either the IOAREA is redefined to provide addressability to the fields of each segment, or separate IOAREAs are defined for each segment.
- The PCBS should be defined in the linkage section of the data division (line 18). When multiple database structures and thus multiple PCBs exist in a program, one PCB must be defined in the linkage section for each PCB in the PSB. However, these PCBs need not be in any specific order.
- Code an ENTRY statement (line 30) at the entry to your program. A parameter of the USING clause should exist for each database structure (PCB) that is used in your program. The order of PCBs in this clause must be the same as the order that is specified in PSB for your program.
- Each DL/I CALL statement should be coded like the statement on line 33. The parameters of the DL/I CALL statement differ in number for different functions and are explained elsewhere in this chapter.
- The status code in the PCB should be checked after each call (line 37). The status-code error routine (line 38) is described in "Status Code Processing" on page 228.

- At the end of processing, control must be returned to DL/I through a GOBACK statement (line 44). Optionally, you can set the COBOL RETURN-CODE (line 39). If DL/I detects no errors, and thus does not set the return code, the COBOL RETURN-CODE value is passed on to the next job step.

PL/I Programming Considerations

A few considerations apply when you are coding DL/I programs in PL/I. In the text that follows Figure 15-13, the numbers between parentheses map to the line numbers in Figure 15-13. Specific parameter values and formats are described throughout this rest of this chapter.

```
/*-------------------------------------------------------------------*/ 000001
/*                 SAMPLE PL/I PROGRAM                               */ 000002
/*-------------------------------------------------------------------*/ 000003
PE2PROD:                                                                 000004
PROCEDURE (DC_PTR,DB_PTR) OPTIONS (MAIN);                                000005
/*        DECLARE POINTERS AND PCBS.                                 */ 000006
 DECLARE                                                                 000007
   PLITDLI ENTRY,                           /* DL/I WILL BE CALLD*/ 000008
   DFSOAST ENTRY OPTIONS (ASSEMBLER INTER),  /* STATISTICS PRINT */ 000009
   DFSOAER ENTRY OPTIONS (ASSEMBLER INTER),  /* STATUS CODE PRINT */ 000010
   DC_PTR POINTER,                          /* CHPAT IN PSB      */ 000011
   DB_PTR POINTER,                      .   /* ORDER DB PCB      */ 000012
  01 CLPC BASED (DC_PTR),                    /* NOT USED IN       */ 000013
     02 DUMMY CHAR (32),                     /* BATCH DL/I        */ 000014
  01 DLPC BASED (DB_PTR),                    /* PHASE 2 ORDER DB  */ 000015
     02 DLPCDBDN CHAR (8),                   /* DBD NAME          */ 000016
     02 DLPCLEVL CHAR (2),                   /* SEGMENT LEVEL     */ 000017
     02 DLPCSTAT CHAR (2),                   /* STATUS CODE       */ 000018
     02 DLPCPROC CHAR (4),                   /* PROCESSING OPTN   */ 000019
     02 OLPCRESV FIXED BINARY(31),           /* RESERVED          */ 000020
     02 DLPCSEGN CHAR (8),                   /* SEGMENT NAME      */ 000021
     02 DLPCKFBL FIXED BINARY(31),           /* KEY FEEDBACK LNG  */ 000022
     02 DLPCNSSG FIXED BINARY(31),           /* NO. OF SENSEGS    */ 000023
     02 DLPCKFBA CHAR (14);                  /* KEY FEEDBACK      */ 000024
/*  DECLARE FUNCTION CODES, I/0 AREA, CALL ARG LIST LENGTHS         */ 000025
 DECLARE                                                                 000026
   IO_AREA CHAR (256),                      /* I/0 AREA          */ 000027
   GU_FUNC STATIC CHAR (4) INIT ('GU'),     /* CALL FUNCTION     */ 000028
   FOUR STATIC FIXED BINARY (31) INIT ( 4 ), /* ARG LIST LENGTH  */ 000029
   ERROPT1 CHAR (4) INIT ('0') STATIC,      /* OPTN FOR DFSOAER  */ 000030
   ERROPT2 CHAR (4) INIT ('2') STATIC,      /* FINAL OPTN:DFSOAER*/ 000040
   DERRID CHAR (8) INIT ('DERFORO1') STATIC; /* ID FOR DFSOAER   */ 000041
```

continues

Figure 15-13 Example of a PL/I Batch Program

```
/* DECLARE SEGMENT SEARCH AFGUMENT (SSA) - ORDER SEGMENT.     */ 000042
  DECLARE                                                         000043
    01 SSA007_GU_SE2ORDER,                                        000044
       02 SSA007_BEGIN CHAR (19) INIT ('SE2ORDER(FE2OGPEF ='),    000045
       02 SSA007_FE2OGPEF CHAR (6),                               000046
       02 SSA007_END CHAR (1) INIT ('1');                        000047
/* PROCESSING PORTION OF THE PROGRAM                          */ 000048
  SSA007_FE2OGPEF = 'XXXXXX';                /* SET SSA VALUE  */ 000049
  CALL PLITDLI (FOUR,GU_FUNC,DB_PTR,IO_AREA, /* THIS CALL WILL */ 000050
            SSA007_GU_SE2ORDER);             /* RETURN 'GE' STAT */ 000060
  IF DLPCSTAT ^= ' ' THEN DO;                /* CALL ERROR PRINT */ 000061
     CALL DFSOAER (DLPC,DERRID,IO_AREA,ERROPT1);                  000062
     CALL DFSOAER (DLPC,DERRID,IO_AREA,ERROPT2);/* FINAL CALL TO ERR */ 000063
  END;                                                            000064
/* RETURN TO CALLER.                                          */ 000065
  END PE2PROD;                                                    000066
```

Figure 15-13   Example of a PL/I Batch Program (Continued)

When DL/I invokes your PL/I program, it passes the addresses, in the form of pointers, to each PCB that is required for execution. These pointers are passed in the same sequence as specified in the PSB. To use the PCBs, you must code parameters in your PROCEDURE statement, and declare them to have the attribute POINTER.

In Figure 15-13, DC_PTR and DB_PTR are specified in the PROCEDURE statement (line 5) and declared as POINTER variables (lines 11 and 12). Use these pointer variables to declare the PCBs as BASED structures (lines 13 and 15), and in calling DL/I (line 50).

The format of the PL/I CALL statement to invoke DL/I (line 50) is:

```
CALL PLITDLI (parmcount, function, pcb-ptr, io-area,ssa1,...,ssan):
```

parmcount

The number of arguments in this call that follow this argument. The value of parmcount must have the attributes FIXED BINARY (31). See line 29.

function

The DL/I function code. The function code must be a fixed-length character string of length four.

pcb-ptr

A pointer variable that contains the address of the PCB. The pcb-ptr is normally the name of one of the parameters passed to your program at invocation.

io-area

The storage in your program into which and from which DL/I stores or fetches data. The io-area can be a major structure, a connected array, a fixed-length character string (CHAR (n)), a pointer to any of these, or a pointer to a minor structure. The io-area cannot be the name of a minor structure of a character string with the attribute VARYING.

ssa1...

One or more optional segment search arguments. Each SSA must be in one of the same PL/I forms allowed for io-areas. See line 44 in Figure 15-13 on page 264.

Upon completion of your program, you should return control to DL/I by either using a RETURN statement or by executing the main procedure END statement.

PROCESSING DATABASES WITH LOGICAL RELATIONSHIPS

Generally, there is no difference between the processing of physical databases and logical databases: all call functions are available for both. Some considerations do apply, however, when accessing a logical child of a concatenated segment.

Accessing a Logical Child in a Physical Database

When accessing a logical child in a physical DBD, you should remember the layout of the logical child. A logical child always consists of the logical parent concatenated key (that is, all the consecutive keys from the root segment down to and including the logical parent) plus the logical child itself: the intersection data (see Figure 15-5 on page 251). Understanding the layout of the logical child is especially important when inserting a logical child. You receive an IX status code when you try to insert a logical child and its logical parent does not exist (except at initial load time), which typically happens when you forget the logical parent's concatenated key (LPCK) in front of the logical child (LCHILD).

> **N O T E:** In general, do not use physical databases to process logical relationships.

Accessing Segments in a Logical Database

The following considerations apply for each call function when accessing segments in logical DBDs.

Retrieve Calls with a Logical Database

Retrieve calls work as described in "Retrieving Segments" on page 248 with the same status codes. However, the concatenated segment always consists of the logical child segment plus, optionally (dependent on the logical DBD), the destination parent segment.

Replace Calls with a Logical Database

In general, replace calls work the same as described in "Updating Segments" on page 252. When replacing a concatenated segment, you can replace both the logical child segment and the destination parent. However, you cannot change a sequence field. The following sequence fields can occur in a concatenated segment:

- Destination parent concatenated key.
- Real logical child sequence field: the sequence of the physical twin chain as defined for the real logical child. This field can partially overlap the logical parent concatenated key.
- Virtual logical child sequence field: that is, the sequence of the logical twin chain as defined for the virtual logical child. This field can partially overlap the physical parent concatenated key.
- The key of the destination parent itself.

If any of the sequence fields is changed during a replace operation, a DA status code is returned, and no data is changed in the database.

Delete Calls with a Logical Database

In general, delete calls work the same as described in "Deleting Segments" on page 253. However, if you delete a concatenated segment (either of the two versions), only the logical child and its physical dependents (the dependents of the real logical child) are deleted. The destination parent can be deleted only through its physical path: the delete is not propagated upwards across a logical relation. You can delete only those dependents of concatenated segments that are real dependents of the logical child. For example:

- If, in the logical DBD of Figure 7-6 on page 76, a PART segment is deleted, the associated STOCK and DETAIL segments are also deleted. However, the associated CUSTOMER ORDER and SHIPMENT segments remain.
- If, in the logical DBD of Figure 7-6 on page 76, a CUSTOMER ORDER segment is deleted, the associated DETAIL and SHIPMENT segments are also deleted. However, the associated PART and STOCK segments remain.

The logical child and its physical dependents are always deleted whenever one of its parents is deleted.

Insert Calls with a Logical Database

When you insert a concatenated segment, the destination parent must already exist in the database. You can provide the destination parent together with the logical child in the IOAREA, but that destination is not used. In addition to the normal status codes, an IX status code is returned when the destination parent does not exist.

PROCESSING DATABASES WITH SECONDARY INDEXES

Access to segments through a secondary index allows a program to process segments in an order that is not the physical sequence of the database. The order segment in Figure 7-6 on page 76 is a good example of how secondary indexes can be used. To process an order when only the customer order number is known, the ORDER segment can be accessed by using the customer order number. This is the simplest form of a secondary index.

Another basic use for a secondary index is to provide a method of processing a subset of the segments in a database without having to read the entire database. An example of this would be to provide a secondary index on a Balance-owing field in the customer database. The secondary index database could be defined to only contain those database records for which a non-zero balance is owing.

Accessing Segments by Using a Secondary Index

The format of the CALL statement parameters for accessing segments through a secondary index are identical to those used to access segments through the primary path. The difference is in how the PCB is coded in the PSB. The second PCB in the PSB in Figure 15-14 shows how to define a PCB that can be used to access a segment through a secondary index.

```
*
* PSB with Secondary index PCB
*
          PCB     TYPE=DB,PROCOPT=G,
                      DBDNAME=BE2CUST,,KEYLEN=6

          PCB     TYPE=DB,PROCOPT=G,
                      DBDNAME=BE2CUST,,PROCSEQ=FE2CNAM,,KEYLEN=20
*
                  SENSEG NAME=SE2PSCUST

    PSBGENG,LANG=COBOL,PSBNAME=SE2PCUST,CMPAT=YES
    END
```

Figure 15-14   Example of a PSB with a Secondary Index Defined

Retrieving Segments Using a Secondary Index

The same calls are used as described in "Retrieving Segments" on page 248. However, the index search field, which is defined by an XDFLD statement in the DBD, is used in the SSA for the get unique call of the root segment. The index search field defines the secondary processing sequence.

After the successful completion of this get unique call, the PCB and IOAREA look the same as after the basic get unique call in Figure 15-2 on page 248, except that the key feedback area now starts with the Customer name field.

When using the secondary processing sequence, consecutive get next calls for the CUSTOMER ORDER segment present the CUSTOMER ORDER segments in Customer name sequence.

If both the primary and the secondary processing sequence are needed in one program, you should use two PCBs, as shown in Figure 15-15.

```
77  GU-FUNC                        PICTURE XXXX     VALUE 'GUbb

01  SSA002-GU-SE2PCUST.
    02  SSA002-BEGIN               PICTURE x(19) VALUE 'SE2PCUSTb(FE2PCNAMb='.
    02  SSA002-FE2PCNAM PICTURE X(20).
    02  SS1002-END                 PICTURE X       VALUE ')'.

01  IOAREA                         PICTURE X(256).
---------------------------------------------------------------------------
MOVE CUSTOMER-NAME TO SSA002-FE2PCNAM.
CALL 'CBLTDLI' USING GU-FUNC,PCB-NAME,IOAREA,SSA002-GU-SE2PCUST.
---------------------------------------------------------------------------
STATUS CODES:
-------------
    bb:   succesfull call
    GE:   exceptional but correct condition
  other:  error condition
```

Figure 15-15   Example of a Get Unique Call Using a Secondary Index

Replacing Segments Using a Secondary Index

To replace segments in the indexed database, you can use a combination of get hold and replace calls, but you cannot change sequence fields. However, you can change index search fields. If you change an index search field, DL/I automatically updates the index database by deleting the old pointer segment and inserting a new pointer segment.

> **N O T E:** When you use a secondary processing sequence, you might need to access the database record again later.

Deleting Segments Using a Secondary Index

When using a secondary processing sequence, you cannot delete the index target segment (the root segment that depends on the definitions). If you must delete the index target segment, use a separate PCB with a primary processing sequence.

Inserting Segments Using a Secondary Index

When you use a secondary processing sequence, you cannot insert the index target segment. In all other cases, the insert call will work as described in "Inserting Segments" on page 254.

Creating Secondary Indexes

You can create a secondary index during the initial load of the indexed database, or later. The secondary index database is created by the DL/I reorganization utilities. No application programs are required.

LOADING DATABASES

When you design an application program to load databases, there are planning considerations for the application program and the PSB used. The following sections describe these considerations and describe the process of loading databases.

Overview of Loading Databases

When the load program inserts segments into the database, it builds the segments and inserts them in the database in hierarchical order. Often the data to be stored in the database already exists in one or more files, but merge and sort operations might be required to present the data in the correct sequence.

The process of loading a database is different than that of updating a database that is already populated with segments. Before the database can be used by most application programs, it must be initialized. A database can be initialized in several ways:

- Data reloaded by the Database Recovery utility
- Data loaded by a database reload utility
- Data loaded by a program with the processing option specified as PROCOPT=L (for full-function databases only)

After the database is initialized it remains so until it has been deleted and redefined. Therefore, it is possible to have an empty initialized database. A database that is not empty cannot be used by a PSB with a PROCOPT=L specified, nor can it be recovered or loaded with a reload utility.

If the database does not have secondary indexes or logical relationships, then the load process is very straightforward. Any program with PROCOPT=L specified can load the database. After that program completes and closes the database, the database can be used by any program for read or update purposes.

The loading of databases with logical relationships and secondary indexes is discussed in "Loading a Database That Has Logical Relationships" on page 271 and "Loading a Database That Has Secondary Indexes" on page 271.

Loading an HDAM Database

When you initially load an HDAM database, you should specify PROCOPT=L in the PCB. DL/I does not need to insert the database records in root key order, but you must still insert the segments in their hierarchical order.

For performance reasons, it is advantageous to sort the database records into sequence. The physical sequence should be the ascending sequence of the block and root anchor point values as generated by the randomizing module. You can achieve this sequence by using the Physical Sequence Sort for Reload tool, which is part of the IBM IMS High Performance Load for z/OS, V2 tool. This tool provides a sort exit routine that gives each root key to the randomizing module for address conversion and then directs the z/OS SORT utility to sort the database records based on the value that was generated from the address plus the root key.

Related Reading: For information about the IMS tools available from IBM, see Chapter 26, "IBM IMS Tools," on page 443.

Status Codes for Loading Databases   Table 15-5 shows the possible status codes returned when you load databases after issuing an insert call.

Table 15-5   Database Load Status Codes

Returned Status Code	Explanation
bb or CK	The segment is inserted in the database
LB	The segment already exists in the database
LC	The key field of the segment is out of sequence
LD	No parent has been inserted for this segment in the database
other	Error situation

Status Codes for Error Routines   Errors for status codes fall into two categories: those caused by application program errors, and those caused by system errors. Sometimes, however, a clear split cannot be made immediately.

Table 15-5 contains all the status codes you should expect using the examples in this book. See the DL/I status codes in *IMS Version 9: Messages and Codes, Volume 1* for a complete listing of all status codes.

Loading a HIDAM Database

When initially loading a HIDAM database, you must specify PROCOPT=LS (load segments in ascending sequence) in the PCB. Also, database records must be inserted in ascending root sequence and segments must be inserted in their hierarchical sequence.

Loading a Database That Has Logical Relationships

IMS provides a set of utility programs to establish the logical relationships during an initial load of databases with logical relationships. You must use the utilities because the sequence in which the logical parent is loaded is normally not the same as the sequence in which the logical child is loaded. To sort this out, IMS automatically creates a work file (whenever you load a database) that contains the necessary information to update the pointers in the prefixes of the logically related segments.

Logical relationship utilities do not apply to HALDBs. You cannot use a logical DBD when initially loading a database.

Figure 15-16 on page 272 illustrates the process of loading a database with logical relationships. The steps are as follows:

1. The pointers in the prefixes of the logically related segments are processed with the Database Prereorganization utility. This utility generates a control data set (DFSUR-CDS) that is used in subsequent utilities in this process (the HD Reorganization Reload utility, Database Prefix Resolution utility, and Database Prefix Update utility).

2. The databases are loaded with the HD Reorganization Reload utility. This utility generates a work file (DFSURWF1) that is used as input to the Database Prefix Resolution utility and also updates the information about the databases in the RECON data set. You must load all databases involved in the logical relationship and pass the work files to the Database Prefix Resolution utility

3. The work file (DFSURWF1) is sorted in physical database sequence by the Database Prefix Resolution utility. This utility also checks for missing logical parents and generates another work file (DFSURWF3).

4. The segment prefixes are then updated with the Database Prefix Update utility. After this step, the databases are ready to use.

If any of the databases involved in the logical relationship also have secondary indexes, then the process for loading a database with secondary indexes must be used as well. See Figure 15-18 on page 274 for an illustration of the complete process.

Loading a Database That Has Secondary Indexes

To load a database that has secondary indexes, the primary database must be uninitialized, as shown in Figure 15-17 on page 273. IMS extracts the required information into the work file to build the secondary index databases.

Figure 15-18 on page 274 illustrates the process of loading a database that has both logical relationships and secondary indexes.

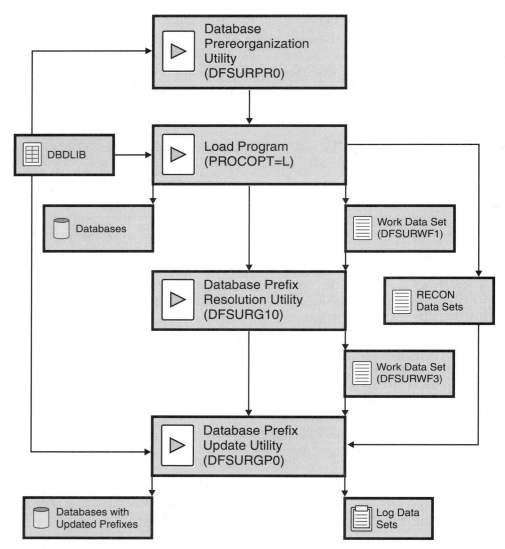

Figure 15-16   Loading a HIDAM Database That Has Logical Relationships

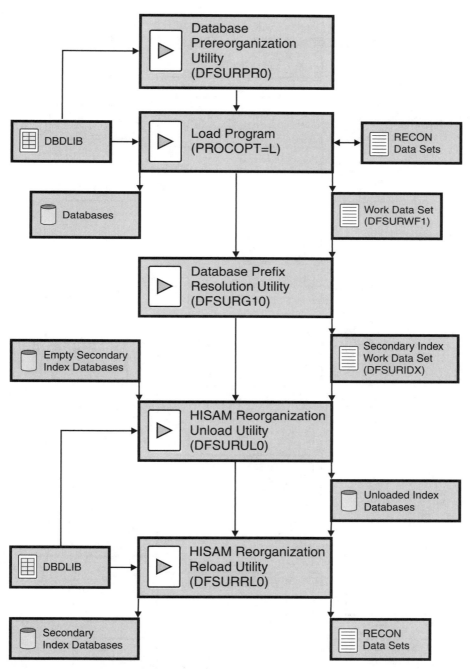

Figure 15-17 Loading a Database That Has Secondary Indexes

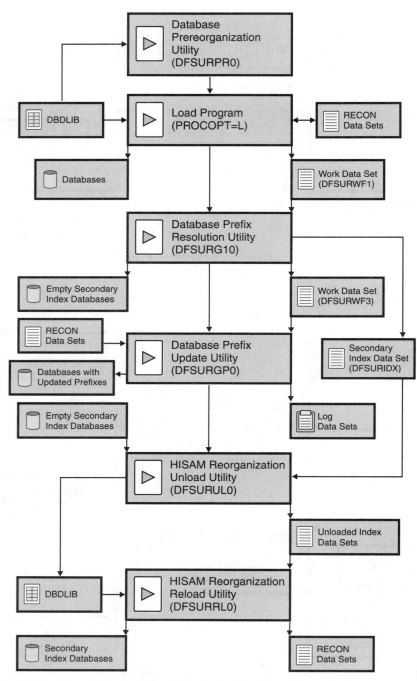

Figure 15-18   Loading a Database That Has Logical Relationships and Secondary Indexes

USING BATCH CHECKPOINT/RESTART

The DL/I batch checkpoint/restart facility allows long-running programs to be restarted (after a failure) at an intermediate point (not the beginning of the program). At regular intervals during application program execution (when the application issues CHKP calls), DL/I saves the designated working storage areas in the user's program, the position of GSAM databases, and the key feedback areas of non-GSAM databases. DL/I saves all this information on its log data set.

For each checkpoint, a checkpoint ID (message DFS681I) is written to the z/OS system console and to the job system output.

At restart, the restart checkpoint ID is supplied in the PARM field of the EXEC statement of the job. DL/I repositions the GSAM databases and restores the designated program areas as a result of a special restart call (XRST), which must be the first DL/I call in the program. At initial program execution, the XRST call identifies the potential program areas to be checkpointed by later CHKP calls.

For compatibility with BMP execution, always plan on restarting from the last successful checkpoint rather than from any previous checkpoint.

To use the DL/I checkpoint/restart function for batch programs, consider the following guidelines:

- All the data sets that the program uses must be DL/I databases. GSAM should be used for sequential input and output files, including SYSIN and SYSOUT. Any other file cannot be repositioned by DL/I and can result in duplicate or lost output.
- The GSAM output data sets should use DISP=(NEW,KEEP,KEEP) for the initial run, and DISP=(OLD,KEEP,KEEP) at restarts.
- SYSOUT should not be used directly. The output should be written to a GSAM file and printed with the additional job step. The DFSMSdfp IEBGENER (Sequential Copy/Generate Data Set) utility can be used for this purpose.
- The first call issued to DL/I must be an XRST call.
- You determine the frequency of the checkpoint call. A basic recommendation is one checkpoint for every 50 to 500 update transactions. Design your program so that you can easily adjust this frequency factor.
- After each checkpoint call, you must reposition your program in non-GSAM databases by issuing a get unique call for each of those databases. Repositioning of GSAM databases is done by DL/I, and you should proceed with a get next (input) or an insert (output) call.

The following sections discuss the restart call ("Using the Restart Call" on page 276) and the checkpoint call ("Using the Checkpoint Call" on page 277).

Using the Restart Call

Upon receiving the restart call (XRST), DL/I checks whether a checkpoint ID has been supplied in the PARM field of the EXEC card or in the work area pointed to by the restart call. If no ID has been supplied, a flag is set to trigger storing of repositioning data and user areas on subsequent checkpoint calls. That is, DL/I assumes that this is the initial program execution, not a restart.

If the checkpoint at which restart is to occur is supplied, the IMS batch restart routine reads backward on the log defined in the IMSLOGR DD statement in order to locate the checkpoint records. User program areas are restored.

The GSAM databases that are active at the checkpoint are repositioned for sequential processing. Key feedback information is provided in the PCB for each database active at the checkpoint. The user program must reposition itself on all non-GSAM databases, just as it must do after taking a checkpoint.

The format of the restart call in COBOL is:

```
CALL 'CBLITDLI'  using
call-func,IOPCB-name, I/O-area-len,work-area
[,1st-area-len, 1st rea,...,nth-area-len,nth-area].
```

The format of the restart call in PL/I is:

```
CALL PLITDLI
(parmcount,call-func,IOPCB-name. I/O-area-len,work-ar
[,1st-area-len,1st-area,...,nth-area-len,nth-area]):
```

The format of the restart call in Assembler is:

```
CALL
ASMTDLI,(call-func,IOPCB-name,I/O-area-len,work-area[,1st-area-len,
1st-area,...,nth-area-len,nth-rea]),
```

parmcount
> The name of a field that contains the number of arguments that follow. parmcount is mandatory for PL/I (as a fullword) and optional for other languages (as a halfword).

call-func
> The name of a field that contains the call function, XRST.

IOPCB-name
> The name of the I/O PCB or the dummy I/O PCB that is supplied by the CMPAT option in PSEGEN.

I/O-area-len

The name of the length field of the largest I/O area used by the user program. I/O-area-len must be a fullword.

work-area

The name of a 12-byte work area. This area should be set to blanks (X'40') before the call and tested on return. If the program is started normally, the area is unchanged. If the program is restarted from checkpoint, the ID supplied by the user in that checkpoint call and restart JCL is placed in the first eight bytes of the work area. If the user wants to restart the program from a checkpoint using a method other than IMS program restart, the user can use the restart call to reposition GSAM databases by placing the checkpoint ID in this work area before issuing the call. The checkpoint ID is the eight-byte left-aligned, user-supplied ID.

1st-area-len

The name of a field that contains the length of the first area to be restored. The field must be a fullword.

1st-area

The name of the first area to be restored.

nth-area-len

The name of a field that contains the length of the nth area to be restored. The maximum value for n is 7. The field must be a fullword.

Guidelines for Using the Restart Call

- The number of areas specified on the restart call must be equal to the maximum number that is specified on any checkpoint call.
- The lengths of the areas specified on the restart call must be equal to or larger than the lengths of the corresponding (in sequential order) areas of any checkpoint call.
- The restart call is issued only once, and it must be the first request made to DL/I.
- The only correct status code is bb. Any other status code implies an error condition.
- All area-len fields in PL/I must be defined as substructures. The name of the major structure should, however, be specified in the call.

Using the Checkpoint Call

When DL/I receives a checkpoint (CKPT) call from a program that initially issued a restart call, the following actions are taken:

- All database buffers modified by the program are written to DASD.
- A log record is written, specifying this ID, to the system console and job output data stream.

- The user-specified areas (for example, application variables and control tables) are recorded on the DL/I log data set. The user-specified areas should be specified in the initial restart call.
- The fully qualified key of the last segment processed by the program on each DL/I database is recorded in the DL/I log data set.

The format of the checkpoint call in COBOL is:

```
CALL 'OCBLTDLI' using
call-func,IOPCB-name, I/O-area-len,I/O=area
[,1st-area-len,1st-area,...,nth-area-len,nth-area]).
```

The format of the checkpoint call in PL/I is:

```
CALL PLITDLI [parmcount,
call-func,IOPCB-name,I/O-area-len, I/O-area
[,1st-area-len,1st-area,...,nth-area-len,nth-area]):
```

The format of the checkpoint call in Assembler is:

```
CALL ASMTDLI,
(call-func,IOPCB-name,I/O-area-len,I/O-area
[,1st-area-len,1st-area,...,nth-area-len,nth-area]):
```

parmcount
(PL/I only) The name of a binary fullword field that contains the number of arguments that follow.

call-func
The name of a field that contains the call function: CKPT.

IOPCB-name
The name of the I/O PCB or the dummy I/O PCB in batch.

I/O-area-len
The name of the length field of the largest I/O area used by the application program. I/O-area-len must be a fullword.

I/O-area
The name of the I/O area. The I/O area must contain the 8-byte checkpoint ID, which is used for operator or programmer communication and should consist of EBCDIC characters. In PL/I, this parameter should be specified as a pointer to a major structure, an array, or a character string.

The recommended format is MMMMnnnn, where:

MMMM   The 4-character program identification.

nnnn   The 4-character checkpoint sequence number, which is incremented at each checkpoint call.

1st-area-len (optional)

The name of a field that contains the length of the first area to checkpoint. 1st-area-len must be a fullword.

1st-area (optional)

The name of the first area to checkpoint.

nth-area-len (optional)

The name of the field that contains the length of the nth area to checkpoint. The maximum value for *n* is 7. nth-area-len must be a fullword.

nth-area (optional)

The name of the *n*th area to checkpoint. The maximum value for *n* is 7.

Guidelines for Using the Checkpoint Call

- The only correct status code in batch is bb. Any other specifies an error situation.
- Before restarting a program after failure, you must always correct the failure and recover or back out your databases. You must reestablish your position (issue a get unique call) in all IMS databases (except GSAM) after control returns from the checkpoint.
- All area-len fields in PL/I must be defined as substructures.
- Because the log data set is read forward during restart, the checkpoint ID must be unique for each checkpoint.

Application Programming for the IMS Transaction Manager

This chapter describes how to write application programs that run in the IMS TM environment.

In This Chapter:

- "Application Program Processing"
- "Transaction Manager Application Design" on page 289

APPLICATION PROGRAM PROCESSING

Online message processing (the work performed by an MPP) can be divided into six phases. Figure 16-1 on page 282 illustrates these phases, and the following list describes the phases.

The six phases of the flow of an MPP are:

1. Initialization

Initialization is the clearing of working storage, which might contain data that is left from processing a message from another terminal.

2. Retrieval of the scratch pad area (SPA) and input message

The application issues a DL/I message call (GU) to IMS TM to retrieve a message from the message queue. The application retrieves the SPA first if the transaction is conversational.

3. Status code check

The application checks the status code from IMS TM that indicates whether the message was successfully retrieved or not.

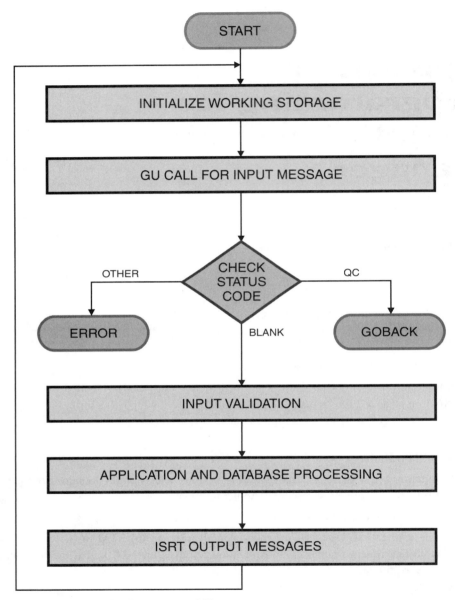

Figure 16-1   General MPP Structure and Flow

4. Input syntax check

IMS TM checks the syntax of the input message. All checks which can be done without accessing the database, including a consistency check with the status of the conversation as maintained in the SPA, are performed.

5. Database processing

Database processing is performed, preferably in one phase, which means that the retrieval of a database segment is immediately followed by its update. An example of database processing in more than one phase is to initially retrieve all the segments that the program requires and then perform a second retrieve and then update.

6. Output processing

The application builds an output message and sends it (by issuing DL/I message calls) to the originating (or other) logical terminal. The SPA is also inserted in the message queue if the transaction is conversational.

After finishing the processing of one input message, the program goes back to step 1 and requests a new input message. If there are no more input messages, IMS returns a status code indicating that, and then the MPP must return control to IMS.

Role of the PSB

In addition to database PCBs, the program specification block (PSB) for an MPP or a BMP contains one or more PCBs for logical terminal linkage. The first PCB (called the *I/O PCB*) always identifies the originating logical terminal. The I/O PCB must be referenced in the get unique (GU) and get next message (GN) calls. The I/O PCB must also be used when inserting output messages to that logical terminal. In addition, one or more alternate output PCBs (TP PCBs) can be defined. Their logical terminal destinations can be defined in the PCBs or set dynamically with change destination calls.

DL/I Message Calls

The same DL/I language interface that is used for the access of databases is used to access the message queues.

The principal DL/I message calls are:

GU (get unique)

Used to retrieve the first, or only, segment of the input message.

GN (get next)

Used to retrieve second and subsequent message segments.

ISRT (insert)

Used to insert an output message segment into the output message queue. These output messages are not sent until the MPP terminates or requests another input message by issuing a get unique call.

CHNG (change destination)

Used to set the output destination for subsequent insert calls.

The IMS Java function provides Java methods for the DL/I message calls. Examples are `IMS-MessageQueuegetNextMessage` and `IMSMessageQueue.insertMessage`.

For a detailed description of the DL/I database calls and guidelines for their use, see Chapter 15, "Application Programming for the IMS Database Manager," on page 241.

Conversational Processing

You can define a transaction code as belonging to a conversational transaction during IMS system definition. If the transaction code is defined as belonging to a conversational transaction, an application program that processes that transaction can interrelate messages from a given terminal. The vehicle to accomplish this is the scratch pad area (SPA). A unique SPA is created for each physical terminal that starts a conversational transaction.

Each time an input message is entered from a physical terminal in conversational mode, its SPA is presented to the application program as the first message segment (the actual input being the second segment). Before terminating or retrieving another message (from another terminal), the program must return the SPA to IMS with a message ISRT call.

The first time a SPA is presented to the application program when a conversational transaction is started from a terminal, IMS formats the SPA with binary zeroes (X'00'). If the program wants to terminate the conversation, it can indicate this by inserting the SPA with a blank transaction code.

Output Message Processing

As soon as an application reaches a synchronization point, its output messages in the message queue become eligible for output processing. A synchronization point is reached whenever the application program terminates or requests a new message from the input queue by issuing a GU call.

In general, output messages are processed by Message Format Service (MFS) before they are transmitted through the telecommunications access method.

Different output queues can exist for a given LTERM, depending on the message origin. They are, in transmission priority:

1. Response messages: messages that are generated as a direct response (same PCB) to an input message from this terminal.
2. Command responses.
3. Alternate output messages: messages generated through an alternate PCB.

Message Switching

A message switch is when a user wishes to send a message to another user. The basic format of a message switch is the destination LTERM name followed by a blank and the message text.

A program-to-program switch or program-to-program message switch is a program that is already executing that requests a new transaction be put on the IMS message queues for standard scheduling and execution.

This new transaction can:

- Continue the processing of the first transaction (which, in this case, has probably terminated) and respond (if required) to the originating terminal, which is probably still waiting for a response.
- Be a second transaction, purely an offshoot from the first, without any relationship or communications with the originating terminal. In this case, the original transaction must respond to the terminal, if required.

Application Program Termination

Application programs can terminate in two ways: normally or abnormally. The following sections describe both.

Normal Termination

Normal termination involves the program returning control to IMS TM when it finishes processing. When your program runs in a BMP or DB batch region, the program can set the return code and pass it to the next step in the job. If your program does not use the return code in this way, set the return code to zero as a programming convention.

> **RESTRICTION:** MPPs cannot pass return codes.

Abnormal Termination

When a message or batch-message processing application program is abnormally terminated for reasons other than a deadlock resolution, internal commands are issued to prevent rescheduling. These commands are the equivalent of a /STOP command, and they prevent continued use of the program and the transaction code in process at the time of abnormal termination. The master terminal operator can restart either or both stopped resources.

At the time abnormal termination occurs, a message is sent to the master terminal and to the input terminal that identifies the application program, transaction code, and input terminal. The message also contains the system and user completion codes. In addition, the first segment of the input transaction, in process by the application at abnormal termination, is displayed on the master terminal.

The database changes of a failing program are dynamically backed out. Also, its output messages inserted in the message queue since the last synchronization point are cancelled.

Logging and Checkpoint/Restart Processing

To ensure the integrity of its databases and message processing, IMS uses logging and checkpoint/restart processing. In case of a system failure, either software or hardware, IMS can be restarted. This restart includes the repositioning of users' terminals, transactions, and databases.

Logging

During IMS execution, all information necessary to restart the system in the event of hardware or software failure is recorded on an online log data set (OLDS). The following critical system information is recorded on the OLDS:

- The receipt of an input message in the input queue
- The start of an application program
- The receipt of a message by an application program for processing
- Before and after images of database updates by an application program
- The insert of a message into the queue by an application program
- The termination of an application program
- The successful receipt of an output message by the terminal

In addition to this logging, all previous database record unchanged data is written to the log data set. This log information is used only for dynamic backout processing of a failing application program. As soon as the application program reaches a synchronization point, the dynamic log information of this program is discarded.

Related Reading: For further information on IMS logging facilities, see Chapter 22, "IMS Logging," on page 367.

Emergency Restart

In case of failure, IMS is restarted with the log data set that is active at the time of failure. Restart processing backs out the database changes of incomplete MPPs and BMP programs. The output messages that are inserted by these incomplete MPPs are deleted.

After backout, the input messages are re-enqueued, the MPPs restarted, and the pending output messages are retransmitted. If a BMP is active at the time of failure, it must be resubmitted by using a z/OS job. If the BMP uses the restart and checkpoint calls, it must be restarted from its last successful checkpoint. In this way, missing or inconsistent output is avoided.

Program Isolation and Dynamic Logging

When processing DL/I database calls, the IMS *program isolation* function ensures database integrity.

With program isolation, all activity (database modifications and message creation) of an application program is isolated from any other application programs running in the system until an application program commits, by reaching a synchronization point, the data it has modified or created. This ensures that only committed data can be used by concurrent application programs. A synchronization point is established with a get unique call for a new input message (single mode) or a checkpoint call (BMP programs only), or program normal termination (GOBACK or RETURN). Program normal termination is not always sufficient; for example, Fast Path aborts the last unit of work if the program just returns without a synchronization point. Therefore, a good coding practice is to end the program immediately after a synchronization point.

Program isolation allows two or more application programs to concurrently execute with common data segment types even when the processing intent is segment update, add, or delete. IMS accomplishes this concurrency by using a dynamic enqueue/dequeue routine, which enqueues the affected database elements (segments, pointers, and free space elements) between synchronization points.

At the same time, the dynamic log modules log the prior database record images between those synchronization points. This logging makes it possible to dynamically back out the effects of an application program that terminates abnormally, without affecting the integrity of the databases controlled by IMS. The logging does not affect the activity of other application programs running concurrently in the system.

With program isolation and dynamic backout, it is possible to provide database segment occurrence level control to application programs. A means is provided for resolving possible deadlock situations in a manner transparent to the application program.

The following sequence of events is an example of a deadlock:

1. Program A updates database element X.
2. Program B updates database element Y.
3. Program A requests Y and must wait for the synchronization point of program B.
4. Program B in turn requests X and must wait for the synchronization point of program A.

A deadlock has now occurred: both programs are waiting for each other's synchronization point. The dynamic enqueue/dequeue routines of IMS intercept possible deadlocks during enqueue processing (in the above example, during enqueue processing of event 4).

When a deadlock situation is detected, IMS abnormally terminates (pseudo abends) one of the application programs involved in the deadlock. The activity of the terminated program is dynamically backed out to a previous synchronization point. Its held resources are freed, which allows the other program to process to completion. The transaction that was being processed by the abnormal terminated program is saved. If the application program is an MPP, it is rescheduled. For a BMP region, the job must be restarted. This process is transparent to application programs and terminal operators.

There are two situations where the enqueue/dequeue routines of program isolation are not used in processing a database call:

- If PROCOPT=GO (read only) is specified for the referenced segments of the call.
- If PROCOPT=E (exclusive) is specified for the referenced segments in the call, except in a data sharing environment.

Possible conflicts with exclusive extent are resolved during scheduling time and, as such, cannot occur at call time.

Keep the following considerations in mind when using PROCOPT=GO or PROCOPT=E :

- With the PROCOPT=GO option, a program can retrieve data that has been altered or modified by another program still active in another region, and database changes made by that program are subject to being backed out.
- Exclusive intent might be required for long-running BMP programs that do not issue checkpoint calls. Otherwise, an excessively large enqueue/dequeue table in main storage might result.
- Even when PROCOPT=E is specified, dynamic logging will be done for database changes. The ultimate way to limit the length of the dynamic log chain in a BMP is by using the restart and checkpoint calls. The chain is deleted at each checkpoint call because it constitutes a synchronization point.

- If one MPP and one BMP program are involved in a deadlock situation, the MPP is subject to the abnormal termination, backout, and reschedule process. IMS gives preference to the task that is less easily restarted.

Internal Resource Lock Manager (IRLM)

When an IMS is involved in a data-sharing environment with other IMS systems, IRLM is used instead of program isolation for lock management. See "Internal Resource Lock Manager" on page 43 for further details.

TRANSACTION MANAGER APPLICATION DESIGN

This section distinguishes between the following areas in the IMS database and data communication application design process:

- Online program design
- Message Format Service (MFS) design
- Database design

"Online Transaction Processing Concepts" describes some of the concepts that are important to designing application programs that run in IMS TM.

"Online Program Design" on page 292 concentrates on the design of message processing programs (MPPs).

"Basic Screen Design" on page 293 describes some of the concepts of 3270 screen layouts that IMS TM application programs must deal with if the application programs do not use the message format service (MFS). Chapter 17, "Editing and Formatting Messages," on page 297 discusses how MFS provides facilities to deal with 3270 screen layouts and operator interaction.

Although each of the above areas is discussed in separate sections, you need to realize that they depend upon each other. Therefore, an overall system design must be performed initially and an overall system review must follow the design phase of each section

Online Transaction Processing Concepts

In an IMS online environment, a transaction can be viewed from three different points:

- The application, by its processing characteristics and database accesses
- The terminal user
- The IMS system

Each of these views constitutes a set of characteristics. These characteristics are described in the following sections.

Application Characteristics

Generally, applications have two basic characteristics:

- Applications that collect or retrieve data (with no previous database access). This is not a typical IMS application but can be part of an IMS application system.
- Applications that update data. This normally involves database reference and the subsequent updating of the database. Most IMS applications have this characteristic.

In a typical IMS multi-application environment, these application characteristics are often combined. However, a single transaction normally has only one of the characteristics.

Terminal User Characteristics

From the terminal user's point of view, there exist:

- Single-interaction transactions
- Multi-interaction transactions

Single-interaction transactions do not impose any dependencies between an input message, its corresponding output, and the next input message.

Multi-interaction transactions constitute a dialogue between the terminal and the MPPs. Both the terminal user and the message processing rely on a previous interaction for the interpretation and processing of a subsequent interaction.

IMS System Characteristics

From the IMS system point of view, there exist:

- Non-response transactions
- Response transactions
- Conversational transactions

You define these IMS transaction characteristics for each transaction during IMS system definition.

With non-response transactions, IMS accepts multiple input messages (each being a transaction) from a terminal without a need for the terminal to first accept the corresponding output message, if any.

With response transactions, IMS does not accept further transaction input from the terminal before the corresponding output message is sent and interpreted by the user.

Conversational transactions are similar to response transactions, in that no other transactions can be entered from the terminal until the terminal is out of conversational mode. With response mode, the terminal is locked until a reply is received, but not for conversational mode. Another difference between the two is that for conversational transactions, IMS provides a unique scratch pad area (SPA) for each user to store vital information across successive input messages.

Transaction Response Time Considerations

In addition to the application, terminal user, and IMS system characteristics, the transaction response time is an important factor in the design of online systems. The *transaction response time* is the elapsed time between the entering of an input message by the terminal operator and the receipt of the corresponding output message at the terminal.

In general, two main factors constitute the transaction response time:

- The telecommunication transmission time, which is dependent on factors such as:
  - Terminal network configuration
  - Data communication access method and data communication line procedure
  - Amount of data transmitted, both input and output
  - Data communication line utilization
- The internal IMS processing time, which is mainly determined by the MPP service time. The MPP service time is the elapsed time required for the processing of the transaction in the MPR.

Choosing the Correct Characteristics

Categorize each IMS transaction by one of the previously described characteristics. Some combination of the characteristics are more likely to occur than others. The combinations depend on your application's needs.

Choose which combination is attributed to a given transaction. Selecting the appropriate characteristics is an essential, deliberate part of the design process, rather than determining the characteristics after implementation.

Following are some examples:

- Assume you need to design an inquiry for the customer name and address, with the customer number as input. The most straightforward way to implement this is as a non-conversational response-type transaction.
- The entry of new customer orders could be done by a single response transaction. The order number, customer number, detail information, part number, and quantity all could be entered at the same time. The order would be processed completely with one interaction. This is most efficient for the system, but it might be cumbersome for the terminal user who has to reenter the complete order in the case of an error.

Quite often, different solutions are available for a single application. Choose your solution based on a trade-off between system cost, functions, and user convenience. The following sections will highlight this for the different design areas.

Online Program Design

Online program design is second in importance to database design. In this section, discussion of this broad topic is limited to the typical IMS environment.

The following sections discuss a number of considerations that can influence your program design decisions.

Single versus Multiple Passes

A transaction can be handled with one interaction or pass, or with two or more passes. Each pass bears a certain cost in transmission time and in IMS and MPP processing time. In general, you should use as few passes as possible. Whenever possible, use the current output screen to enter the next input. This is generally easy to accomplish for transactions that query or retrieve data (with no updates), where the lower part of the screen can be used for input and the upper part for output (see "Basic Screen Design" on page 293).

For update transactions, the choice is more difficult. The basic alternatives are:

One-pass update

> After input validation, the database updates are all performed in the same pass, which is the most efficient way from the system point of view. However, correcting errors after the update confirmation is received on the terminal requires additional passes or the reentering of data. You must evaluate the expected error rate.

Two-pass update

> On the first pass, the input is validated, including database access, and a status message is sent to the terminal. If the terminal operator agrees, the database is updated in the second pass. With this approach, making corrections is generally much simpler, especially when a scratch pad area is used. However, the database is accessed twice.

> Except for the SPA, no correlation exists between successive interactions from a terminal. So the database can be updated by another user and the MPP can process a message for another terminal between the two successive passes.

Multi-pass update

> In a multi-pass update, each pass partially updates the database. The status of the database and screen is maintained in the SPA. Take this approach only for complex transactions. Also, remember that the terminal operator experiences response times for each interaction. You also must consider the impact on database integrity. IMS backs out only the database changes of the current interaction in the case of project or system failure.

> An IMS emergency restart with a complete log data set repositions the conversation. The terminal operator can proceed from the point at the time of failure. When a conversational application program terminates abnormally, only the last interaction is backed out, so the application must reposition the conversation after correction. For complex situations, IMS

provides the Conversational Abnormal Termination exit routine (DFSCONE0). For more information about this exit routine, see *IMS Version 9: Customization Guide*.

Conversational Transactions versus Non-Conversational Transactions

Conversational transactions are generally more expensive in terms of system cost than non-conversational ones. However, conversational transactions give better terminal operator service. Use conversational transactions only when required. Also, with the proper use of MFS, the terminal operator procedures sometimes can be enhanced to almost the level of conversational processing.

Transaction or Program Grouping

As the program designer, it is your choice how much application function is implemented by one transaction or program. The following considerations apply:

- Inquiry-only transactions should be simple transactions and normally should be implemented as non-conversational transactions. Also, simple transactions can be defined as "non-recoverable inquiry-only". If, in addition, the associated MPPs specify read without integrity (PROCOPT=GO) in all their database PCBs, no dynamic enqueue and logging will be done for these transactions and reading is without integrity.
- Limited-function MPPs are smaller and easier to maintain. However, a very large number of MPPs costs more in terms of IMS resources, such as control blocks and path lengths.
- Transactions with a long MPP service time involving many database accesses should be handled by separate programs.

As mentioned in "Message Switching" on page 285, IMS TM provides a program-to-program message switch capability. You can split transaction processing in two or more phases by using message switches. The first (foreground) MPP does the checking and switches a message (and, optionally, the SPA) to a background MPP in a lower-priority partition. The background MPP performs the lengthy part of the transaction processing, thus making the foreground MPP available to service other terminals. Also, if no immediate response is required from the background MPP and the SPA is not switched, the terminal is more readily available for entering another transaction.

Basic Screen Design

When you design 3270-type screen applications that use MFS, you need to understand basic screen design, which is described in this section. For more information about screen design and MFS, see:

- *IMS Version 9: Administration Guide: Transaction Manager*
- *IMS Version 9: Application Programming: Transaction Manager*

Generally, a screen can be divided into five areas, from top to bottom:

1. Primary output area: contains general, fixed information for the current transaction. The fields in this area should generally be protected.
2. Detail input/output area: used to enter or display the more variable part of the transaction data. Accepted fields should be protected (under program control) because fields in error can be displayed with high intensity and unprotected to allow for corrections.
3. MPP error message area: In general, one line is sufficient. The MPP error message area can be the same line as a system message field.
4. Primary input: the requested action or transaction code for next input, and the primary database access information.
5. System message field: used by IMS to display system messages and by the terminal operator to enter commands.

For readability, separate the screen areas by at least one blank line. IBM recommends that you develop a general screen layout and a set of formats that can be used by incidental programs and programs in their initial test, which can significantly reduce the number of format blocks needed and simplify maintenance.

Installation standards should be defined for a multi-application environment.

General Screen Layout Guidelines
Observe the following performance guidelines when you design screen layouts:

- Avoid full-format operations. IMS knows what format is on the screen. If the format for the current output is the same as the format that is on the screen, IMS need not retransmit all the literals and unused fields.
- Avoid unused fields, such as undefined areas on the screen. Use the attribute byte (non-displayed) of the next field as a delimiter, or expand a literal with blanks. Each unused field causes 5 additional control characters to be transmitted across the line during a full-format operation. Weigh the cost of transmitting the 5 additional control characters against the benefits of user convenience.

Including the Transaction Code in the Format
IMS requires a transaction code as the first part of an input message. With MFS, this transaction code can be defined as a literal. In doing so, the terminal operator always enters data on a preformatted screen. The initial format is retrieved with the /FORMAT command.

To allow for multiple transaction codes in one format, part of the transaction code can be defined as a literal in the message input descriptor (MID). The rest of the transaction code can then be entered by using a DFLD statement in the format. This method is very convenient for the terminal operator, who does not have to be aware of the actual transaction codes.

General IMS TM Application Design Considerations

Keep the following points in mind when you design IMS TM applications that use MFS:

- A conversation is terminated (a blank transaction code is inserted in the SPA) after each successfully completed transaction. This termination is transparent to the terminal operator because the output format is linked to a MID that contains the transaction code, so the operator does not need to reenter the transaction code.

- Each output message should contain all the data (except the literals that are defined in the message output descriptor) to be displayed. Do not rely on already existing data on the screen because a clear screen operation or a restart operation might have destroyed the data.

- Using secondary indexing can significantly increase the accessibility of online databases. Therefore, a wider use of this facility is discussed in "Secondary Index Databases" on page 77.

CHAPTER 17

Editing and Formatting Messages

IMS uses two methods to edit and format messages to and from terminals: Message Format Service (MFS) and basic edit routines. IMS also provides exit routines to edit:

- Input and output from a terminal
- Transaction codes
- Input message fields
- Input message segments
- Message switching

This chapter presents an overview of MFS, introduces MFS control blocks for message formatting, summarizes the responsibilities of the MFS administrator, and presents an overview of the IMS basic edit function.

Related Reading:

- For more information about the exit routines that are delivered with IMS, see *IMS Version 9: Customization Guide*.
- For more information about MFS and the basic edit function, see *IMS Version 9: Administration Guide: Transaction Manager*.

In This Chapter:

MESSAGE FORMAT SERVICE

MFS is an IMS facility that formats messages to and from terminals so that IMS application programs need not deal with device-specific characteristics in input or output messages.

MFS formats messages to and from user-written programs in remote controllers and subsystems so that host application programs need not deal with terminal-specific characteristics of the remote controller.

> **RESTRICTION:**   MFS does not support LU 6.2 devices. The LU 6.2 Edit exit routine (DFSLUEE0), which is supplied with IMS, can edit both input and output messages from LU 6.2 devices when the implicit API support is used.

MFS uses control blocks that the user specifies to indicate to IMS how input and output messages are arranged.

- For input messages, MFS control blocks define how the message that is sent by the device to the application program is arranged in the program's I/O area.
- For output messages, MFS control blocks define how the message that is sent by the application program to the device is arranged on the screen or at the printer. Data such as literals that appear on the screen but not in the program's I/O area can also be defined.

In IMS systems, data that is passed between the application program and terminals or remote programs can be edited by MFS or the basic edit function. The facilities provided by MFS depend on the type of terminals or secondary logical units (SLUs) your network uses.

MFS allows application programmers to deal with logical messages instead of device-dependent data; this simplifies application development. The same application program can deal with different device types using a single set of logic, whereas device input and output varies for specific device types.

Figure 17-1 on page 299 shows how MFS can make an application program device-independent by formatting input data from the device or remote program for presentation to IMS, and by formatting the application program data for presentation to the output device or remote program.

The presentation of data on the device or operator input can be changed without changing the application program. Full paging capability is provided by IMS for display devices. Input messages can be created from multiple screens of data.

With MFS, you do not need to design your program for the physical characteristics of the device that is used for input and output messages unless the program uses very specific device features.

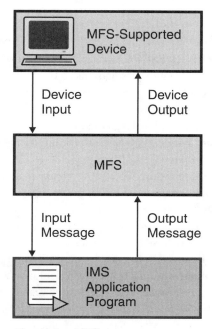

Figure 17-1 Message Formatting Using MFS

Even when these features are used, the program can request that MFS assist in their presentation to the program or the device.

MFS supports SLU-type devices SLU-1, SLU-2, SLU-P, Finance, and LU 6.1. MFS also supports older devices, including IBM 2740, 2741, 3270, and 3600.

For IBM 3270 or SLU-2 devices, device control characters or orders can be sent directly from or received by the program using the MFS bypass function. This gives the application program more direct control of the data stream. The program uses reserved format names that cause MFS not to edit:

- Output messages
- The next input message that is received from the display terminal

Using MFS bypass is usually confined to special application programs such as those that invoke Graphical Data Display Manager (GDDM) to display graphical data.

Both logical and physical paging facilities are provided for the IBM 3270 and 3604 display stations. These facilities allow the application program to write large quantities of data that MFS can divide into multiple display screens on the terminal. The terminal operator can then page forward and backward to different screens within the message.

MFS Components

MFS has several components:

- **MFS Language utility (DFSUPAA0):** Executes offline to generate control blocks from user-written control statements and places the control blocks in a format data set named IMS.FORMAT. The control blocks describe the message formatting that is to take place during message input or output operations. The control blocks are generated according to a set of utility control statements.
- **MFS message editor:** Formats messages according to the control block specifications generated by the MFS Language utility.
- **MFS pool manager:** Keeps the MFS control blocks that are required by the MFS message editor in the main-storage MFS buffer pool.
- **MFS Service utility (DFSUTSA0):** Used for maintenance of the control blocks in IMS.FORMAT. The MFS Service utility provides a method for additional control of the format control block data sets. It executes offline and is able to create and maintain an index of control blocks for online use by the MFS pool manager.
- **MFSTEST pool manager:** Replaces the MFS pool manager when the MFS Language utility is being used in test mode. The /TEST command with the MFS keyword places a logical terminal into MFSTEST mode. For each terminal in MFSTEST mode, combining temporary format blocks with the use of other blocks that are already in production mode allows new applications and modifications to existing applications to be tested without disrupting production activity.
- **MFS Device Characteristics Table (MFSDCT) utility (DFSUTB00):** Defines new screen sizes in a descriptor member of the IMS.PROCLIB library without performing an IMS system definition. These new screen size definitions are added to the screen sizes that were previously defined.

IMS online change also plays an important part in updating the MFS libraries, even though it is not part of MFS. Briefly, online change allows the control block libraries to be modified while the IMS control region is running.

Related Reading: For a complete description of online change, see *IMS Version 9: Administration Guide: System.*

Figure 17-2 on page 301 shows an overview of the MFS utilities and their output. For information about these utilities, see *IMS Version 9: Utilities Reference: Database and Transaction Manager.*

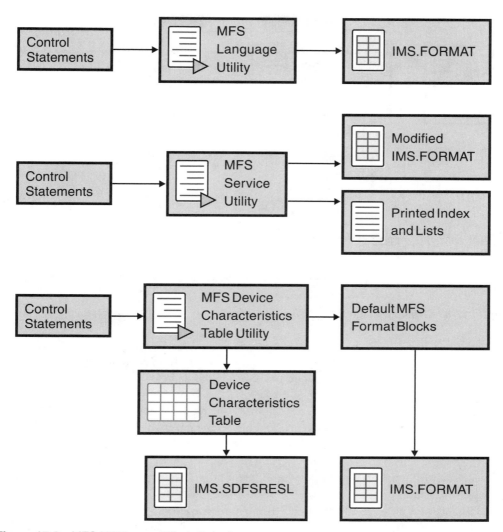

Figure 17-2   MFS Utilities and Their Output

Figure 17-3 on page 302 shows the MFS online environment. The steps that follow correspond to the numbers in Figure 17-3.

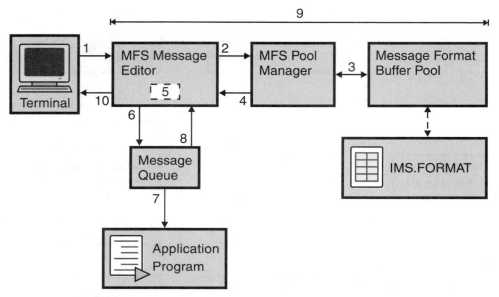

Figure 17-3   Overview of the MFS Online Environment

1. An input message is sent to the MFS message editor from the terminal.
2. The MFS message editor requests a pointer (the address) to the MFS control blocks from the MFS pool manager.
3. The MFS pool manager checks the message format buffer pool to see if the control blocks exist in the pool. If the control blocks are not in the buffer pool, the MFS pool manager reads the control blocks from IMS.FORMAT and places them in the buffer pool.
4. The MFS pool manager sends the address of the MFS control blocks to the MFS message editor.
5. The MFS message editor formats the input message for the application program.
6. The MFS message editor sends the formatted input message to the message queue to be processed.
7. The application program processes the message and sends the output message to the message queue.
8. The output message is sent from the message queue to the MFS message editor.
9. MFS processes the output message for the terminal just as it processed the input message (steps 2 through 6).
10. The formatted output message is sent to the terminal.

Figure 17-4 show the MFS test environment. The steps that follow correspond to the numbers in Figure 17-4.

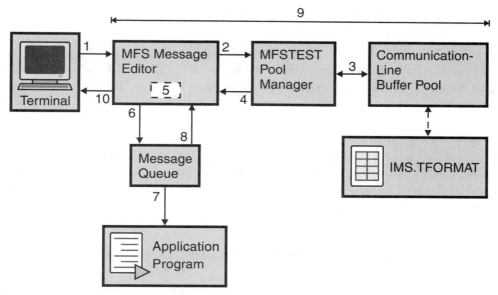

Figure 17-4 Overview of the MFS Test Environment

1. The input message is sent to the MFS message editor from the terminal.

2. The MFS message editor requests a pointer to MFS control blocks from the MFSTEST pool manager.

3. The MFSTEST pool manager checks the communication-line buffer pool to see if the control blocks exist in the buffer pool. If the blocks are not in the buffer pool, the MFS pool manager reads the blocks from IMS.TFORMAT and places them in the buffer pool.

4. The MFSTEST pool manager sends the address of the MFS control blocks to the MFS message editor.

5. The MFS message editor formats the input message for the application program.

6. The MFS message editor sends the formatted input message to the message queue to be processed.

7. The application program processes the message and sends the output message to the message queue.

8. The output message is sent from the message queue to the MFS message editor.

9. MFS processes the output message for the terminal just as it processed the input message (steps 2 through 6).

10. The formatted output message is sent to the terminal.

The MFS message editor and MFS pool manager operate online during the normal production mode of operation. The MFS message editor performs the actual message formatting operations using the control block specifications.

In MFS test mode, the MFS Language utility can run at the same time as the online IMS control region. However, you must use the online change procedure to modify MFS formats when not in IMS test mode.

Administering MFS

To take full advantage of the flexible message formatting options offered by MFS and to ensure efficient MFS operation, you should appoint an MFS administrator. The MFS administrator is responsible for MFS implementation and administration and should coordinate MFS application design and programming for the installation.

The responsibilities of an MFS administrator include:

- Establishing procedures for the submission of MFS control block requests by application development personnel.
- Establishing procedures and controls for the application of changes to the IMS.TFOR-MAT library.
- Defining MFS control blocks most efficiently in keeping with the requirements of the specific application and the overall system.
- Minimizing device character transmission, sharing MFS control blocks, and ensuring the most efficient use of MFS without jeopardizing application requirements or operator considerations.
- Establishing and documenting operator guidelines and system standards for MFS. The many options that MFS offers can result in confusing practices, unless you establish and follow standard procedures. Be sure to standardize certain aspects of format design in order to minimize terminal operator training and error rates.
- Deciding if and how the optional index directory should be used and determining buffer pool requirements.
- Monitoring the use of the MFS control blocks and of the MFS buffer pool with the IMS /DISPLAY command and IMS Monitor report output, and modifying MFS parameters as required.
- Making end users aware of the operating characteristics of the different device types and terminal subsystems.
- Informing others about the differences between the various partition formats.
- Establishing and informing others about naming conventions and guidelines. In particular, the MFS administrator should be able to discuss naming conventions for the partition descriptor blocks and the sizes of the display screen, the viewports, and the display characters.
- Communicating information about conventions for and restrictions on MFS formats.

- Defining screen sizes and feature combinations that are not included in the IMS stage–1 system definition.
- Creating the MFS device characteristics table control statements for processing by the MFSDCT utility (DFSUTB00). The MFS device characteristics table entries and default format control blocks are used for ETO terminals.
- Defining input message field edit routines and segment edit routines. MFS and all MFS-supported devices are able to use message edit routines. You can use these exit routines for such common editing functions as numeric validation or the conversion of blanks to zeros.

  IMS provides a sample of both a field edit and a segment edit routine.

  Related Reading: For information about the timing within the MFS editing processing when these routines are activated, and the coding requirements for the routines, see *IMS Version 9: Application Programming: Transaction Manager.*

The MFS administrator should be technically competent in all aspects of IMS relative to MFS, including:

- Online transaction processing
- IMS API for message processing
- Operation with remote controllers
- MFS implementation, device characteristics, and capabilities
- Interpretation of MFS statistics and related IMS Monitor report output

The administrator should also be familiar with the hardware and remote programs for SLU-P, Finance remote programs, or ISC subsystems if such programs are going to operate with MFS by using distributed presentation management.

In addition, the administrator should be familiar with the terminal hardware characteristics because one administrative responsibility is minimizing device character transmission.

An MFS administrator must communicate with IMS system administrators and application developers, as well as programmable workstation developers and end users. The MFS administrator must be able to enforce installation standards and to modify application specifications for MFS control blocks when necessary to benefit overall system performance. The procedures of related programming groups should recognize this authority of the MFS administrator.

MFS Control Blocks

MFS uses the following four types of control blocks to format input and output messages for application programs, terminals, or remote programs:

- **Message output descriptors (MODs):** Define the layout of messages that MFS receives from the application program

- **Device output formats (DOFs):** Describe how MFS formats messages for each of the devices with which the program communicates
- **Device input formats (DIFs):** Describe the formats of messages MFS receives from each of the devices with which the program communicates
- **Message input descriptors (MIDs):** Describe how MFS formats messages so that the application program can process them

A MID and MOD that work together as a set are collectively called a *message descriptor*. A DIF and DOF that work together as a set are collectively called a *device format*.

Because each MOD, DOF, DIF, and MID deals with a specific message, both a MOD and DOF must exist for each unique message that a program sends, and both a DIF and MID must exist for each unique message that a program receives.

Figure 17-5 shows how the input data from a terminal in formatted mode is mapped by MFS (using a DIF and a MID) to the message format that is presented to the application program.

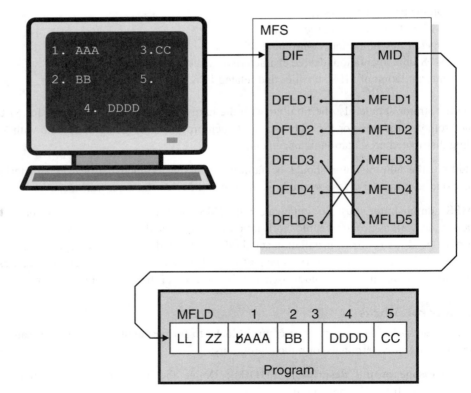

Figure 17-5   MFS Input Formatting

In Figure 17-5, the DIF contains a list of device descriptor fields (DFLDs) that define what data is expected from which part of the device (that is, the location on the screen). The MID contains a list of message descriptor fields (MFLDs) that define the layout of the input segment as it is presented to the application program. MFS maps the data of the DFLDs into the corresponding MFLDs. The application program is primarily device independent because different physical inputs can be mapped into the same input segment. When the application program finishes its processing, the reverse mapping process occurs to deliver the result back to the device.

MFLD statements define:

- The device fields (DFLDs) defined in the DIF, the contents of which are included in the message presented to the application program.
- Constants, defined as literals to be included in the message: A common use of literals is to specify the transaction code.

In addition, the MFLD statement defines:

- The length of the field expected by the application program
- Left or right justification and the fill character to be used for padding the data received from the device
- A 'nodata' literal for the MFLD if the corresponding DFLD does not contain any input data

Advantages to Using MFS

Two primary advantages to using MFS are that it:

- Simplifies the development and maintenance of terminal-oriented application systems
- Improves online performance

To simplify IMS application development and maintenance, MFS performs many common application program functions and gives application programs a high degree of independence from specific devices or remote programs.

With the device independence (the ability to communicate with different types of terminals without having to change the way it reads and builds messages) offered by MFS, one application program can process data to and from multiple device types while still taking advantage of their different capabilities. Thus, MFS can eliminate or minimize the changes in application programs when new terminal types are added.

When the application program receives a message from a terminal, how the message appears in the program's I/O area is independent of the type of terminal that sent it; the appearance depends on the MFS options specified for that program. If the next message that the application program receives is from a different type of terminal, the user does not need to do anything to the application program. MFS shields the application program from the physical device that is sending the message in the same way that a database program communication block (PCB) shields a program from the data in the database and how it is stored.

Other common functions MFS performs include left or right justification of data, padding, exit routines for validity checking, time and date stamping, page and message numbering, and data sequencing and segmenting. When MFS performs these functions, the application program handles only the actual processing of the message data.

Related Reading: For information on user-written exit routines and how to use them, see *IMS Version 9: Customization Guide*.

MFS also improves online performance of a terminal-oriented IMS by using control blocks that are designed for online processing. The MFS control blocks are compiled offline, when IMS is not being executed, from source language definitions. MFS can check their validity and make many decisions offline to reduce online processing. In addition, during online processing, MFS uses look-aside buffering of the MFS control blocks in order to reduce CPU usage and the channel costs of input/output activity.

Online storage requirements are also reduced because MFS control blocks are reentrant and can be used for multiple applications. Optional main-storage indexing and anticipatory fetching of the control blocks can also reduce response time. IMS gains additional performance improvements because multiple I/O operations can execute concurrently in loading the format blocks from the MFS format library.

In addition, MFS uses z/OS paging services to reduce page faults by the IMS control region.

Finally, MFS can reduce the volume of data that travels across communication lines. Compressing and transmitting only the required data reduces line load and improves both response time and device performance.

BASIC EDIT FUNCTION

If you do not use MFS, the IMS basic edit function performs message editing.

For input messages, the basic edit function:

- Translates messages to uppercase, if specified by the EDIT=UC parameter on the system definition TRANSACT macro.
- Removes leading control characters from the first segment of each message. Leading blanks are also removed from the first segment if the message is not the continuation of a conversation or a message from a terminal that is in preset mode.
- Removes leading control characters from all subsequent message segments, if the message type is a transaction or a command (except the /BROADCAST command).
- Removes line control characters from all segments.

- Removes trailing carriage return and end-of-block characters from all segments of a transaction.
- Eliminates backspaces, on a one-for-one basis, from all segments when the entering or transmission of backspaces is a normal correction procedure on the entering terminal.
- Removes the password and replaces it with a blank when necessary to provide separation between the transaction code, logical terminal, or command verb and the data that follows.
- Inserts, in front of data that is entered in the first segment of a message, the transaction code or logical terminal name defined by the prior / SET command. A blank is inserted following the transaction code if it is necessary to obtain separation between the inserted transaction code and the entered data.
- Adds a non-conversational transaction code to the first segment of the next input message, if a terminal is in conversation mode and the application terminates the conversation by inserting a non-conversational transaction code into the SPA.
- Removes the function management header (FMH), if any, that appears at the beginning of the first transmission of a chain for VTAM-supported devices.
- Deblocks message segments at each interrecord separator (IRS) control character, and discards the IRS control character for input from a SLU–1 card reader, a transmit data set (TDS), or a user data set (UDS).
- Deblocks message segments at each new line or form-feed control character if the optional MFS editing is not selected for SLU–1 consoles. This character can be discarded, depending on the criteria previously described.
- Treats the presence of a TRN (X'35') character immediately followed by a length in the next byte as transparent data.

For output messages, the basic edit function:

- Changes nongraphic characters in the output message before the data goes to the device
- Inserts any necessary idle characters after new-line, line-feed, and tab characters
- Adds line control characters for the operation of the communication line

For basic edit support of SLU–1 transparent data, basic edit does not alter or delete characters following the destination and password fields if transparent processing has been requested. Indicate transparent processing by specifying:

- BINPDSB1=BINTRNDS on the bind image for VTAM-type SLU–1 terminals
- Edit option BASIC=TRN on the COMPT1 parameter of the IMS TERMINAL macro or ETO descriptors for SLU–1 terminals

Related Reading: For more information about the basic edit function, see *IMS Version 9: Administration Guide: Transaction Manager.*

CHAPTER 18

Application Programming in Java

The IMS Java function implements the JDBC API, which is the standard Java interface for database access. JDBC uses SQL (structured query language) calls. The IMS's implementation of JDBC supports a selected subset of the full facilities of the JDBC 2.1 API. The IMS-supported subset of SQL provides all of the functionality (select, insert, update, delete) of traditional IMS applications.

The IMS Java function also extends the JDBC interface for storage and retrieval of XML documents in IMS. For more information, see "XML Storage in IMS Databases" on page 321.

In addition to JDBC, the IMS Java function has another interface to the IMS databases called the *IMS Java hierarchical database interface*. This interface is similar to the standard IMS DL/I database call interface and provides lower-level access to IMS database functions than the JDBC interface. However, JDBC is the recommended access interface to IMS databases, and this chapter focuses on JDBC. For information about the IMS Java hierarchical database interface, see Appendix C, "IMS Java Hierarchical Database Interface" in *IMS Version 9: IMS Java Guide and Reference*.

In This Chapter:

DESCRIBING AN IMS DATABASE TO THE IMS JAVA FUNCTION

In order for a Java application to access an IMS database, it needs information about the database. This information is contained in the PSB (program specification block) and in DBDs (database descriptions), which you must first convert into a form that you can use in the Java application: a subclass of the `com.ibm.ims.db.DLIDatabaseView` class called the IMS Java metadata class. The DLIModel utility generates this metadata from the IMS PSBs, DBDs, COBOL copybooks, and other input specified by utility control statements.

In addition to creating metadata, the DLIModel utility also:

- Generates XML schemas of IMS databases. These schemas are used when retrieving XML data from or storing XML data in IMS databases.
- Incorporates additional field information from XMI input files that describe COBOL copybooks.
- Incorporates additional PCB, segment, and field information, or overrides existing information.
- Generates a DLIModel IMS Java Report, which is designed to assist Java application programmers. The DLIModel IMS Java Report is a text file that describes the Java view of the PSB and its databases.
- Generates an XMI description of the PSB and its databases.

The DLIModel utility can process most types of PSBs and databases. For example, the utility supports:

- All database organizations except MSDB, HSAM, SHSAM, and GSAM
- All types and implementations of logical relationships
- Secondary indexes, except for shared secondary indexes
- Secondary indexes that are processed as standalone databases
- PSBs that specify field-level sensitivity

The DLIModel utility is a Java application, so you can run it from the UNIX System Services prompt, or you can run it using the z/OS-provided BPXBATCH utility.

Figure 18-1 on page 313 shows the inputs to and outputs from the DLIModel utility.

Related Reading: For more information about the DLIModel utility, see *IMS Version 9: Utilities Reference: System.*

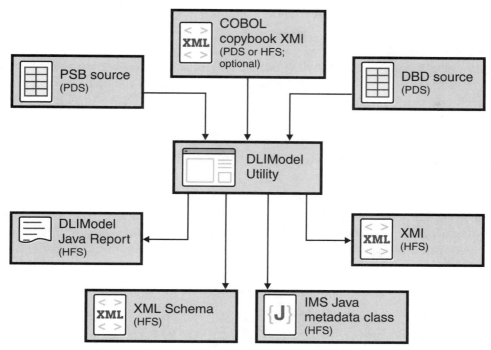

Figure 18-1 DLIModel Utility Inputs and Outputs

SUPPORTED SQL KEYWORDS

Table 18-1 contains the portable SQL keywords that are currently supported by the IMS Java function. None of the keywords are case-sensitive.

Table 18-1 SQL Keywords Supported by the IMS Java Function

ALL	INSERT
AND	INTO
AS	MAX
ASC	MIN
AVG	OR
COUNT	ORDER BY
DELETE	SELECT
DESC	SUM
DISTINCT	UPDATE
FROM	WHERE
GROUP BY	

DEVELOPING JMP APPLICATIONS

JMP applications access the IMS message queue to receive messages to process and to send output messages. Therefore, you must define input and output message classes by subclassing the `IMSFieldMessage` class. The IMS Java class libraries provide the capability to process `IMSFieldMessage` objects. JMP applications commit or roll back the processing of each message by calling `IMSTransaction.getTransaction().commit()` or `IMSTransaction.getTransaction().rollback()`.

JMP applications are started when IMS receives a message with a transaction code for the JMP application and schedules the message. JMP applications end when there are no more messages with that transaction code to process.

A transaction begins when the application gets an input message and ends when the application commits the transaction. To get an input message, the application calls the `getUniqueMessage` method. The application must commit or roll back any database processing. The application must issue a commit call immediately before calling subsequent `getUniqueMessage` methods.

Figure 18-2 shows the general flow of a JMP application program.

```
public static void main(String args[]) {

    conn = DriverManager.getConnection(...); //Establish DB connection

    while(MessageQueue.getUniqueMessage(...)){ //Get input message, which
                                               //starts transaction

        results=statement.executeQuery(...); //Perform DB processing
        ...
        MessageQueue.insertMessage(...);       //Send output messages
        ...
        IMSTransaction.getTransaction().commit(); //Commit and end transaction
    }

    conn.close();                             //Close DB connection
    return;
}
```

Figure 18-2   JMP Application Example

JMP Applications and Conversational Transactions

A conversational program runs in a JMP region and processes conversational transactions that are made up of several steps. It does not process the entire transaction at the same time. A conversational program divides processing into a connected series of terminal-to-program-to-terminal interactions. Use conversational processing when one transaction contains several parts.

A nonconversational program receives a message from a terminal, processes the request, and sends a message back to the terminal. A conversational program receives a message from a terminal and replies to the terminal, but it saves the data from the transaction in a scratch pad area (SPA). Then, when the person at the terminal enters more data, the program has the data it saved from the last message in the SPA, so it can continue processing the request without the person at the terminal having to enter the data again. The application package classes enable applications to be built using the IMS Java function.

Related Reading: For details about the classes you use to develop a JMP application, see the IMS Java API Specification, which is available on the IMS Java Web site. Go to http://www.ibm.com/ims and link to the IMS Java page.

DEVELOPING JBP APPLICATIONS

JBP applications do not access the IMS message queue, and therefore you do not need to subclass the `IMSFieldMessage` class.

JBP applications are similar to JMP applications, except that JBP applications do not receive input messages from the IMS message queue. The program should periodically issue commit calls, except for applications that have the PSB PROCOPT=GO parameter.

Unlike BMP applications, JBP applications must be non-message-driven applications.

Similarly to BMP applications, JBP applications can use symbolic checkpoint and restart calls to restart the application after an abend. The primary methods for symbolic checkpoint and restart are:

- `IMSTransaction().checkpoint()`
- `IMSTransaction().restart()`

These methods perform analogous functions to the following DL/I system service calls: (symbolic) CHKP and XRST.

Figure 18-3 shows a sample JBP application that connects to a database, makes a restart call, performs database processing, periodically checkpoints, and disconnects from the database at the end of the program.

```
public static void main(String args[]) {

    conn = DriverManager.getConnection(...);       //Establish DB connection

    IMSTransaction.getTransaction().retart();  //Restart application
                                               //after abend from last
                                               //checkpoint
    repeat {

        repeat {
            results=statement.executeQuery(...); //Perform DB processing
            ...
            MessageQueue.insertMessage(...);       //Send output messages
            ...
        }

        IMSTransaction.getTransaction().checkpoint(); //Periodic checkpoints
                                                      // divide work

    }

    conn.close();                                  //Close DB connection
    return;
}
```

Figure 18-3   JBP Application Example

Related Reading: For details about the classes you use to develop a JBP application, see the IMS Java API Specification, which is available on the IMS Java Web site. Go to http://www.ibm.com/ims and link to the IMS Java page.

ENTERPRISE COBOL INTEROPERABILITY WITH JMP AND JBP APPLICATIONS

IMS Enterprise COBOL for z/OS and OS/390 Version 3 Release 2 supports interoperation between COBOL and Java languages when running in a JMP or JBP region. With this support, you can:

- Call an object-oriented (OO) COBOL application from an IMS Java application by building the front-end application, which processes messages, in Java and the back end, which processes databases, in OO COBOL.
- Build an OO COBOL application containing a main routine that can invoke Java routines.

> **RESTRICTION:** COBOL applications that run in an IMS Java dependent region must use the AIB interface, which requires that all PCBs in a PSB definition have a name.

You can access COBOL code in a JMP or JBP region because Enterprise COBOL provides object-oriented language syntax that enables you to:

- Define classes with methods and data implemented in COBOL
- Create instances of Java and COBOL classes
- Invoke methods on Java and COBOL objects
- Write classes that inherit from Java classes or other COBOL classes
- Define and invoke overloaded methods

Related Reading: For details on building applications that use Enterprise COBOL and that run in an IMS Java dependent region, see *IMS Version 9: IMS Java Guide and Reference* and *Enterprise COBOL for z/OS and OS/390: Programming Guide*.

ACCESSING DB2 UDB FOR z/OS DATABASES FROM JMP OR JBP APPLICATIONS

A JMP or JBP application can access DB2 UDB for z/OS databases by using the DB2 JDBC/SQLJ 2.0 driver or the DB2 JDBC/SQLJ 1.2 driver. The JMP or JBP region that the application is running in must also be defined with DB2 UDB for z/OS attached by the DB2 Recoverable Resource Manager Services attachment facility (RRSAF).

Related Reading: For information about attaching DB2 UDB for z/OS to IMS for JMP or JBP application access to DB2 UDB for z/OS databases, see *IMS Version 9: IMS Java Guide and Reference*.

DEVELOPING JAVA APPLICATIONS THAT RUN OUTSIDE OF IMS

The following sections briefly describe using Java application programs to access IMS databases from products other than IMS.

Related Reading: For the details of the requirements for running Java applications from these products, see *IMS Version 9: IMS Java Guide and Reference*.

WebSphere Application Server for z/OS Applications

You can write applications that run on WebSphere Application Server for z/OS and access IMS databases when WebSphere Application Server for z/OS and IMS are on the same LPAR (logical partition).

To deploy an application on WebSphere Application Server for z/OS, you must install the IMS JDBC resource adaptor (the IMS Java class libraries) on WebSphere Application Server for z/OS, and configure both IMS open database access (ODBA) and the database resource adapter (DRA).

Figure 18-4 shows an Enterprise JavaBean (EJB) that is accessing IMS data. JDBC or IMS Java hierarchical interface calls are passed to the IMS Java layer, which converts the calls to DL/I calls. The IMS Java layer passes these calls to ODBA, which uses the DRA to access the DL/I region in IMS.

Remote Data Access with WebSphere Application Server Applications

With the IMS Java function remote database services, you can develop and deploy applications that run on non-z/OS platforms and access IMS databases remotely. Unlike other Java solutions for IMS, you do not need to develop a z/OS application or access a legacy z/OS application to have access to IMS data. Therefore, the IMS Java function is an ideal solution for developing IMS applications in a WebSphere environment.

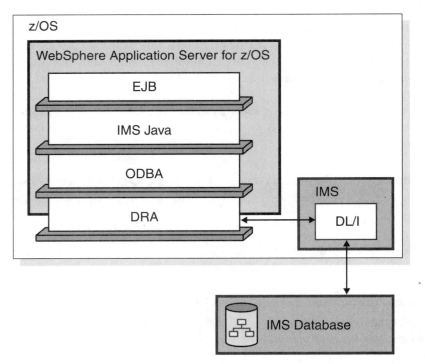

Figure 18-4   WebSphere Application Server for z/OS EJB Using the IMS Java Function

Figure 18-5 shows the components that are required for an enterprise application (in this case, an EJB) on a non-z/OS platform to access IMS DB.

DB2 UDB for z/OS Stored Procedures

You can write DB2 UDB for z/OS Java stored procedures that access IMS databases.

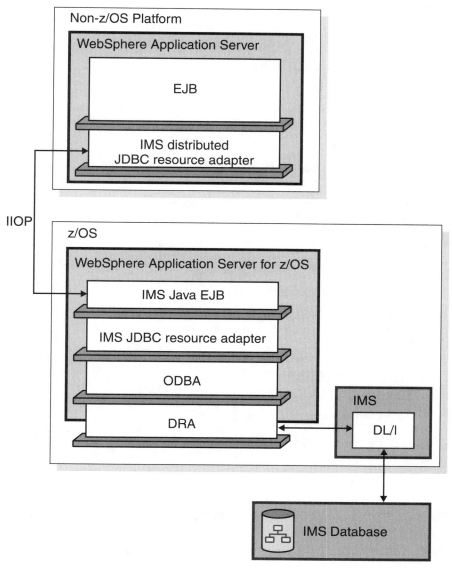

Figure 18-5   The IMS Java Function and WebSphere Application Server Components

To deploy a Java stored procedure on DB2 UDB for z/OS, you must configure IMS Java, ODBA, and DRA.

Figure 18-6 shows a DB2 UDB for z/OS stored procedure using IMS Java, ODBA, and DRA to access IMS databases.

CICS Applications

Java applications that run on CICS Transaction Server for z/OS can access IMS databases by using IMS Java.

Java applications use the IMS Java class libraries to access IMS. Other than the IMS Java layer, access to IMS from a Java application is the same as for a non-Java application.

Figure 18-7 on page 321 shows a JCICS application accessing an IMS database using ODBA and IMS Java.

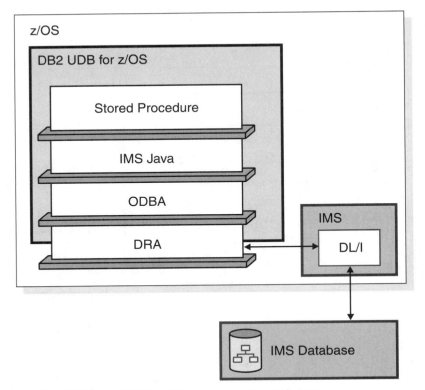

Figure 18-6   DB2 UDB for z/OS Stored Procedure Using IMS Java

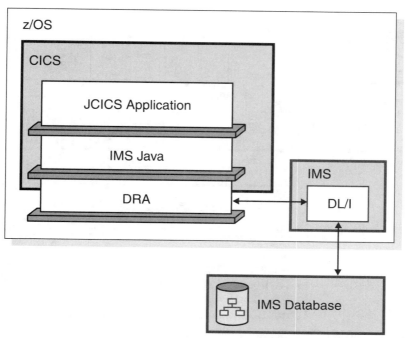

Figure 18-7   CICS Application Using IMS Java

Related Reading: For information about configuring CICS for the IMS Java function and for information about developing a Java application that runs on CICS and accesses IMS databases, see *IMS Version 9: IMS Java Guide and Reference*.

XML Storage in IMS Databases

To store XML in an IMS database or to retrieve XML from IMS, you must first generate an XML schema and the IMS Java metadata class using the DLIModel utility. The metadata and schema are used during the storage and retrieval of XML. Your application uses the IMS Java JDBC user-defined functions (UDFs) storeXML and retrieveXML to store XML in IMS databases, create XML from IMS data, or retrieve XML documents from IMS databases.

Figure 18-8 on page 322 shows the overall process for storing and retrieving XML in IMS.

retrieveXML UDF

The retrieveXML UDF creates an XML document from an IMS database and returns an object that implements the java.sql.Clob interface. It does not matter to the application whether the data is decomposed into standard IMS segments or the data is in intact XML documents in the IMS database.

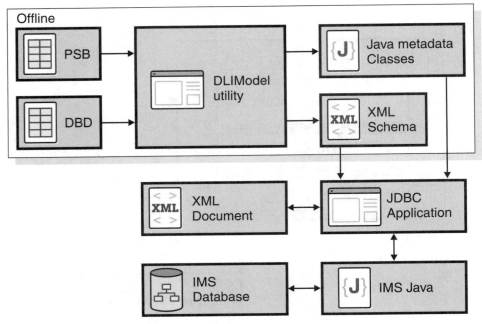

Figure 18-8   Overview of XML Storage in IMS

The Clob JDBC type stores a character large object as a column value in a row of the result set. The getClob method retrieves the XML document from the result set. Figure 18-9 shows the relationship between the retrieveXML UDF and the getClob method.

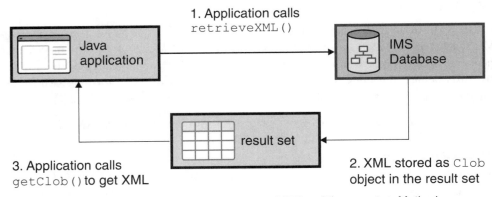

Figure 18-9   Creating XML Using the retrieveXML UDF and the getClob Method

To create an XML document, use a `retrieveXML` UDF in the SELECT statement of your JDBC call. Pass in the name of the segment that will be the root element of the XML document (for example, `retrieveXML(Model)`). The dependent segments of the segment that you pass in will be in the generated XML document if they match the criteria listed in the WHERE clause.

The segment that you specify to be the root element of the XML document does not have to be the root segment of the IMS record. The dependent segments are mapped to the XML document based on the generated XML schema.

storeXML UDF

The `storeXML` UDF inserts an XML document into an IMS database at the position in the database that the WHERE clause indicates. IMS, not the application, uses the XML schema and the Java metadata class to determine the physical storage of the data into the database. It does not matter to the application whether the XML is stored intact or decomposed into standard IMS segments.

An XML document must be valid before it can be stored into a database. The `storeXML` UDF validates the XML document against the XML schema before storing it. If you know that the XML document is valid and you do not want IMS to revalidate it, use the `storeXML(false)` UDF.

To store an XML document, use the `storeXML` UDF in the INSERT INTO clause of a JDBC prepared statement. Within a single application program, you can issue INSERT calls that contain `storeXML` UDFs against multiple PCBs in an application's PSB.

The SQL query must have the following syntax:

```
INSERT INTO PCB.Segment (storeXML())
VALUES ( ? )
WHERE Segment.Field = value
```

Decomposed Storage Mode for XML

In decomposed storage mode, all elements and attributes are stored as regular fields in optionally repeating DL/I segments. During parsing, all tags and other XML syntactic information are checked for validity and then discarded. The parsed data is physically stored in the database as standard IMS data, meaning that each defined field in the segment is of an IMS standard type. Because all XML data is composed of string types (typically Unicode) with type information existing in the validating XML schema, each parsed data element and attribute can be converted to the corresponding IMS standard field value and stored into the target database.

Inversely, during XML retrieval, DL/I segments are retrieved, fields are converted to the destination XML encoding, tags and XML syntactic information (stored in the XML schema) are added, and the XML document is composed.

Figure 18-10 shows how XML elements are decomposed and stored into IMS segments.

Decomposed storage mode is suitable for data-centric XML documents, where the elements and attributes from the document typically are either character or numeric items of known short or medium length that lend themselves to mapping to fields in segments. Lengths are typically, though not always, fixed.

The XML document data can start at any segment in the hierarchy, which is the root element in the XML document. The segments in the subtree below this segment are also included in the XML document. Elements and attributes of the XML document are stored in the dependent segments of the root element segment. Any other segments in the hierarchy that are not dependent segments of that root element segment are not part of the XML document and, therefore, are not described in the describing XML schema.

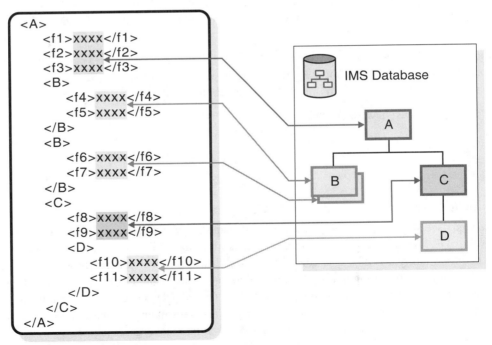

Figure 18-10 How XML Is Decomposed and Stored in IMS Segments

When an XML document is stored in the database, the value of all segment fields is extracted directly from the XML document. Therefore, any unique key field in any of the XML segments must exist in the XML document as an attribute or simple element.

The XML hierarchy is defined by a PCB hierarchy that is based on either a physical or a logical database. Logical relationships are supported for retrieval and composition of XML documents, but not for inserting documents.

For a legacy database, either the whole database hierarchy or any subtree of the hierarchy can be considered as a decomposed data-centric XML document. The segments and fields that comprise the decomposed XML data are determined only by the definition of a mapping (the XML schema) between those segments and fields and a document.

One XML schema is generated for each database PCB. Therefore, multiple documents may be derived from a physical database hierarchy through different XML schemas. There are no restrictions on how these multiple documents overlap and share common segments or fields.

A new database can be designed specifically to store a particular type of data-centric XML document in decomposed form.

Intact Storage Mode for XML

In intact storage mode, all or part of an XML document is stored intact in a field. The XML tags are not removed and IMS does not parse the document. XML documents can be large, so the documents can span the primary intact field, which contains the XML root element, and fields in overflow segments. The segments that contain the intact XML documents are standard IMS segments and can be processed like any other IMS segments. The fields, because they contain unparsed XML data, cannot be processed like standard IMS fields. However, intact storage of documents has the following advantages over decomposed storage mode:

- IMS does not need to compose or decompose the XML during storage and retrieval. Therefore, you can process intact XML documents faster than decomposed XML documents.
- You do not need to match the XML document content with IMS field data types or lengths. Therefore, you can store XML documents with different structure, content, and length within the same IMS database.

Intact XML storage requires a new IMS database or an extension of an existing database because the XML document must be stored in segments and fields that are specifically tailored for storing intact XML.

To store all or part of an XML document intact in an IMS database, the database must define a base segment, which contains the root element of the intact XML subtree. The rest of the intact XML subtree is stored in overflow segments, which are child segments of the base segment.

The base segment contains the root element of the intact XML subtree and any decomposed or non-XML fields. The format of the base segment is defined in the DBD.

The overflow segment contains only the overflow XML data field. The format of the overflow XML data field is defined in the DBD.

Side Segments for Secondary Indexing

IMS cannot search intact XML documents for specific elements within the document. However, you can create a side segment that contains specific XML element data. IMS stores the XML document intact, and also decomposes a specific piece of XML data into a standard IMS segment. This segment can then be searched with a secondary index.

Figure 18-11 shows a base segment, an overflow segment, and the side segment for secondary indexing.

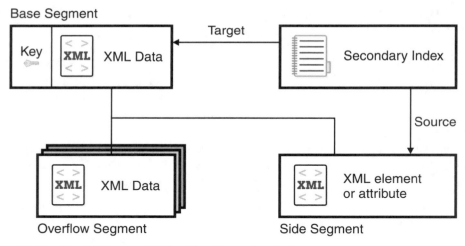

Figure 18-11   Intact Storage of XML with a Secondary Index

IMS System Administration

The IMS System Definition Process

he IMS system definition process:

- Describes the IMS resources to IMS:
  - — At installation time
  - — When maintenance is applied
  - — When standard application definition changes are required
- Assumes a working knowledge of the z/OS system modification program/extended (SMP/E). SMP/E is required for installation and is used as part of the IMS system definition process.
- Is evolving to be more dynamic (versus static) over time.

Related Reading: For information about SMP/E, see the *SMP/E V3R2.0 User's Guide*.

Extended Terminal Option (ETO), a separately priced feature of IMS TM, enables you to define resources dynamically, without shutting down IMS. With ETO, you can dynamically add or delete VTAM terminals and users to your IMS outside of the IMS system definition process. For more information about ETO, see "The Extended Terminal Option (ETO)" on page 338.

In This Chapter:

OVERVIEW OF THE IMS SYSTEM DEFINITION PROCESS

The IMS system definition process comprises many steps. Some steps occur only for certain types of IMS definitions (see "Types of IMS System Definitions" on page 332). The basic steps involved in IMS system definition are:

1. Modify or tailor IMS-supplied macro statements and procedures (JCL) to define the IMS system that your business requires. These macro statements and procedures are the building blocks for your IMS system (see "IMS System Definition Macros" on page 335).
2. Run the IMS preprocessor to check the macros and procedures for correctness (see Figure 19-1).
3. Stage 1 assembly, in which you run the JCL that you modified in step 1 through the z/OS High Level Assembler program to assemble your program into the JCL that is required as input to stage 2 (see "Stage 1 of the IMS System Definition Process" on page 333).
4. Stage 2 assembly, in which you build the IMS executable load modules and, optionally, build MFS default formats and perform updates to IMS.PROCLIB (see "Stage 2 of the IMS System Definition Process" on page 333).
5. JCLIN, which is an SMP/E process that tells SMP/E how to assemble and bind modules (see "JCLIN Processing" on page 334).
6. Use the SMP/E APPLY command to process any maintenance that has not been processed using the SMP/E ACCEPT command (see "SMP/E Maintenance" on page 334).
7. Optionally, perform an IMS Security Maintenance utility generation, which generates a set of secured-resource tables (see "IMS Security Maintenance Utility Generation" on page 334).

Figure 19-2 on page 331 shows an overview of the stage 1 and stage 2 components of the system definition process.

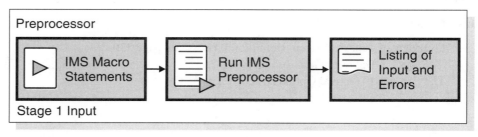

Figure 19-1   Overview of the Preprocessor Stage of the System Definition Process

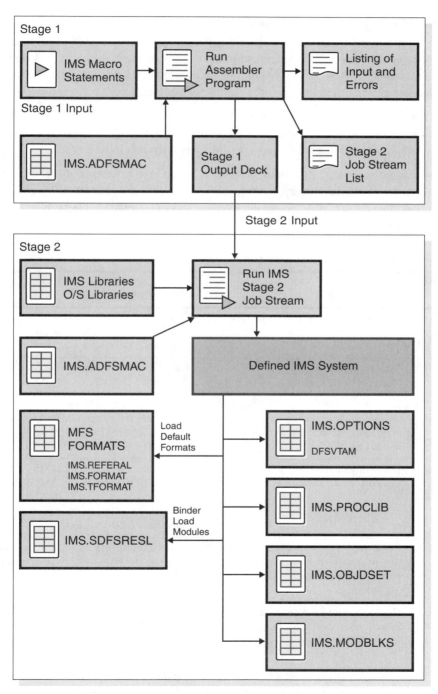

Figure 19-2 Overview of Stage 1 and Stage 2 of the System Definition Process

Types of IMS System Definitions

There are seven different types of IMS system definitions. You use the IMSCTRL macro statement to describe the type of IMS system definition to be performed, the basic IMS control program options, and the z/OS system configuration under which IMS is to execute. The IMSCTRL options that specify the different types of system definitions are described in Table 19-1.

After your initial system definition, the ON-LINE, CTLBLKS, and NUCLEUS types of system definition can be used to implement changes. The ON-LINE, CTLBLKS, and NUCLEUS types of system definitions require a cold start of the IMS online system to take effect.

For certain changes to your IMS system, however, you can take advantage of the online change method using the MODBLKS type of system definition. With the MODBLKS type of system definition, the changes are made active during the execution of the online system and do not require a restart operation.

Table 19-1   Types of IMS System Definitions

IMSCTRL Option	When to Use	Description
BATCH	Only to define a batch environment.	Generates modules and procedures that are needed to build a complete batch IMS system.
MSVERIFY	Only appropriate for MSC.	Builds control blocks for the Multiple Systems Verification utility (DFSUMSV0).
MODBLKS	Use when online changes are required to the IMS system, such as changes to programs, transactions, and database definitions.	Generates control block members for resources to be added online (for example, APPLCTN, DATABASE, TRANSACT, and RTCODE macros).
CTLBLKS	Use to rebuild the existing IMS nucleus and to create communications definitions.	Generates modules for all IMS control blocks (for example, TERMINAL and LINE macros). The CTLBLKS type of system definition includes the MODBLKS and MSVERIFY types too.
NUCLEUS	Use when performing major maintenance that affects the contents of the IMS nucleus, or when a new nucleus with a new suffix is required.	Generates an IMS nucleus for the control region. The NUCLEUS type of system definition includes the CTLBLKS type too.
ON-LINE	Use to perform a major update, or during initial system definition. Often required for maintenance.	Builds all the modules and procedures needed for the online IMS environment. The ON-LINE type of system definition includes the NUCLEUS type too.
ALL	Use during a typical initial system definition. Often required for maintenance.	Builds most IMS modules and procedures. Includes BATCH and ON-LINE types too.

Related Reading: For the details about the different types of system definition, see "Using the Macro Table" in *IMS Version 9: Installation Volume 2: System Definition and Tailoring.*

Stage 1 of the IMS System Definition Process

Stage 1 of the system definition process uses the z/OS High Level Assembler program and uses the IMS macros as input, as described in "IMS System Definition Macros" on page 335. Other references are to the IMS distribution macro libraries (IMS.ADFSMAC).

The output from stage 1 of the IMS system definition process includes:

- Standard assembler listing output with any appropriate error messages.
- Stage 2 system definition input JCL, which is also used for the JCLIN process.

Depending on what is specified in the IMSGEN macro[1] for stage 1, stage 2 of the system definition process can be divided up into a single job with multiple steps, or into many jobs with fewer steps.

Stage 2 of the IMS System Definition Process

Stage 2 of the system definition process assembles and binds all the modules that are required to build the necessary load modules, depending on what type of system definition is being run.

The steps involved in stage 2 refer to the IMS distribution macro library (IMS.ADFSMAC) at assembly time, and the distribution load library (IMS.ADFSLOAD) at bind time.

The output of stage 2 of the system definition process includes:

- Executable load modules in data sets IMS.SDFSRESL and IMS.MODBLKS.
- IMS options definitions in the data set IMS.OPTIONS.
- Assembled object code for use in later system definition steps in the data set IMS.OBJDSET.
- Optionally, the runtime IMS. PROCLIB data set.

  The PROCLIB= parameter in the IMSGEN stage 1 macro determines whether the IMS.PROCLIB data set is to be populated by this system definition. The IMS.PRO-CLIB library contains IMS started tasks and JCL procedures, as well as the IMS.PRO-CLIB members required by IMS and IMS utilities to provide options.

- Optionally, the runtime IMS default MFS screens in data sets IMS.FORMAT, IMS.TFORMAT, and IMS.REFERAL.

  The MFSDFMT= parameter in the IMSGEN stage 1 macro determines whether the default message format screens are built as part of stage 2 of the system definition process.

---

1. You specify the assembler and binder data sets and options, and the system definition output options and features in the IMSGEN macro.

JCLIN Processing

Because the stage 2 system definition process actually assembles and binds the IMS modules based on the definitions for that particular system and is run outside of SMP/E control, the input JCL for system definition stage 2 must be used as input to the JCLIN process. This input JCL ensures that SMP/E knows how to manage any maintenance that is added to the system following this IMS system definition.

Run the JCLIN process following any IMS system definition, to ensure that SMP/E is always synchronized with the updated IMS.

SMP/E Maintenance

All IMS system definitions use the IMS SMP/E distribution libraries and the IMS stage 1 macros as input. As a result, any SMP/E maintenance (SYSMODs - PTFs, APARs or USERMODs) that processed using the SMP/E APPLY command, but not processed using the SMP/E ACCEPT command, prior to an IMS system definition, might be regressed as a result of that IMS system definition, depending on the type of IMS system definition, and the impact of the SYSMOD.

> **RECOMMENDATION:**   Any maintenance that has been processed using the SMP/E APPLY command, but not processed using the SMP/E ACCEPT command, should be processed again (using both commands) following an IMS system definition, unless further investigations have shown specific cases where this is not necessary.

Related Reading: For more information about performing SMP/E maintenance on IMS, see "IMS Service Considerations" in *IMS Version 9: Installation Volume 1: Installation Verification*.

IMS Security Maintenance Utility Generation

For security beyond that provided by default terminal security, you can use the various security options provided by the Security Maintenance utility (SMU) or by RACF (or equivalent product). You define the RACF security for IMS resources outside of the IMS system definition process.

The SMU is executed offline *after* the completion of stage 2 of the system definition process. The output of the SMU is a set of secured-resource tables, which are placed in the MATRIX data set. The tables are loaded at system initialization time and, for certain options, work with exit routines and RACF during online execution to provide resource protection.

IMS SYSTEM DEFINITION MACROS

The IMS system definition macros change from release to release of IMS. See a specific version of *IMS Installation Volume 2: System Definition and Tailoring* for version-specific details about the system definition macros. The IMS Version 9 system definition macros are briefly summarized here:

APPLCTN

The APPLCTN macro allows you to define the program resource requirements for application programs that run under the control of the IMS DB/DC environment, as well as for applications that access databases through DBCTL. An APPLCTN macro combined with one or more TRANSACT macros defines the scheduling and resource requirements for an application program. Using the APPLCTN macro, you only describe programs that operate in message processing regions, Fast Path message-driven program regions, batch message processing regions, or CCTL threads. You also use the APPLCTN macro to describe application programs that operate in batch processing regions. When defining an IMS data communication system, at least one APPLCTN macro is required.

BUFPOOLS

The BUFPOOLS macro specifies default storage buffer pool sizes for the DB/DC and DBCTL environments. The storage buffer pool sizes specified are used unless otherwise expressly stated for that buffer or pool at control program execution time for an online system.

COMM

The COMM macro specifies general communication requirements that are not associated with any particular terminal type. The COMM macro is always required for terminal types that are supported by VTAM, and might also be required to specify additional system options, such as support for MFS on the master terminal.

CONFIG

The CONFIG macro statement provides the configuration for a switched 3275 terminal. Because the configuration provided by the CONFIG macro is referenced when the named 3275 dials into IMS, differently configured 3275 terminals can use the same communication line. All CONFIG macro statements must be between the LINEGRP macro and the LINE macros. LINE macros can refer to named CONFIG macros defined previously in this line group or in previously defined line groups.

CTLUNIT

The CTLUNIT macro specifies 2848, 2972, and 3271 control unit characteristics. The CTLUNIT macro is valid only for 3270 remote line groups.

DATABASE

The DATABASE macro defines the set of physical databases that IMS manages. One DATABASE macro statement must be specified for each HSAM, HISAM, HDAM, or PHDAM database. Two DATABASE macro statements are required for each HIDAM or PHIDAM database: one for the INDEX DBD and one for the HIDAM or PHIDAM DBD. One DATABASE macro instruction must be included for each secondary index database that refers to any database that is defined to the online system. For Fast Path, a DATA-BASE macro statement must be included for each main storage database (MSDB) and data entry database (DEDB) to be processed.

FPCTRL

The FPCTRL macro defines the IMS Fast Path options of the IMS control program, and the DBCTL environment. The FPCTRL macro is ignored when the IMSCTRL statement specifies that only a BATCH or MSVERIFY system definition is to be performed.

IDLIST

The IDLIST macro statement is used to create a terminal security list for switched 3275s.

IMSCTF

Defines additional options and system parameters under which IMS is to operate.

IMSCTRL

The IMSCTRL macro statement describes the basic IMS control program options, the z/OS system configuration under which IMS is to execute, and the type of IMS system definition to be performed.

The IMSCTRL macro instruction must be the first statement of the system definition control statements.

IMSGEN

IMSGEN specifies the assembler and binder data sets and options, and the system definition output options and features.

The IMSGEN macro must be the last IMS system definition macro, and it must be followed by an assembler END statement.

LINE

The LINE macro provides the address and characteristics of one line in the line group specified by the LINEGRP statement. The LINE macro describes both switched and non-switched communication lines to IMS.

LINEGRP

The LINEGRP macro defines the beginning of a set of macro instructions that describe the user's telecommunications system.

MSGQUEUE

The MSGQUEUE macro defines the characteristics of the three message queue data sets: QBLKS, SHMSG, and LGMSG. The information you specify in this macro is also used in a shared-queues environment. The MSGQUEUE macro is required for all DB/DC and DCCTL systems.

MSLINK

The MSLINK macro defines a logical link to another system.

MSNAME

The MSNAME macro provides a name for the remote and local system identifications that it represents.

MSPLINK

The MSPLINK macro defines a physical MSC link.

NAME

The NAME macro defines a logical terminal name (LTERM) that is associated with a physical terminal. You might need to provide a NAME macro for the following macros: TERMINAL, SUBPOOL, MSNAME.

POOL

The POOL macro describes a pool of logical terminals that are associated with a set of switched communication lines.

RTCODE

The RTCODE macro is used one or more times with the APPLCTN macro that defines a Fast Path application program. The RTCODE macro specifies the routing codes that identify the program named in the preceding APPLCTN macro. A TRANSACT macro that specifies an IMS Fast Path-exclusive transaction builds an internal RTCODE macro with a routing code that is identical to the transaction code.

SECURITY

The SECURITY macro specifies optional security features that are in effect during IMS execution unless they are overridden during system initialization.

STATION

The STATION macro describes the physical and logical characteristics of System/3 or System/7 remote intelligent stations.

SUBPOOL

The SUBPOOL macro, when used in a VTAM macro set, is a delimiter between groups of NAME macros that create LU 6.1 LTERM subpools.

When the SUBPOOL macro is used in a switched communication device macro set, the SUBPOOL macro defines a set of logical terminals.

TERMINAL

The TERMINAL macro defines physical and logical characteristics of VTAM nodes and non-VTAM communication terminals.

TRANSACT

The TRANSACT macro is used one or more times with each APPLCTN macro to identify transactions as IMS exclusive, IMS Fast Path potential, or IMS Fast Path exclusive. The TRANSACT macro specifies the transaction codes that cause the application program named in the preceding APPLCTN macro to be scheduled for execution in an IMS message processing region. The TRANSACT macro also provides the IMS control program with information that influences the application program scheduling algorithm.

TYPE

The TYPE macro defines the beginning of a set of communication terminals and logical terminal description macros that include the TERMINAL and NAME macros. The TYPE macro begins a description of one set, which contains one or more terminals of the same type. The TYPE macro defines terminals attached to IMS through VTAM and is equivalent to the LINEGRP and LINE macro set that is used to define terminals attached to IMS by means other than VTAM.

VTAMPOOL

The VTAMPOOL macro, required for parallel session support, begins the definition of the LU 6.1 LTERM subpools.

THE EXTENDED TERMINAL OPTION (ETO)

The IMS Extended Terminal Option (ETO) allows you to dynamically add VTAM terminals and users to your IMS: they do not need to be predefined during system definition. ETO is a separately priced feature of the IMS Transaction Manager (TM) and provides additional features such as output security, automatic logoff, and automatic signoff.

By using ETO, you can achieve each of the following goals:

- Improved system availability by reducing the scheduled down time that is associated with adding or deleting VTAM terminals.
- Faster system availability to users, because they can establish an IMS session from any VTAM terminal in the network.
- Improved IMS security by relating output messages to users, rather than to terminals.
- Reduced number of macros required to define the terminal network. This reduces system definition time and storage requirements.
- Reduced checkpoint and restart time. For ETO terminals and user structures, resources are not allocated until they are actually required; similarly, when they are no longer required, they are deleted.

- Reduced number of skilled system programmer resources that are required for maintaining static terminal definitions.

Related Reading: For more information about ETO, see *IMS Version 9: Administration Guide: Transaction Manager.*

ETO Terminology

The following sections describe the terms that have ETO-specific meanings. These meanings are important for understanding ETO.

Terminals

A terminal is a physical VTAM logical unit (LU) that establishes a session with IMS. A physical terminal is represented using a control block.

When a terminal is not built by ETO but is defined at system definition, it is called a *static terminal*. A static terminal can be a VTAM node. When messages are sent to a static terminal they are queued to a logical terminal (LTERM) message queue, where they await retrieval by the recipient.

When a terminal is not defined at system definition and ETO builds a terminal, that terminal is called a *dynamic terminal*, or an ETO terminal. For dynamic terminals, the logical terminal (LTERM) is known as a dynamic user message queue, and the LTERM associates the messages with the user, rather than with the physical terminal. Associating messages with the users provides more security for these users, because they can access their messages only when they sign on using their unique user ID. In addition, all users in the network can access their messages from any physical terminal, instead of being restricted to using a particular physical terminal.

Dynamic User

A *dynamic user* is a user who signs on to a dynamic terminal and who has a unique identification (user ID) that IMS uses for delivering messages. The user is usually associated with a person but can also be associated with another entity, such as a printer.

Terminal Structure

A *terminal structure* is a control block that represents a specific terminal that is known to IMS. A terminal structure is created when the individual terminal logs on to IMS and is deleted when the terminal logs off with no remaining associated activity.

User Structure

A *user structure* is a set of control blocks, including a user block and one or more LTERM blocks. The message queues are associated with the dynamic user, as opposed to the physical terminal, and they are queued to the user ID. Usually, a user structure represents a person who uses IMS.

The dynamic user structure connects to the physical terminal only when the user signs on. This provides a secure environment, because different users accessing the same terminal cannot receive each other's messages.

IMS creates a user structure when either of the following events takes place:

- A dynamic user signs on to IMS.
- Output messages that are destined for a dynamic user are sent to the user, but the user has not signed on to IMS.

The user structure name is usually the same as the user ID. A user structure can also represent a logical destination, such as a printer. In this case, the user structure name can be the same as or different from the LTERM name that your installation uses in its application programs and its exit routines. For example, you can assign the same name to a user structure for a printer that you assign to its LTERM destination node name. However, output is then queued according to the terminal, and not to the user.

Figure 19-3 illustrates:

- A physical terminal (Node LU1)
- Two logical terminals (LTERM LT1A and LTERM LT1B) that are defined as being associated with Node LU1
- The message queues that are associated with logical terminals LTERM LT1A and LTERM LT1B
- The traditional, static system definition for LU1, LTERM LT1A, and LTERM LT1B

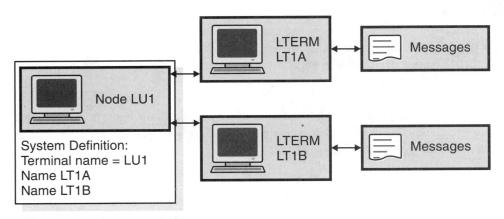

Figure 19-3   Static Resources: Node and Static Terminals

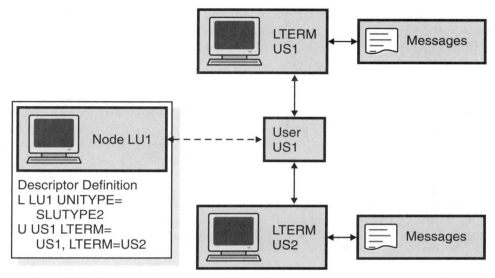

Figure 19-4   ETO Dynamic Resources: User and Dynamic Terminals

Figure 19-4 illustrates:

- A physical terminal (Node LU1)
- A dynamic user (US1)
- Two dynamic logical terminals (LTERM US1 and LTERM US2) that are dynamically associated with user US1
- The dynamically built user message queues that are associated with logical terminals LTERM US1 and LTERM US2
- The dynamic definition (descriptor) that IMS builds for LU1, US1, LTERM US1, and LTERM US2

Descriptors

A descriptor provides information to IMS when IMS builds a dynamic resource for a logon or a signon. IMS stores the descriptors in two IMS.PROCLIB members, DFSDSCMx and DFSD-SCTy. For more information about these PROCLIB members, see *IMS Version 9: Installation Volume 2: System Definition and Tailoring*.

IMS uses four types of descriptors:

- Logon descriptors
- User descriptors
- MSC descriptors
- MFS device descriptors

Logon Descriptors   A logon descriptor is a skeleton that IMS uses to build an ETO dynamic terminal. It provides information regarding a terminal's physical characteristics. IMS uses logon descriptors in conjunction with exit routines to create terminal structures.

IMS uses three types of logon descriptors:

Generic

A generic logon descriptor provides characteristics for all terminals of a particular type. For example, all SCS printers might share a single generic descriptor. Similarly, all 3270 terminals might share a generic logon descriptor.

Group

A group logon descriptor provides characteristics for a collection of terminals, each of which has compatible hardware characteristics and is defined to IMS in the same manner. The characteristics of these terminals are usually identical, but they can differ. IMS uses the group logon descriptor to derive their characteristics.

Specific

A specific logon descriptor provides characteristics for a single terminal, and these characteristics apply only to that terminal. The specific descriptor name matches the name of the terminal that it describes.

> **RECOMMENDATION:**   Although you might need to use specific logon descriptors during the actual migration to ETO, use generic logon descriptors or group logon descriptors after you have migrated to ETO; these types of descriptors ease network administration.

User Descriptors   A user descriptor is a skeleton from which IMS builds a user structure. A user descriptor can provide user options and queue names.

MSC Descriptors   IMS uses an MSC descriptor to create a remote LTERM, which is an LTERM that does not exist on the local IMS. The physical terminal definition (either static or dynamic) for the remote LTERM is in the remote IMS.

Each MSC descriptor for a remote LTERM is loaded during IMS initialization and tells IMS which MSC link to use for output destined for that remote LTERM.

MFS Device Descriptors   An MFS device descriptor allows you to add new device characteristics for MFS formatting without requiring an IMS system definition. The MFS Device Characteristics Table utility (DFSUTB00) uses MFS device descriptors to update default formats in the MFS library.

IMS also uses MFS device descriptors to update the MFS device characteristics table. IMS loads this table only during initialization; therefore, updates are not effective until the next IMS initialization.

How Structures are Created and Used

Structures are created in the following situations:

- Logon
- Signon
- Output is queued to your LTERM
- /ASSIGN command is used to assign an LTERM to a non-existent user
- /ASSIGN command is used to assign a non-existent LTERM to a user
- /CHANGE USER *user* AUTOLOGON command is directed to a non-existent user

In all cases, IMS searches for an existing terminal or user structure before creating a new one.

IMS creates and deletes user structures in the following sequence:

1. When you establish a session between IMS and an undefined terminal, IMS selects a logon descriptor.
2. Using the information in the logon descriptor, the customization defaults, and VTAM information, IMS builds an IMS terminal control block (called a *VTAM terminal control block* or VTCB) that describes the new terminal.
3. When you sign on, if a user structure does not exist, IMS builds one, using information from a user descriptor that it selects, and then connects this user structure to the terminal structure.
4. IMS deletes terminal structures or user structures when they are no longer needed to maintain sessions. User structures are typically deleted when you sign off, if no special status needs to be maintained and if no messages remain queued. IMS deletes terminal structures when no terminal status exists (such as trace mode), no user is signed on, and the terminal is idle.

   If you are using the Resource Manager and a resource structure, IMS normally maintains status in the resource structure instead of the local control blocks. Therefore, IMS deletes the resource structures.

This sequence applies only to terminal logon and logoff and to user signon and signoff. When asynchronous output is queued to a user, IMS creates the user structure, as needed.

Related Reading: For more information about the Resource Manager, see "Resource Manager" on page 498 or *IMS Version 9: Common Service Layer Guide and Reference*. For more information about how IMS manages terminal and user structures, see *IMS Version 9: Administration Guide: Transaction Manager*.

Descriptors and Exit Routines

Using descriptors and exit routines, you can assign characteristics to dynamic terminals and assign user structures to be associated with those dynamic terminals.

A descriptor provides the basic information for the dynamic terminal. An exit routine completes or changes this information. Two methods of using descriptors and exit routines are:

- You can use many descriptors and code little or no processing logic in exit routines.
- You can use few descriptors and code exit routines to perform much of the processing.

How Descriptors Are Created and Used

All descriptors are created during IMS initialization, prior to IMS startup. You must specify that you want ETO support and ensure that the ETO initialization exit routine (DFSINTX0) does not disable ETO support.

During IMS initialization, IMS reads and validates all ETO descriptors. IMS initialization then continues, and the descriptors remain in storage for the duration of IMS execution. Any changes you make to descriptors become effective after the next initialization of IMS.

IMS uses descriptors to create both terminal and user structures. IMS rebuilds structures during an IMS restart, if appropriate. For example, if messages are queued for a structure and IMS shuts down, the structures are rebuilt when IMS restarts. IMS rebuilds these structures to be the same as they were before the IMS restart. IMS does not use the descriptors or exit routines to rebuild these structures. Therefore, any changes you make to descriptors are only reflected in new structures that are built after IMS restart, and the changes are not reflected in structures that are rebuilt during IMS restart.

Example   USERA signs on using descriptor DESCA, which specifies an auto signoff time of 20 minutes (ASOT=20). USERA starts an IMS conversation, and then IMS abnormally terminates. The system programmer changes DESCA to ASOT=10. After the IMS restart, USERB signs on using DESCA. USERA's structure was rebuilt during the IMS restart. USERA still has a value of 20 minutes for the auto signoff time (ASOT=20), and USERB has a value of 10 minutes for the auto signoff time (ASOT=10).

Summary of ETO Implementation

Figure 19-5 on page 345 shows an overall view of an ETO implementation. The steps that follow correspond to the highlighted numbers in Figure 19-5.

1. The system-defined descriptors that are built during system definition are stored in IMS.PROCLIB as member DFSDSCMx.
2. Your user-defined descriptors that are written to override the system definition defaults are stored in IMS.PROCLIB as member DFSDSCTy. MFS descriptors that are

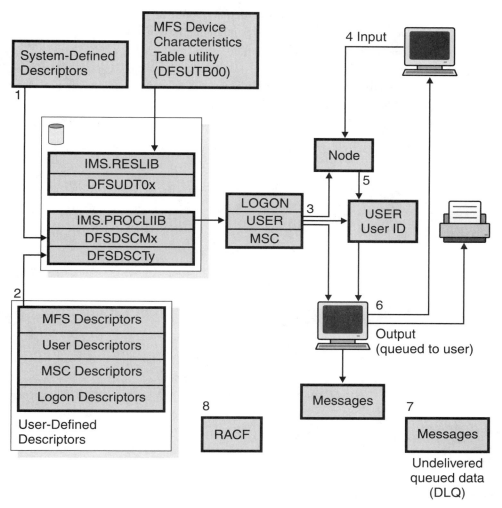

Figure 19-5 Summary of ETO Implementation

processed by the MFS Device Characteristics Table utility (DFSUTB00) are stored in the device characteristics table.

3. Logon, user, and MSC descriptors are loaded at IMS initialization using the input from IMS.PROCLIB.
4. The Logon and Logoff exit routines are called during logon and logoff.
5. The Signon and Signoff exit routines are called during signon and signoff.
6. Output is delivered to the destination specified in the Output Creation exit routine, unless the user is created during signon.

7. If IMS is unable to determine where output should be delivered, the messages are added to the dead-letter queue. Messages might not be delivered because:

- The user name is not a valid user ID.
- The user signon is rejected.
- A physical-to-logical relationship does not exist between the device and the LTERM.

8. RACF (or an equivalent product) manages security in the ETO environment.

CHAPTER 20

Customizing IMS

Customizing IMS is the process of tailoring IMS functions to fit the specific needs of your installation.

Some customization tasks are required before you can use IMS, but most are optional. If you elect not to do optional customization on a specific IMS function, that function then works according to IBM-provided defaults. If IMS is new to your installation, you initially might want to do a minimum amount of optional customization. You can use IMS and you can do additional customization when performance or IMS capabilities indicate the need to do so.

There are a number of ways for you to customize IMS. IMS provides:

- Initialization values you can change.
- Macros you can use.
- Procedures you can change.
- User exits (places in IMS's logic flow) for which you can write exit routines to perform special processing. IMS calls exit routines at various points and allows you to control how IMS performs its work.

One example of customizing might be to interrogate an in-flight message (in an MSC environment) to determine if it originated from a test or production system. If it came from a test system, you might want to route that message to an application that collects data about the test system. If the message originated from a production system, you probably would not want to change its destination.

To perform the interrogation of the message, you would code a TM and MSC Message Routing and Control User Exit routine. If you name this routine DFSMSCE0, place it in the IMS.SDFS-RESL library, and bind it to that library (or a concatenated library), IMS calls your exit routine when IMS receives the message. When your exit routine is done with its processing, the exit routine returns control to IMS and then IMS resumes processing the message to either the original destination or the test application.

Certain exit routines are required and others are optional. Some IBM-supplied exit routines can be used as is and some require modification before using.

> **RECOMMENDATION:** Write IMS exit routines in assembler language rather than high-level languages. IMS does not support exit routines running under Language Environment for z/OS. If an exit routine is written in a high-level language executing in the Language Environment for z/OS, you might incur performance problems or abends.

In This Chapter:

- "What You Can Customize"
- "Naming the Routines" on page 349
- "Changeable Interfaces and Control Blocks" on page 349
- "IMS Standard User Exit Parameter List" on page 349
- "Binding the Routines" on page 349
- "Saving Registers" on page 350
- "IMS Callable Services" on page 350
- "Considering Performance" on page 351
- "Summary of IMS Exit Routines" on page 352

WHAT YOU CAN CUSTOMIZE

Using exit routines, you can:

- Edit messages
- Check security
- Edit transaction code input, message switching input, and physical terminal input and output
- Perform additional application clean-up
- Initialize dependent regions
- Control the number of buffers that the RECON data sets use
- Keep track of updated segments

You can write or include additional routines to customize your IMS system.

You can replace a default exit routine that does not meet your needs by writing one of your own. If you use IMS macros in your exit routine, you must reassemble the routine with the current release level macro library.

NAMING THE ROUTINES

Using standard z/OS conventions, each routine can have any name up to eight characters in length. Be sure that this name is unique and that it does not conflict with the existing members of the data set into which you place the routine. Because most IMS-supplied routines begin with the prefix "DFS", "DBF", "DSP", "DXR", "BPE","CQS", or "CSL", you should not choose a name that begins with these letters, unless the specific routine requires it. Also, specify one entry point for the routine.

Related Reading: See *IMS Version 9: Administration Guide: Database Manager* for more information about establishing naming conventions.

CHANGEABLE INTERFACES AND CONTROL BLOCKS

The interfaces that IMS supplies for use by the exit routines might change in future releases of IMS. IMS control blocks such as the SCD, PST, DMB, or VTCB might also change. Therefore, if you write an exit routine that uses these services or control blocks, you might need to change or reassemble the routine accordingly when you migrate to a new release of IMS.

IMS STANDARD USER EXIT PARAMETER LIST

Many of the IMS user exit routines use a standard user exit interface. This interface allows the exit routines to use callable services to access IMS blocks. At the same time, this interface creates a clearly differentiated programming interface (CDPI) between IMS and the exit routine. Part of the interface consists of a standard user exit parameter list. The list contains items such as a pointer to a version number and a pointer to a function-specific parameter list. All standard user exit parameter lists that have the same version number will contain the same parameters. If a new parameter is added, it is added to the end of the parameter list and the version number is increased by one.

If an exit routine is written to use a parameter that was added in a later version, and the exit routine can execute in an environment in which earlier versions of the parameter list could be received, the exit routine should check the version of the parameter list it received to ensure that the data is available to the exit routine.

BINDING THE ROUTINES

Most modules receive control and must return control in AMODE=31, and must be able to execute in cross-memory and TASK modes.

RECOMMENDATIONS:

- RMODE=ANY is recommended.
- All TM exit routines can be entered simultaneously by multiple dispatchable tasks. Therefore, it is highly recommended that all TM exit routines be coded as *reentrant* (RENT).

All routines receive control and must return control in 31-bit addressing mode (AMODE=31) and must be able to execute in RMODE ANY and AMODE=31.

If you bind an exit routine as reentrant (RENT), it must be truly reentrant (for example, it cannot depend on *any* information from a previous iteration and it cannot store into itself).

If you bind an exit routine as reusable (REUSE), it must be truly reusable (it cannot depend on *any* information in itself from a previous iteration), but it can depend on information that it saves in the specific block passed to it. If you bind a routine that is serially reusable, it must be used for a single database only.

If you bind an exit routine as neither RENT nor REUSE, it can store into itself and depend on the information saved in the block that is passed to it.

If you bind an exit routine as reentrant, it is loaded in key 0 storage to automatically protect the exit routine from being accidentally or intentionally modified.

SAVING REGISTERS

IMS exit routines need to save registers in the save area pointed to by Register 13. This save area is provided at entry. In general, the save area passed to the exit is in 31-bit storage. You should save and restore registers in 31-bit mode.

There are two types of save areas that exit routines use to save registers:

- A prechained save area passed to the exit routine by IMS or the calling application
- A single save area used by exit routines that use the standard user exit parameter list

IMS CALLABLE SERVICES

IMS Callable Services are services provided by IMS for use by IMS exit routines. These services provide clearly defined interfaces that allow exit routines to request various functions.

There are three types of IMS Callable Services: storage services, control block services, and automated operator interface (AOI) services.

Storage Services

Storage services support four functions:

- **Get storage:** Used to obtain user storage
- **Free storage:** Used to release user storage previously obtained by the GET storage service
- **Load module:** Used to load a module
- **Delete module:** Used to delete a module previously obtained by the LOAD storage service

Control Block Services

Control block services support two functions:

- **Find control block:** Used to find a specific instance of a control block
- **Scan control block:** Used to scan control blocks of a certain type

Automated Operator Interface Services

AOI services support three functions:

- **Insert message:** Used to insert the first, or a subsequent, message segment into a message buffer
- **Enqueue message:** Used to insert the last or only message segment into the message buffer
- **Cancel message:** Used to cancel messages that have been inserted into the message buffer but not yet enqueued

Using Callable Services

To use a callable service, do the following:

1. Bind your exit routine to the callable service interface module.
2. Initialize callable services for your exit routine each time your exit routine gets control.
3. Initialize the callable services parameter list.
4. Initialize the function-specific parameter list.
5. Invoke the callable service.

Repeat steps 3 through 5 as many times as necessary while your exit routine has control. Not all exit routines perform all five of the preceding steps.

CONSIDERING PERFORMANCE

Efficiency of exit routines is a prime concern for IMS performance. Most routines are called from the IMS control region and get control in key 7 supervisor state. Some routines might be called from mainline processing code running under the IMS Control Region task. The amount and type of processing that is done by those routines can directly contribute to the total path length and time required to complete a unit of work. Other units of work that must wait to run under a task currently in use by an exit routine can also be impacted. An abend in an exit routine that executes in the IMS control region can cause the IMS control region to abend.

Services such as z/OS WAIT calls, SVC calls, and I/O can all contribute to poor performance and should be used sparingly. When an IMS callable service exists, it is recommended that you use it, rather than the z/OS equivalent, because the callable service is usually optimized to perform more efficiently in an IMS subdispatching environment.

RECOMMENDATIONS:
- Code user-written routines in ways that minimize path length and processing time as much as possible.
- Code user exit routines only in assembler. Exit routines written in other languages might functionally work, but unacceptable performance can result. For example, using a high-level language runtime environment (such as Language Environment for z/OS) can result in unacceptable performance with the initialization and termination of the environment.

SUMMARY OF IMS EXIT ROUTINES

Table 20-1, Table 20-2 on page 353, and Table 20-3 on page 358 list most IMS exit routines and briefly describe what the exit routines can be used for.

Related Reading: For details about all of the IMS user exit routines, see *IMS Version 9: Customization Guide*.

Table 20-1   IMS Database Manager Exit Routines and Their Uses

Exit Routine Name	Description
Data Capture exit routine	Receives control whenever a segment for which the exit routine is defined is updated. Possible use is to enable replication of that data to a DB2 database.
Data Conversion User exit routine (DFSDBUX1)	Receives control at the beginning of a DL/I call and at the end of the call. In the exit routine, you can modify segment search arguments, the key feedback area, the I/O area, and the status code.
Data Entry Database Randomizing routine (DBFHDC40/ DBFHDC44)	Required for placing root segments in or retrieving them from a DEDB.

Table 20-1   IMS Database Manager Exit Routines and Their Uses (Continued)

Exit Routine Name	Description
Data Entry Database Resource Name Hash routine (DBFLHSH0)	Used with the IRLM and enables IMS and DBCTL to maintain and retrieve information about the control intervals (CIs) used by sharing subsystems.
Data Entry Database Sequential Dependent Scan Utility exit routine (DBFUMSE1)	Allows you to copy and process a subset of the number of segments that the utility scans at a particular time.
HALDB Partition Selection exit routine (DFSPSE00)	Used to select partitions by some criteria other than high key.
HDAM and PHDAM Randomizing routines (DFSHDC40)	Required routine for HDAM and PHDAM access methods for placing root segments in, or retrieving them from, HDAM or PHDAM databases.
Secondary Index Database Maintenance exit routine	Used to selectively suppress secondary indexing.
Segment Edit/Compression exit routine (DFSCMPX0)	Used to compress and expand segments of data.
Sequential Buffering Initialization exit routine (DFSSBUX0)	Used to dynamically control the use of sequential buffering (SB) for online and batch IMS subsystems, as well as DBCTL.

Table 20-2   IMS Transaction Manager Exit Routines and Their Uses

Exit Routine Name	Description
Build Security Environment exit routine (DFSBSEX0)	Tells IMS whether or not to build the RACF or equivalent security environment in an IMS dependent region for an application that has received its input message from neither OTMA nor an LU 6.2 device.
Conversational Abnormal Termination exit routine (DFSCONE0)	Used to clean up, if required, when a conversation is terminated prematurely.
Fast Path Input Edit/Routing exit routine (DBFHAGU0)	Used to determine the eligibility of an incoming message for Fast Path processing.
Front-End Switch exit routine (DFSFEBJ0)	Allows you to keep the input terminal in response mode while it is waiting for the reply from the processing system for messages entered in an IMS system by a front-end switchable VTAM node and processed in another system (such as IMS or CICS).

continues

Table 20-2   IMS Transaction Manager Exit Routines and Their Uses (Continued)

Exit Routine Name	Description
Global Physical Terminal (Input) edit routine (DFSGPIX0)	Message segments are passed one at a time to this edit routine so that the routine can process the segments in one of the following ways: • Accept the segment and release it for further editing by the IMS basic edit function. • Modify the segment (for example, change the transaction code or reformat the message text) and release it for further editing by the IMS basic edit function. • Cancel the segment. • Cancel the message and request that IMS send a corresponding message to the terminal operator. • Cancel the message and request that IMS send a specific message from the user message table to the terminal operator.
Greeting Messages exit routine (DFSGMSG0)	Allows you to tailor how IMS handles messages issued during the logon and signon process.
IMS Adapter for REXX exit routine (DFSREXXU)	Has the ability to: • Override the EXEC name to be executed. This name defaults to the IMS program name. • Choose not to execute any EXEC and have the IMS adapter for REXX return to IMS. • Issue DL/I calls using the AIB interface as part of its logic in determining what EXEC to execute. • Set REXX variables (through the TSO/E IRXEXCOM variable access routine) before the EXEC starts. • Extract REXX variables (through IRXEXCOM) after the EXEC ends. • Change the initial default IMSRXTRC tracing level.
Initialization exit routine (DFSINTX0)	Used to create two user data areas that can be used by some of your installation's exit routines.
Input Message Field edit routine (DFSME000)	Used to perform common editing functions such as numeric validation or conversion of blanks to numeric zeros.
Input Message Segment edit routine (DFSME127)	Used to perform common editing functions such as numeric validation or conversion of blanks to numeric zeros.

Table 20-2 IMS Transaction Manager Exit Routines and Their Uses (Continued)

Exit Routine Name	Description
Logoff exit routine (DFSLGFX0)	Used to perform processing that complements the Logon exit routine (DFSLGNX0).
Logon exit routine (DFSLGNX0)	Enables you to control the way logons are processed.
LU 6.2 Edit exit routine (DFSLUEE0)	Enables you to edit input and output LU 6.2 messages for IMS-managed LU 6.2 conversations.
Message Control/Error exit routine (DFSCMUX0)	Used to control transactions, responses, and message switches that are in error.
Message Switching (Input) edit routine (DFSCNTE0)	Similar to the Transaction Code Input edit routine and is capable of message switching.
Non-Discardable Messages exit routine (DFSNDMX0)	Tells IMS what to do with the input message that is associated with an abended application program.
OTMA Destination Resolution exit routine (DFSYDRU0)	Determines and changes the final destination of OTMA member names or Tpipe names that are used for OTMA asynchronous output messages.
OTMA Input/Output Edit exit routine (DFSYIOE0)	Modifies or cancels OTMA input and output messages.
OTMA Prerouting exit routine (DFSYPRX0)	Determines whether an asynchronous output message needs to be routed to an OTMA destination or a non-OTMA destination.
Output Creation exit routine (DFSINSX0)	Validates both an unknown destination for a message and the creation of an unknown user.
Physical Terminal Input edit routine (DFSPIXT0)	Message segments are passed one at a time to the Physical Terminal Input edit routine, and the edit routine can handle them in one of the following ways: • Accept the segment and release it for further editing by the IMS basic edit function. • Modify the segment and release it for further editing by the IMS basic edit function. • Cancel the segment. • Cancel the message and request that the terminal operator be notified accordingly. • Cancel the message and request that a specific message from the user message table be sent to the terminal operator.

continues

Table 20-2   IMS Transaction Manager Exit Routines and Their Uses (Continued)

Exit Routine Name	Description
Physical Terminal Output edit routine (DFSCTTO0)	Edits output messages immediately before they are sent to a terminal.
Queue Space Notification exit routine (DFSQSPC0/DFSQSSP0)	This exit routine is activated when a logical record is assigned to or released from a message queue data set. This routine causes a message to be issued when one of the following situations occurs: • The number of records currently in use exceeds the upper threshold percentage value of the maximum number assignable before initiation of automatic shutdown. • The number of records currently in use falls below the lower threshold percentage value of the same maximum.
Security Reverification exit routine (DFSCTSE0)	Reevaluates transaction authorization checking on the DL/I CHNG Call.
Shared Printer exit routine (DFSSIML0)	Decides whether a terminal that is unavailable can be automatically acquired by IMS or an AOI application program.
Sign-On exit routine (DFSSGNX0)	Used for signon processing if ETO=Y is specified.
Signoff exit routine (DFSSGFX0)	Used for signoff processing.
Sign On/Off Security exit routine (DFSCSGN0)	Verifies a user's ID and password. This exit routine can conflict with the Sign-On exit routine (DFSSGNX0).
Time-Controlled Operations (TCO) exit routine (DFSTXIT0)	Inserts messages that are the commands, transactions, and message switches that you specify in the time schedule requests and message sets that make up a script member.
TM and MSC Message Routing and Control User exit routine (DFSMSCE0)	• Provides maximum routing control for TM and MSC messages. • Eases TM and MSC coding and maintenance requirements, and reduces the number of exit modules. • Supports a consistent set of routing capabilities across all of the exit entry points (or functions). • Provides a common parameter list interface and linkage interface to the various entry points (or functions).

Table 20-2   IMS Transaction Manager Exit Routines and Their Uses (Continued)

Exit Routine Name	Description
TM and MSC Message Routing and Control User exit routine (DFSMSCE0) (continued)	• Provides the ability to append an optional user prefix segment to TM and MSC messages which TM and MSC user exit routines can use to communicate and control user-customized routing needs. • Logs routing errors and footprints in the message to indicate those exit routines that reroute the message.
Transaction Authorization exit routine (DFSCTRN0)	Works with the Security Reverification exit routine (DFSCTSE0) and the Sign On/Off Security exit routine (DFSCSGN0) to check an individual user ID for authority to use a transaction.
Transaction Code (Input) edit routine (DFSCSMB0)	Used to edit input messages before they are enqueued for scheduling.
Type 1 Automated Operator exit routine (DFSAOUE0)	This AO exit routine is called continuously for system messages destined for the master terminal, operator-entered commands, and command responses. Use it to: • Ignore selected segments or an entire message. • Send a copy of a system message, command, or command response to an alternate destination. • Send a new message to an alternate destination for a system message, command, or command response. • Change a system message. • Change a system message and send a copy to an alternate destination. • Change a copy of a command or command response and send the copy to an alternate destination. • Delete a system message. • Delete a system message and send a copy to an alternate destination. • Request the edited command buffer (when the input is a command).
2972/2980 Input edit routine (DFS29800)	Required to perform terminal-related functions inherent in the design of the 2972/2980 General Banking Terminal system.
4701 Transaction Input edit routine (DFS36010)	Appends a blank and the 8-byte node name to a transaction input message.

Table 20-3   IMS System Exit Routines and Their Uses

Exit Routine Name	Description
Application Group Name (AGN) exit routine (DFSISIS0)	Provides users without RACF a mechanism for checking authorization to IMS application group names (AGNs). **Recommendation:** Use the Resource Access Security exit routine (DFSRAS00) instead of this exit routine for AGNs.
Buffer Size Specification Facility (DSPBUFFS)	Allows you to control the number of buffers used for RECON data sets when either the local shared resource (LSR) or the nonshared resource (NSR) buffering option is used.
Command Authorization exit routine (DFSCCMD0)	Verifies the authority of a command that is issued from a particular origin.
DBRC Command Authorization exit routine (DSPDCAX0)	Determines (in conjunction with RACF or another security product) the success or failure of DBRC command authorization.
Dependent Region Preinitialization Routines	Dependent Region Preinitialization routines enable you to perform any application-unique dependent region initialization.
Dump Override Table (DFSFDOT0)	Either forces or suppresses dumps for specified abends.
ESAF Indoubt Notification exit routine (DFSFIDN0)	Resolves in-doubt work before restarting a failed IMS.
IMS Command Language Modification Facility (DFSCKWD0)	Modifies the command keyword table.
Large SYSGEN Sort/Split Input exit routine (DFSSS050)	Alters the resource data for user-generated resources.
Large SYSGEN Sort/Split Output exit routine (DFSSS060)	Alters the resource data for user-generated resources.
Log Archive exit routine	Produces an edited subset of the complete IMS log.
Log Filter exit routine (DFSFTFX0)	Controls the amount of log data sent to an RSR tracking subsystem, by acting as a filter.
Logger exit routine (DFSFLGX0)	Processes log data for recovery purposes.
Partner Product exit routine (DFSPPUE0)	Initializes products that run with IMS.
RECON I/O exit routine (DSPCEXT0)	Tracks changes to the RECON data set, which you can log in a journal.

Table 20-3 IMS System Exit Routines and Their Uses (Continued)

Exit Routine Name	Description
Resource Access Security exit routine (DFSRAS00)	Authorizes IMS resources such as transactions, PSBs, or output LTERM names. **Recommendation:** Use this exit routine instead of the Application Group Name exit routine (DFSISIS0) for AGNs.
SCI Registration exit routine (DSPSCIX0)	Used by DBRC to perform an authorization check before allowing a potential SCI client to register with SCI.
System Definition Preprocessor exit routine (Input Phase) (DFSPRE60)	Alters, inserts, or deletes data from stage 1 input before the preprocessor record scan occurs.
System Definition Preprocessor exit routine (Name Check Complete) (DFSPRE70)	Builds tables that contain resource names that have been cross-checked.
Type 2 Automated Operator exit routine (DFSAOE00)	• Modifies the text of IMS system messages. • Deletes IMS system messages. • Directs any message, command, or command response to an Automated Operator (AO) application. • Starts a BMP job (for example, an AO application).
User Message Table (DFSCMTU0)	Used to create your own messages and list them in your own message table.

CHAPTER 21

IMS Security

 his chapter provides an overview of the IMS security features.

In This Chapter:

- "History of IMS Security"
- "Security Overview"
- "Securing Resources" on page 363

HISTORY OF IMS SECURITY

When IMS was developed, security products such as the Resource Access Control Facility (RACF) had not yet been developed, or were not in use by most installations. Before RACF was developed, it was common for each subsystem to implement its own security. Therefore, IMS offered basic levels of protection for IMS resources. These internal IMS security facilities (for example, the Security Maintenance utility, access specifications in DBDs, or command authorization) are available for protecting many IMS resource types and are used by some IMS installations today.

With the development and introduction of security products, such as RACF, more and more installations have implemented security for IMS resources using such security products.

SECURITY OVERVIEW

When you initiate security safeguards, you must balance the requirements of those users who are responsible for the security of resources and those users who legitimately need access to those resources. Because an individual assigned to resource security is held responsible for resources that might be compromised, that person should not allow easy access to dominate protection measures. On the other hand, users performing their assigned tasks need convenient access to the resources. The users and the security specialist should work out a balanced approach between the ease of resource access and the complexity of protecting that resource.

IMS provides ample flexibility in allowing the installation to secure any type of resource.

In an IMS system, you should consider various facets of the security implementation:

- The resource name: For example, a user might be allowed access to the Part database but not to the Customer Order database.
- The level of access: What the user can do to the resource. For example, a user might be allowed to read a file but not to update it.

IMS provides a system definition macro (the SECURITY macro) that allows the installation to code all of the security specifications on one macro. The SECURITY macro specifies security options for IMS internally provided SMU security, RACF security, an installation-provided security exit routine, or any combination of these facilities.

Before you decide what security facilities to use in designing a secure IMS system, you should know which resources within the system need protection. In other words, you should decide what to protect before you decide how to protect it.

Two advantages of using a security product for securing access to resources are:

- One product can be used to implement the security requirements for multiple subsystems, such as IMS, CICS, and other subsystems.
- All of the security information can be kept and maintained in one place, such as the RACF database. One centralized database repository containing all the installation's security specifications eliminates, or significantly minimizes, the problems inherent with using individual product's security functions, namely:
  - Duplicating and distributing security information among several subsystems
  - Coordinating the security enforcement functions implemented in multiple products

RACF offers a wide range of security choices to the installation. For example, RACF contains security features such as user-identification-based security and verification-based security, which are not available with the SMU.

> **RECOMMENDATION:**   IBM recommends that you implement security using only RACF or an equivalent security product because IMS Version 9 is the last version of IMS to support the SMU.

Related Reading: For more information about IMS security, see:

- Chapter 4, "Establishing IMS Security," in the *IMS Version 9: Administration Guide: System*
- *IMS Version 9: Installation Volume 2: System Definition and Tailoring*
- The IBM Redbook *IMS Security Guide*
- *z/OS V1R4 Security Server RACF Security Administrator's Guide*

SECURING RESOURCES

Table 21-1 lists the:

- Resources you can protect
- Valid security options for that resource
- Facilities available to protect that resource
- Applicable environments

Table 21-1   Resources That Can Be Secured, Types of Protection, the Facilities to Protect Them, and Valid Environments

Resource	Type of Protection	Facilities	Valid Environments
Command	Default terminal security	System definition	DB/DC, DCCTL
	LTERM security[a]	SMU	DB/DC, DCCTL
	Password security[a]	SMU	DB/DC, DCCTL
	Transaction command security	SMU, RACF	DB/DC, DCCTL
	Input access security	RACF	DB/DC, DCCTL
	IMSplex command security	RACF	DB/DC, DCCTL
	DBRC command authorization[b]	RACF or exit routine	DB/DC, DCCTL
Database	Segment sensitivity	PSBGEN RACF	DB/DC, DCCTL, DBCTL
	Field sensitivity	PSBGEN RACF	DB/DC, DCCTL, DBCTL
	Password security (for /LOCK, /UNLOCK commands)	SMU or RACF	DB/DC, DCCTL, DBCTL

continues

Table 21-1   Resources That Can Be Secured, Types of Protection, the Facilities to Protect Them, and Valid Environments (Continued)

Resource	Type of Protection	Facilities	Valid Environments
Dependent region	Application group name (AGN) security	SMU and exit routine or SMU and RACF	DB/DC, DCCTL, DBCTL
	APSB security	RACF	DB/DC, DCCTL, DBCTL
	Resource Access Security (RAS)	RACF	DB/DC, DCCTL, DBCTL
IMS online system (control region)	Extended resource protection (using APPL resource class)	RACF	DB/DC, DCCTL, DBCTL
LTERM[a]	Password security (for /IAM, /LOCK, /UNLOCK commands)	SMU or RACF	DB/DC, DCCTL
	AGN security	SMU and exit routine or SMU and RACF	DB/DC, DCCTL
	RAS security	RACF	DB/DC, DCCTL
LU 6.2 inbound and IMS-managed outbound conversations	Allocate verification security	RACF and exit routine	DB/DC, DCCTL
	Input access security	RACF and exit routine	DB/DC, DCCTL
Online application program	Password security (for /IAM, /LOCK, /UNLOCK commands)	SMU or RACF	DB/DC, DCCTL
	Extended resource protection (using APPL keyword)	RACF	DB/DC, DCCTL
PSB	AGN security	SMU and exit routine or SMU and RACF	DB/DC, DCCTL, DBCTL
	RAS	RACF	DB/DC, DCCTL, DBCTL
	APSB security	RACF[c]	DB/DC, DCCTL
PTERM[a]	Signon verification security	SMU and exit routine or RACF and exit routine	DB/DC, DCCTL
	Terminal-user security	RACF	DB/DC, DCCTL
	Password security (for /IAM, /LOCK, /UNLOCK commands)	SMU or RACF	DB/DC, DCCTL

Table 21-1 Resources That Can Be Secured, Types of Protection, the Facilities to Protect Them, and Valid Environments (Continued)

Resource	Type of Protection	Facilities	Valid Environments
System data set	Operating system password protection	z/OS	DB/DC, DCCTL, DBCTL
	Data set protection (VSAM) (using PERMIT, RDEFINE classes)	RACF	DB/DC, DCCTL
Terminals defined with ETO	Signon verification security	RACF and exit routine	DB/DC, DCCTL
	Input access security	RACF and exit routine	DB/DC, DCCTL
Transaction	LTERM security[a]	SMU	DB/DC, DCCTL
	AGN security	SMU and exit routine or SMU and RACF	DB/DC, DCCTL
	Input access security	RACF	DB/DC, DCCTL
	RAS	RACF	DB/DC, DCCTL
	Password security[a] (for /LOCK, /UNLOCK commands)	SMU or RACF	DB/DC, DCCTL
Type 1 Automated Operator Interface (AOI) applications	Transaction command security	SMU or RACF and Command Authorization exit routine	DB/DC, DCCTL
Type 2 AOI applications	Transaction command security	RACF and Command Authorization exit routine	DB/DC, DCCTL

a.   Static terminals only. Not applicable to ETO-defined terminals.

b.   DBRC Command Authorization is an additional command security option for DBRC commands only. DBRC commands are also subject to any other command security options that are active in the IMS system.

c.   Using RACF to secure APSBs applies to CPI-C driven applications only.

CHAPTER **22**

IMS Logging

During IMS execution, all information that is necessary to restart the system in the event of hardware or software failure is recorded in a system log data set. The following critical system information is recorded in the logs:

- The receipt of an input message in the input queue
- The start of an MPP or BMP program
- The receipt of a message by the MPP for processing
- Before and after images of data base updates by the MPP or BMP program
- The insert of a message into the queue by the MPP
- The termination of an MPP or BMP program
- The successful receipt of an output message by the terminal

In This Chapter:

- "IMS System Checkpoints"
- "Database Recovery Control Facility (DBRC)" on page 368
- "IMS Log Components" on page 368

IMS SYSTEM CHECKPOINTS

At regular intervals during IMS execution, checkpoints are written to the log without having to wait to do any physical I/O. A checkpoint is taken after a specified number of log records are written to the log since the previous checkpoint, or after a checkpoint command. Special checkpoint commands are available to stop IMS in an orderly manner.

Related Reading: For information about the commands that are used to stop IMS, see *IMS Version 9: Operations Guide.*

DATABASE RECOVERY CONTROL FACILITY (DBRC)

DBRC is an integral part of IMS logging.

DBRC keeps information about all of IMS's logging activities in the recovery control (RECON) data sets.

Related Reading: For more information about DBRC, see Chapter 23, "Database Recovery Control (DBRC) Facility," on page 375 and *IMS Version 9: Database Recovery Control (DBRC) Guide and Reference.*

IMS LOG COMPONENTS

The IMS logs comprise a number of components, which are described in the following sections:

- "IMS Log Buffers"
- "Online Log Data Sets (OLDSs)" on page 369
- "Write-Ahead Data Sets (WADSs)" on page 371
- "System Log Data Sets (SLDSs)" on page 372
- "Recovery Log Data Sets (RLDSs)" on page 373

IMS Log Buffers

IMS uses the IMS log buffers to write any information required to be logged, without having to do any real I/O.

Whenever a log buffer is full, IMS schedules the complete log buffer to be written out to the online data set (OLDS) as a background, asynchronous task. In a busy system, IMS generally chains these log buffer write operations together.

Should any application or system function require a log record to be externalized (that is, IMS believes that for recoverability, this log record must be physically written to DASD before proceeding), then IMS uses the write-ahead data set (WADS). See "Write-Ahead Data Sets (WADSs)" on page 371.

The OLDS log buffers are used in such a manner as to keep available as long as possible the log records that might be needed for dynamic backout. If a needed log record is no longer available in storage, one of the OLDS buffers is used for reading the appropriate blocks from the OLDS.

The number of log buffers is specified as an IMS startup parameter. The maximum number of log buffers is 999. The size of each log buffer is dependent on the actual block size of the physical OLDS. The IMS log buffers reside in extended private storage, however; there is a log buffer prefix that exists in extended common service area (ECSA).

Online Log Data Sets (OLDSs)

The OLDSs are the data sets that contain all the log records that are required for restart and recovery. These data sets must be pre-allocated, but need not be pre-formatted, on DASD, and hold the log records until they are archived.

The OLDS is written using BSAM. OSAM is used to read the OLDS for dynamic backout.

The OLDS are made up of multiple data sets that are used in a wrap-around manner. At least 3 data sets must be allocated for the OLDS to allow IMS to start, while an upper limit of 100 is supported.

To enhance performance, only complete log buffers are written to the OLDS. Should any incomplete buffers need to be written out, they are written to the WADS. When the WADS is unavailable, such as at IMS shutdown and when IMS is in degraded logging mode (running with too few OLDSs) , then any incomplete buffers are written to the OLDS.

All OLDSs should be dynamically allocated by using the DFSMDA macro, and not hardcoded in the IMS control region JCL.

Dual Logging of OLDS

You can implement dual logging, optionally, with a primary and secondary data set for each defined OLDS.

- A primary and secondary data set are matched and, therefore, the pair should have the same space allocation. Because an OLDS pair contains the same data, extra space allocated to one data set is not used in the other.
- You cannot use secondary extent allocation.
- OLDSs can be allocated on different supported DASDs.
- All OLDSs must have the same block size, and be a multiple of 2 KB (2048 bytes). The maximum allowable block size is 30 KB.

Dynamic Backout

To allow IMS to dynamically back out a failed MPR or BMP program, IMS writes the before images of each database change to the OLDS. These before images show the database record as it was before the program updated it. When the MPR or BMP program issues a synchronization-point call, IMS discards these before images for the program.

Archiving an OLDS

Whenever one of the following situations occurs, the current OLDSs (both primary and secondary) are closed and the next OLDS is used:

- OLDS becomes full.
- I/O error occurs.
- MTO command (such as /SWI OLDS) is issued to force a log switch.
- MTO command (such as /DBR DB without the NOFEOV parameter) is issued to close a database.

When IMS starts using a new OLDS, it automatically notifies DBRC. When this situation occurs, IMS can automatically submit the archive job to the Log Archive utility (DFSUARC0) by using the ARC= IMS startup parameter.

IMS can define whether the log archive process occurs with every log switch or every second log switch. The DBRC skeletal JCL that controls the archiving can be defined to also create one or two system log data sets (SLDSs), and zero, one, or two recovery log data sets (RLDSs). After the last allocated OLDS has been used, the first OLDS is used again in a wrap-around fashion, as long as it has been archived.

The Log Archive utility JCL is in DBRC skeletal JCL, and you can tailor it to create the required SLDS, and optionally dual SLDSs, one or two RLDSs, and any user data sets. Figure 22-1 shows the data sets for the Log Archive utility.

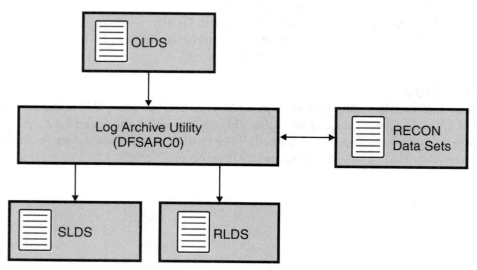

Figure 22-1   Inputs and Outputs of the Log Archive Utility

Related Reading: For the details about the Log Archive utility, see *IMS Version 9: Utilities Reference: System.*

OLDS I/O Errors
In the case of a write error, IMS puts the subject OLDS (or pair of OLDSs) into a stopped status and it is not used again. This action is equivalent to a user issuing the /STO OLDS command.

If using dual OLDS, then the data set without error is used for IMS archives.

If data set errors result in only a single OLDS that remains, IMS internally schedules a /CHE FREEZE command to shut down the IMS system. If an error occurs on the very last OLDS, IMS abends with a U0618 code.

Information about the OLDS for each IMS system is kept in the RECON data set. The data in the RECON data set indicates whether an OLDS contains active log data that must be archived, or whether the OLDS is available for use.

Too Few Available OLDSs
IMS issues messages when it is running out of OLDSs.

- During the use of the last available OLDS, IMS indicates that no spare OLDS are available.
- When all the OLDSs are full, and the archives have not successfully completed, then IMS stops, and waits until at least one OLDS is archived. IMS repeatedly issues messages to indicate that it is out of OLDSs, and is waiting.

Write-Ahead Data Sets (WADSs)
The WADS is a small, high-performance direct access data set that contains a copy of committed log records that are in OLDS buffers but have not yet been written to the OLDS.

When IMS processing requires writing of a partially filled OLDS buffer, a portion of the buffer is written to the WADS. If IMS or the system fails, the log data in the WADS is used to close (terminate) the OLDS, either as part of an emergency restart or as an option on the Log Recovery utility.

The WADS space is continually reused after the appropriate log data is written to the OLDS. The WADS is required for all IMS systems, and must be pre-allocated and formatted at IMS startup when first used.

All WADSs should be dynamically allocated by using the DFSMDA macro, and not hardcoded in the control region JCL.

All WADSs must be on the same device type and have the same space allocation.

Dual WADS Logging

Dual WADS logging is supported to provide backup in the event of a read error while terminating the OLDS from the WADS. The primary and secondary WADS will contain the same data. Single or dual WADS logging is determined from an IMS startup parameter.

Additional WADS

You can define up to ten WADS to any IMS (for example, WADS0, WADS1, ..., WADS9).

WADS0 (and WADS1 if running dual WADS) is active, and the rest remain as spares in case any active WADS has an I/O error. The next spare then replaces the one with the error.

System Log Data Sets (SLDSs)

The SLDS is created by the Log Archive utility, optionally after every OLDS switch. The SLDS is usually written to tape or to a cartridge, but can also reside on DASD. The SLDS can contain the data from one or more OLDS data sets.

The SLDS can also be used as input to all IMS log utilities, and IMS restart.

Information about the SLDS is maintained by DBRC in the RECON data set. Calls to DBRC are made by the Log Archive utility, which identifies the OLDS being archived and the SLDS being created. OLDS that have been archived are then available for reuse by IMS.

Dual Archiving SLDSs

IMS supports dual archiving to two SLDS data sets (primary and secondary).

When archiving to tape or to a cartridge, the user can also force the primary and secondary volumes to contain the same data by specifying the number of log blocks per volume. When this number is reached, a force-end-of-volume (FEOV) occurs on both the primary and secondary SLDSs. In this way, both primary and secondary SLDSs are identical and interchangeable if a subsequent I/O error occurs on one of them.

You can also specify which records are copied from the OLDS to the SLDS. Generally, the SLDS should contain all the log records from the OLDS, but if you want to omit types of log records from the SLDS, you can specify these within the Log Archive utility.

The SLDS must always contain those log records required for database recovery, batch backout processing, or system recovery.

The block size of the SLDS is independent of the block size of the OLDS, and can be specified to maximize space on the SLDS device type.

Recovery Log Data Sets (RLDSs)

When you run the Log Archive utility, you can request that an output data set be created that contains all of the log records needed for database recovery. This output data set is called the recovery log data set (RLDS), and is also known to DBRC.

The RLDS is preferred by many installations. All database recoveries and change accumulation jobs use the RLDS if one exists. Having an RLDS available can considerably speed up any of the recovery processes because the only contents of these data sets are database recovery log records. Other IMS TM, application scheduling, and checkpoint log records are not included on the RLDSs.

The RLDS is optional, and you can also have dual copies of it, as you can with the SLDS.

IMS Log Data Sets and Data Facility Storage Management Subsystem (DFSMS)

Although most IMS data sets can be managed by DFSMS, OLDS data sets should not be managed by DFSMS because if an OLDS is migrated (not very likely in most installations), it might be recalled with different attributes.

OLDS data sets must be allocated in contiguous space. If the OLDS were managed by DFSMS, both the primary and secondary OLDS data sets might be placed on the same volume. If that volume becomes unreadable, this is a major problem. Use management classes to avoid this situation.

Write-ahead data sets (WADS) have a very high write rate and are very sensitive to slow response. These data sets should be placed with some care. DFSMS might not provide a good place to allocate them.

If OLDS, RLDS, SLDS, or image copy data sets are managed by DFSMS, the CATDS parameter must be set for the RECON data set. The CATDS parameter tells DBRC to use the system catalog to find data sets and not be concerned if they are not on the same volumes to which they were originally allocated.

CATDS and cataloging is a good choice even when the data sets are not managed by DFSMS.

CHAPTER 23

Database Recovery Control (DBRC) Facility

 he Database Recovery Control (DBRC) facility includes the IMS functions that:

- Ensure IMS system and database integrity.
- Control log and database recovery.
- Control access to databases by various IMS subsystems sharing those databases.

Related Reading: This chapter contains an overview of DBRC and briefly describes how to use it. For the details about DBRC, see *IMS Version 9: Database Recovery Control (DBRC) Guide and Reference*.

In This Chapter:

Overview of DBRC

DBRC is an integral part of IMS. IMS relies on DBRC to:

- Record and manage information about many items. DBRC keeps this information in a set of VSAM data sets that are collectively called the RECovery CONtrol (RECON) data sets.
- Advise IMS (based on the information in the RECON data sets) about how to proceed for certain IMS actions.

Specifically, DBRC:

- Helps you ensure IMS system and database integrity by recording and managing information associated with the logging process.
- Assists IMS in the restart process by notifying IMS which logs to use for restart.
- Assists IMS to allow or prevent access to databases in data-sharing environments by recording and managing database authorization information.
- Facilitates database and log recovery by:
  — Controlling the use and integrity of the information in the logs.
  — Recording and maintaining information about the databases and logs in the RECON data set.
  — Generating and verifying the JCL for various IMS utility programs.
- Supports Extended Recovery Facility (XRF) by identifying (in the RECON data set) if the subsystem is XRF capable.
- Supports Remote Site Recovery (RSR) by containing the RSR complex definition in the RECON data set and providing other services associated with controlling RSR.
- Supports IMSplexes by notifying all DBRCs in the same IMSplex when one of the DBRCs performs a RECON data set reconfiguration.

DBRC Tasks

DBRC automatically performs the following tasks:

- Records and manages information about logs for IMS
- Records recovery information in the RECON data set
- Verifies that database utilities have the correct input
- Controls the recovery of databases that are registered with DBRC
- Controls the access authorization information for the control and serialization of shared databases

You can perform the following tasks and more when you initiate them by passing commands or requests to DBRC:

- Start or stop the DBRC application programming interface (API)
- Record recovery information in the RECON data set
- Generate JCL for various IMS utilities and generate user-defined output
- List general information in the RECON data set
- Gather specific information from the RECON data set

DBRC COMPONENTS

DBRC includes the following components, which are introduced in this section:

- "RECON Data Set"
- "Database Recovery Control Utility (DSPURX00)"
- "Skeletal JCL" on page 378

RECON Data Set

DBRC stores recovery-related information in the RECON data sets.

> **RECOMMENDATION:** Define three VSAM KSDSs for the RECON data sets when you install DBRC. The first two data sets are active data sets; the third one is a spare. The second active data set is a copy of the first. For most purposes, you can think of the two active RECON data sets as if they were a single data set, the RECON data set.

Related Reading: These data sets are described in "Overview of the RECON Data Sets" on page 395.

Database Recovery Control Utility (DSPURX00)

Use the Database Recovery Control utility to issue DBRC commands.

The DBRC commands allow you to perform all of the following tasks:

- List the information in the RECON data set
- Update the information in the RECON data set
- Use the information in the RECON data set to generate jobs for the IMS utilities

Skeletal JCL

DBRC uses partitioned data set (PDS) members as input models (or templates) for generating input for some of the recovery utilities. These PDS members are distributed with IMS and are called *skeletal JCL*.

DBRC uses the skeletal JCL, information from the RECON data set, and instructions from a GENJCL command to generate the JCL and control statements that are needed to correctly run some of the recovery utilities. Modify the skeletal JCL to reflect your installation's system configuration.

IMS provides PDS members that contain skeletal JCL statements. These PDS members are called skeletal JCL execution members and can be found in the IMS.SDFSISRC target library.

The IMS Installation Verification Program (IVP) customizes the skeletal JCL execution members and places the customized members into the IMS.PROCLIB procedure library. DBRC uses the members (from IMS.PROCLIB) to generate jobs (JCL and control statements) for the IMS utilities. There is also a skeletal JCL execution member, JOBJCL, that produces a JOB statement.

WHEN SHOULD YOU USE DBRC?

Most IMS configurations require DBRC, including:

- Online configurations: DB/DC, DCCTL, or DBCTL
- Data-sharing environments, including IMSplexes
- Configurations that use Extended Recovery Facility (XRF)
- Remote Site Recovery (RSR)

DBRC also plays a key role in managing the log data needed to restart and recover IMS online subsystems.

> **ATTENTION:** DBRC is not required for IMS batch jobs and for some offline utilities. However, if batch jobs and utilities that access registered databases are allowed to run without DBRC, the recoverability and integrity of the databases could be lost. Even if your configuration does not require the use of DBRC (such as in a non-data-sharing, non-RSR batch environment), you can simplify your recovery process by using DBRC to supervise recovery and protect your databases.

Related Reading: *IMS Version 9: Operations Guide* provides detailed descriptions of recovery procedures with and without DBRC.

You need to make two decisions about using DBRC. The first decision is whether or not DBRC is active in your IMS system. If you decide that DBRC is active, the second decision is whether databases must be registered to DBRC.

- **Whether or not DBRC is active:** DBRC is always active in an IMS control region (DBCTL, DCCTL, or DB/DC). You cannot override this. A BMP region does not have a DBRC execution parameter. DBRC is always active in the IMS control region that the BMP connects to.

  For batch and utility regions, you can use module DFSIDEF0 to specify whether or not DBRC is active. In DFSIDEF0, you can set DBRC= to YES, NO, or FORCE. The FORCE parameter forces DBRC usage in all other address spaces. FORCE cannot be overridden in the JCL.

  The YES, NO, and FORCE parameters control whether DBRC is active in an address space. The level of functions available is controlled by information in the RECON data set.

- **Whether or not databases must be registered to DBRC:** The option to force registration or not (NOFORCER or FORCER parameters on the INIT.RECON command) controls whether or not databases *must* be registered DBRC. Whether a database is registered to DBRC or not is recorded in the RECON data set.

  — If NOFORCER is specified, databases might, or might not be listed as being registered in the RECON data set. If a database is not in the RECON as being registered and DBRC is active, you get a warning message each time the database is opened.

  — If FORCER is specified and if DBRC is active in the address space, all databases must be listed in the RECON data set as registered. If the database is not registered, DBRC rejects authorization and the job abends (in DBCTL environments, the PSB fails to schedule, but the DBCTL region stays up).

If a database is listed in the RECON data set as registered and you run a job with DBRC=N, the next time you run a job with DBRC=Y, a warning message is issued flagging the fact the database has been accessed outside of DBRC control. You might want to take an image copy at that point. When you run a job with DBRC=N, there is an incomplete record of updates, which is useless for recovery purposes.

COMMUNICATING WITH DBRC

Use DBRC batch and online commands or DBRC API requests to obtain services from DBRC. The following sections discuss these commands and requests in more detail.

DBRC Commands

Use DBRC batch and online commands to:

- Add, change, and delete information in the RECON data sets
- Generate the JCL and the control statements necessary to run the various IMS utilities used in database recovery

The following is a list of the DBRC batch commands:

- BACKUP.RECON: Used to create backup copies of the RECON data set.
- CHANGE: Used to modify information in a RECON data set.
- DELETE: Used to delete information from a RECON data set.
- GENJCL: Used to generate JCL and utility control statements that run the various IMS recovery utilities.
- INIT: Used make the following changes to a RECON data set:
  — Create entries
  — Create change accumulation (CA) groups
  — Register DBDSs or DEDB areas
  — Define global service groups
  — Register HALDB partition
  — Initialize a RECON data set
- LIST: Used to produce a formatted printout of all or selected information contained in a RECON data set.
- NOTIFY: Used to add information to a RECON data set that is normally written there automatically.
- RESET.GSG: Used to remove obsolete recovery information from an original active site RECON data set.

You issue these batch commands to DBRC by including them in the JCL job that runs the Database Recovery Control utility (DSPURX00).

You can issue a variation of some of the DBRC batch commands online using the /RMxxxxxx command (for example, /RMCHANGE.RECON).

Related Reading: For more information about the DBRC commands, see Part 2, "DBRC Command Reference" in *IMS Version 9: Database Recovery Control (DBRC) Guide and Reference.*

DBRC Application Programming Interface (API)

The DBRC API was introduced with IMS Version 9. You can write programs that issue requests to the DBRC API instead of issuing DBRC batch commands that are embedded in the JCL job that runs the Database Recovery Control utility. Use DBRC API requests to:

- Start and stop DBRC.
- Query information from the RECON data set.

The following is a list of the DBRC API requests:

- STARTDBRC: Used to initialize the DBRC API and to start DBRC.
- QUERY: Used to retrieve information from the RECON data set.
- RELBUF: Used to release storage that was acquired as a result of a DBRC query request.
- STOPDBRC: Used to terminate the DBRC API and to stop DBRC.

Related Reading: For more information about the DBRC API and the API requests, see the chapter titled "Using the DBRC API" in *IMS Version 9: Database Recovery Control (DBRC) Guide and Reference.*

DBRC FUNCTIONS

The following sections describe DBRC's major functions:

- "Recording and Controlling Log Information"
- "How DBRC Helps in Recovery" on page 385
- "Recording Information about Opening and Updating Databases" on page 390
- "Supporting Data Sharing" on page 391
- "Supporting Remote Site Recovery" on page 394
- "Supporting IMSplexes" on page 395

Recording and Controlling Log Information

As IMS operates, it constantly records its activities in the IMS logs. The IMS logs contain information about:

- IMS startups and shutdowns
- Changes made to databases
- Transaction requests received and responses sent
- Application program initializations and terminations
- Application program checkpoints
- IMS system checkpoints

The IMS logs consist of the:

- Write-ahead data set (WADS)
- Online log data set (OLDS)
- System log data set (SLDS)
- Recovery log data set (RLDS)

Figure 23-1 shows the log data sets and restart data set (RDS) that IMS produces and the RECON data set that DBRC creates and maintains.

Related Reading: See *IMS Version 9: Operations Guide* for detailed discussions of the IMS logging process.

After you have initialized DBRC, it participates in the IMS logging process by recording and controlling information about IMS's logging activities. This information is recorded in the RECON data set. If you want DBRC to control the recovery of your database data sets (DBDSs), you must register them with DBRC.

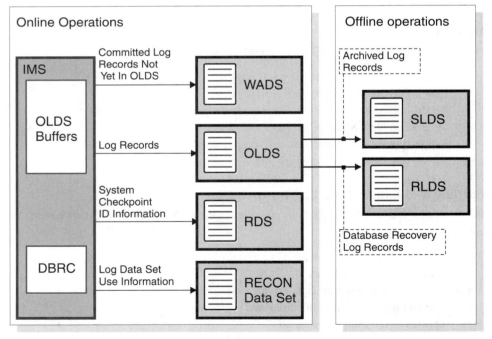

Figure 23-1   Logs Produced for Recovery and Restart

DBRC automatically records many items in the RECON data set, including:

- Information about log data sets
- Information about database data sets
- Information about events, such as:
  - Database updates
  - Database authorizations
  - Creation of database image copies
  - Reorganizations of databases
  - Recoveries of databases
  - Archiving of an OLDS and creation of the corresponding SLDS and RLDS
  - Execution of the Log Recovery utility
  - Subsystem sign-on
- Definitions and information about events for Remote Site Recovery

IMS uses this information for restarting itself and for database recovery jobs (if the databases are registered with DBRC). DBRC also tracks the archiving requirements of the OLDS and, if requested, generates and submits the JCL for archiving jobs.

DBRC also provides unit-of-recovery management for all attached subsystems. DBRC provides information about these units of recovery for batch backout, dynamic backout, partial backout, and restart.

For logs produced by batch systems, you are not required to use DBRC. The advantage of using DBRC for batch jobs is that DBRC records information about all the log data sets that are produced by batch jobs and prevents batch update jobs from executing if you specify a dummy or null log data set.

Changing Log Records in the RECON Data Set

Use the CHANGE.PRILOG or CHANGE.SECLOG commands to modify the information about OLDSs, RLDSs, or SLDSs in the log record of the RECON data set. Update the log record to indicate when errors have occurred on the data sets or that volume serial numbers have changed. You do not normally need to use these commands.

Archiving an OLDS

Run the Log Archive utility to archive an OLDS to an SLDS so that IMS can reuse the OLDS. How frequently you should archive depends on the load on the subsystem and the number of log records written to the OLDSs.

The Log Archive utility always produces an SLDS. The SLDS contains all log records that are required for both database recovery and for online IMS restart.

You can ask the Log Archive utility to produce an RLDS in addition to an SLDS. The RLDS contains only those log records that are required for database recovery.

If you request an RLDS, information about the output RLDS data sets is recorded in the PRILOG record in the RECON data set and information about the SLDS data sets is recorded in the PRISLD record. If you do not request an RLDS, the same information about the SLDS data sets is recorded in both the PRILOG and PRISLD records.

If there is a secondary OLDS, or if you request that dual logs be produced from a single OLDS, the information about the secondary-log output is recorded in corresponding SECLOG and SECSLD records.

> **IMPORTANT:**   Log data sets that are output from IMS batch jobs are technically SLDSs, but the information about them is recorded in the PRILOG and SECLOG records.

Run the Log Archive utility by issuing the `GENJCL.ARCHIVE` command. DBRC then determines which OLDSs are full, and generates the appropriate JCL.

Related Reading: See Member DFSVSMxx in *IMS Version 9: Installation Volume 2: System Definition and Tailoring* for more information on the ARCHDEF statement and automatic archiving.

> **RECOMMENDATION:**   Whether you use automatic archiving or invoke archiving yourself, make sure the archive jobs run as quickly as possible. The online subsystem only reuses an OLDS after it has been archived. If the archive job is not run and all the OLDS become full, the online subsystem waits. One way to ensure that archive jobs run quickly is to use an initiator that runs with a fairly high priority and is not used by many other users. This ensures that the archive jobs do not remain on the internal reader queue for too long.

If DBRC has marked an OLDS in the RECON data set as having errors, the `GENJCL` function does not submit it for archiving. If one of a pair of OLDSs has been destroyed or is unavailable, you can choose to mark it in the RECON data set as having errors.

The following references point to where you can find more information about archiving log records.

Related Reading:

- See *IMS Version 9: Operations Guide* for more information about automatic, manual, and custom archiving of log records.
- See *IMS Version 9: Utilities Reference: System* for more information about specifying entry points and running the Log Archive utility.
- Refer to *IMS Version 9: Customization Guide* for more information about the Log Archive and the Logger exit routines.

DBRC Log-Related Commands

Use the following commands to perform DBRC log-related functions in your operational procedures:

- `CHANGE.PRILOG`
- `CHANGE.RECON`
- `CHANGE.SECLOG`
- `DELETE.LOG`
- `GENJCL.ARCHIVE`
- `GENJCL.CLOSE`
- `LIST.LOG`
- `NOTIFY.PRILOG`
- `NOTIFY.SECLOG`

In addition to the `LIST.LOG` command, you can use a LOG or OLDS query API request to retrieve log-related information from the RECON data set.

How DBRC Helps in Recovery

DBRC can generate JCL for executing a database recovery, because DBRC records this information in the RECON data set. Whether you use the `GENJCL` commands to generate JCL or provide the JCL yourself, DBRC uses information in the RECON data set to determine exactly which data sets are required for input. The Database Recovery utility runs only if DBRC verifies that the JCL is correct.

You can omit all logged changes after a certain time from the input by performing a *time-stamp recovery*. A time-stamp recovery is equivalent to backing out the omitted changes from the database.

Most time-stamp recoveries require DBRC in order to be successful. When you involve DBRC in your request for a time-stamp recovery, DBRC selects the correct logs and, at execution time, communicates to the Database Recovery utility where to stop processing the input to correctly perform your request.

Figure 23-2 on page 386 shows how DBRC works with the Database Recovery utility.

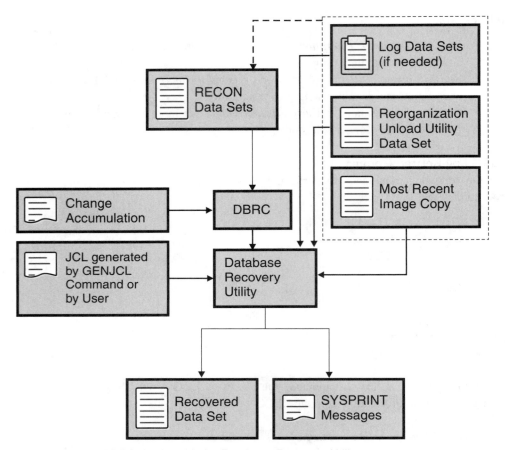

Figure 23-2   How DBRC Works with the Database Recovery Utility

> **RECOMMENDATION:**   Implement DBRC in phases,
> defining at first only a few recoverable databases in the RECON data
> set. This allows you to gain experience in the use of DBRC, and gives
> you an opportunity to assess, make, and test any changes needed in
> your backup, recovery, and operational procedures.

Information for a database recovery can come from any or all of the following sources:

- Image copies of the database
- Database reorganization data sets
- Log data sets (SLDSs and RLDSs)
- Change accumulation data sets

You can use DBRC to track all of these information sources, greatly simplifying the task of database recovery.

Related Reading: Refer to *IMS Version 9: Operations Guide* for more information about the recovery process.

If you register recoverable databases in the RECON data set, DBRC records the association of the databases to the log data sets containing database change records.

DBRC also records information about:

- Database image copies
- Reorganizations (except DEDB online reorganizations)
- Recoveries
- Change accumulations
- Backout

DBRC is invoked by recovery tools and utilities to provide information about the resources required for database recovery. These resources can include information about image copies, logs, change accumulations, and database data sets.

DBRC can:

- Generate JCL that can be used to run various utilities (see "Generating Recovery JCL").
- Validate the input to those utilities (see "Validating Utility JCL" on page 389).
- Record the result (in the RECON data set) of running the utilities (see "Recording the Result" on page 390).

Generating Recovery JCL

You can use the GENJCL.RECOV command to generate the JCL that is necessary to recover a registered database data set. Using information recorded in the RECON data set, DBRC:

1. Selects the image copy data set to use for loading the most recent image copy.
2. Selects the change accumulation and log data sets that are to be input to apply all the changes that were logged since the image copy was created.

If change accumulation input is required (because of data sharing), but it is not present or usable, DBRC informs you of that fact and the GENJCL.RECOV command fails.

The GENJCL.USER command can generate user-defined output, which can include JCL. No skeletal JCL execution members are supplied to support the GENJCL.USER command. If you want to enter GENJCL.USER commands, you must supply the members to support them.

Issue the GENJCL command to request that DBRC generate JCL in batch or issue the /RMGEN-JCL command online. When you enter either command, DBRC reads skeletal JCL and replaces symbolic parameters with actual values based on the information recorded in the RECON data set to build the appropriate JCL. For example, if you request that DBRC generate JCL to recover a database, DBRC retrieves the skeletal JCL member from the library and completes the JCL with information about the latest image copy, change accumulation, and log data sets, if necessary. Your databases must be registered in order for DBRC to generate JCL to process them.

The amount of time and effort required to recover a database can be significantly reduced by using the GENJCL to generate the JCL and control statements necessary for the recovery. Using the GENJCL command also eliminates the causes of many recovery errors. You could spend a large amount of time during database recoveries determining which input data sets should be provided in what order to the Database Recovery utility.

When change accumulation data sets or PRILOG records (in the RECON data set) are available, DBRC selects them rather than the SLDS for recovery. This results in quicker database recoveries if you run the Database Change Accumulation regularly. DBRC knows which log data sets are required and ensures that IMS processes all volumes in the correct order. DBRC also selects the most recent image copy for database recovery.

DBRC always selects the optimum input for the Database Recovery utility by using change accumulation data sets whenever possible. If you have not used the Database Change Accumulation utility, or if that utility did not process some log data sets, DBRC selects the required log data sets from the PRILOG (or SECLOG) records, which can contain RLDS, SLDS, or both RLDS and SLDS entries.

Related Reading:

- See *IMS Version 9: Installation Volume 2: System Definition and Tailoring* for more information about the tailoring actions for IMS.PROCLIB members, the DBRC procedure, and the JCLOUT and JCLPDS DD statements.
- See *IMS Version 9: Database Recovery Control (DBRC) Guide and Reference* for details about customizing your own skeletal JCL and about the contents of IMS-supplied skeletal JCL.

> **RECOMMENDATION:** For increased availability of data entry databases (DEDBs), use the DEDB Area Data Set Create utility to provide additional usable copies of an online area. It does not provide backup copies for recovery. The DEDB Area Data Set Create utility uses the RECON data set as part of its input.

Validating Utility JCL

When a recovery utility processes a registered database data set, the utility presents its input to DBRC for validation. Whether the recovery JCL was created by you or by DBRC, DBRC verifies that the input JCL to the utility is correct (according to the current information in the RECON data set). It is possible, even if you created the JCL with the GENJCL command, that intervening events could invalidate the input JCL before the utility is run.

DBRC is invoked by the following IMS utilities and services to validate input and record the results:

- Index/ILDS Rebuild utility (DFSPREC0)
- Database Image Copy utility (DFSUDMP0)
- Database Image Copy 2 utility (DFSUDMT0)
- Online Database Image Copy utility (DFSUICP0)
- Database Change Accumulation utility (DFSUCUM0)
- Batch Backout utility (DFSBBO00)
- Database Recovery utility (DFSURDB0)
- Log Recovery utility (DFSULTR0)
- Log Archive utility (DFSUARC0)
- HALDB online reorganization
- HD Reorganization Unload utility (DFSURGU0)
- HD Reorganization Reload utility (DFSURGL0)
- HISAM Reorganization Unload utility (DFSURUL0)
- HISAM Reorganization Reload utility (DFSURRL0)
- Database Prefix Update utility (DFSURGP0)
- DEDB Area Data Set Create utility (DBFUMRI0)
- /RECOVER commands

Figure 23-3 on page 390 shows DBRC's role in running the previously mentioned utilities.

Related Reading: See *IMS Version 9: Utilities Reference: Database and Transaction Manager* for more information on the IMS recovery utilities.

When you run the Batch Backout utility (DFSBBO00), DBRC determines the complete set of logs that are needed for a particular backout job. In addition, DBRC manages information about the logs so that backout and restart jobs can be easily coordinated.

> **E X C E P T I O N:**   DBRC does not verify the JCL input for the HD and the HISAM Reorganization utilities, but does record information about their execution in the RECON data set.

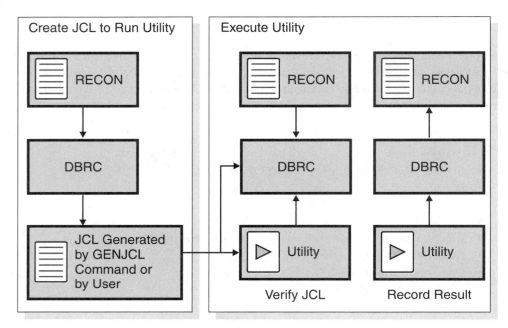

Figure 23-3   DBRC's Role in Utility Execution

Recording the Result

When the recovery completes successfully, DBRC records information about the recovery in the RECON data set. If you performed a time-stamp recovery, DBRC records information about the range of omitted changes.

> **REQUIREMENT:**   If a time-stamp recovery is performed within a database allocation interval, you must immediately create an image copy to ensure a valid starting point for subsequent recovery attempts. DBRC then prevents the changes from being reapplied on any subsequent recovery.

Recording Information about Opening and Updating Databases

After IMS opens a database, DBRC passes back the RECON data set initialization token (RIT) and any extended error queue elements (EEQEs) associated with each DBDS. The RIT allows IMS to determine whether the database has been used without DBRC or whether the database has been controlled by a different RECON data set.

Related Reading: See *IMS Version 9: Operations Guide* for information on EEQEs.

When changes to DBDSs and areas occur, DBRC records information about these changes in the RECON data set. DBRC subsequently uses this information to determine which log data sets might contain change records for a given DBDS or area.

When a DBDS that is registered in the RECON data set is first opened for updates (or allocated), IMS tells DBRC to create an ALLOC record. In the case of a DEDB area, the ALLOC record is created when the area is first opened for update. The ALLOC record identifies the DBDS or area and contains the time stamp of the first update and the open time stamp of the corresponding PRILOG.

When DBRC creates the ALLOC record, DBRC also enters the name of the DBDS or area being changed in the LOGALL record for the PRILOG that is active at the time of the change.

When you deallocate (close) a DBDS or area using a /DBRECOVERY command from the operator console of the online IMS subsystem, DBRC writes a deallocation time stamp in the ALLOC record. If no deallocation time is recorded, DBRC uses the closing time of the associated log as the deallocation time. Thus the RECON data set contains a list of the names of DBDSs or areas for which change records might exist on a given log data set (LOGALL record), a list of the time ranges where changes could exist for a specific DBDS or area (ALLOC records), and a list of the logs containing the changes.

Supporting Data Sharing

Data sharing introduces the concept of database authorization. Database authorization determines if an online IMS or batch IMS can have access to the requested databases. DBRC authorizes or refuses to authorize access to the databases depending on the current authorizations and the access intent of the IMS system.

Data sharing requires that the databases be registered with DBRC. DBRC checks that subsystems have authority to perform the requested task and that other subsystems are not currently reserving the database.

Related Reading: See *IMS Version 9: Operations Guide* and *IMS Version 9: Administration Guide: System* for more information on data sharing.

Access Intent

DBRC determines access intent. When IMS tries to allocate a database:

- For a batch job, DBRC uses the processing option (PROCOPT) of the PSB for each database to determine the access intent. If the PSB has multiple PCBs for the same database, the highest intent level for that database is used.
- For an IMS TM online system, the value specified on the ACCESS keyword of the DATABASE macro sets the access intent. You can change this access intent by issuing a /STA DB command.

There are four levels of access intent for a database. Table 23-1 shows these attributes in reverse order, from the highest access intent (the most restrictive) to the lowest (the least restrictive)

Table 23-1   Database Access Intent Attributes

ACCESS Keyword Values	Description
Exclusive access (EX)	The IMS system requires exclusive access of the database. No sharing is allowed regardless of the share options registered in DBRC. • **Batch:** PROCOPT of L or xE (where x = A,D,G,I, or D) • **Online:** ACCESS of Ex
Update access (UP)	The IMS system can update the database. Even if no updates actually take place, the database is held in update mode. Any logs created with actual changes during this process are required for recovery or change accumulation. • **Batch:** PROCOPT of A,I,R, or D • **Online:** ACCESS of UP
Read with integrity access (RD)	The IMS system only reads the database, but it also checks any enqueue or lock held by other IMS systems. The IMS system waits for the lock to be released before processing. • **Batch:** PROCOPT of G • **Online:** ACCESS of RD
Read without integrity access (RO)	The IMS system only reads the database and it does not check for any lock or enqueue held by other IMS systems. • **Batch:** PROCOPT of GO • **Online:** ACCESS of RO

Levels of Data Sharing

DBRC supports the two levels of IMS data sharing:

Database level

The entire database or DEDB area is a resource that can be accessed for update by a single IMS system at a time. For area resources this can also be called *area-level sharing*.

Block level

A database or DEDB area can be accessed by multiple IMS subsystems concurrently. Data integrity is preserved for the IMS subsystems that access the shared data. Within a database or area, resources are reserved at the block level.

> **DEFINITION:**
>
> For OSAM databases, the *block* is a physical data block that is stored on DASD. For VSAM databases and DEDBs, the block is a control interval (CI).

Recording Data-Sharing Information in the RECON Data Set

DBRC records the following data-sharing information in the RECON data set for all registered databases:

- Sharing level allowed for each database
- Names of databases or areas currently authorized for processing
- Names of IMS subsystems that are involved
- Statuses of the IMS subsystems
- Database statuses from a recovery viewpoint

Assigning a Sharing Level with DBRC

The sharing level of a database or DEDB area determines whether a request for access is granted. DBRC allows you to establish one of four sharing levels.

The following sharing levels are defined using the INIT.DB command and modified with the CHANGE.DB command.

SHARELVL 0

The database is not to be shared. The database can be authorized for use by one IMS system at a time. SHARELVL 0 is equivalent to specifying ACCESS=EX on the /START command.

SHARELVL 1

Sharing is at the database level. One IMS system can be authorized for update at one time; any sharing systems can only be authorized for read-only processing. Another configuration for SHARELVL 1 is to authorize all IMS systems for read-only processing of the shared data.

SHARELVL 2

Sharing is at the block level but only within the scope of a single IRLM and a single z/OS. Sharing requires that IMS subsystems sharing a database use the same RECON data set. Multiple IMS systems can be authorized for update or read processing.

SHARELVL 3

Sharing is at the block level by multiple IMS subsystems using multiple instances of IRLM. Multiple IMS systems can be authorized for non-exclusive access. The IMSs can be on multiple z/OS images using different IRLMs. As with SHARELVL 2, all IMS subsystems sharing a database must use a single RECON data set.

> **N O T E:** To ensure the integrity of databases in data-sharing
> environments when batch jobs running without IRLM support access
> SHARELVL 3 databases, DBRC authorizes batch jobs that have
> update access only if all other IMS systems and batch jobs that are
> currently authorized by DBRC to the database have read-only access.
>
> If IRLM=N is specified in the IMSCTRL macro or DBBBATCH proce-
> dure, DBRC authorizes a batch job for update access to a database
> only if all other IMS systems and batch jobs that are currently autho-
> rized by DBRC to the database have read-only access.
>
> When a batch IRLM=N job has authorization for update, authoriza-
> tion for an online system or other batch job fails unless it is for read-
> only access.

Supporting Remote Site Recovery

DBRC assists you with the definition and management of IMS components in the RSR complex.
In support of RSR, DBRC provides:

- Commands to define, update, and display the status of the RSR complex.

  The RECON data set contains the definition of an RSR complex.

- Services that are used by an active subsystem to identify the tracking subsystem and the
  databases covered by RSR.

  An active subsystem obtains the identity of its tracking subsystem from DBRC. As
  databases are updated by the active subsystem, DBRC tells the database component
  whether the database is covered by RSR. If the databases are being tracked by RSR, the
  active subsystem sends its log data to the tracking subsystem.

- Services used by a tracking subsystem to record information about log data that is
  received from an active subsystem.

  As logs are received and stored at the tracking site, DBRC records the receipt of the log
  data. When begin-update records are received for registered databases, DBRC records
  the database update.

- Tracking subsystem database support:
  - Two types of tracking (called *shadowing*): Database-Level Tracking (DBTRACK)
    or Recovery-Level Tracking (RCVTRACK).
  - Maintains log data set information for online forward recovery.
  - Records which database change records have actually been applied to the covered
    databases.

- Services to assist in the takeover process.

  During a remote takeover, DBRC changes the state information of the registered databases at the new active site to indicate that they are now the active databases.

Related Reading: See *IMS Version 9: Administration Guide: System* for more information about controlling database recovery in an RSR environment.

Supporting IMSplexes

When an I/O error occurs on a RECON data set in an IMSplex and a spare data set is available, the instance of DBRC that noticed the error copies the good RECON data set to the spare, activates the spare, and deallocates the original RECON data set.

At this point in the processing, the DBRC that noticed the I/O error can automatically notify the other DBRCs in the IMSplex about the reconfiguration. Then, after the original RECON data set is deallocated, it can be deleted and redefined as the spare RECON data set.

Related Reading: See *IMS Version 9: Common Service Layer Guide and Reference* for more information about IMSplexes.

Overview of the RECON Data Sets

The RECON data set is the most important data set for the operation of DBRC and data sharing. The RECON data set holds all of the resource information and event tracking information that is used by IMS.

The RECON data set can consist of one, two, or three data sets:

1. The original data set
2. A copy of the original data set
3. A spare data set

The original data set and the copy are a pair of VSAM clusters that work as a pair to record information. A third RECON can be used as a spare. IMS normally works with two active RECON data sets. If one becomes unavailable, the spare will be activated if it is available.

The best solution, from an availability point of view, is to use all three data sets. This is strongly recommended. Using three data sets for the RECON causes DBRC to use them in the following way:

- The first data set is known as copy1. It contains the current information. DBRC always reads from this data set, and when some change has to be applied, the change is written first to this data set.
- The second data set is known as copy2. It contains the same information as the copy1 data set. All changes to the RECON data sets are applied to this copy2 only after the copy1 has been updated.

- The third data set (the spare) is used in the following cases:
  — A physical I/O error occurs on either copy1 or copy2.
  — DBRC finds, when logically opening the copy1 RECON data set, that a spare RECON has became available, and that no copy2 RECON data set is currently in use.
  — The following command is executed: `CHANGE.RECON REPLACE(RECONn)`

When the third RECON data set starts to be used, the remaining valid data set is copied to the spare. When the copy operation is finished, the spare becomes whichever of the data sets was lost, missing, or in error.

RECON Records

The individual records in the RECON contain the information that DBRC keeps track of.

Types of RECON Records

There are six general types of RECON records:

Control records

Control records control the RECON data set and the default values used by DBRC. This class of records includes the RECON header record and header extension record.

Log records

Log records track the log data sets used by all subsystems. This class of records includes:

- Primary Recovery Log (PRILOG) and Secondary Recovery Log (SECLOG) records (including interim log records), which describe a recovery log data set (RLDS) created by an IMS TM system, a CICS online system, a DB batch job, or the Log Archive utility.
- Log Allocation (LOGALL) record, which lists the DBDSs for which database change records have been written to a particular log.
- Primary OLDS (PRIOLD) and Secondary OLDS (SECOLD) records (including interim OLDS records), which describe the IMS TM online data sets (OLDS) that are defined for use.
- Primary System Log (PRISLDS) and Secondary System Log (SECSLDS) records (including interim SLDS records), which describe a system log SLDS created by an IMS TM system.

Change accumulation records

Change accumulation records track information about change accumulation groups. This class of records includes change accumulation group, execution, and data set records.

DBDS group records

Database data set group (DBDSGRP) records define the members of a DBDS group. The only record type in this class is a DBDS group record.

Subsystem records

Subsystem records contain information about the subsystem and related recovery information, including:

- Subsystem name and type (online or batch)
- IRLM identification
- Abnormal-end flag and the recovery-process start flag
- List of authorized databases
- Time stamp that correlates the subsystem entry with the appropriate log records

Database records

Database records track the state of databases, DBDSs, and resources required for recovery of the DBDSs. This class of records includes:

- Database record (IMS, HALDB, or PARTition)
- Area authorization record
- DBDS record (non-Fast Path or Fast Path)
- Allocation record
- Image copy record
- Reorganization record
- Recovery record

Database-Related Information

A database and its associated data sets should be defined in only one RECON data set.

The fundamental principle behind the RECON data set is to store all recovery-related information for a database in one place. It is not possible to use multiple RECON data sets in the recovery processing for the same database.

IMS Systems and the RECON

An IMS system can be connected to only one set of RECON data sets.

All databases that are accessed by IMS TM systems under the control of DBRC must be registered in the RECON referenced by the online IMS system only if the RECON has the FORCER option set on.

All batch IMS systems that access any database accessed by the online IMS system should reference the same RECON data sets that are referenced by the online IMS system.

Database Names in the RECON Data Set

The database names (DBD names) defined in one RECON data set must all be unique.

The database records stored in the RECON data set are registered with a key based on the DBD name. Therefore, DBRC cannot be used to control both test and production databases that use the same RECON data sets, unless you adopt a naming convention.

As a general rule, more than one set of RECON data sets is necessary if all the following conditions are true:

- Multiple versions of the same database exist (for example, test and production).
- The same DBD name is used for the different versions of the database.
- More than one version of the databases can be used, but only one can be registered to DBRC in the RECON data set. The other versions are treated as not registered (unless the FORCER option is set in the RECON).

The application of the previous rules usually results in the need for at least two different sets of RECON data sets: one shared between the production systems, and one for the test systems.

> **N O T E:** On the `INIT.DBDS` command, which is used to create the database data set record in the RECON, you must supply the database data set name (DSN). When IMS opens the database, DBRC checks the DSN against the name that is registered in the RECON data set. If this name does not match, DBRC treats this database as if it was not registered. In this case, the test database (with a DSN different than the production database, even if with the same DBD name) and data set name, can coexist with the production environment, but not under the control of DBRC.

DEFINING AND CREATING THE RECON DATA SETS

The RECON data sets are VSAM KSDSs. They must be created by using the VSAM AMS utilities. The RECON data sets:

- Must all use the same record size and CI size.
- Should be given different FREESPACE values so that CA and CI splits do not occur at the same time for both active RECON data sets.
- Should have different space allocation specifications to increase availability. The spare data set should be the largest RECON data set.

Figure 23-4 shows an example of a RECON data set definition.

```
DELETE STIMS220.RECONB

 SET LASTCC=0

DEFINE CLUSTER (NAME(STIMS220.RECONB) -
       VOLUMES (SBV010)                -
       INDEXED                         -
       KEYS (24 0)                     -
       CYLINDERS C5 2)                 -
       RECORDSIZE (128 32600)          -
       SPANNED                         -
       FREESPACE (30 80)               -
       CISZ(4096)                      -
       NOREUSE                         -
       NERAS SPEED REPL IMBD           -
       UNORDERED                       -
       SHAREOPTIONS (3 3))             -
 INDEX (NAME(STIMS220.RECONB.INDEX))   -
  DATA (NAME(STIMS220.RECONB.DATA))
```

Figure 23-4   Example of a RECON Data Set Definition

Placement Considerations for the RECON Data Sets

The placement of the RECON data sets in the DASD configuration is critical. The primary rule is to configure for availability. In doing so, you isolate possible failures. This means, for example, to place all three RECON data sets on:

- Different volumes
- Different control units
- Different channels
- Different channel directors

INITIALIZING THE RECON DATA SETS

After you create the RECON data sets, you must initialize them by using the INIT.RECON command (issued as an input command JCL statement to the Database Recovery Control utility). This causes the RECON header records to be written in both current RECON data sets.

The RECON header records must be the first records written to the RECON data sets because they identify the RECON data sets to DBRC.

ALLOCATING THE RECON DATA SETS TO AN IMS SYSTEM

You can use one of two methods to allocate the RECON data sets to an IMS system:

- Point to the RECON data sets by inserting the DD statements in the startup JCL for the IMS system.
- Use dynamic allocation.

If a DD statement is specified for the RECON data sets, DBRC does not use dynamic allocation. Otherwise, DBRC uses dynamic allocation.

> **RECOMMENDATION:**   With multiple IMS systems sharing the same databases and RECON data sets, use dynamic allocation for both the RECON data sets and the associated databases. Doing so ensures that:
>
> - Correct and current RECON data sets are used.
> - Correct RECON data sets are associated with the correct set of databases.

Dynamic allocation also makes the recovery of a failed RECON data set easier because DBRC dynamically deallocates a RECON data set if a problem is encountered with it.

To establish dynamic allocation, you must add a special member that names the RECON data sets to the IMS.SDFSRESL library or to an authorized library that is concatenated to the IMS.SDFSRESL library. Add the member to IMS.SDFSRESL using the IMS DFSMDA macro. Figure 23-5 shows an example of the required DFSMDA macros for dynamic allocation of the RECON data sets.

```
//DYNALL JOB..
//STEP     EXEC IMSDALOC
//SYSIN    DD  *
    DFSMDA TYPE=INITIAL
    DFSMDA TYPE=RECON,DSNAME=PROD.RECON01,
             DDNAME=RECON1
    DFSMDA TYPE=RECON,DSNAME=PROD.RECON02,
             DDNAME=RECON2
    DFSMDA TYPE=RECON,DSNAME=PROD.RECON03,

DDNAME=RECON3
```

Figure 23-5   Example JCL for Allocating RECON Data Sets Dynamically

RECON data sets are always dynamically allocated with DISP=SHR specified.

When using multiple RECON data sets (for example, test and production), be sure that each IMS uses the correct RECON data set group. You can ensure that the correct RECON data set group is being used by altering the SYSLMOD DD statement in the IMSDALOC procedure to place the dynamic allocation parameter lists for the different RECON data set groups in different IMS.SDFSRESL libraries. The appropriate IMS.SDFSRESL or concatenated IMS.SDFSRESL libraries must be included for each IMS startup JCL.

> **I M P O R T A N T:** When multiple IMSs running on different processors are accessing the same RECON data set, you must keep the dynamic allocation parameter lists being used by the different processors synchronized in the IMS.SDFSRESL libraries. This synchronization does not happen automatically. Also, using dynamic allocation in some IMS systems and JCL allocation in others is not recommended.

MAINTAINING THE **RECON** DATA SETS

You can use several procedures and commands to maintain the RECON data sets.

Backing Up the RECON Data Sets

Set up operational procedures to ensure that regular backups of the RECON data sets are taken using the DBRC `BACKUP.RECON` command. The `BACKUP.RECON` command includes a reserve mechanism to ensure that no updating of the RECON data sets takes place during the backup. If possible, take the backup when no IMS systems are active.

The backup copy is created from the copy1 RECON data set. The command to create the backup copy invokes the AMS `REPRO` command, with its normal defaults and restrictions. For instance, the data set that is receiving the backup copy must be empty.

Deleting Inactive Log Records from the RECON Data Sets

When DBRC becomes aware that an image copy has been taken of a database data set (DBDS), DBRC automatically deletes, reuses, or updates the records in the RECON that are associated with that particular DBDS. After this automatic processing, certain log records are considered inactive, but are not deleted from the RECON.

A log is considered inactive when the following conditions are all true:

- The log volume does not contain any DBDS change records that are more recent than the oldest image copy data set known to DBRC. This check is performed on a DBDS basis.
- The log volume is not opened in 24 hours.
- The log has either been terminated (nonzero stop time) or has the ERROR flag in the PRILOG and SECLOG record set on.

The only recovery-related records in the RECON that are not automatically deleted are the log records (for example, the PRILOG and LOGALL records). You can delete these records using the DELETE.LOG INACTIVE command. You can also add the DELETE.LOG INACTIVE command to the job that takes a backup of the RECON data sets.

Monitoring the RECON Data Sets

In addition to the regular backups, you should monitor the status of the individual RECON data sets on a regular basis. There are two ways to do this: using the LIST.RECON STATUS command and using the DBRC API Query request.

Monitoring the RECON Data Sets Using the LIST.RECON STATUS Command

Use the LIST.RECON STATUS command regularly to monitor the status of the individual RECON data sets.

The LIST.RECON command produces a formatted display of the contents of RECON data sets. The copy1 RECON data set is used as a source. DBRC ensures that the second RECON data set contains the same information as the first RECON data set.

You can use the optional STATUS parameter to request the RECON header record information and the status of all RECON data sets. The use of this parameter suppresses the listing of the other records.

Issue a LIST.RECON STATUS command two or three times a day during the execution of an online system to ensure that problems have not been encountered with these data sets.

Monitoring the RECON Data Sets Using the DBRC API Query Request

Use the DBRC API Query request (DSPAPI FUNC=QUERY) along with the TYPE parameter to retrieve the following types of information from the RECON data sets:

- Backout (TYPE=BACKOUT): Retrieves backout information for a specific subsystem or all subsystems.
- Database (TYPE=DB): Returns database registration and status information for:
  — Full-function databases.
  — Fast Path databases.
  — HALDB databases.
  — DBDS or area information and supporting recovery-related information for each DBDS or area (allocation, image copy, recovery, and reorganization).
- Group and member information for the following group types:
  — Change accumulation (TYPE=CAGROUP). CA execution information can also be returned.
  — DBDS (TYPE=DBDSGROUP).

  — Database (TYPE=DBGROUP).
  — Recovery (TYPE=RECOVGROUP).
  — Global Service Group (TYPE=GSGROUP).
- Log, recovery, and system log data set (TYPE=LOG).
- Online log data set (TYPE=OLDS).
- RECON status (TYPE=RECON): Returns RECON header information, as well as the status of the RECON configuration.
- Subsystem (TYPE=SUBSYS).

REORGANIZING RECON DATA SETS

Because all current levels of VSAM support CI reclaim (and DBRC does not turn CI reclaim off), the requirement to reorganize RECON data sets to reclaim space is diminished. For instance, when all the records in a CI are erased, the CI is returned to the free CI pool in the CA. Some users reorganize their RECON data sets on a monthly basis.

A plan for reorganizing the RECON data sets to reclaim this space on a regular basis must be considered. The RECON data sets can be reorganized while the IMS online systems are active.

The RECON data sets can be reorganized easily and quickly with the use of a few DBRC and AMS commands. The AMS REPRO command copies one RECON data set to another, reorganizing it during the process. This command, combined with a DELETE and a DEFINE of the RECON data sets, is enough to complete a reorganization.

Additional information to consider when designing the RECON data set reorganization procedures, related to the IMS TM status, are as follows:

- If the online system is active, a reorganization of the RECON data sets should be scheduled:
  — During a period of low RECON data set activity.
  — When no batch, DL/I, or DBB jobs or utilities are running.

  Each online system that uses the RECON data sets must issue a LIST.RECON STATUS command after the CHANGE.RECON REPLACE command is issued, in order to deallocate the RECON data set before deleting and redefining it.

- If the online system is not active, a reorganization of the RECON data sets should be scheduled:
  — After the RECON has been backed up (using the BACKUP.RECON command).
  — When no subsystems are allocating the RECON data sets.

RECREATING THE RECON DATA SETS

You might need to recreate the RECON data sets, for instance:

- In a disaster recovery site
- After the loss of all the RECON data sets when no current backup is available

Recreating the RECON data sets can be a long and slow process. When designing procedures to handle this process, there are two basic alternatives:

- Restore the RECON data sets from the last backup (if available) and update it to the current status required
- Recreate and reinitialize the RECON data sets

Both of these procedures have advantages and disadvantages. The best alternative for an installation depends on:

- The timeframe in which the system must be recovered and available
- The point in time to which it is acceptable to recover
- The type of processing environment (24-hour online availability or batch)

SUMMARY OF RECOMMENDATIONS FOR RECON DATA SETS

Keep the following recommendations in mind when planning for your RECON data sets:

- Use three RECON data sets: two current and one spare.
- Define the three RECON data sets with different space allocations.
- Separate the RECON data sets (for example, put them on different devices and channels).
- Use dynamic allocation.
- Do not mix dynamic allocation and JCL allocation.
- Define the RECON data sets for *availability*, but keep performance implications in mind.

CHAPTER **24**

Operating IMS

Operating IMS consists of many tasks. These tasks are discussed in the following sections of this chapter.

In This Chapter:

Related Reading: For more detailed information on the above topics, see *IMS Version 9: Operations Guide*.

MONITORING THE SYSTEM

Monitor the status of the system on a regular schedule to gather problem determination and performance information. For example, to determine if you should start an extra message region, you might monitor the status of the queues during peak load.

To determine the current status of the system: Issue `/DISPLAY` commands along with the appropriate keywords.

To monitor the status of the IRLM: Issue the z/OS MODIFY *irlmproc*, STATUS command.

To help diagnose system operation problems: Issue the /TRACE command. This command turns on or off various IMS traces, which record use of IMS control blocks, message queue and I/O line buffers, and save area sets. IMS records trace information on the IMS log unless you request that the traces be recorded on an external trace data set. See "IMS Trace Facility" on page 418 for more information. You can also use the /TRACE command to trace locking activities and to start and stop the IMS Monitor (see "IMS Monitor" on page 414).

Related Reading: For more information on monitoring, see *IMS Version 9: Administration Guide: Database Manager.*

PROCESSING IMS SYSTEM LOG INFORMATION

The system log data sets are a basic source for statistics about the processing performed by the online system. Individual log record types contain data that can be analyzed in many ways. For example, you can select and format all activity pertaining to a specified user ID or about IMS pools.

Using IMS System Log Utilities

IMS provides several utilities to assist with extracting log records from the system log. These utilities also assist with reducing and merging data that is spread across several log data sets. The sections that follow describe several of these utilities:

- "File Select and Formatting Print Utility"
- "Fast Path Log Analysis Utility" on page 407
- "Log Transaction Analysis Utility" on page 407
- "The Statistical Analysis Utility" on page 408
- "Knowledge-Based Log Analysis" on page 408

File Select and Formatting Print Utility

You can use the File Select and Formatting Print utility (DFSERA10) if you want to examine message segments or database change activity in detail. This utility prints the contents of log records contained in the OLDS, SLDS, or the CQS log stream. Each log record is presented as one or more segments of 32 bytes. The printed output gives each segment in both character and hexadecimal formats.

You can specify selection criteria for a subset of the records rather than printing all records. You can also specify a starting record number and the number of records to process. You can use an exit routine to customize the selection and formatting of the log records.

Although you can use the File Select and Formatting Print utility to copy entire input logs, you can more conveniently use the Log Archive utility to do so. You use one or more SLDSs as input and specify a user data set as output. Also, you need to specify DBRC=NO in the EXEC statement to prevent DBRC from making entries in the RECON data set about your backup log. Making backup copies of the system log data sets can be useful to obtain an alternative input source for statistics and other monitoring activities that occur in parallel with production use of the system log.

Fast Path Log Analysis Utility

Use the Fast Path Log Analysis utility (DBFULTA0) to prepare statistical reports for Fast Path, based on data recorded on the IMS system log. This utility is an offline utility and produces three data sets, one of which contains the following formatted reports:

- Detail Listing of Exception Transactions
- Summary of Exception Detail by Transaction Code for IFP Regions
- Overall Summary of Transit Times by Transaction Code for IFP Regions
- Overall Summary of Resource Usage and Contentions for All Transaction Codes and PSBs
- Summary of Region Occupancy for IFP Regions by PST
- Summary of VSO Activity
- Recapitulation of the Analysis

These reports are useful for system installation, tuning, and troubleshooting. The Fast Path Log Analysis utility is not related to the IMS Monitor or the Log Transaction Analysis utility. For more information about the IMS Monitor, see "IMS Monitor" on page 414.

Log Transaction Analysis Utility

In an IMS DB/DC or DCCTL environment, you can use the Log Transaction Analysis utility (DFSILTA0) to collect information about individual transactions, based on records in the system log. Many events are tabulated in the Log Analysis report that is produced by this utility, including total response time, time on the input queue, processing time, and time on the output queue.

You can select a start time for the report tabulation; analysis begins at the first checkpoint after the start time. To control how much transaction activity is tabulated, you can specify an interval (in minutes) of elapsed time from the start time before the utility ends the tabulation, or you can relate the activity reported to a number of IMS checkpoints.

You can retitle a Log Analysis report or change the sequence in which the detailed transaction lines are printed. You can sort by transaction code or by any of the fields in the report. You can also suppress printing so that the output is stored on a DASD data set.

Using the Log Transaction Analysis utility, you can create an output data set (in system log format) that is a copy of all or part of the input system logs. By having a copy of the system log, you can monitor system activity without impacting the use of the OLDS for recovery.

The Statistical Analysis Utility

In an IMS DB/DC or DCCTL environment, you can produce several summary reports using the IMS Statistical Analysis utility (DFSISTS0). You can use these reports to obtain actual transaction loads and response times for the system. The statistics produced are dependent on the input system log data sets. The following set of reports is produced by the IMS Statistical Analysis utility:

- Telecommunication line and terminal (distributed traffic over a 24-hour day)
- Transaction (distributed activity over a 24-hour day)
- Transaction response
- Messages queued but not sent (listing by destination and by transaction code)
- Program-to-program messages (listing by destination and by transaction code)
- Application accounting
- IMS accounting

Knowledge-Based Log Analysis

Knowledge-Based Log Analysis (KBLA) is a collection of IMS utilities that select, format, and analyze log records. KBLA also provides an ISPF interface to create and run the jobs for various log-related utilities, and to access other ISPF applications. KBLA uses an ISPF panel-driven user interface to simplify JCL job creation and to prevent JCL errors. KBLA generates the JCL and control statements necessary to run the supported utilities. This JCL preparation allows you to focus on the output of the utility used rather than on how to code JCL to extract information.

The following KBLA log-formatting routines help you examine and display data from IMS log data sets:

- The Knowledge-Based Formatting Print routine (DFSKBLAK) provides a clear, simple description of each event represented by a log record, including the meaning of the various fields and flags. It does not display null fields.
- The Knowledge-Based Summary Formatting Print routine (DFSKBLAS) prints and displays the header and description of a log record, but not the record itself. This information is useful when you need a general understanding of the log records associated with a particular resource.
- The Knowledge-Based Basic Formatting Print routine (DFSKBLA3) is similar in function to the Record Format and Print Module (DFSERA30), but its output also provides a brief description of the log record identifier (or log record type). This information can be useful if you are unfamiliar with the record types present in an IMS log. The Knowledge-Based Basic Formatting Print routine also interprets the prefix fields for the IMS type X'01' and type X'03' log records.

The following KBLA routines help with log analysis and diagnosis:

DBCTL Transaction Analysis Utility (DFSKDBC0)

The DBCTL Transaction Analysis utility (DFSKDBC0) performs the functions of both the Log Transaction Analysis utility (DFSILTA0) and the Fast Path Log Analysis utility (DBFULTA0). The DBCTL Transaction Analysis utility also performs a sort of the data. The DBCTL Transaction Analysis utility uses the X'07' and X'5937' log records or the X'5938' log record to gather statistics.

Deadlock Trace Record Analysis Utility (DFSKTDL0)

The Deadlock Trace Record Analysis utility is used to format and summarize data extracted from X'67FF' pseudoabend records for database-related deadlocks. These records are identified by a four-character requester identification that indicates a pseudo-abend condition, and an eight-character element identification that indicates deadlock.

The Deadlock Trace Record Analysis utility processes the logical deadlock events and the individual deadlocks to produce reports that:

- Provide details about the deadlock
- Show the hierarchy of the participants in the deadlocks (relative to the victim in each deadlock)
- Summarize the deadlock activity, including deadlocks by:
  — Hour
  — DBMS
  — State
  — Lock type
  — DBD
  — PSB
  — Lock name
  — RBA

IMS Records User Data Scrub Utility (DFSKSCR0)

The IMS Records User Data Scrub utility (DFSKSCR0) performs a scan of all of the IMS logs. The utility deletes those record parts that might contain sensitive or confidential customer business transaction information, in particular, X'01', X'03', X'50', X'5901', X'5903', X'5950', and X'67'. The deletion does not compromise the integrity or the content of the vital IMS system data. This scrub is useful when you must send IMS log data to an outside organization for analysis.

IRLM Lock Trace Analysis Utilities (DFSKLTA0, DFSKLTB0, DFSKLTC0)

IRLM Lock Trace Analysis consists of three programs (DFSKLTA0, DFSKLTB0, and DFSKLTC0) that run serially to perform IRLM Lock Trace Analysis. DFSKLTA0 is run first to create the control file of global data management block (DMB) numbers and their respective database names. DFSKLTB0 is then used to create the lock wait detail and summary records. DFSKLTC0 formats and prints the information and creates the optional output data set.

The IRLM Lock Trace Analysis utilities can be useful in finding database or application issues that impact transaction response times by causing frequent and long lock waits.

You can save the report to a data set, which you can then sort using either the Knowledge-Based Log Analysis ISPF tools or an editor's SORT command. The IRLM Lock Trace Analysis panel provides some pre-defined sort options, such as Sorted by Database Name and Sorted by RBA.

Log Record Processing Rate Analysis Utility (DFSKRSR0)

The Log Record Processing Rate Analysis utility (DFSKRSR0) is used to generate reports that summarize the volume of log data that is being generated by an IMS subsystem. The volume of log data is expressed in number of records per second and number of bytes per second. The detailed log record processing rate data is broken down by log record type, and by subtype within record type, if requested.

The Log Record Processing Rate Analysis utility can be used to:

- Determine the size of log data sets or archiving frequency
- Track data volume for Remote Site Recovery (RSR)

Selection criteria for the DFSKRSR0 trace table entries can include:

- Log record type
- Subtypes within log record types
- Time range data
- Log sequence number ranges
- Number of records to be processed or skipped

Log Summary Utility (DFSKSUM0)

The Log Summary utility (DFSKSUM0) can create a summary of the content of the log data sets, characteristics of the IMS system that produced the log data (when statistical log records are present), and some statistical information related to transactions, programs, and databases. The Log Summary utility also includes the following information:

- Input IMS logs used for the utility execution
- IMSID
- First and last Log Sequence Number (LSN) in the log
- Time stamp (UTC) and local time of the first and last log record
- Difference between UTC and local time (HHMM format)
- Elapsed time on selected logs
- Total number of log records in the log data set

- Presence of internal trace record, system restarts, dump log record, and system checkpoint
- Number of log records present for each record ID
- Statistics related to individual transactions, programs, and databases
- Gaps in the log

MSC Link Performance Formatting Utility (DFSKMSC0)

The MSC Link Performance Formatting utility (DFSKMSC0) uses the IMS MSC link trace log records to provide information about link response times, which can be used to help isolate performance problems with MSC links. You can specify either of the following types of analysis:

Detail

The Detail Selection routine (DFSKBST0) produces a report that contains the individual response times in milliseconds of every send data and receive data for each MSC link that is traced.

Summary

The Summary Selection routine (DFSKMSCD) produces a report that contains the average response time in milliseconds of the total number of send data and receive data values for each link trace.

The enhanced log formatting routines produce formatted output only if the IMS input logs contain X'6701' records generated using the /TRACE SET ON LIN-K*link#* command.

RECON Query of Log Data Set Names Utility (DFSKARC0)

The RECON Query of Log Data Set Names utility (DFSKARC0) analyzes the RECON data sets to find appropriate log data set names. Based on the control statements that you provide, it can determine the following information:

- Data set names for OLDS, SLDS, or PRILOG data sets
- The names for the primary or secondary log data sets
- The volume serial numbers for these data sets

The logs can be selected by any or all of the following parameters:

- Starting date and time
- Ending date and time
- SYSID

Information from the RECON data sets can be extracted from either of the following places:

- The RECON data sets themselves, when available on the system that executed DFSKARC0
- A pre-existing report generated by the DBRC LIST.LOG command

Statistic Log Record Analysis Utility (DFSKDVS0)

The Statistic Log Record Analysis utility (DFSKDVS0) processes the X'45' log records that are generated at each IMS checkpoint and formats a report that is a verbal description and interpretation for all of the fields contained in the X'45' log record, including its subcodes. This information can be used to look for bottlenecks within the IMS system or to detect trends in internal resource usage that can help to determine if tuning is necessary. You must use the /CHECKPOINT STATISTICS command to ensure that the X'45' log record contains the information required for this enhanced formatting.

Trace Record Extract Utility (DFSKXTR0)

The need for information for problem diagnostics or accumulation of statistics drives trace table logging, which often generates a large number of records. The Trace Record Extract utility (DFSKXTR0) reads an IMS log data set (OLDS or SLDS) or trace data set (DFSTRAxx) to produce a subset of information that meets specific selection criteria.

Unlike DFSERA10, which searches entire log records for specific strings, DFSKXTR0 searches individual trace table entries using selection criteria. Trace table entries are relatively small, 32- or 64-byte entries. Although the data in the entries can vary depending on what is specifically being traced, the structure is a constant eight words of data.

Search criteria are entered as a paired specification identifying the word, halfword, or byte to be examined, and the associated data value. Optionally, the entire log record containing the matching trace table entries can be extracted as well.

After searching the trace table entries, DFSKTXR0 stores the entries that match selection criteria into new log records. These new log records can subsequently be passed to the DFSERA60 exit routine for formatting.

Selection criteria for the trace table entries can include:

- Trace table IDs
- Character string searches at the trace entry level
- Specific words, halfwords or bytes in the trace entries
- Time range data
- Entire log records to be matched
- Number of records during processing
- Mode of SCAN to read the log records without actual processing

Related Reading: For detailed information about the KBLA routines and utilities, see *IMS Version 9: Utilities Reference: System*.

Using the IMS Performance Analyzer for z/OS

The IMS Performance Analyzer for z/OS, program number 5697-B89, gives you the information you need to increase your IMS system performance. The IMS Performance Analyzer for z/OS provides more than 30 reports that can help optimize IMS system and application performance.

Specifically, the IMS Performance Analyzer for z/OS:

- Offers an ISPF CUA-compliant user interface to build, maintain, and submit report requests
- Provides revised, enhanced, and new reports
- Supports IMS Versions 7, 8, and 9 from a single load library
- Allows the optional use of GDDM® for selected graphical reports
- Saves selected report data for reporting using PC tools
- Requires no dependency on GPAR

Related Reading:

- For more information about the IMS Performance Analyzer for z/OS, see "IBM IMS Performance Analyzer for z/OS, V3.3" on page 451.
- IBM offers a number of other IMS database productivity tools. IMS Tools is a set of database performance enhancements for your IMS environment. These tools can help you automate and speed up your IMS utility operations. They can also assist you in analyzing, managing, recovering, and repairing your IMS databases. To learn more about these tools, see Chapter 26, "IBM IMS Tools," on page 443 or go to the DB2 and IMS Tool Web site at http://www.ibm.com/software/data/db2imstools/.

CHOOSING TOOLS FOR DETAILED MONITORING

Many of the monitoring tools you can use to collect detailed data are also used for general diagnostics. The principal tool provided by IMS for collecting and analyzing data is the IMS Monitor, which allows you to monitor online subsystems. For a standalone IMS DB batch system driven by an SLDS, use the DB Monitor. The DB Monitor can be active during the entire execution of an IMS batch job, or you can stop and restart it from the system console.

You can also use the IMS Performance Analyzer, program isolation and lock traces, and the external trace facility.

Related Reading:

- For complete information about the IMS Monitor, see *IMS Version 9: Utilities Reference: System.*
- For complete information about the DB Monitor, see *IMS Version 9: Utilities Reference: Database and Transaction Manager.*

IMS Monitor

The IMS Monitor collects data while the online IMS subsystem is running. It gathers information for all dispatch events and places it, in the form of IMS Monitor records, in a sequential data set. Use the IMSMON DD statement in the IMS control region JCL to specify the IMS Monitor data set. IMS adds data to this data set when you activate the IMS Monitor using the /TRACE command. The IMS MTO can start and stop the IMS Monitor to obtain snapshots of the system at any time. However, the IMS Monitor adds to system overhead and generates considerable amounts of data.

Controlling IMS Monitor Output

Plan to run the IMS Monitor for short intervals and to control its operation carefully. Shorter intervals also prevent the overall averaging of statistics, so that problems within the system can be more readily identified. The IMS Monitor's output can be constrained by:

- Type of activity monitored
- Database or partition or area
- Dependent region
- Time interval

IMS Monitor Output Data Sets

The IMS Monitor output can be either a tape or a DASD data set. Using DASD eliminates the need to have a tape drive allocated to the online system. If you want to use the IMS Monitor frequently, you might find that permanently allocated space for a DASD data set is convenient. One technique is to code DISP=SHR on the IMSMON DD statement so that the reports can be generated as each IMS Monitor run completes.

You must coordinate the report generation with the operator because each activation of the IMS Monitor writes over existing data. Although this overwriting does not occur for tape data sets, new volumes must be mounted. The volume is rewound, and a mount request is issued each time you start the IMS Monitor.

RECOMMENDATIONS:

- Do not catalog IMS Monitor data sets. The IMS Monitor can produce multiple output volumes while IMS is running if the data sets are not cataloged.

  If you want IMS to dynamically allocate the IMS Monitor data set, do not include the IMSMON DD statement in the IMS control region JCL.

- Allow IMS to dynamically allocate IMS Monitor tape data sets. A tape drive is not permanently reserved for the control region for dynamically allocated data sets.

Selecting Monitor Traces

After you establish monitoring requirements, you might be able to restrict the scope of the IMS Monitor activity. Restricting the scope has the advantage of reducing the impact of the IMS Monitor on system throughput. However, you should not compromise the collection of useful data.

You can control what specific types of events are traced by using specific keywords on the /TRACE command. For example, you can monitor line activity, scheduling and termination events, activity between application programs and message queues, activity between application programs and databases, or all activity.

Obtaining IMS Monitor Reports

You can obtain reports based on the IMS Monitor's output by using the IMS Performance Analyzer for z/OS or the IMS Monitor Report Print utility (DFSUTR20). For information about the IMS Performance Analyzer for z/OS, see "Using the IMS Performance Analyzer for z/OS" on page 413.

The IMS Monitor Report Print utility summarizes and formats the raw data produced by IMS and presents the information in a series of reports. You can suppress the reports pertaining to DL/I calls and tabulated frequency distributions.

The duration of the monitored events is determined by the entries for start and stop of the IMS Monitor. You cannot select a different time period for reporting, because many of the timed events are not captured continuously—only when the IMS Monitor is started and stopped. For this reason, you should ensure that the IMS Monitor is stopped before taking any action to stop the IMS control region.

//DFSSTAT Reports

The //DFSSTAT reports give you the number of database and data communications calls issued by an application program and describe the buffering activity. These reports are described in *IMS Version 9: Utilities Reference: System.*

z/OS Generalized Trace Facility

You can use the z/OS generalized trace facility (GTF) to record a wide range of system-level events. The trace activity is controlled from the z/OS system console using the MODIFY command. Output is spooled to a sequential data set that is used by a generalized formatting utility. You can write exit routines that are called by the formatting utility to edit the trace records and present the data as desired.

For more information about the z/OS generalized trace facility, see *z/OS V1R4.0 MVS Diagnosis: Tools and Service Aids.*

z/OS Component Trace (CTRACE) Service

IRLM 2.1 uses the z/OS component trace (CTRACE) service to trace IRLM activity. Because the trace output is in z/OS CTRACE format, you can use IPCS CTRACE format, merge, and locate routines to process the buffer data.

Use the z/OS TRACE CT command to start, stop, or modify an IRLM diagnostic trace. This command can be entered only from the z/OS master console. Entering the commands requires an appropriate level of z/OS authority. IRLM does not support all the options available on the command. You can also start the IRLM tracing by placing TRACE=YES in the IRLM procedure.

Related Reading: For information on the TRACE CT command for IRLM, see *IMS Version 9: Command Reference*. For complete information on the command, see *z/OS MVS System Commands*.

Obtaining Program Isolation and Lock Traces

In an IMS DB/DC or DBCTL environment, you can detect contention for a database segment by examining the output produced by the Program Isolation Trace Report utility (DFSPIRP0). To get the source data for the utility, issue the /TRACE SET ON PI OPTION ALL command. To stop gathering source data, issue the /TRACE SET OFF PI command. A control statement for the utility can select a start or stop time relative to a specified date.

Tracing the program isolation function can create additional log records. These records contain the enqueue or dequeue requests issued by the program isolation function between sync points as a result of database updates, checkpoints, and message handling events.

The Program Isolation Trace Report utility reports only those events that require wait time. The report identifies the data management block (DMB) name, database control block (DCB) number, the relative byte address (RBA), the program specification block (PSB) name, and the transaction code. The utility sorts all activity by RBA number (shown as ID in the report). The report lists elapsed times for enqueues that required a wait during the trace interval, and totals the number of enqueues for each ID, DCB, and DMB. The requesting PSB or transaction is considered the holding PSB or transaction of the next enqueue waiting for the same segment. A sample report is shown in Figure 24-1 on page 417. In this report, no elapsed wait time is recorded for Fast Path.

Related Reading: For details about how to run the Program Isolation Trace Report utility, see *IMS Version 9: Utilities Reference: Database and Transaction Manager*.

```
                        P R O G R A M   I S O L A T I O N   T R A C E   R E P O R T          PAGE    1
    DATE:  08/10/04
    TIME:  16:36  TO   16:37
    DCB *** REQUESTING *** ELAPSED    **** HOLDING *** ID TOTAL DCB TOTAL DMB      TOTAL
    DMB NAME NUM  ID  TRAN AND PSB NAMES   TIME      TIME    TRAN AND PSB NAMES ENQ'S ENQ'S ENQ'S
    TABLEDBQ 1 0022D020  DE1Q     PROGDE1Q  16:36:54  0:00.061  DE2Q     PROGDE2Q
                                                                                         1
               003BE00C  DE2Q     PROGDE2Q  16:36:51  0:00.027  DE1Q     PROGDE1Q
                                                                                         1
               007D901C  DE2Q     PROGDE2Q  16:36:34  0:00.036  DE1Q     PROGDE1Q
                                                                                         1
               008EF014  DE2Q     PROGDE2Q  16:36:49  0:00.038  DE1Q     PROGDE1Q
                                                                                         1
               0090401C  DE1Q     PROGDE1Q  16:36:50  0:00.072  DE2Q     PROGDE2Q
                                                                                         1
               00A06010  DE2Q     PROGDE2Q  16:36:38  0:00.046  DE1Q     PROGDE1Q
                                                                                         1
               00A1401C  DE1Q     PROGDE1Q  16:36:50  0:00.008  DE2Q     PROGDE2Q
                                                                                         1       7     7
    TABLEDBR 1 002A901C  DE2R     PROGDE2R  16:36:40  0:00.034  DE1R     PROGDE1R
                                                                                         1
               0045801C  DE2R     PROGDE2R  16:36:41  0:00.043  DE1R     PROGDE1R
                                                                                         1
               0072F024  DE1R     PROGDE1R  16:36:30  0:00.053  DE2R     PROGDE2R
```

Figure 24-1   Sample Program Isolation Trace Report

You can use the File Select and Formatting Print utility to select and print trace table and PI entries in the log records in the following ways:

- Specify an OPTION statement with the PRINT parameter and COND=E and EXITR=DFSERA40 keyword parameters. The output is a report containing the program isolation (PI) trace records formatted in sequential order.

  Related Reading: For an example of this report and an explanation of the headings, see *IMS Version 9: Utilities Reference: System.*

- Select only the log records that contain the trace using the IMS Trace Table Record Format and Print module (DFSERA60), which is an exit routine that receives type X'67FA' log records from the File Select and Formatting Print utility and formats the records on the SYSPRINT data set.

  Specify an OPTION statement with the PRINT parameter and COND=E and EXITR=DFSERA60 keyword parameters. The output is a report containing the PI trace entries, the DL/I trace entries, and the lock trace entries formatted to show these entries in sequential order. For an explanation of the headings, see an assembly listing of the macro IDLIVSAM TRACENT.

You can use an output report from the IMS Trace Table Record Format and Print module to find out more information:

- The level of control (LEV) column shows read only, share, exclusive control, and single update activity.
- The return code (RC) column shows return codes from DFSFXC10 or the IRLM. You can determine whether the caller had to wait for the requested resource, or if the transaction caused a deadlock situation.
- The PST post code (PC) column shows the cause of the wait. If the entry is X'60', a deadlock occurred.

You can reduce the number of records examined by specifying an additional OPTION statement to the File Select and Formatting Print utility so that only records confirming deadlock are printed.

IMS automatically resolves deadlock situations by using dynamic backout. But the detection of deadlocks is important so that you can modify your application design to prevent future deadlocks.

The advantage of the Program Isolation Record Report is that it shows where contention for a particular segment or range of segments occurs. The report also shows which transactions are competing within a database. It also shows high wait times that might explain a delay in response time. One way to handle the segment contention might be to change the database design to separate some of the fields into an additional segment type.

IMS Trace Facility

You can use the IMS trace facility to write IMS trace tables internally or to an external trace data set. IMS can write this external trace data set to either DASD or tape:

- DASD data sets can be allocated by JCL or can be dynamically allocated.
- Tape data sets must be dynamically allocated.

You can also write the trace tables to the OLDS, but this could adversely affect OLDS performance. The external trace data sets are independent of the OLDS, so you can write trace tables to the external trace data sets even if the OLDS is unavailable.

To display the status of traces, use the /DISPLAY TRACE command. This command can be used to determine the status of the IMS traces in effect and the status of any external trace data sets in use.

Related Reading:

- See *IMS Version 9: Diagnosis Guide and Reference* for information about when and why trace tables are used.
- See *IMS Version 9: Messages and Codes, Volume 2* for information about the `DFS2867A` message when using external tracing to OLDS.
- See *IMS Version 9: Installation Volume 2: System Definition and Tailoring* for information about defining and setting up trace facilities and using the DFSMDA macro to create the dynamic allocation members.

EXECUTING RECOVERY-RELATED FUNCTIONS

While IMS is running, an IMS system programmer or operator might need to complete tasks to recover the system. These tasks include:

- "Using DBRC Commands"
- "Creating a Dump of the Message Queues" on page 420
- "Recovering the Message Queues" on page 420
- "Archiving the OLDS" on page 421
- "Making Databases Recoverable or Nonrecoverable" on page 421
- "Running Recovery-Related Utilities" on page 421

Using DBRC Commands

You can use the `/RMxxxxxx` commands to perform the following DBRC functions:

- Start or stop the DBRC application programming interface (API)
- Record recovery information in the RECON data set
- Generate JCL for various IMS utilities and generate user-defined output
- List general information in the RECON data set
- Gather specific information from the RECON data set

> **RECOMMENDATION:** Allow operators to use the `/RMLIST` and `/RMGENJCL` commands. Restrict the use of `/RMCHANGE`, `/RMDELETE`, and `/RMNOTIFY` commands because they update the RECON data set.

Related Reading: For information about using DBRC commands in a data-sharing environment, see "Supporting Data Sharing" on page 391.

Creating a Dump of the Message Queues

If you want to save the message queues in a non-shared-queues environment, use the /CHECK-POINT SNAPQ command. This command writes a dump of the message queues to the log without terminating the online system.

> **RECOMMENDATION:** Schedule the /CHECKPOINT SNAPQ regularly because it shortens the time required for emergency restart if a problem occurs on the message queue data sets. Consider the following intervals:
>
> - Whenever the OLDS is switched
> - Once each hour
> - Once each shift
> - Twice each day (midnight and noon)
> - Once each day

For a shared-queues environment, use the /CQCHKPT SHAREDQ command to dump the shared message queues.

Recovering the Message Queues

In a non-shared-queues environment, you can recover the message queues during an IMS restart if the previous shutdown included the DUMPQ or the SNAPQ keyword. Specify the BUILDQ keyword on the /NRESTART or /ERESTART command to restore the messages to the message queue data sets from the IMS log. Specify the FORMAT keyword on the /NRE or /ERE command if you also want to reinitialize the message queue data sets.

In order to use the /NRE BUILDQ command, the system must be shut down using either a /CHECKPOINT DUMPQ or a /CHECKPOINT PURGE command. Before you can issue the /ERE BUILDQ command, you need to issue a /CHECKPOINT SNAPQ command.

> **RESTRICTION:** If a /NRE BUILDQ or /ERE BUILDQ command fails and you cold start IMS, messages are lost and are not processed.

You can use the IMS Queue Control Facility for z/OS program product (5697-I08) to select messages from the OLDS (or SLDS) and reinsert them into the IMS message queues after an IMS cold start.

Related Reading: For more information, see "IBM IMS Queue Control Facility for z/OS, V2" on page 462.

For a shared-queues environment, CQS automatically rebuilds the message queues if the coupling facility fails. You can also use the `SETXCF START,REBUILD` command to rebuild the queues manually.

Archiving the OLDS

As mentioned in "Archiving an OLDS" on page 383, you should archive the OLDS to an SLDS at regular intervals. If you are not using automatic archiving, the MTO should use the DBRC `GENJCL` command at regular intervals to generate the JCL for the Log Archive utility and should run the utility.

Making Databases Recoverable or Nonrecoverable

After you delete recovery-related records from the RECON data set, you can change recoverable full-function databases and DEDBs to nonrecoverable by using the DBRC `CHANGE.DB NON-RECOV` command. You can change nonrecoverable full-function databases and DEDBs to recoverable again by using the DBRC `CHANGE.DB RECOVABL` command.

Use the DBRC `LIST.DB` command to display whether a database is recoverable.

Running Recovery-Related Utilities

Depending on your recovery strategy, the MTO might be responsible for running various recovery-related utilities at regular intervals. These could include:

- Database Image Copy utility
- Database Image Copy 2 Utility
- Online Database Image Copy utility
- Database Change Accumulation utility

The MTO should also run these utilities when a database changes from nonrecoverable to recoverable.

Related Reading: For complete information about these utilities, see *IMS Version 9: Utilities Reference: Database and Transaction Manager*.

MODIFYING AND CONTROLLING SYSTEM RESOURCES

You establish the initial settings of IMS resources during IMS system definition. The MTO, and other operators authorized to do so, can change various system resources using IMS commands.

"Modifying the Operating State of Specific IMS Resources" on page 422 describes how you can modify the operating state of specific resources using specific IMS commands.

"List of Commands with Similar Functions for Multiple Resources" on page 425 describes how many IMS commands perform similar control functions for different types of resources.

Related Reading: For details about the IMS commands, see *IMS Version 9: Command Reference*.

Modifying the Operating State of Specific IMS Resources

You can use certain commands to affect the operating state of specific resources, as described in the following sections.

Modifying Dependent Regions

Use the /ASSIGN command to modify the assignment of classes to regions. Do this to adjust the processing load among message regions.

Modifying Telecommunication Lines

Use the /RSTART command to start lines, lines and physical terminals, logical links, nodes, and users when you do not want to reset all associated conditions, such as a conversation or special operating mode. Use the /DEQUEUE command to discard response-mode output messages before you issue an /RSTART LINE command.

Modifying Terminals

Use the /ASSIGN LTERM command to modify the assignment of logical terminals to physical terminals or nodes. The new assignment remains in effect until the next cold start or until you issue another /ASSIGN command.

Use the /DEQUEUE command to discard response-mode output so that the /RSTART command can reset terminal response mode.

Use the /COMPT command for VTAM terminals (nodes) to notify IMS that a terminal component is operable or inoperable.

IMS provides a VTAM I/O timeout facility to detect VTAM hung nodes and determine what action, if any, should be taken. Use the /TRACE command to start and stop the VTAM I/O timeout facility. Use the /IDLE command to deactivate a node and the /ACTIVATE command to activate a node. Use the /DISPLAY command to display all nodes that have I/O outstanding for a time period greater than that specified during system definition.

Modifying Transactions

Use the /ASSIGN command to reassign the scheduling priorities established for transactions during system definition. The new assignments remain in effect until the next cold start or until you issue another /ASSIGN command.

In a shared-queues environment, you can use the /ASSIGN command to control which IMS subsystems can run certain types of transactions by assigning transactions to particular classes.

For example, you can define TRANA to class 4 on IMSA and to class 255 on IMSB and IMSC, so that only IMSA can run TRANA. If IMSA fails, you can reassign TRANA on either IMSB or IMSC to a class that these IMS subsystems can run.

> **RECOMMENDATION:** Do not use the /STOP TRANSACTION command to control which IMS subsystems can run certain types of transactions.

Modifying Databases

Use the /DBDUMP command to stop online update access to a database and produce an offline dump of the database.

Use the /DBRECOVERY command to stop all online access to a database. Use it to recover a database offline.

Normally, IMS switches to using the next OLDS when you enter the /DBDUMP or /DBRECOVERY command. This switch does not occur if you specify the NOFEOV keyword on either command.

Specify the GLOBAL keyword on the /DBDUMP command or /DBRECOVERY command to have the command apply to all subsystems sharing the database. The IRLM must be active if you use this keyword. The default is LOCAL, which specifies that the command applies only to the subsystem on which you enter the command.

You must restart IMS after you issue a command with the GLOBAL keyword.

Modifying ISC Users (Subpools)

Use the /ASSIGN command to change the assignment of a static LTERM to an ISC user (also called a subpool). The new assignment remains in effect until the next cold start or until you issue another /ASSIGN command.

Modifying ETO Users

For dynamic user IDs, use the /ASSIGN command to change the assignment of a user ID to another user or to an LTERM. The new assignment remains in effect until the next cold start or until you issue another /ASSIGN command.

Use the /DISPLAY USER DEADQ command to list all message queues that are eligible for dead letter status. IMS refers to data that cannot be delivered as a *dead letter*. Use the /ASSIGN command to assign a dead letter queue to another user ID. Use the /DEQUEUE command to discard a dead letter queue.

In a shared-queues environment, use the /DISPLAY QCNT MSGAGE command to determine which messages, if any, are eligible for dead letter status.

424   Chapter 24   Operating IMS

Modifying MSC Resources

Use the /MSVERIFY command to verify the consistency of MSC system identifications (SYSIDs) and logical link paths (MSNAMEs) across two systems. You can use the /MSASSIGN command to change the assignment of MSNAMEs and SYSIDs to logical links.

All changes made by an /MSASSIGN command remain in effect until the next cold start or until you issue another /MSASSIGN command.

After using the /MSASSIGN command, you should use the /MSVERIFY command to ensure that the assignment produced a valid configuration.

Modifying Security Options

Use the /CHANGE command to update a current password with a new password. The current password must be known to IMS.

> **RESTRICTION:**   IMS does not allow different user IDs to use the same passwords.

Use the /MODIFY PREPARE RACF and /MODIFY COMMIT commands to reinitialize RACF information if you are not using a RACF data space. If you are using a RACF data space, use the RACF SETROPTS RACLIST command rather than the IMS /MODIFY command.

Use the /DELETE command to delete terminal or password security for the specified system resource.

Use the /SECURE APPC command to control the RACF security level for input from LU 6.2 devices. Use the /DISPLAY APPC command to show the security level that is currently in effect. When IMS starts, the default is full security.

Use the /SECURE OTMA command to control the RACF security level for input from OTMA clients. Use the /DISPLAY OTMA command to show the security level that is currently in effect. When IMS starts, the default is full security.

Modifying Conversations

Use the /DISPLAY CONV command to show the status of all conversations, held or active. You can terminate a conversation if necessary with the /EXIT command, but you should do this only after warning the end user.

Modifying Subsystems

Use the /CHANGE command to delete an invalid network identifier (NID). If you need to disconnect from a specific subsystem, use the /STOP command. If the /STOP command does not work, use the z/OS MODIFY command.

List of Commands with Similar Functions for Multiple Resources

You can use many IMS commands to perform similar control functions for different types of resources. The tables in this section show the relationship between these commands and resources, and provide answers to a series of specific questions. For example, after a command is issued, can a resource:

- Receive input?
- Send output?
- Perform output message queuing?

The following tables show what IMS commands affect certain resources. The resources are:

- Telecommunications Line, Physical Terminal, or Node Resources (Table 24-1)
- Logical Terminal Resources (Table 24-2)
- Logical Link Resources (Table 24-3)
- Logical Link Path Resources (Table 24-4)
- Transaction Resources (Table 24-5)
- Transaction Class Resources (Table 24-6)
- Program Resources (Table 24-7)
- Database Resources (Table 24-8)
- Subsystem Resources (Table 24-9)

Telecommunications Line, Physical Terminal, or Node Resources

Table 24-1   IMS Commands That Affect Telecommunications Line, Physical Terminal, or Node Resources

IMS Command	Receive Input	Send Output	Output Message Queuing
/ASSIGN	Y	Y	Y
/LOCK	N	N	Y
/MONITOR[a]	Y	N	Y
/PSTOP[a]	N	N	Y
/PURGE[a]	N	Y	Y
/RSTART[a]	Y	Y	Y
/START	Y	Y	Y
/STOP	N	N	Y
/UNLOCK	Y		Y

a.   /MONITOR, /PSTOP, /PURGE, and /RSTART refer to the telecommunication line or physical terminal, not to the node.

Logical Terminal Resources

Table 24-2   IMS Commands That Affect Logical Terminal Resources

IMS Command	Receive Input	Send Output	Queuing from Other Terminals	User
/ASSIGN	Y	Y	Y	Y
/LOCK	N	N	N	
/PSTOP	N	N	Y	
/PURGE	N	Y	N	
/RSTART				Y
/START	Y	Y	Y	Y
/STOP	N	N	N	Y
/UNLOCK		Y	Y	

Logical Link Resources

Table 24-3   IMS Commands That Affect Logical Link Resources

IMS Command	Receive Input	Receive Output
/PSTOP	N	N
/RSTART	Y	Y

Logical Link Path Resources

Table 24-4   IMS Commands That Affect Logical Link Path Resources

IMS Command	Queue Primary Requests Not Continuing Conversation	Transmit Queue Message to Partner Systems
/ASSIGN	Y	Y
/PURGE	N	Y
/START	Y	Y
/STOP	N	N

Transaction Resources

Table 24-5 IMS Commands That Affect Transaction Resources

IMS Command	Message Scheduling by Transaction	Message Queuing by Transaction
/ASSIGN	Y	Y
/LOCK	N	Y
/MSASSIGN	Y	
/PSTOP	N	Y
/PURGE	Y	N
/START	Y	Y
/STOP	N	N
/UNLOCK	Y	Y

Transaction Class Resources

Table 24-6 IMS Commands That Affect Transaction Class Resources

IMS Command	Transaction Scheduling by Class
/ASSIGN	Y
/MSASSIGN	Y
/START	Y
/STOP	N

Program Resources

Table 24-7 IMS Commands That Affect Program Resources

IMS Command	Execute
/ASSIGN	Y
/LOCK	N
/START	Y
/STOP	N
/UNLOCK	Y

Database Resources

Table 24-8 IMS Commands That Affect Database Resources

IMS Command	Use
/ASSIGN	Y
/START	Y
/STOP	N
/UNLOCK	Y

Subsystem Resources

Table 24-9 IMS Commands That Affect Subsystem Resources

IMS Command	Attach
/ASSIGN	Y
/START	Y
/STOP	Y

CONTROLLING DATA SHARING

Controlling data sharing involves:

- "Monitoring the Data-Sharing System"
- "Controlling Data Sharing Using DBRC" on page 431

Monitoring the Data-Sharing System

To monitor data sharing, you obtain information on the status of the IRLM, IMS subsystems and databases, the RECON data sets, and coupling facility structures that are participating in data sharing.

Obtaining the Status of IRLM Activity

To display the status of an IRLM on either your system or on another connected system, enter the following z/OS command:

```
MODIFY irlmproc,STATUS,irlmx
```

irlmproc is the name of the procedure that you used to start the IRLM, and *irlmx* is the name of the IRLM whose status you want to display. This command returns:

- The IMS IDs of IMS subsystems using this IRLM.
- The number of locks that are held and waiting for each subsystem on this IRLM.
- Identification of this IRLM: its subsystem name and IRLM number.

You can use the ALLD keyword to display the names and status of every IMS identified to an IRLM in a data-sharing group. Or, you can use the ALLI keyword to display the names and status of every IRLM in a data-sharing group.

Related Reading: For a complete description of the commands for the IRLM, see *IMS Version 9: Command Reference*.

Displaying Components and Resources

Monitoring components and resources in a data-sharing environment requires the same types of procedures as in a non-data-sharing environment. For more information about monitoring, see "Monitoring the System" on page 405.

Table 24-10 lists keywords for the /DISPLAY command that you can use to obtain information about various IMS resources.

Table 24-10 /DISPLAY Command Keywords That Provide Information about IMS Resources

Resources	/DISPLAY Command Keywords
Active control regions	ACTIVE REGION
Active jobs	ACTIVE
Programs, transactions, and conversations	CONVERSATION PROGRAM PSB STATUS PROGRAM STATUS TRANSACTION SYSID TRANSACTION TRANSACTION
Databases	DATABASE AREA STATUS DATABASE

continues

Table 24-10   /DISPLAY Command Keywords That Provide Information about IMS
                  Resources (Continued)

Resources	/DISPLAY Command Keywords
Terminals, lines, links, and nodes	ACTIVE DC ASSIGNMENT LINE ASSIGNMENT LINK ASSIGNMENT NODE LINE LINK LTERM MASTER MSNAME NODE PTERM STATUS LINE STATUS LINK STATUS LTERM STATUS MSNAME STATUS NODE STATUS PTERM
External subsystems and connections to external subsystems	CCTL OASN SUBSYS SUBSYS
VTAM	TIMEOVER

For example, to determine whether the database is started, you can use the /DISPLAY
DATABASE command after you enter a /START DATABASE command.

Related Reading: For detailed information about the /DISPLAY command, see *IMS
Version 9: Command Reference*.

Monitoring Structures on a Coupling Facility

The following z/OS operator commands are especially useful in monitoring structure activity:

- DISPLAY XCF, STRUCTURE: Used to display the status of structures defined in your
  active policy.
- DISPLAY XCF, STRUCTURE, STRNAME=: Used to display detailed information
  about a specific structure. The three structures that are important to IMS are the IRLM,
  OSAM, VSAM, shared MSGQ, and shared EMHQ structures.

These commands let you look at structures on a coupling facility to determine resource status
and, for failures, gather information for problem determination.

Related Reading: For detailed information about these commands, see *z/OS MVS System Commands*.

Controlling Data Sharing Using DBRC

DBRC allows you to control access to data by IMS subsystems that participate in data sharing. Using DBRC, you can modify, initiate, and delete the current status indicators in the RECON data set to change:

- The access intent of online IMS subsystems
- The share level of registered databases

Your data sharing environment depends on the status of the databases and subsystems as indicated in the RECON data set.

Related Reading: For more information about how DBRC participates in data sharing, see "Supporting Data Sharing" on page 391.

You can modify the share level indicator using a form of one of the DBRC online change commands, /RMCHANGE.

CONTROLLING LOG DATA SET CHARACTERISTICS

From time to time, you need to tune and modify log data set characteristics, for example, in the following circumstances:

- After monitoring
- After changing your requirements for system availability, integrity, or operator handling

For summaries of actions required to change log data set design, see:

- "Controlling the Online Log Data Set"
- "Controlling the Write-Ahead Data Set" on page 434
- "Controlling the System Log Data Set" on page 435
- "Controlling the RECON Data Sets" on page 435

Controlling the Online Log Data Set

Because you can restart IMS (warm start or emergency restart) with all input in an SLDS, you can reallocate the OLDSs between a shutdown (or failure) and a subsequent restart. To restart IMS using SLDSs as input, you must delete the PRIOLDS and SECOLDS records from the RECON data sets.

Table 24-11 on page 432 lists the actions required to change OLDS characteristics.

Table 24-11   Changing OLDS Characteristics

Modification	Actions Required
BLKSIZE[a]	1. Shut down IMS. 2. Archive all OLDSs. 3. Delete PRIOLDS and SECOLDS records from the RECON data sets using the DELETE.LOG command. 4. Scratch all OLDSs. 5. Reallocate OLDSs with the new BLKSIZE. 6. Verify WADS space allocation. 7. Restart IMS (from SLDS).
Single to dual[b]	1. Shut down IMS. 2. Archive all OLDSs. 3. Allocate dual OLDSs. 4. Delete the OLDS records from the RECON data sets, using the DELETE.LOG command. The primary OLDS records are deleted. 5. Change OLDSDEF specification to dual. 6. Change IMS startup procedure (OLDS DD statements), if required. 7. Compile DFSMDA macros, if required. 8. Modify operating procedures. 9. Restart IMS.
Dual to single[b]	1. Shut down IMS. 2. Archive all OLDSs. 3. Delete OLDS record from the RECON data sets, using the DELETE.LOG command. The primary and secondary OLDS records are deleted. 4. Delete secondary OLDSs. 5. Change IMS startup procedure. 6. Modify operating procedures. 7. Restart IMS.
BUFNO[c]	1. Shut down IMS. 2. Change the OLDSDEF specification for BUFNO. 3. Verify CSA size. 4. Verify WADS space allocation. 5. Restart IMS.
Space, location, or allocation[d]	1. Shut down IMS. 2. Archive all OLDSs. 3. Delete PRIOLDS and SECOLDS records in the RECON data sets, using the DELETE.LOG command. 4. Scratch and reallocate OLDSs. 5. Restart IMS (from SLDS).

a.   **Changing OLDS Block Size:** Changing OLDS block size affects WADS space allocation. For information on how to calculate WADS space requirements, see *IMS Version 9: Installation Volume 1: Installation Verification*. To change WADS space allocation, see Table 24-12 on page 434. All OLDSs must have the same block size.

b. **Changing the Mode:** You must change your OLDSDEF specification in the DFSVSMxx member in IMS.PROCLIB. IMS initialization requires that at least three pairs of OLDSs be available. You must also reconsider data set placement.

When changing from single to dual OLDS, each data set in a pair of OLDSs must have the same space allocation (number of blocks).

Changing the mode from single to dual or from dual to single requires changes in the following operating procedures:

- Skeletal JCL for the Log Archive utility (ARCHJCL member)
- Skeletal JCL for the Log Recovery utility (LOGCLJCL member)
- Batch JCL for Log Recovery utility
- Batch backout JCL for online transactions and BMPs

If you warm start the IMS subsystem after changing from single to dual OLDSs, the /DISPLAY OLDS command does not show the secondary OLDSs as IN USE until they have been archived once. The command does, however, show dual OLDS logging.

c. **Changing the Number of OLDS Buffers:** Change the BUFNO keyword on the OLDSDEF statement in the DFSVSMxx member in IMS.PROCLIB.

When you modify the BUFNO keyword, you should consider also modifying the region size for the VSAM common segment area (CSA). The amount of storage fixed for OLDS buffers is BUFNO * BUFFERSIZE.

WADS space is also affected by the value specified on the BUFNO keyword. To change WADS space allocation, see Table 24-12 on page 434.

Related Reading: For information on how to calculate WADS space requirements, see *IMS Version 9: Installation Volume 1: Installation Verification.*

d. **Changing Space, Location, or Allocation:** For the recommended method of changing the space or location of your OLDS, or for reallocating an OLDS on the same volume and with the same space, follow the procedure for changing the BLKSIZE in note a.

You can modify space, location, or allocation without shutting down IMS in a non-XRF environment by using the following procedure:

1. /STOP OLDS *nn*
2. Archive all OLDSs.
3. Delete PRIOLDS and SECOLDS records in the RECON data sets, using the DELETE.LOG command.
4. Scratch and reallocate OLDSs.
5. /START OLDS *nn*

Using Newly Initialized Volumes for OLDS

If a newly initialized (or reinitialized, but unformatted) volume is to contain an OLDS, you must format either the volume or the space occupied by the OLDS before the online system uses it. If you do not format the volume, or if the block size of the new OLDS data set is not the same as the existing OLDS data set, you can expect severe performance degradation and excessive device and channel usage until IMS completely fills the OLDS once. This problem is especially noticeable during emergency restart and during XRF tracking and takeover.

You can use any of the following techniques to format a volume for an OLDS:

- Copy an existing OLDS (of the same size) into the new OLDS.
- Copy an existing volume into the new volume, scratch the volume table of contents (VTOC), and allocate the new OLDS.
- Use another IMS subsystem to fill the OLDS: turn on all traces to the log and issue checkpoint commands until the OLDS fills.
- Write a program that either writes at least one byte of data into each track on the volume or fills the OLDS with maximum logical record length (LRECL) blocks.

Controlling the Write-Ahead Data Set

Table 24-12 lists the actions required to change WADS characteristics.

Table 24-12   Changing WADS Characteristics

Modification	Actions Required
Single to dual[a]	1. Shut down IMS. 2. Allocate new WADS. 3. Define a DFSMDA member. 4. Add DD statement in IMS JCL, if necessary. 5. Code WADS=D in IMS JCL. 6. Modify operating procedures. 7. Restart IMS with FORMAT WADS keywords.
Dual to single[a]	1. Shut down IMS. 2. Code WADS=S in IMS JCL. 3. Delete DFSMDA member. 4. Remove DD statement in IMS JCL, if necessary. 5. Modify operating procedures. 6. Restart IMS.
Adding spare	1. Allocate a spare WADS. 2. Update WADSDEF specification in the DFSVSMxx member of IMS.PROCLIB. 3. Define DFSMDA member. 4. Add DD statement in IMS JCL, if necessary. 5. Modify operating procedures. 6. /START WADS *n* (or wait until IMS restart).

Table 24-12   Changing WADS Characteristics (Continued)

Modification	Actions Required
Removing spare	1. `/STOP WADS n` (and wait for dynamic deallocation). 2. Scratch spare WADS. 3. Update WADSDEF statement in the DFSVSMxx member of IMS.PROCLIB. 4. Remove DD statement in IMS JCL. 5. Modify operating procedures.
Space, location, or allocation[b]	1. Shut down IMS. 2. Scratch and reallocate WADSs. 3. Restart IMS with `FORMAT WADS` keywords.

a.   **Changing the Mode:** WADS can be dynamically allocated and deallocated.

    To reflect the new mode for WADSs, you must update the:

      • Skeletal JCL for the Log Recovery utility (LOGCLJCL member).

      • IMS startup procedure (WADS= execution parameter).

      • All recovery procedures implemented to recover WADS errors or to close unclosed OLDSs using WADS.

b.   **Changing the Space, Location, or Allocation:** All WADS must have the same space allocation (number of tracks) and be on the same type of device.

Controlling the System Log Data Set

Converting from single to dual SLDSs requires modification in the skeletal JCL (ARCHJCL member) and in all your operational procedures that use SLDSs. In the operational procedures, consider using the secondary SLDS when you experience errors in the primary SLDS. No modification is required for online processing because IMS dynamically allocates SLDSs.

Changing the BLKSIZE requires modification in the skeletal JCL (ARCHJCL member). All SLDSs required for online processing must have the same BLKSIZE.

Controlling the RECON Data Sets

Table 24-13 on page 436 lists the actions required to change RECON data set characteristics.

Table 24-13   Changing RECON Data Set Characteristics

Modification	Actions Required
Adding spare	1. Define a spare RECON data set. 2. Compile DFSMDA macro for the spare data set or add DD statement in IMS JCL and batch JCL if you do not use dynamic allocation. The spare data set must be in VSAM CREATE mode.
Removing spare	1. Delete cluster. 2. Delete DFSMDA member in IMS.SDFSRESL or remove DD statement from IMS JCL and batch JCL if you do not use dynamic allocation.
Replacing active	**Recommendation:** Stop all IMS subsystems and batch jobs that access the RECON data sets. 1. Define a spare data set with new space or allocate a spare data set at a new location. 2. CHANGE.RECON REPLACE (RECON*n*) 3. Define a new spare data set. 4. Continue normal processing.
Single to dual	**Recommendation:** Stop all IMS subsystems and batch jobs that access the RECON data sets. 1. Define a spare RECON data set. 2. CHANGE.RECON DUAL 3. Define a new spare data set. 4. Continue normal processing.

RECOMMENDATION: For both online and batch, use dynamic allocation for RECON data sets, and run with at least three RECON data sets.

CONNECTING AND DISCONNECTING SUBSYSTEMS

Before an IMS subsystem can access databases in an external subsystem (another program executing in a z/OS address space) such as DB2, you must connect the IMS subsystem to this other subsystem. IMS can connect to another subsystem only if that subsystem is identified in the subsystem member in IMS.PROCLIB. Specify the subsystem member name in the SSM EXEC parameter. When specified to and accessed by IMS, the subsystem member name cannot be changed without stopping IMS.

Related Reading: For information on the SSM EXEC parameter, see *IMS Version 9: Installation Volume 2: System Definition and Tailoring*.

Connections between an IMS subsystem and another subsystem can occur with or without operator intervention, and without regard to which subsystem is available first.

- Automatic connection: When the SSM EXEC parameter is specified, IMS automatically establishes the connection when it processes the parameter.
- Operator-controlled connection: When the SSM EXEC parameter is not specified, the connection is established when the /START SUBSYS SSM command is entered. The /START SUBSYS SSM command specifies the subsystem member in IMS.PROCLIB that IMS uses to connect to subsystems.

Disconnecting IMS from another subsystem is initiated with the /STOP SUBSYS command, and normally completes without operator intervention. IMS quiesces all dependent region external subsystem activity prior to stopping the subsystem.

IMS System Recovery

I MS has many features that provide high availability and complete recovery of the IMS system in all operating environments. The major features are:

- Extended Recovery Facility (XRF)
- Remote Site Recovery (RSR)
- IMS running in a Parallel Sysplex environment and using shared queues, shared data, or both

This chapter describes XRF and RSR. For more information about IMS in a Parallel Sysplex environment, see Part VI, "IMS in a Parallel Sysplex Environment," on page 465.

XRF and RSR are two features of IMS that can, optionally, be used to increase the availability of IMS systems and the data in IMS databases. Both rely on duplicating IMS subsystems and data on another z/OS system.

The first of these is the XRF. The XRF functions are delivered as an integral part of IMS and are intended to provide increased availability of IMS subsystems. There is an overhead, both in machine usage and support, in using XRF. However, if you have an application that can only tolerate minimal outages, then you might consider using XRF.

The second of these features is RSR. RSR is a separately priced component available with IMS. It provides similar facilities to XRF, but with some differences.

Both features rely on having another IMS subsystem, situated on another z/OS system, that tracks the update activity of the primary IMS subsystem (only one for XRF, one or more for RSR) to provide a backup.

The differences between the two features are discussed in "Comparison of XRF and RSR" on page 441.

In This Chapter:

- "Overview of Extended Recovery Facility (XRF)"
- "Overview of Remote Site Recovery (RSR)"
- "Comparison of XRF and RSR" on page 441
- "Summary of When to Use XRF or RSR" on page 442

OVERVIEW OF EXTENDED RECOVERY FACILITY (XRF)

XRF works by having a second, alternate, IMS running. The alternate IMS runs on a separate z/OS image that, preferably, is on a physically separate machine that is channel-attached to the first one. The alternate IMS tracks the work of the active IMS system by reading the IMS log data sets of the active IMS system. XRF provides the ability to perform hardware maintenance and maintenance on other system software products without interrupting the availability of the IMS application.

The principal drawbacks of XRF are:

- XRF does not protect against application errors. If the outage is caused by an application error, the same application message might be re-presented on the alternate IMS and cause it to fail.
- XRF does not protect against network outages. You must plan for this separately.
- XRF does not support DB2 databases.
- Occasionally, you must apply IMS maintenance to both the active and standby IMS systems at the same time.

Although XRF can prevent most unplanned and planned outages, it cannot keep the IMS system available indefinitely. You must eventually plan outages for software maintenance, upgrades, and some changes to the IMS configuration. IMS systems running with XRF have achieved continuous availability for years.

OVERVIEW OF REMOTE SITE RECOVERY (RSR)

RSR is a separately priced feature available with IMS.

RSR can track details of IMS full-function databases and Fast Path DEDBs at an alternate site. The remote site is connected to the site with the active systems by a network connection using the VTAM APPC protocol. The VTAM connection is between separate IMS transport manager subsystems (TMSs) on the active and tracking machines.

The IMS logger component on the active machines sends the log data from all active IMS systems (DB/DC, DCCTL, DBCTL and batch) that are defined for RSR tracking to the tracking machine.

The TMS on the tracking machine receives this data and passes it to a single IMS region. This region processes the data and records it using normal IMS processing. Depending on what level of tracking has been requested, the IMS region might also apply the updates to the IMS databases.

If any interruptions to the network connection occur, RSR notes the gaps in the logging, obtains the missing log data, and performs catch-up processing when the link is reestablished.

The IMS system on the tracking machine normally can process only input from the TMS. The tracking machine only becomes a fully functioning system if it has to take over.

Not all databases are tracked. You define the databases that are tracked when you register them to DBRC.

Related Reading: For more information about RSR, see *IMS Version 9: Administration Guide: System.*

COMPARISON OF XRF AND RSR

Table 25-1 provides a comparison between the features of XRF and RSR.

Table 25-1   Comparison between XRF and RSR Features

XRF	RSR
Uses same physical log data sets and database data sets for active IMS and alternate IMS.	Uses completely separate log data sets and database data sets.
Active and alternate IMSs must be within the distance restrictions of the channel-to-channel connection between them.	Active and tracking systems are connected by network. Only limit on separation is network response.
Active IMS and alternate IMS must use IMS TM.	Active IMS can be any system updating IMS resources: DB/DC, TM only, DB only, or batch. The tracking IMS can be DB/DC or DBCTL.
One-to-one relationship between active IMS and alternate IMS.	One tracking IMS tracks many active IMSs.
All committed updates recorded on alternate IMS.	If there is a gap in the log data at the time of an unplanned takeover, any log data that comes after the gap is removed to ensure system integrity.
Switching to or from alternate IMS is comparatively simple.	Takeovers are more complex than for XRF.
Switch to alternate IMS takes one minute.	Switch to alternate takes less one hour.

Summary of When to Use XRF or RSR

XRF is suitable for situations where you have a single IMS DB/DC system that requires very high system availability (greater than 99.5%). However, the second z/OS containing the tracking IMS system must be channel-attached to the z/OS system that the first IMS is running on.

RSR is suitable for situations where you have one or more IMS subsystems running in a number of address spaces on a single z/OS system and you want to minimize data loss in a failure situation, but can tolerate outages of approximately one hour. RSR uses network connections between the two z/OS systems, so there are no restrictions on the distance separating them.

CHAPTER **26**

IBM IMS Tools

■ **T**he IBM IMS tools are specifically designed to enhance the performance of IMS. The tools support the newest version of IMS right when it becomes available, making it easy to migrate from version to version and still benefit from tools support. The IMS tools are categorized into sections that contain the highlights of each tool.

In This Chapter:

Related Reading: The information in this chapter about the IBM IMS tools is current as of the writing of this book. For complete and up-to-date information about the IBM IMS tools, click on the "IBM DB2 and IMS Tools" link on the IMS Web site at www.ibm.com/ims.

DATABASE ADMINISTRATION TOOLS

The following sections describe the IBM IMS database administration tools.

IBM Data Encryption for IMS and DB2 Databases, V1

The IBM Data Encryption for IMS and DB2 Databases tool:

- Provides user-customizable, pre-coded exit routines for encryption of IMS and DB2 data.
- Conforms to the existing OS/390 and z/OS security model and is implemented using standard IMS and DB2 exit routines.
- Exploits zSeries and S/390 Crypto Hardware features, which results in low overhead encryption and decryption.
- Uses the ANSI Data Encryption Algorithm (DEA), which is also known as the U.S. National Institute of Science and Technology (NIST) Data Encryption Standard (DES) algorithm.
- Works at the IMS segment level, and can be customized at that level. For DB2, encryption and decryption is customizable at the table level.

Program number: 5799-GWD

IBM IMS Database Repair Facility for z/OS, V1.2

The IBM IMS Database Repair Facility for z/OS:

- Interactively repairs VSAM- and OSAM-organized IMS databases that contain pointer or data errors.
- Performs repairs quickly, thereby reducing the amount of time that the affected database is taken offline.
- Supports IMS Fast Path DEDB databases.
- Features VSAM and OSAM pointer repair, pointer navigation, a backout safety feature, and an ISPF front end.
- Runs in interactive mode, in which you can view entire blocks of data of individual IMS segments and can navigate to other segments. Any changes made are tracked and can be undone.
- Runs in batch mode, in which you can dump blocks from the data set or submit changes to the block data.

Program number: 5655-E03

IBM IMS Hardware Data Compression - Extended for z/OS, V2.2

The IBM IMS Hardware Data Compression - Extended for z/OS tool:

- Replaces and extends the dictionary creation and Segment Edit/Compression exit routine creation utilities of IMS.
- Provides HDC enhanced analysis capability, including extended reporting and multiple input sources.

- Offers dictionary archival and evaluation services.
- Supports compression of HDAM, HIDAM, HISAM, and Fast Path databases.

Program number: 5655-E02

IBM IMS High Availability Large Database (HALDB) Conversion and Maintenance Aid for z/OS, V2

The IBM IMS High Availability Large Database (HALDB) Conversion and Maintenance Aid for z/OS:

- Guides DBAs through HALDB conversions with ease.
- Performs index pointer healing.
- Speeds the conversion process with partition modeling.
- Enables conversion with minimal manual intervention.
- Requires no HALDB experience and little IMS expertise.
- Creates DBD and DBRC definitions as well as the conversion JCL.
- Provides additional conversion options such as Initial HALDB Load assistance and Status Code 'BA' Aid.
- Includes a Partition Maintenance Aid that supports split partitions, DBRC functions for HALDB, creation of backup and recovery JCL, and generation of reorganization utilities.

Program number: 5655-K47

IBM IMS Library Integrity Utilities for z/OS, V1

The IBM IMS Library Integrity Utilities for z/OS:

- Includes and replaces all of the features and functions of the IMS Library Management Utilities:
  — Managing IMS ACB, PSB, and DBD libraries
  — DBD/PSB/ACB Compare, DBD/PSB/ACB Reversal, and DBD/PSB/ACB Mapper and IMS Advanced ACB Generator
  — Providing a high-speed generation process that greatly reduces the time needed to process large volumes of IMS ACBs
  — Reporting information in a tabular form
  — Checking results from your desktop and ensuring that all PSBs and DBDs were processed as expected
- Includes an Integrity Checker to help prevent system outages caused by databases corrupted by using the wrong DBD.
- Includes a Consistency Checker function to ensure that all the necessary definitions have been created for a database.

Program number: 5655-I42

IBM IMS Online Reorganization for z/OS, V1

The IBM IMS Online Reorganization for z/OS tool:

- Enables reorganization of IMS full-function databases with a short outage (a short period of time called *takeover time*).
- Reorganizes databases to shadow data sets, captures the changes during this period, and applies them to the reorganized shadow data sets.
- Requires databases and their data sets to be registered with DBRC.
- Reorganizes HISAM, HIDAM, HDAM, and SHISAM databases, and recreates their associated index data sets.
- Reorganizes PHIDAM and PHDAM databases as single partitions.
- Makes selected DBD changes during the reorganization process that are automatically propagated to the participating online systems without the need of launching an online change.
- Allows predefinition of the period when takeover time may occur.
- Automatically creates the shadow data sets: SMS allocation uses the same SMS constructs; non-SMS allocation uses the same volume serial, and user predefinition.
- Supports a user exit during reload that can be called to process any changes.

Program number: 5655-H57

IBM IMS Parameter Manager for z/OS, V1

The IBM IMS Parameter Manager for z/OS tool:

- Enables IMS administrators to control the specification and maintenance of IMS parameter library members.
- Simplifies parameter management and provides increased levels of parameter control.
- Supports the 19 startup parameter members in an IMS system startup.
- Allows parameter specification by ISPF dialog panels or the integrated ISPF editor.
- Contains extensive online help and parameter descriptions.
- Provides parameter syntax and value checking, and automatic parameter statement construction.
- Provides a view of active (current) parameter members by IMS system.
- Enables the creation of a "back-up" member immediately prior to applying changes.
- Automatically collects previous version histories for altered parameter members.
- Includes facilities to assist with IMS software version migration.

Program number: 5655-L69

IBM IMS Sequential Randomizer Generator for OS/390, VI

The IBM IMS Sequential Randomizer Generator for OS/390:

- Creates a randomizer that enables the user to access HDAM and DEDB database segments either directly or sequentially.

- Allows access to HDAM and DEDB databases in logical key sequence without sacrificing their efficient direct access capabilities.
- Optimizes the distribution of database records by adjusting the randomizing module if the number of synonyms or the control interval (CI) or block utilization exceeds the user-specified value.

Program number: 5655-E11

APPLICATION MANAGEMENT TOOLS

The following sections describe the IBM IMS application management tools.

IMS Batch Backout Manager for z/OS, VI

The IMS Batch Backout Manager for z/OS:

- Helps automate the normally manual task of backing out database updates after an IMS batch application failure.
- Reduces the downtime associated with an application failure and improves database availability.
- Provides automation of the batch backout process after specific application abends.
- Dynamically handles log close and allocation.
- Forces allocation of batch SLDSs for jobs with no logs allocated (either by specific or by generic job name).

Program number: 5697-H75

IBM IMS Batch Terminal Simulator for z/OS, V3

The IBM IMS Batch Terminal Simulator for z/OS:

- Provides a comprehensive way to test and check IMS application program logic, IMS application interfaces, teleprocessing activity, 3270 format control blocks, and database activity.
- Simulates the operation of IMS applications in TSO and batch environments.
- Operates transparently to the applications, requiring no changes to IMS code, control blocks, libraries, or application load modules.
- Accesses DL/I and DB2 databases from TSO terminals.

- Provides a stable online system in test and production environments to execute applications properly before they are put online.
- Provides audit reporting and Java language support.

Program number: 5655-J57

IBM IMS Connect for z/OS, V2.2

The IBM IMS Connect for z/OS tool:

- Supports communications with IMS between one or more TCP/IP clients and one or more IMS systems.
- Supports SMP installability; dump and trace formatting enhancements for increased serviceability; user exit routines, command improvement, and asynchronous output support for enhanced usability.
- Provides Unicode support, enabling a Unicode application to send data to an IMS host application, such as a Java application that is running in IMS.
- Provides ACK/NAK required notification support without additional testing of data received.
- Reduces the design and coding effort of a client application by including the full message length preceding the output message to the client.
- Uses the VisualAge® for Java IMS Connector for Java to create Java applications that can access IMS transactions from WebSphere Application Servers for z/OS and OS/390.
- Offers WebSphere Adapter support with the addition of the IMS Connector for Java J2EE Runtime support.
- Supports two-phase commit for distributed environments across TCP/IP, providing for a WebSphere Application Server in a non-OS/390, non-z/OS environment to connect to IMS through IMS Connect (with IMS and IMS Connect initially in the same LPAR).
- Provides enhanced security items, such as Secure Sockets Layer (SSL), the capability to control the security environment, and "trusted user" support.
- Provides Message Format Services (MFS) Web Services support to enable IMS customers to publish existing MFS-based IMS applications on the Internet as Web Services.
- Includes command enhancements for ease of manageability.
- Contains Commit Mode 0 / Persistent Socket to improve performance.
- Supports IMS Connect Extensions for z/OS, V1.1, to enhance performance and availability reporting.
- Has cancel timer support to enhance usability.
- IMS Connector for Java also adds Commit Mode 0 / Persistent Socket for improved performance, socket timeout for enhanced usability, and retry to broaden availability.

Program number: 5655-K52

IBM IMS Connect Extensions for z/OS, V1

The IBM IMS Connect Extensions for z/OS, V1:

- Enhance the basic capabilities of the IMS Connect for z/OS, V2.2, tool.
- Provide performance monitoring capabilities by creating and collecting performance and accounting information for IMS Connect activities.
- Provide enhanced services for customer user exit routines: dynamic exit reload without interruption of IMS Connect execution, and adding or removing exits without interruption of IMS Connect execution.
- Include flexible resource definitions for the grouping of resource types, such as data store and transactions.
- Have expanded control of client input messages, which includes dynamic routing of messages to multiple Data Stores, and includes dynamic resource controls.
- Allow external control of IMS Connect Extension by the ISPF console.
- Include security items, such as a special RACF class for client access control, USERID SAF profile caching, refreshing of SAF profiles by command, and verifying client access to IMS Connect resources.
- Contain performance monitoring extensions that provide performance measurements and basic reporting, with more extensive reporting being provided by the IBM IMS Performance Analyzer for z/OS tool.

Program number: 5655-K48

IBM IMS Message Format Services Reversal Utilities for z/OS, V1

The IBM IMS Message Format Services Reversal Utilities for z/OS:

- Include the MFS Reversal and MFS Compare utilities in the package.
- Convert Message Format Services MID, MOD, DIF, and DOF control blocks back into Message Format Services utility control statements.
- Help you recover the source and compare deltas if you lose your MFS source library or suspect a difference between the generated control blocks and the source.
- Provide useful summary reports of the IMS FORMAT library that show the relationships among the members.

Program number: 5655-F45

IBM IMS Program Restart Facility for OS/390, V2

The IBM IMS Program Restart Facility for OS/390:

- Automatically assigns the most recent checkpoint ID to jobs that are restarted because of an earlier abnormal termination.
- Forces an extended restart to occur for all jobs that require restart.

- Helps prevent corruption resulting from restarting an abended job without specifying a restart checkpoint ID.
- Saves costly and time-consuming database recoveries caused by manual restart errors.
- Reduces the risk of data being unavailable or becoming corrupt.

Program number: 5655-E14

PERFORMANCE MANAGEMENT TOOLS

The following sections describe the IBM IMS performance management tools.

IBM IMS Buffer Pool Analyzer for z/OS, V1

The IMS Buffer Pool Analyzer for z/OS tool:

- Provides modeling facilities to assist with making informed decisions about the addition of buffers to an existing pool, or sizing requirements for a new buffer pool.
- Helps you determine the impact of buffer pool changes before they are made to take the guesswork out of the process.
- Analyzes IMS database buffer pools (OSAM and VSAM) to provide statistical analysis of the impact of changes that affect the buffer pools.
- Provides I/O rates and buffering requirements for a specific database.
- Allows for better allocation of real memory resources.
- Identifies databases that most heavily use each database subpool.
- Performs "what if" scenario analysis, such as identifying the impact of splitting a specific database into a new buffer pool.
- Determines the performance effects for a given buffer pool when you add or reduce the number of buffer pools.

Program number: 5697-H77

IBM IMS Network Compression Facility for z/OS, V1

The IMS Network Compression Facility for z/OS:

- Replaces the IMS Data Stream Tuner; provides support for IMS Version 6, IMS Version 7, and IMS Version 8; and adds several new features and functionality improvements.
- Provides several new options for compression of 3270 data streams:
  - Compresses all repeated characters, not just spaces, nulls, asterisks, and dashes
  - Allows 3270 Field Merge, blank elimination, and elimination of non-display fields
  - Eliminates redundant 3270 Set Buffer Address (SBA) commands

- Makes installation easier by eliminating the need for the XCM address space and sub-system, and for SYS1.PARMLIB updates, except APF authorization of one data set.
- Includes a utility to convert current options to the new PROCLIB member format.
- Improves flexibility by allowing cross-MVS system inquiries and updates to Network Compression Facility information and options.

Program number: 5655-E41

IBM IMS Performance Analyzer for z/OS, V3.3

The IBM IMS Performance Analyzer for z/OS tool:

- Provides comprehensive reporting for the IMS log and IMS Monitor, and for IMS Connect Extensions for z/OS event collection.
- Contains a New Dashboard report that provides a quick overview of critical system performance indicators.
- Includes a new BMP Checkpoint report that measures batch checkpoint frequency that can impact online performance and system restartability.
- Generates the Transaction History File that collects detailed transaction performance data and exports it into DB2.
- Provides additional information to aid in the interpretation of reports.
- Provides a wide variety of reports that can help shorten transaction response times and increase resource availability.
- Offers automatic DBRC log selection of the required SLDS log files to simplify report requests.
- Produces IMS log and Monitor reports to "health check" your system.
- Enhanced DBCTL reporting.
- Provides log reports: Transaction Statistics, System Checkpoint, and Deadlock.
- Provides ISPF dialog interface enhancements to manage IMS system and sysplex definitions, and tailor and submit report requests.
- Comprehensive reporting for the Fast Path Monitor, including DEDB, BALG/EMH, Fast Path Buffer, OTHREAD, and VSO.
- Complements IMS Problem Investigator for z/OS (5655-K50) in the investigation of IMS performance-related problems.

Program number: 5655-E15

IBM IMS Performance Monitor for z/OS, V1

The IBM IMS Performance Monitor for z/OS:

- Provides real-time status monitoring and alerts for an active IMS subsystem.
- Detects active IMS subsystems when they are started and any IMS subsystems that may subsequently become active.

- Allows multiple IMS subsystems to be viewed from a single monitoring station, and these subsystems can be logically grouped as desired (for example, in data-sharing groups and shared-queues groups).
- Reports as much information as possible to help isolate or point to problem areas that include sysplex functions.
- Features general IMS information such as release levels, configurations, and system startup parameters.
- Allows user-specified thresholds for setting alerts.
- Provides current IMS resource information to assist in tuning.

Program number: 5655-G50

IMS Problem Investigator for z/OS, V1

The IMS Problem Investigator for z/OS tool:

- Provides an enhanced level of problem-determination services for IMS TM and IMS DB systems.
- Includes navigation aids, formatted and personalized reporting, and investigative procedures for IMS log, trace, and other data.
- Offers powerful automated features to help reduce the amount of time required to identify and analyze defects or other events of interest in the IMS log.
- Accesses services by an ISPF dialog or a batch reporting utility.

Program number: 5655-K50

RECOVERY MANAGEMENT TOOLS

The following sections describe the IBM IMS recovery management tools.

Application Recovery Tool for IMS and DB2 Databases, V1.2

The Application Recovery Tool for IMS and DB2 Databases:

- Includes enhancements for IMS applications.
- Supports HALDB (High Availability Large Databases) by adding a HALDB (Y|N) parameter to all IMS-related functions.
- Supports IMS sysplex data sharing.
- Adds the new member IMSDSGS to the PARMLIB.

Program number: 5697-F56

IMS Database Recovery Facility for z/OS, V2

The IMS Database Recovery Facility for z/OS:

- Is a high performance, state of the art database recovery product supporting all recoverable IMS databases.
- Provides a high performance tool for recovering IMS database data sets and Fast Path areas.
- Works in an online environment, with a single pass of input data.
- Speeds recovery by applying database changes to multiple data sets simultaneously.
- Increases database availability by reducing recovery time.
- Provides recovery to any prior point in time through a time stamp recovery function.
- Follow-on version of the IMS Online Recovery Service for z/OS tool (5655-E50), containing all the features and functions of that product, and adding several key features such as:

  — IMS Database Recovery Facility initiation by submitting an MVS batch job
  — Batch invocation of the IMS Database Recovery Facility that does not require an active IMS region
  — Online invocation of the IMS Database Recovery Facility that does not use IMS region resources to update the database
  — Reading multiple image copy data sets and writing multiple database data sets in parallel
  — Use of DFSORT to order the input log records in several concurrent processes and apply changes in a single pass of the database
  — Analysis of recovery execution and provision of a formatted report summarizing inputs, outputs, and processing
  — Generation of a setup report/list without running the recovery process
  — Reporting of all open units of work that contain updates not applied in a point-in-time recovery
  — Parallel and concurrent processing to provide dramatic gains in performance

Program number: 5655-I44

IBM IMS DEDB Fast Recovery for z/OS, V2.2

The IBM IMS DEDB Fast Recovery for z/OS tool:

- Assists in the operation and maintenance of data integrity of IMS databases.
- Is designed as a fast alternative to emergency restart (ERE) failure recovery.
- Corrects online log data sets (OLDSs) by invalidating logging for transactions that did not reach the sync point.
- Significantly reduces the amount of time needed to recover DEDBs after an IMS failure.

- Generates the JCL for the MSDB Dump Recovery utility to be processed before an IMS cold start for MSDB (main storage database) recovery.
- Shortens the recovery time of an unscheduled IMS cold start while maintaining the integrity of the IMS databases.
- Supports multiple IMS releases from a single Load Library.

Program number: 5655-E32

IBM IMS High Performance Image Copy for z/OS, V3.2

The IBM IMS High Performance Image Copy for z/OS tool:

- Helps you process and manage image copies more efficiently.
- Enables you to run the image copy function with the hash checking of the IMS High Performance Pointer Checker for z/OS tool, V2, under the control of the IMS Parallel Reorganization for z/OS tool, V3.
- Reduces the run time of the reorganization process for an IMS full function database.
- Allows accuracy checking of an image copy and supports processes in parallel within an IMS Parallel Reorganization.
- Contains a new optional parameter for controlling the secondary image copy data set.
- Supports dynamic allocation for the specification of SMS classes for new output image copy data sets.
- Provides a Creation Image Copy function that creates new copies from IMS standard image copy data sets, ICE compressed image copy data sets, IMS Online Image Copy data sets, and IMS Image Copy 2 data sets, while simultaneously creating up to seven copies from the original data set.

Program number: 5655-K96

IBM IMS High Performance Change Accumulation for z/OS, V1.2

The IMS High Performance Change Accumulation for z/OS tool:

- Replaces the IMS Parallel Change Accumulation tool; supports IMS Versions 6, 7, and 8; and adds numerous new features and functional improvements.
- Improves operations by triggering a single job through the internal reader, without the need to submit the JCL manually. The job functions as a multitask address space, ensuring parallel streaming of both input and output data.
- Eliminates the need for the XCM address space and subsystem for easier installation.
- Processes input data (from RLDSs) and output data (new CAs) in parallel to ensure that elapsed execution time is as short as possible; also provides the option for users to control the number of parallel processes.

- Provides ISPF interfaces that allow for customization, setup, execution, and batch interfaces for operations.
- Supports DBRC.
- Provides processing report improvements that consolidate the status of associated address spaces into a single report and extends diagnostic capabilities with new error reporting messaging.
- Supports an extended batch interface that makes it easier to run automated job scheduling facilities.

Program number: 5655-F59

INFORMATION INTEGRATION MANAGEMENT TOOLS

The following sections describe the IBM IMS Information Integration management tools.

IBM IMS DataPropagator for z/OS, V3

The IBM IMS DataPropagator for z/OS tool:

- Supports IBM WebSphere MQ for z/OS-based, asynchronous, near real-time propagation that allows:
  — The Capture Component to capture IMS database changes performed by IMS Batch, IMS BMP, and IMS TM application programs
  — The Apply Component to transform the IMS database changes into relational format and apply them to DB2 tables on the same or on different systems from the IMS databases
  — The transmission of the database changes from the Capture to the Target Component through the recoverable, buffered, and queued asynchronous messaging services of WebSphere MQ
- Reduces elapsed time between the IMS database updates and the DB2 table updates to as little as a few seconds.
- Supports point-in-time propagation, allowing the content of the DB2 target tables to reflect clearly identified logical points in time of the IMS source databases, for example, the logical end of a business day.
- Exploits the well-established, high-performance, reliable queued messaging services of WebSphere MQ and allows enterprises to leverage their WebSphere MQ administration and operations skills.
- Improves performance by transmitting multiple IMS database changes within the same WebSphere MQ message, by compressing WebSphere MQ message data, and by exploiting the caching services of the Virtual Lookaside Facility (VLF) of z/OS.

Program number: 5655-E52

IBM DB2 Information Integrator Classic Event Publisher for IMS, V8.2

DB2 Information Integrator Classic Event Publisher for IMS makes it easy to link data events with business processes. This tool captures database changes in IMS by:

1. Reading the active or recovery log
2. Formatting the changes into XML messages, and then
3. Publishing them to WebSphere MQ

Any application or service that integrates either with WebSphere MQ directly or supports Java Message Service (JMS) can asynchronously receive the data changes as they occur. DB2 Information Integrator Classic Event Publisher for IMS also enables database events to initiate business processes; for example a change in an inventory value could be used to drive restocking of the product.

With this tool, businesses can realize faster time to market based on integration that captures the event in a single location and is easier to maintain.

Program number: 5655-M38

IBM DB2 Information Integrator Classic Event Publisher for VSAM, V8.2

DB2 Information Integrator Classic Event Publisher for VSAM makes it easy to link data events with business processes. This tool captures database changes in VSAM by:

1. Reading the active or recovery log
2. Formatting the changes into XML messages, and then
3. Publishing them to WebSphere MQ

Any application or service that integrates either with WebSphere MQ directly or supports Java Message Service (JMS) can asynchronously receive the data changes as they occur. DB2 Information Integrator Classic Event Publisher for VSAM also enables database events to initiate business processes; for example, a change in an inventory value could be used to drive restocking of the product.

With this tool, businesses can realize faster time to market based on integration that captures the event in a single location and is easier to maintain.

Program number: 5655-M35

UTILITIES MANAGEMENT TOOLS

The following sections describe the IBM IMS utilities management tools. These tools are grouped into the following categories:

- "Fast Path Utilities Management" on page 457

Fast Path Utilities Management

The following sections describe the IBM IMS utilities management tools for Fast Path databases.

IBM IMS Fast Path Basic Tools for z/OS, V1.2

The IBM IMS Fast Path Basic Tools for z/OS:

- Analyze, maintain, tune, and migrate IMS Fast Path DEDB databases without bringing up an IMS online system environment.
- Include DEDB Pointer Checker, DEDB Tuning Aid, and DEDB Unload/Reload utilities.
- Provide the new control statement parameter ACCESS=FAST in the DEDB Unload utility to support high performance read access to the DEDB area data set by using DFSMS Media Manager interfaces.
- Feature a new DEDB Reload utility that allows you to produce image copies for reloaded DEDB areas and provide automatic notification of them to DBRC.

Program number: 5655-E30

IBM IMS Fast Path Online Tools for z/OS, V2

The IBM IMS Fast Path Online Tools for z/OS:

- Extends IMS Fast Path Basic Tools to an online IMS environment.
- Includes the DEDB Online Pointer Checker tool and the DEDB Online Data Extract tool.
- Boosts system availability by allowing you to perform a variety of key functions without having to take your IMS database offline.
- Uses the Fast Path Online Area Extender tool to expand the size of DEDB areas online, which results in 24×7 availability of an IMS Fast Path DEDB area.

Program number: 5655-F78

IBM IMS High Performance Fast Path Utilities for z/OS, V2

The IBM IMS High Performance Fast Path Utilities for z/OS:

- Provides all the features and functions available in the IMS Fast Path Basic Tools for z/OS, V1.2, and the IMS Fast Path Online Tools for z/OS, V2.
- Contains the new High Performance Fast Path Reorganization Tool component, which:
  - Determines utility use based on control state
  - Supports dynamic allocation of databases and Sort work data sets
  - Provides support for making DEDBs available to IMS after reloading

— Allows a single SYSIN DD statement
— Supports multiple area data sets (ADSs)
— Provides SYSIN: Non-positional control statement

Program number: 5655-K94

Full-Function Utilities Management Tools

The following sections describe the IBM IMS utilities management tools for full-function databases.

IBM IMS High Performance Load for z/OS,V2

The IBM IMS High Performance Load for z/OS tool:

- Provides a high performance database reloading capability for IMS full-function databases.
- Supports IMS Parallel Reorganization for z/OS V3 capabilities, such as image copy creation during database reorganization.
- Supports reorganization reload of HALDB partitions, including online-reorganization-capable HALDB partitions of IMS Version 9.
- Supports various formats of the unloaded data sets.
- Includes the Physical Sequence Sort for Reload (PSSR) utility.
- Gives you the option to load compressed data that was previously unloaded by IBM IMS High Performance Unload for OS/390 in a compressed format.
- Accepts multiple standard formats for load data sets.
- Provides JCL statement compatibility with IMS High Performance Load V1 JCL streams without modification.

Program number: 5655-M26

IBM IMS High Performance Unload for OS/390,V1

The IBM IMS High Performance Unload for OS/390 tool:

- Provides an API that enables application programs to leverage the tool's high performance retrieval techniques efficiently.
- Allows you to unload broken data sets.
- Gives you the option to unload compressed data without decompression overhead.
- Provides multiple standard formats for unload data sets.
- Includes a variety of statistical reports for improved tuning.

Program number: 5655-E06

IBM IMS High Performance Prefix Resolution for z/OS, V3

The IBM IMS High Performance Prefix Resolution for z/OS tool:

- Enables you to resolve and update prefixes of IMS databases involved in logical relationships as a single job step.
- Uses the HPPRPIPE data transfer service to eliminate the intermediate Work File 2 (WF2) and Work File 3 (WF3) data sets.
- Helps you avoid much of the I/O, tape handling, and DASD requirements that are often associated with prefix resolution and prefix update.
- Executes the prefix resolution and prefix update functions as replacements for the IMS Prefix Resolution and IMS Prefix Update utilities.
- Supports IMS Parallel Reorganization for z/OS, V3 single job step execution of database reorganization, prefix resolution, and prefix update tasks.

Program number: 5655-M27

IBM IMS High Performance Pointer Checker for z/OS, V2

The IBM IMS High Performance Pointer Checker for z/OS:

- Enables you to analyze corrupt databases quickly and reduce the amount of time spent to diagnose and repair them.
- Generates reports that facilitate system tuning, report space utilization, and detect and report problems in primary and secondary indexes.
- Provides the ability to set several new thresholds, including available extents, CA and CI splits, and database and data set last extents.
- Has significant improvements in performance to Full Checking capabilities: improved usability with simplified setup and operation; parallel processing of databases; and improved reporting.

When the IMS High Performance Pointer Checker is used in conjunction with the IMS Database Repair Facility, the tools work together to help detect and correct database errors and repair them with a minimum of downtime.

Program number: 5655-K53

IBM IMS Index Builder for z/OS, V2.3

The IBM IMS Index Builder for z/OS:

- Offers several features that improve overall performance and enhance ease of use.
- Builds or rebuilds primary and secondary indexes quickly.
- Allows the user to specify an optional output file where records that are needed for prefix resolution can be split off and written as they are read in.
- Eliminates the need to image copy indexes.

- Provides an ISPF front end for easy JCL generation.
- Creates a separate address space for sorting index records.
- Recognizes index records that have duplicate keys and writes the duplicate keys to a SYSOUT data set.
- Supports building IMS HALDB primary indexes.

Program number: 5655-E24

IBM IMS Parallel Reorganization for z/OS, V3

The IBM IMS Parallel Reorganization for z/OS tool:

- Provides infrastructure to integrate IBM IMS tools for database reorganization and to operate them in a single job step.
- Improves administrative productivity for reorganizing IMS full-function databases.
- Drives IMS HP Unload for z/OS, IMS HP Load for z/OS, V2; IMS Index Builder for z/OS, V2.3; IMS HP Image Copy for z/OS, V3.2; IMS HP Pointer Checker for z/OS, V2; and IMS HP Prefix Resolution for z/OS, V3.
- Executes the image copy task with optional hash pointer checking in a parallel reorganization job step, concurrently with the unload, reload, and index builder steps.
- Executes the prefix resolution and update task in a parallel reorganization job step for a database that has internal logical relationships.
- Supports the IMSDALIB DD statement used for specifying the library of dynamic allocation members.
- Provides optional deletion of the old database data sets at successful completion of parallel reorganization.
- Supports parallel reorganization of HISAM and SHISAM databases.
- Supports parallel reorganization of HALDB partitions, including online-reorganization-capable HALDB partitions of IMS Version 9.
- Provides JCL statement compatibility with IMS Parallel Reorganization V2 JCL streams without modification.

Program number: 5655-M28

Administration Utilities Management Tools

The following sections describe the IBM IMS utilities management tools for IMS administration.

IBM IMS Database Control Suite for z/OS, V3

The IBM IMS Database Control Suite for z/OS:

- Provides a day-to-day IMS database environment management tool for DBAs, system programmers, and application support specialists.

- Enables you to collect and build on the data that is required to generate job control language (JCL) for database backup/recovery/reorganization management using IMS Base Utilities and IBM High Performance Tools.
- Provides an ISPF interface for the IMS Library Integrity Utilities.
- Includes a simplified user interface; reduction and consolidation of the number of data sets, ISPF panels, and process steps; and more flexibility for local standards.
- Automates tedious manual IMS maintenance functions to make database management easier.
- Is a functional replacement for the IMS DBICF (Database Integrity Control Facility) tool.
- Provides improved usability and productivity because the build process, during which JCL skeletons for utilities are built, is no longer required.
- Provides improved product panels and panel navigation; field-level help for all help panels; and fuller integration with DBRC terminology.

Program number: 5655-L08

TM MANAGEMENT TOOLS

The following sections describe the IBM IMS TM management tools.

IBM IMS Command Control Facility for z/OS, V1

The IBM IMS Command Control Facility for z/OS:

- Issues commands for DBCTL, DCCTL, or DB/DC regions.
- Issues IMS commands from a batch utility or from a TSO session from an ISPF interface by an ISPF interface.
- Ensures successful processing of database START, STOP, DBR, and DBD commands.
- Processes IMS commands across all regions in a sysplex using the batch command processor.
- Synchronizes online change and database commands across all regions in a sysplex using the batch command processor.

Program number: 5655-F40

IBM IMS Extended Terminal Option Support for z/OS, V2.2

The IBM IMS Extended Terminal Option Support for z/OS tool:

- Provides a frontend to the IMS Extended Terminal Option (ETO) feature.
- Offers capabilities to help manage, implement, customize, and exploit the benefits of ETO in your systems environment to manage resources effectively.
- Supports tailoring of all parts of ETO, including sign-on processing.

- Lets you set global options for the entire user community and override options for specific terminals or user IDs.
- Allows LTERM names that start with a numeric value.
- Supports multiple versions of IMS.
- Extends shared-queues support to issue SYSTEMS level ENQ for all LTERM names that are associated with a user at sign-on.
- Offers SLU type P support and SLU 1 console support that allow you to supply a variety of options on an LU-by-LU basis (for example, Logmode, Logon Description, ASOT, ALOT).

Program number: 5655-L61

IBM IMS High Performance System Generation (SYSGEN) Tools for z/OS, V1

The IBM IMS High Performance System Generation (SYSGEN) Tools for z/OS:

- Includes Fast System Generation (SYSGEN), Merge Clone, and System Generation (SYSGEN) Compare.
- Performs IMS SYSGENs for application resource changes (transactions, programs, databases, and route codes) in a single-step batch job or online.
- Reduces the time needed to perform IMS SYSGENs for application resource changes (transactions, programs, databases, and route codes) and consumes far less CPU time.
- Creates and maintains IMSplex SYSGEN configurations.

Program number: 5655-F43

IMS Multi-Dialog Manager for z/OS, V1

The IMS Multi-Dialog Manager for z/OS:

- Enables your IMS users to more quickly change between IMS sessions.
- Improves the usability of your IMS online system and the productivity of your users.
- Complements the existing IMS support for conversational transactions by managing the process of holding and resuming conversations for the end user.

Program number: 5697-H91

IBM IMS Queue Control Facility for z/OS, V2

The IBM IMS Queue Control Facility (QCF) for z/OS:

- Manages IMS message queues in both shared and non-shared queue environments.
- Allows greater flexibility in configuration, and additional support of sysplex environments.

- Implements improved security using the SAF/RACF security interface, which is accepted as a standard for security authorization.
- Uses information maintained by the IMS Database Recovery Control (DBRC) facility that automates several functions that were previously performed manually in the areas of Automatic Checkpoint Location, Automatic Log Selection, and Cold Queue Recovery for IMS/SMQ.
- Provides support for the INCLUDE and EXCLUDE statements of the LOAD function.
- Allows message re-queueing between different LTERMs.
- Accepts multiple-line commands in the Display Destination panels.
- Conforms to user installation standards for execution libraries.
- Provides improved product customization and documentation.

Program number: 5697-I08

IBM IMS Workload Router for z/OS, V2.4

The IBM IMS Workload Router for z/OS tool:

- Works with IMS TM to provide transparent routing or balancing of a transaction workload among two or more IBM systems.
- Uses IMS Multiple Systems Coupling (MSC).
- Is adaptable to a variety of system configurations.

Program number: 5697-B87

MISCELLANEOUS IMS TOOLS

The following older IMS tools also support IMS:

- IMS ADF, Version 2
- IMS Data Refresher, Version 1.1.1
- OS/VS DB/DC Data Dictionary, Version 6

IMS in a Parallel Sysplex Environment

CHAPTER 27

Introduction to Parallel Sysplex

I n 1990, IBM announced the *sysplex* as the strategic direction for large systems computing environments, described as "a collection of z/OS systems that cooperate, using certain hardware and software products, to process work." The term *sysplex* is derived from the words *SYStems comPLEX*. At the time of this first announcement, and for several years thereafter, there was no Parallel Sysplex—only a base sysplex. The base sysplex provided improvements in interprocessor communications between systems and any subsystems that wanted to exploit those services, but no data-sharing services.

The Parallel Sysplex was introduced later in the 1990s and added hardware and software components to provide for sysplex data sharing. In this context, *data sharing* means the ability for sysplex member systems and subsystems to store data into, and retrieve data from, a common area. In short, a Parallel Sysplex can have multiple central processor complexes (CPCs) and multiple applications (like IMS) that can directly share the workload.

Although the Parallel Sysplex environment is complex, it basically consists of three elements:

- Two z/OS components: cross-system coupling facility (XCF) and cross-system extended services (XES)
- One hardware component called the coupling facility (CF)

Since IMS Version 5, each release of IMS has added more features that are based on Parallel Sysplex technology. Most of these features are discussed in the following sections of this chapter:

- Data sharing
- Shared queues
- VTAM Generic Resources

- VTAM multinode persistent sessions
- Automatic restart management
- Sysplex communications
- Operations Manager and single point of control
- Resource Manager and sysplex terminal management
- Coordinated global online change
- Automatic RECON loss notification

In this book, the term *sysplex* is synonymous with Parallel Sysplex.

Related Reading:

- For a further discussion of IMS in a sysplex environment, see Chapter 28, "IMSplexes," on page 495 and *IMS Version 9: Administration Guide: System.*
- For a detailed discussion of IMS in a sysplex environment, see:
  — The IBM Redbook *IMS in the Parallel Sysplex: Volume I: Reviewing the IMSplex Technology*
  — The IBM Redbook *IMS in the Parallel Sysplex: Volume II: Planning the IMSplex*
  — The IBM Redbook *IMS in the Parallel Sysplex: Volume III: IMSplex Implementation and Operations*

In This Chapter:

- "Goals of a Sysplex Environment"
- "IMS and the Sysplex Environment" on page 469
- "Other Advantages of Running IMS TM in a Sysplex Environment" on page 485

GOALS OF A SYSPLEX ENVIRONMENT

The goals of a sysplex environment are:

- High availability
- Capacity
- Workload balancing

High availability means that the end user has access to the facilities and resources needed to perform some business function when it is needed. Parallel Sysplex allows you to have multiple IMS systems that can do the same work. These systems are called *clones*, which means that each IMS system definition is the same. The clones must have access to the same data and the capability to process the same transactions or work requests. High availability requires that you survive both planned outages, such as upgrades, and unplanned outages, such as abends. Even with clones, you need the capability to quickly restore any failed system.

Adequate capacity means that the servers have the resources to satisfy all of the work requests from their end users within the needed time frame. Parallel Sysplex allows you to meet capacity needs by easily adding and deleting cloned IMS systems. When you change your configuration in this way, you can route the work to the systems that can handle it.

Workload balancing is the spreading of work across the systems that can do it and spreading that work appropriately. Parallel Sysplex provides capabilities to automatically balance workloads. Proper balancing allows you to more easily handle unexpected peaks in workloads. Work balancing operates at its best when it can dynamically adjust to changes in the workload and changes in your hardware and software configurations.

IMS and other products, when used in a Parallel Sysplex, provide the facilities to increase availability, enhance capacity, and more easily balance workloads.

IMS AND THE SYSPLEX ENVIRONMENT

Phase in the following sysplex capabilities (in the following order) to enable IMS to make the most of the sysplex environment:

1. Implement data sharing among multiple IMS DBs within the sysplex. For more information on this topic, see "IMS DB and the Sysplex Environment."
2. Distribute the transaction workload of multiple IMS TMs within the sysplex. This involves distributing connections and transactions. For more information on this topic, see "IMS TM and the Sysplex Environment" on page 474.

IMS DB and the Sysplex Environment

The foundation in using Parallel Sysplex with IMS is the implementation of data sharing by IMS DB. Data sharing allows multiple IMS subsystems to access and update the same IMS databases.

Block-level data sharing means that each IMS server has the authority to access and update all shared data. As many as 255 IMS subsystems on up to 32 z/OS images can share IMS databases. Each IMS has full capability to access and update with integrity.

Figure 27-1 on page 470 shows a data-sharing configuration with four IMS systems running on four z/OS images sharing the same set of IMS databases. Each IMS system has its own database buffer pools. Each IMS reads and updates the databases. To support the integrity requirements, IMS utilizes structures in coupling facilities. A lock structure is used to hold locking information that is shared by the lock managers (IRLMs) used by the IMS systems. Information about database blocks and their locations in the buffer pools is stored in cache structures. These locks are used to maintain the integrity of the buffer pools when an IMS updates a block.

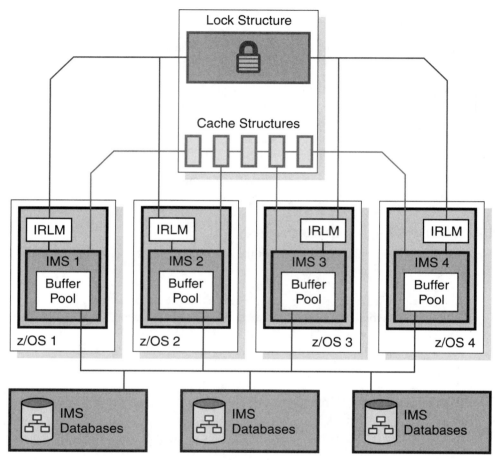

Figure 27-1   Example of Sysplex Data Sharing with Four IMSs

RESTRICTIONS:
- MSDBs cannot participate in data sharing. They must be converted to DEDBs.
- GSAM and HSAM databases cannot participate in data sharing.

IMS does not force data affinities on an installation because all IMS data can be shared. A data affinity occurs when some data, such as a database, is not shared (access to the database can only occur from one system). Without data affinities, a transaction or batch process is capable of running on any system. It does not have to be routed to a particular IMS because that is the only one with access to the data.

Dependent Regions and Grouped IMSs in a Sysplex

Outside of the sysplex environment, an application runs with only one control region. You do not move an application from one IMS to another. With Parallel Sysplex you might want this ability, especially for applications executing as BMPs. Use the IMSID parameter in the dependent region to specify to which control region the dependent region will connect. Each IMS has a unique IMSID, which makes moving a dependent region, such as a BMP, difficult. Before you can move the dependent region, you must change the JCL to specify a different IMSID. In Figure 27-2, we want to execute dependent region BMPY (which has IMSID=IMS2 specified) on z/OS3 where IMSID=IMS3 is running. This will not work. The job fails because BMPY is associated with IMS2 (IMSID=IMS2) and you cannot dynamically change the IMSID that is specified in BMPY.

The IMSGROUP parameter allows IMS to be known by both its IMSID and its IMSGROUP name. All the IMSs must have unique IMSIDs, but they can have the same IMSGROUP name. The IMSs register to this group name using z/OS token services and their own unique IMSID. The BMP has an IMSID equal to the IMSGROUP name. The BMP uses token services to see if there is an IMSID using the "IMS" as an IMSGROUP parameter. In Figure 27-3 on page 472, BMPY is running on the same z/OS with IMS3. It would connect to IMS3. In this way, if IMS2 is not running or that system is very busy, the BMP could be routed to any z/OS that has any IMS in the group.

You can use the Program Restart Facility for OS/390 (5655-E14) to easily restart a failed BMP on another IMS system. This further extends the capabilities to use BMPs with Parallel Sysplex. For more information about the Program Restart Facility for OS/390, see "IBM IMS Program Restart Facility for OS/390, V2" on page 449.

Fast Database Recovery

You can use Fast Database Recovery (FDBR) to greatly reduce the effect of the failure of an IMS system on data availability to other IMS systems.

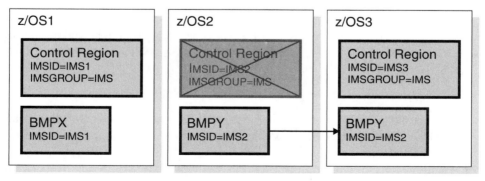

Figure 27-2 Moving a Dependent Region Between IMSs

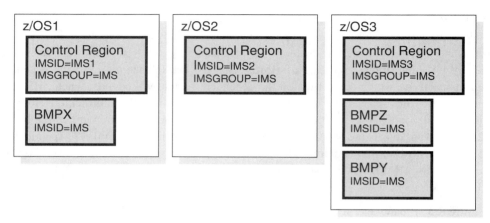

Figure 27-3   Example of a Dependent Region Running with a Different Control Region

If an IMS system fails, the update locks are retained. They must be kept until the inflight work of the failed system is backed out. Without FDBR, the inflight work is backed out during IMS emergency restart. Locked records cannot be accessed by other IMS systems. These systems do not wait for the release of the locks. Instead, their applications get a lock reject condition when they ask for a lock that is retained for the failed system. This lock reject condition typically causes an application abend. The failure of one IMS system affects the other IMS systems. The IMS systems that are still running do not have access to some data until the inflight transactions are backed out.

FDBR is the solution for the locked records problem. FDBR is an independent region that runs in its own address space. An FDBR region tracks one IMS control region. For maximum effectiveness, the tracking FDBR region should run on a different operating system than where the tracked IMS is running. Figure 27-4 on page 473 illustrates a sample FDBR configuration.

In Figure 27-4, IMS A and its FDBR run on different systems. IMS B and its FDBR run on different systems. If z/OS A or IMS A fails, FDBR A backs out all of the inflight work from IMS A. It also releases the retained locks held for the inflight work of IMS A. This allows IMS B to access all of the IMS data.

Tracking is accomplished by implementing either one of the following methods:

- An FDBR and its IMS system join the same XCF group as the IMS that is being tracked. This allows FDBR to be immediately aware when the tracked IMS address space or z/OS terminates.
- FDBR continually reads the tracked IMS's log (OLDS). If IMS abends, its ESTAE routine writes a failure log record (type X'06'). FDBR can read this log record before the IMS address space terminates.

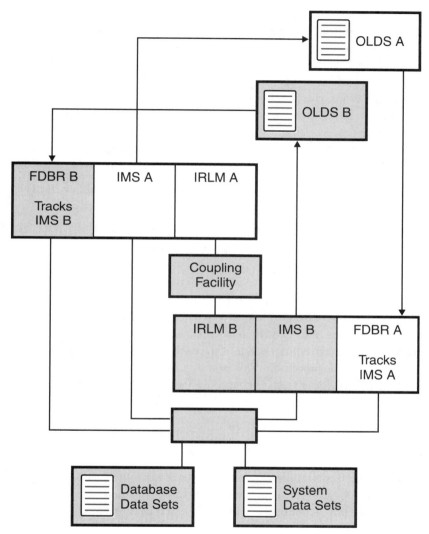

Figure 27-4 Sample FDBR Configuration

When either of these tracking methods makes FDBR aware of the IMS failure, FDBR restores the databases to the last point of consistency. For full-function databases, this means FDBR backs out inflight units of work. For DEDBs, this means that FDBR invokes REDO processing for incomplete output threads. These are the same actions that emergency restart would take. When these actions are complete, FDBR releases the locks held by the failed IMS, emulating what emergency restart does.

FDBR is much quicker than emergency restart. FDBR does not have to wait for the restart of IMS nor does it have to wait for the loading of the IMS modules. FDBR does not have to wait for the reading of the log except for the last few records. FDBR is much better because it eliminates many of the potential lock rejects and application abends on the surviving IMSs.

Summary of IMS DB and the Sysplex Environment

Higher availability is provided by the data-sharing configuration, which allows work that might otherwise have to wait for the restart of a failed IMS to run on a surviving IMS. FDBR reduces the impact of the failure by monitoring an active IMS and performing dynamic backout or DEDB REDO processing (or both) sooner than an IMS emergency restart would.

Work can run on any IMS in the sysplex data-sharing group because multiple IMSs have access to the same data. Up to 32 z/OS images can be used to provide maximum capacity.

If every IMS can access all the data, then every IMS can process any of the work. This allows an installation to create IMS clones. In fact, a single system definition can be used for all the IMSs. Cloning allows you to distribute the work to the systems that have the capacity to handle it.

IMS TM and the Sysplex Environment

After data sharing is in place, the next logical step in using Parallel Sysplex with IMS TM is the distribution of connections. For VTAM, connections are sessions. For TCP/IP, they are socket connections. Distributing connections is one of the methods for distributing the workload across multiple IMSs and multiple processors. This is known as *static distribution*. That is, after a user is connected to an IMS, the user remains connected until the connection is broken. Another connection is required to use this method to distribute the workload to another IMS.

Distributing Transaction Workload

To distribute the transaction workload, use one of the following two basic techniques:

* Distribute the logons so that not all users are logged on to the same IMS. Whichever IMS they are logged on to is the one that processes the transaction.
* Distribute the transactions between IMSs after a transaction has been received from the network.

There is a combination whereby users' logons are distributed and the transactions submitted by these users are also distributed after they are entered.

It does not matter where the transaction is processed if you use data sharing.

Distributing Logons Manually The earliest approach to distributing logons was to tell the end user which IMS to log on to. Some IMS shops might still use this technique. There are several problems with this technique:

- Balancing the logons becomes an administrative responsibility which must be monitored continuously as users come and go.
- As new IMSs join the group, either no users log on to that IMS (because they do not know about it), or the administrator must reassign users to the new IMSs.
- If an IMS fails, users have to be instructed either to wait for it to restart or to log on to another IMS. After a user knows of another IMS, the user might decide arbitrarily to log on to it instead of his primary IMS, defeating the balancing goal.

Distributing Logons Automatically Distributing logons can be done automatically using several techniques.

For SNA networks, VTAM Generic Resources can be used to dynamically route a logon request to an active IMS. The IMS is chosen based on Workload Manager (WLM) information or the number of users currently logged on. This capability is available with IMS Version 6 and later releases.

Prior to IMS Version 6, logons could be distributed automatically using a VTAM USERVAR exit routine. This exit routine can be used to direct the logon request to one of several IMSs in the group. Although this method is still supported, IBM recommends using VTAM Generic Resources.

For TCP/IP, connection distribution can be accomplished using such tools as Domain Name Server/Workload Manager (DNS/WLM), Interactive Network Dispatcher (IND), or the Sysplex Distributor.

The following sections discuss these techniques.

VTAM USERVAR Exit USERVAR is a VTAM capability that can change the value specified for the VTAM application name in a logon request. USERVAR support includes an optional exit routine. The exit routine can choose from multiple application names. A USERVAR exit routine can be used to route a logon to any IMS that it knows about. But, it might not know of configuration changes or of the availability of any particular IMS in the group. For example, in Figure 27-5 on page 476, if IMS1 fails, the exit routine might continue to route logons to IMS1. Similarly, if IMS4 is added to the configuration, the exit routine might not route any logons to it. A sophisticated routine might be able to modify its decisions, but there is no automatic notification to the routine of changes in the configuration.

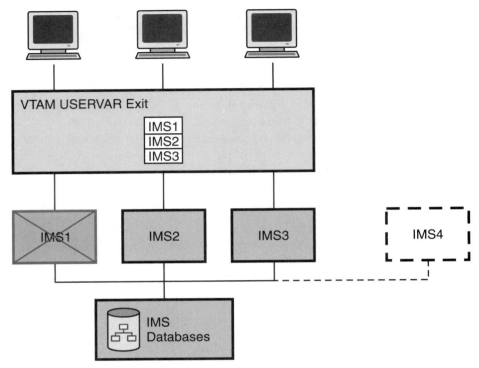

Figure 27-5   Example of VTAM USERVAR Exit Routing IMS Logons

VTAM Generic Resources   VTAM Generic Resources (VGR) is a service provided by VTAM in a Parallel Sysplex. VGR minimizes the knowledge that an end user needs to log on to one of several like instances of an application, such as IMS. Each instance of an application joins a Generic Resource Group by specifying both the group name and its specific VTAM application name. End users specify the group name when logging on. VTAM selects a member of the group for the session.

D E F I N I T I O N S:

- *Logging on* to a terminal establishes a session with IMS for that terminal.
- *Signing on* to a terminal identifies a user to IMS.
- *Logging off* from a terminal ends a session with IMS for that terminal.
- *Signing off* from a terminal ends an identification of a user to IMS.

Generic Resource Groups are dynamic. When a new IMS opens its VTAM ACB, it joins the group and is a candidate for subsequent logons. When an IMS terminates, it is removed from the group. It is then no longer a candidate for logons.

Information about the members of a group is kept in a coupling facility structure, as in Figure 27-6.

APPC/IMS can use VGR, but the support for this configuration is not built into IMS. This support is provided by APPC/MVS.

There are many benefits of VGR over other techniques for distributing logon requests. Some of these benefits are:

Availability

VTAM knows by looking in the coupling facility structure which IMSs are active. It routes requests only to active IMSs. If an IMS fails, its users can immediately log on again using the same generic name. The users are connected to one of the active IMSs.

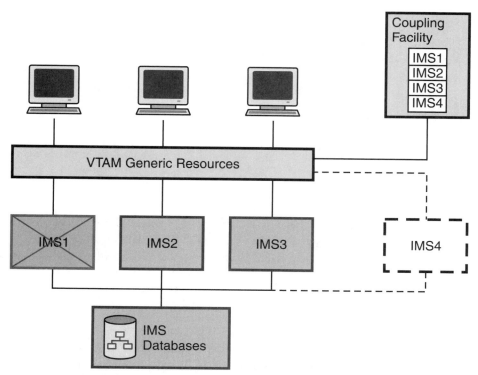

Figure 27-6   VTAM Generic Resources Distributing IMS Logons in a Sysplex

Capacity

If another IMS is needed to handle the workload, it immediately becomes eligible for user logons. User procedures do not have to be modified.

Workload Balancing

VTAM attempts to balance logons across the available IMSs. It has two ways of doing this.

- If Workload Manager (WLM) goal mode is used, VGR routes a logon to the system with the most available capacity.
- If WLM goal mode is not used, VGR attempts to balance the number of logons for each IMS system.

You can implement a VGR user exit routine to override the VGR decision.

Web and TCP/IP Connections to IMS   Many installations access their IMS systems using TCP/IP. This includes connections from the Web. Web servers can use many different ways of connecting to IMS. The most typical connection types are:

APPC

If the Web server sends requests to z/OS using APPC protocols, then the connections to IMS can be distributed using APPC/MVS support for VTAM Generic Resources.

TCP/IP Telnet

TN3270 allows 3270-style users to use TCP/IP protocols. The end user is a TN3270 client. The TN3270 client communicates with a TN3270 server using TCP/IP. The TN3270 server uses LU2 (3270) protocols to communicate with IMS through VTAM. VGR can be used with TN3270 servers to provide connection balancing.

TCP/IP Sockets

If the Web server uses sockets, the server can communicate with IMS Connect for z/OS, which communicates with IMS. IMS Connect executes in its own address space. It communicates with its client, in this case the Web server, using TCP/IP socket protocols. It communicates with IMS using the IMS Open Transaction Manager Access (OTMA) protocol. OTMA uses z/OS Cross System Coupling Facility (XCF), which allows programs running in different address spaces, possibly on different z/OS images in the Parallel Sysplex, to send and receive messages from each other. The distribution of connections from Web servers to IMS Connect must be done with TCP/IP socket protocols.

Domain Name Server/Workload Manager (DNS/WLM) can be used in conjunction with TN3270 to distribute the connection requests across multiple TN3270 servers in the Parallel Sysplex. The TN3270 client request goes to one DNS/WLM, which then uses the WLM to decide which TN3270 server should get the connection request. After the DNS/WLM chooses a TN3270 server, it is no longer involved (communications go directly between the TN3270 client and the TN3270 server). The TN3270 server can then use VTAM Generic Resources to distribute sessions across the IMS members. VGR always uses a local IMS if one is available. A local IMS is an IMS that is using the same VTAM as the TN3270 server is using. However, if the TN3270 server is on a z/OS image without an IMS, VGR can send the logon request to an available IMS on any z/OS.

Figure 27-7 illustrates the use of Telnet 3270. The diagram shows four systems:

- One system (in the upper portion of the diagram) consisting of a DNS/WLM, a TN3270 Server, and an IMS
- The other three systems in the Parallel Sysplex being second copies of the DNS/WLM, TN3270 Server, and IMS

The second DNS/WLM in the diagram is a backup for the first (in case the first one fails).

While the configuration illustrated in Figure 27-7 provides good connection balancing, it is fairly expensive, in CPU usage, to establish and terminate the connection. Therefore, this is not a good configuration for connections that are short term.

The Interactive Network Dispatcher (IND) can be used to distribute connection requests from a Web server to one of several IMS Connect address spaces in the Parallel Sysplex. IND is much more efficient than DNS/WLM at handling connection requests, but requires a separate

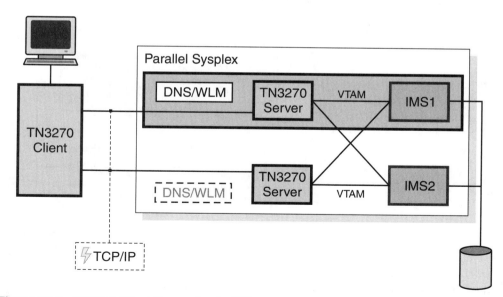

Figure 27-7   TN3270 Client Connecting to IMS

hardware box (such as an IBM 2216 router) and so can be more expensive. IMS Connect then sends work to one of several IMSs using XCF services and IMS OTMA, as is illustrated in Figure 27-8.

In Figure 27-8, both IMSs can be reached through either instance of IMS Connect. Exit routines in IMS Connect can be used to choose which IMS the request is sent to. These routines can access information that describes which IMSs are currently active.

The network dispatching function of IND is included in IBM WebSphere Edge Server. There are WebSphere Edge Servers for Linux, AIX, Windows, and Sun Solaris.

A better product for both long and short connections is the Sysplex Distributor, which is part of the z/OS Communications Server. The Sysplex Distributor is software that runs on the host system and distributes sockets across multiple target systems. Like DNS/WLM, a backup Sysplex Distributor can be running on another z/OS image in the sysplex.

The example in Figure 27-9 on page 481 uses multiple instances of IMS Connect. Input messages go through the Sysplex Distributor. Responses do not go through the Sysplex Distributor. In Figure 27-9, the responses go directly from IMS Connect to the Web Server.

Distributing Transactions

After the connections are distributed within the sysplex, the next step in using Parallel Sysplex with IMS TM is the distribution of transactions. This involves processing a transaction on a system other than the one that initially received the input message.

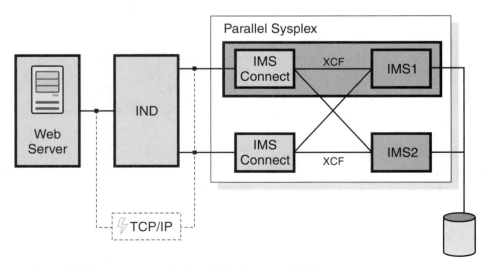

Figure 27-8 IND Connecting to Multiple IMSs through IMS Connect

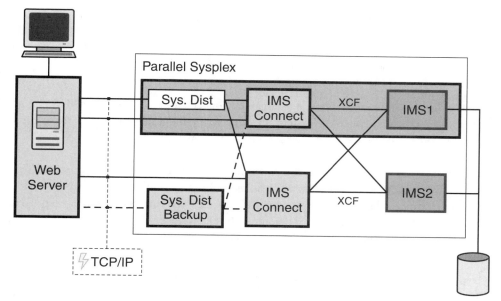

Figure 27-9   Web Connections to IMS Using the Sysplex Distributor and IMS Connect

The techniques used to distribute connections from users across IMS systems might not balance the workload. Several possible causes are:

- A large batch workload on one system might overload it. Users who are already connected to that system remain connected to it. Their response times could be affected by this overload.
- The volumes of inputs from connected users might vary. This could result in peak loads on one system while another system has a lull in inputs.
- Other factors could also cause unbalanced workloads across the systems.

The techniques to address this imbalance involve distributing transactions to other IMS TM systems.

When you distribute transactions, an input transaction can be routed from one IMS to another for processing. There are two methods of doing this in IMS.

Multiple Systems Coupling (MSC)

With MSC, multiple IMS systems are connected by communication links. An IMS system can send a message across one of these links to another IMS. The receiving system processes the transaction and sends its reply to the original system. The original system sends the reply to the user.

IMS Shared Message Queues

With shared queues, IMS systems share one set of message queues. They are stored in list structures in coupling facilities. Any IMS system can process a transaction because the queues are available to all the IMS systems. It is a "pull" implementation. Those with more processing capacity tend to process more transactions.

With either of these implementations, a user can be connected to any system and have an input message processed on another IMS system. In some cases, input messages from these connections must be processed by the system where the connection exists.

Routing Messages with MSC   As illustrated in Figure 27-10, MSC is comprised of VTAM sessions between multiple IMS systems. When an IMS transaction is received by any IMS, its definitions determine where that transaction is to execute. The transaction might be processed locally (on the IMS system that receives the transaction). However, the transaction might be processed remotely (on another system). If the transaction is defined to run remotely, the IMS system that receives the message sends it to the remote system.

MSC can be used to distribute transactions across multiple IMSs. The definitions are static. An IMS makes its decision about whether or not to process a transaction based on the transaction code. This decision is not dynamic. Decisions are not based on workloads. It is relatively

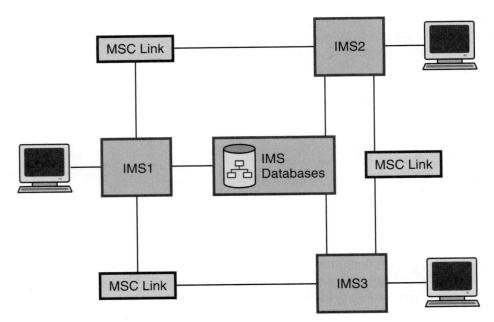

Figure 27-10   VTAM Sessions of Three IMSs Connected Using MSC

difficult to add a new IMS system to the complex. A new IMS system requires changes in the definitions for the other existing IMS systems.

MSC definitions can be used to distribute the workload, but they do not balance the workload. MSC definitions in a shared-queues group are subsumed by the shared queues, and workload balancing is automatic.

A link failure or an IMS failure can mean that a transaction cannot be processed until the failure is corrected.

MSC users can include MSC exit routines to override the definitions of where transactions are processed. This adds some dynamic capabilities to MSC routing. The IBM IMS Workload Router (WLR) for z/OS (product number 5697-B87) provides a set of these exit routines.

The IBM IMS Workload Router for z/OS (WLR) uses MSC directed routing to distribute transactions across multiple IMSs without regard to how they have been defined. For example, if TRANA is received at IMS1, it can be processed on IMS1, IMS2, or IMS3. The WLR can be directed to process a certain percentage of transactions locally and to send others to remote IMSs. This provides some workload balancing capability.

Related Reading: For more information about the IMS Workload Router product, see the *IBM IMS Workload Router for z/OS User's Guide.*

Distributing Transactions Using Shared Message Queues   IMS TM is a queue-driven system. Transaction input messages can be received from terminals or programs. Output messages can be sent to terminals or programs. All of these messages are placed in message queues.

In conventional (non-shared queues) systems, each IMS has its own set of queues; see Figure 27-11 on page 484. These queues are accessible only by the IMS system that owns them. When MSC is used, one IMS sends a message from its queues to another IMS system, which places the message in its queues. In any case, a message can be processed only by the IMS system on whose queues it resides.

With shared queues, the message queues are moved to list structures in coupling facilities where they are available to any IMS in the shared-queues group. See Figure 27-12 on page 484. A terminal is connected to one IMS system. Input messages from the terminal are placed in the shared queues. They are accessible from any IMS using those queues. This means that another IMS system, not the one to which the terminal is connected, can process the input message.

All messages (input and output) go into the shared queues. IMS subsystems register interest in specific queues, such as the queue for transaction TRANA or for terminal TERMX. An IMS system registers interest for queues it can process. This includes the queues for the terminals connected to it and the transactions that are defined to it.

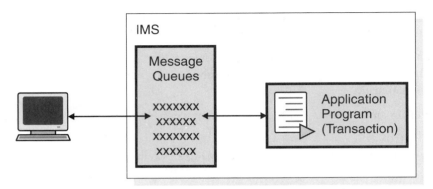

Figure 27-11   A Single IMS with a Single Message Queue

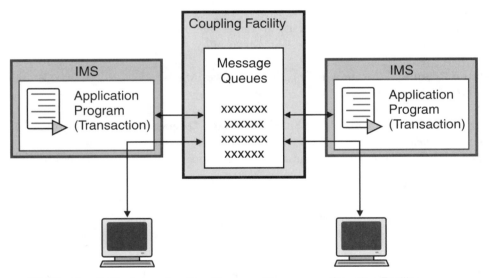

Figure 27-12   Two IMSs Accessing One Message Queue on a Coupling Facility

When there is work on a registered queue, the IMS systems that have registered interest in the queue are notified. When an IMS has the resources available to process the transaction, such as an available dependent region, it attempts to read a message from the shared queue. If it receives a message, it processes it and puts the response back on a shared queue. Multiple IMSs can attempt to retrieve messages from a queue, but only one will receive an individual message. Terminal output messages are retrieved from the queue by the IMS to which the terminal is connected. This IMS sends the output message to the terminal.

Only those IMS systems with available resources ask for and process the transaction because any IMS can process a shared-queues message. This tends to distribute the workload to the systems best able to handle it. Those systems with the most free resources ask for work most frequently.

By using shared queues, the application workload is balanced dynamically. If there is any processing capacity available anywhere in the shared-queues group, queued transactions are scheduled and processed. The user is not forced to wait because a single IMS is overloaded.

Shared queues can also be used in conjunction with connection balancing provided by VTAM Generic Resources or one of the techniques used for TCP/IP.

Summary of IMS TM and the Sysplex Environment

In a Parallel Sysplex environment, you can take advantage of multiple capabilities:

- VTAM Generic Resources provides connection balancing for SNA sessions. It improves availability for users connected via VTAM and makes it easy to add new systems without changing user logon procedures.
- The various TCP/IP distributors provide connection balancing for TCP/IP users. The distributors provide improved availability for these users and make it easy to add capacity for systems with these users.
- The IMS Workload Router provides workload balancing capabilities for users of conventional queueing.
- Shared queues provide:
  - Dynamic workload balancing by allowing an IMS system with available capacity to process any transaction in the shared-queues group.
  - Availability benefits by allowing any active IMS to process transactions when another IMS fails or is stopped. Capacity is easily added because modifications to the previously existing IMS systems are not necessary.

OTHER ADVANTAGES OF RUNNING IMS TM IN A SYSPLEX ENVIRONMENT

The next few sections discuss additional IMS functions that take advantage of the sysplex environment:

- "Rapid Network Reconnect"
- "Sysplex Failure Recovery" on page 488

Rapid Network Reconnect

Rapid Network Reconnect (RNR) is IMS's support for VTAM persistent sessions for non-XRF systems. RNR can provide great benefits for some environments, but it is not appropriate for all environments. RNR is optional.

VTAM persistent session support eliminates session cleanup and restart when a host failure occurs. There are two kinds of persistent session support:

- Single node persistent sessions (SNPSs) provide support only for IMS failures. With SNPS, the VTAM instance must not fail.
- Multinode persistent sessions (MNPSs) provide support for all types of host failures. These include failures of IMS, VTAM, z/OS, or the processor.

With persistent sessions, end users do not lose their sessions for the supported failures. In fact, they remain logged on. Even though their IMS system fails, their sessions are not terminated. This means that the unbind traffic does not flow through the network when the failure occurs. Secondly, when their IMS system is restarted, their sessions do not have to be reestablished and the bind traffic does not flow. For LU types that typically have users, such as SLUTYPE2 and SLUTYPE1 (CONSOLE), a sign-on is required. For LU types that typically are programmable, such as SLUTYPEP, or do not have direct users, such as LU1 (PRINTER1), a sign-on is not required.

Single Node Persistent Sessions

When using RNR with SNPS, only outages due to IMS abends are mitigated. The VTAM used by this IMS must not fail.

The scenario illustrated in Figure 27-13 shows how SNPS works. The numbers in Figure 27-13 refer to the descriptions in the following list.

1. When a session is established, session data is stored in a z/OS data space associated with the VTAM address space.
2. If the IMS system abends but VTAM does not, the session stays active and the session data remains.

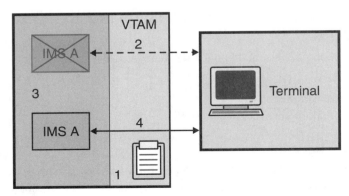

Figure 27-13   SNPS Example Scenario: Logon Is Not Terminated When Its IMS Fails

3. The failed IMS is restarted.

4. The users' sessions are given to the restarted IMS. The users have remained logged on even though their IMS system had failed.

Multinode Persistent Sessions

With MNPS, the session data is stored in a coupling facility structure where it is available to other systems in the sysplex. All types of failures are supported with MNPS. As with SNPS support, when IMS is restarted, the users are automatically reconnected in a "logged on" state.

When using RNR with MNPS, all outages of the IMS, VTAM, or processor are mitigated.

The scenario illustrated in Figure 27-14 shows how MNPS works. The numbers in Figure 27-14 refer to the descriptions in the following list.

1. When a session is established, session data is stored in a coupling facility structure.

2. CPCA fails and IMSA also fails because it is running on CPCA. The session data is not lost, however, because it is on the coupling facility. Another VTAM in the sysplex detects the error, and the session survives the failure of CPCA.

3. IMSA is restarted on another processor (CPCB) in the sysplex.

4. When IMSA is restarted on CPCB, the users, sessions are given to the restarted IMS. These users have remained logged on even though their IMS system failed.

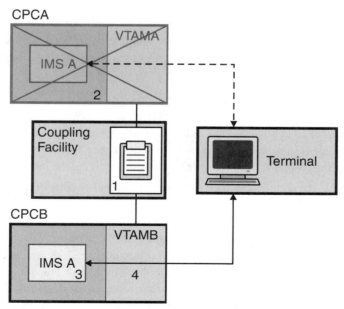

Figure 27-14 MNPS Example Scenario: Logon Is Not Terminated When Its IMS Fails

Benefits of Rapid Network Reconnect

The benefit of RNR is the maintenance of the sessions when IMS fails. RNR eliminates the time required to terminate and reestablish the sessions. This eliminates the bind and unbind traffic that would otherwise flow through the network, which can be time consuming. Service to the end users is reestablished more quickly.

Of course, the IMS system must be restarted. When using RNR, the end user does not have the option of logging on to another IMS in the Parallel Sysplex. The value of RNR depends on how quickly IMS is restarted. If the restart is slow, there is not much benefit. If the restart is quick, the benefit can be substantial. However, if another system with the same capabilities is available, the users would get quicker restoration of service by logging onto it, which means that RNR is probably not a good solution for IMS systems with clones.

Persistent session support for IMS users of APPC (LU 6.2) is provided by APPC/MVS, not IMS. With APPC, the sessions are persistent, but the conversations are not.

Sysplex Failure Recovery

Parallel Sysplex adds more components to a system. These include clones of systems and subsystems and new components such as coupling facilities and coupling facility links. Even though you might have another component available to do your work when one component fails, you want to restore the sysplex to full robustness as soon as possible. Recoveries from most failures in a sysplex can be automated.

Advantages of Multiple Copies of Servers

The main advantage in a sysplex is that you have multiple copies of your servers. When one fails, another is available to do its work. This applies to subsystems, processors, and coupling facilities.

- If IMS fails, other IMS instances are available. You can use the routing and balancing capabilities to distribute the work to the active IMS systems.
- If a processor or LPAR fails, the z/OS Automatic Restart Manager (ARM) can be used to restart failed subsystems on surviving processors or LPARs.
- If a coupling facility fails, there are two ways of surviving the loss:
  — Rebuild the coupling facility structures on another coupling facility.
  — Use multiple copies of the structures.

Recovery Using the Automatic Restart Manager (ARM)

When IMS fails, you need to restart it as quickly as possible. Even though other IMS systems might be available to do work, the failed IMS might have inflight or indoubt work that needs to be resolved. This resolution releases locks on database resources and releases DBRC authorizations and allows new work to have access to all of the data.

ARM can be used to provide rapid restarts of IMS. ARM is a sysplex capability that allows an automatic restart of subsystems such as IMS, DB2, CICS, and IRLM. If the subsystem abends, the restart is on the same z/OS instance (LPAR). If the z/OS (LPAR) fails, the restart is on another z/OS instance in the sysplex.

Figure 27-15 illustrates the actions of ARM when an IMS abends.

In Figure 27-15, IMS is restarted on the same z/OS system. This IMS was providing DBCTL services to a CICS and was using a DB2 subsystem. You must restart IMS on the same z/OS so that services between these subsystems can be restored. For example, indoubt threads must be resolved.

In the case of a z/OS or processor failure, IMS is restarted on another candidate z/OS (see Figure 27-16 on page 490). The z/OS is chosen according to a user-defined ARM policy. Subsystems that must remain together can be restarted as a group on the same z/OS. In the example in Figure 27-16, an IMS subsystem is using DB2 for database services. A CICS AOR (Application Owning Region) is using the same DB2 and the IMS for database services. When the z/OS system fails, the IMS, the DB2, and the CICS AOR must be moved together, but the CICS TOR (Terminal Owning Region) can be restarted on another z/OS in the sysplex because CICS AORs and TORs can communicate with other z/OS systems.

For ARM to restart subsystems, it must be active in the sysplex. ARM is controlled by a policy that the user defines. The policy is stored in an ARM couple data set. The policy is used to group subsystems for restart together. It also controls whether or not a subsystem is restarted. For example, an installation might not want to restart test subsystems.

ARM only restarts subsystems that register with ARM. Subsystems register with ARM when they initialize. IMS uses the ARMRST parameter to control whether or not IMS registers with ARM. ARMRST=Y is the default.

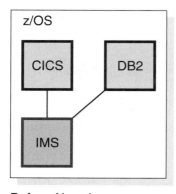
Before Abend

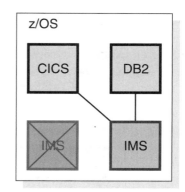
After Abend and ARM Restart

Figure 27-15 ARM Restarting an Abended IMS

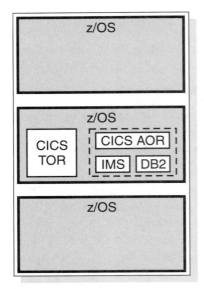 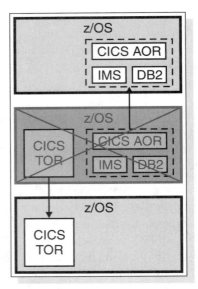

Before Failure   After Failure and ARM Restart

Figure 27-16   ARM Restarting IMS, CICS, and DB2 after a z/OS Failure

IMS has full ARM support. ARM can be used to restart IMS control regions, Common Queue Server regions, Fast Database Recovery regions, Common Service Layer components, and IRLMs. ARM does not directly restart IMS dependent regions. These are typically started by automation when the control region is started.

ARMWRAP is a program that registers an address space for ARM restarts. It is used for a step in a job. If the following step fails, ARM restarts the job. IMS Connect does not register with ARM. ARMWRAP can be used to get ARM support for IMS Connect.

Recovery After Coupling Facility Failures
Much of the sysplex support is provided through the use of coupling facility structures. If a CF is lost, it is important to have access to structures elsewhere.

If a CF survives, but you lose all of the links from a processor to the CF, you need to resolve the problem. This can be treated like the loss of the CF itself. You can either rebuild its structures on CFs that have connectivity to the processors that require it or you can use duplicate structures.

Recovery Using Structure Rebuild   Some structures can be rebuilt automatically when either a CF failure or a CF link failure occurs. These include IRLM lock structures, OSAM and VSAM cache structures, and IMS shared-queues structures. The example in Figure 27-17 on page 491 uses an IRLM lock structure.

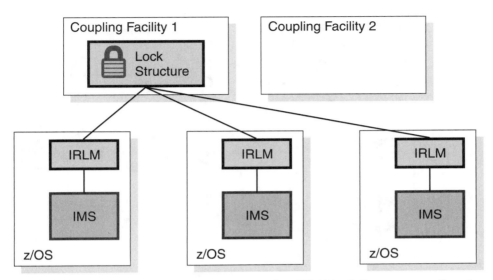

Figure 27-17   Three IMSs on Three z/OSs Sharing One IRLM Lock Structure on a Coupling
Facility

Figure 27-17 shows an IRLM structure on CF1 before a CF failure.

Figure 27-18 on page 492 shows a scenario where CF1 (on which the IRLM structure resides) fails. When the CF fails, the system automatically recognizes the loss and rebuilds the lock structure on another CF (CF2). Each IRLM retains the information necessary to restore its lock information in the structure. The IRLMs together rebuild the lock structure on another CF. Data sharing is resumed. Similar rebuild and recovery occurs for OSAM, VSAM, and shared-queue structures.

In Figure 27-19 on page 492, the CF does not fail. Instead, the connectivity between one of the processors and the CF fails. This case is treated the same as the loss of the CF. That is, the system automatically rebuilds the structure on another CF. All processors have connectivity to this CF. This means that data sharing can continue. Similar rebuild and recovery occurs for OSAM, VSAM, and shared-queue structures.

Recovery Using Structure Duplexing   Fast Path shared VSO does not rebuild its cache structures. Instead, it relies on a duplicate copy to provide failure survival. The duplicate copy can be created in either of two ways.

- Fast Path can build two structures. This is called user-managed duplexing.
- By using appropriate hardware prerequisites, you can have the system build duplexed structures. This is system-managed duplexing. System-managed duplexing is also available for IRLM lock structures and shared-queues structures.

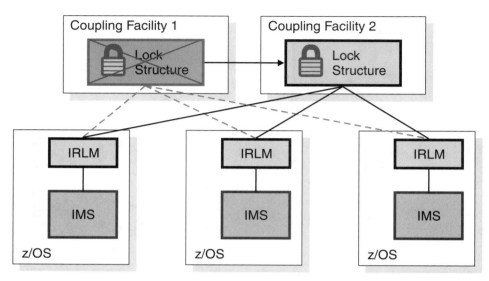

Figure 27-18   IRLM Structure on Failed Coupling Facility Is Rebuilt on Another Coupling Facility

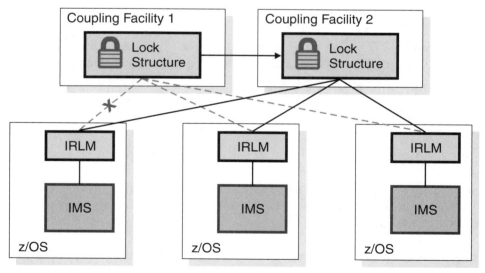

Figure 27-19   IRLM Structure Rebuilt on Another Coupling Facility After a Connectivity Failure

Figure 27-20 shows a duplexed DEDB VSO structure on two coupling facilities that are being shared by three IMSs.

If a CF is lost (as shown in Figure 27-21 on page 494), then a duplicate structure on another CF is used. With system-managed duplexing, a duplicate is immediately built if another CF is available. If another CF is not available, a duplicate structure is built when another CF becomes available.

Similarly, if connectivity to a CF is lost, then the use of its structure is discontinued. The duplicate structure on another CF is used instead.

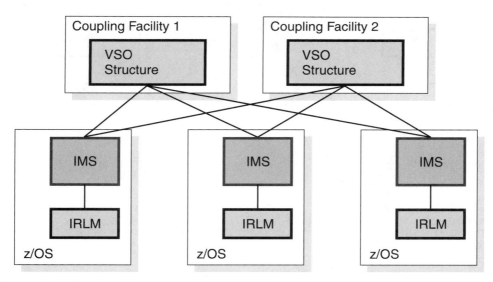

Figure 27-20   Shared VSO Structure Duplexed on Two Coupling Facilities

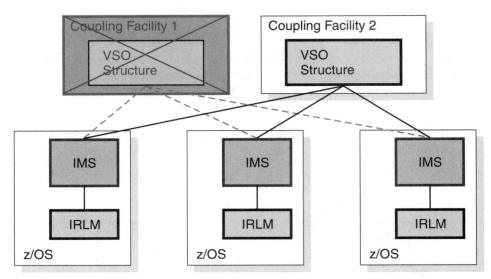

Figure 27-21   System-Managed Duplicate Shared VSO Structure Is Used After a Coupling
Facility Failure

CHAPTER **28**

IMSplexes

A n IMSplex is one or more IMS address spaces that work together as a unit. Typically, but not always, these address spaces:

- Share either databases, resources, or message queues (or any combination)
- Run in a z/OS Parallel Sysplex environment
- Include an IMS Common Service Layer (CSL)

The address spaces that can participate in the IMSplex are:

- Control region address spaces
- IMS manager address spaces (OM, RM, SCI)
- IMS server address spaces (Common Queue Server [CQS])

An IMSplex provides the ability to manage multiple IMS systems as if they were one system (a single-system perspective). An IMSplex can exist in a non-sysplex environment or can consist of multiple IMS subsystems (in sharing groups) in a sysplex environment.

Related Reading:

- For complete details about setting up a sysplex, see *z/OS MVS Setting Up a Sysplex*.
- For the details of IMSplex components, see *IMS Version 9: Common Service Layer Guide and Reference*.

This chapter discusses an IMSplex with a CSL included.

In This Chapter:

- "Components of an IMSplex"
- "Requirements for an IMSplex" on page 498
- "Operating an IMSplex" on page 499

COMPONENTS OF AN IMSPLEX

The following sections discuss the components of an IMSplex:

- "Common Queue Server"
- "Common Service Layer"

Common Queue Server

Common Queue Server (CQS) is a generalized server delivered with IMS that manages data objects on a coupling facility list structure, such as a queue structure or a resource structure, on behalf of multiple clients. CQS receives, maintains, and distributes data objects from shared queues on behalf of multiple clients. Each client has its own CQS access the data objects on the coupling facility list structure. IMS is one example of a CQS client that uses CQS to manage both its shared queues and shared resources.

Related Reading: For more information about CQS, see "Common Queue Server Address Space" on page 40.

Common Service Layer

The CSL provides the infrastructure for improving IMS systems management. The CSL is made up of three IMS address spaces:

- The Operations Manager (OM)
- The Resource Manager (RM)
- The Structured Call Interface (SCI)

The CSL components and IMS subsystems in an IMSplex can be called IMSplex components.

Related Reading: For complete information about CSLs, see *IMS Version 9: Common Service Layer Guide and Reference*.

Figure 28-1 on page 497 illustrates a sample IMSplex configuration that includes the CSL, a single point of control (SPOC), and automated procedures:

- The operating system image includes address spaces for OM, SCI, RM, an IMS control region, and IMS CQS.
- The operating system image shares a coupling facility and databases.
- A SPOC application, an automation application, a master terminal, and an end-user terminal all access the z/OS image.

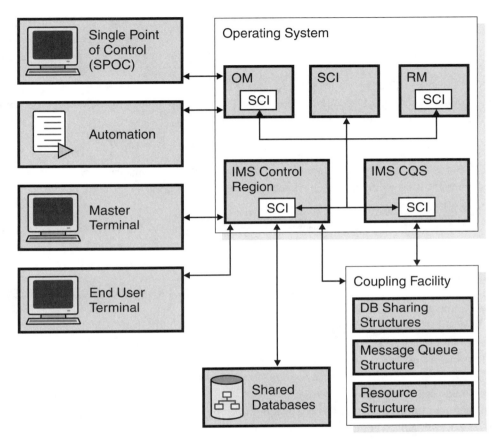

Figure 28-1   Sample IMSplex Configuration with a CSL

Operations Manager

The Operations Manager (OM) controls the operations of an IMSplex. OM provides an application programming interface (the OM API) through which commands can be issued and responses received. With a single point of control (SPOC) interface, you can submit commands to OM. The SPOC interfaces include the TSO SPOC, the REXX SPOC API, and the IMS Control Center. You can also write your own application to submit commands.

Specifically, OM can:

- Route IMS commands to IMSplex members registered for the command.
- Consolidate command responses from individual IMSplex members into a single response and provide that response to the originator of the command.
- Provide an API for automated operator commands.

- Provide a general user interface to register commands to support any command-processing client.
- Provide user exits for command and response edit and command security.

One OM must be defined in the IMSplex to use OM functions. Each z/OS image can have more than one OM. If multiple OMs are defined in the IMSplex, any OM defined can perform work from any z/OS image in the IMSplex.

Resource Manager

The Resource Manager (RM) is the component of the CSL that manages global resources and coordinates IMSplex-wide processes on behalf of its clients. IMS is an example of one such client. IMS uses RM to:

- Manage the following resources: transactions, LTERMs, MSNAMEs, nodes, users, user IDs, and APPC descriptor names.
- Ensure that a resource that is defined as a transaction, LTERM, or MSNAME is defined as the same resource type for all the IMSs in the IMSplex.
- Coordinate IMSplex-wide processes, such as performing global online changes.

RM uses the Common Queue Server (CQS) to maintain global resource information in a resource structure. A resource structure is a coupling facility list structure that all CQSs in the IMSplex can access.

Structured Call Interface

The Structured Call Interface (SCI) is the component of the CSL that provides the communication between IMSplex components, whether they are on one z/OS image or multiple z/OS images.

REQUIREMENTS FOR AN IMSPLEX

The minimum configuration for an IMSplex is an IMS control region and one set of CSL components (an OM, an RM, and an SCI) in one z/OS image and another (one or more) z/OS image (forming the sysplex) with a single SCI and a single IMS. Figure 28-2 on page 499 illustrates a similar configuration: one z/OS image with an IMS and one each of the CSL components, and two other z/OS images each with a single IMS and a single SCI.

All IMSs in an IMSplex must have a unique IMSID.

A single point of control (SPOC) application is required if you want to use certain CSL functions, such as performing a global online change.

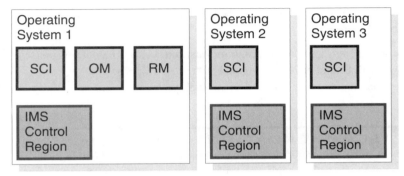

Figure 28-2 Minimum CSL Configuration for an IMSplex

> **RESTRICTION:** The maximum configuration for an IMSplex is 32 control regions, 32 CQSs, and a maximum of 1023 total system address spaces.

OPERATING AN IMSPLEX

Operating an IMSplex differs from operating a single IMS. The individual IMS subsystems in an IMSplex must be defined and set up individually; however, once this up-front work is done, they can be operated as a group, the IMSplex.

In general, you operate an IMSplex by issuing commands through the Operations Manager and analyzing the responses to those commands. You cannot issue commands directly to OM, however. OM has an application programming interface (API) that is designed to accept commands from and pass command responses to an application program. The IMS TSO SPOC application and the IMS Control Center are examples of such application programs.

The IMS Control Center, which supports IMS Version 8 and later and is part of the DB2 Universal Database Control Center, is another application program that accesses the OM API. With the IMS Control Center, you can manage your IMSplex using a graphical interface. The IMS Control Center uses the SPOC functions of the OM API. For more information about the IMS Control Center, go to www.ibm.com/ims and link to the IMS Control Center page.

You can design an application program that allows an operator to enter the commands and view the responses or you can design an automated operator program that issues commands and makes decisions based on the responses. The commands that are issued are the same in both instances. The differences are:

- The automated application program must anticipate what the responses to the commands will be and have logic to deal with those responses.
- The operator (issuing commands through an application) must have procedures to follow.

> **RECOMMENDATION:** When designing the automated operator programs or creating operator procedures, keep in mind that there might be IMSplex-wide ramifications for some actions. For example, if you tell an operator (or code your AOP) to shut down a particular SCI for a particular reason, the IMSs that used that particular SCI can no longer communicate with the IMSplex after that SCI is shut down. This might not be the solution you were hoping for, so plan accordingly.

The following list briefly covers the operations of the IMSplex.

- **Starting or restarting an IMSplex**

  Start an IMSplex in the following manner:

  1. Start the CSL components that are local to the IMS control region with a z/OS `START` command.
  2. Start the local IMS control region with the appropriate parameters specified on the appropriate PROCLIB members.
  3. Start the other individual IMSplex components (other IMSs, SCIs, OMs, and RMs).

  An IMSplex or its components can be restarted (after a failure or shutdown) by either manually starting the individual components (with a z/OS `START` command) or by using the z/OS Automatic Restart Manager (ARM). If ARM is used for restart purposes, it is specified on the IMSplex components' startup procedures or in their individual initialization PROCLIB members.

- **Querying statistics from an IMSplex**

  Any IMSplex member (for example, an Automated Operations Program [AOP]) can query statistics about the components of a CSL using a CSLZQRY request.

- **Shutting down an IMSplex**

  Shut down an IMSplex using two basic steps:

  1. Shut down the IMS components that participate in that IMSplex (issuing a `/CHE FREEZE` or similar command to the individual IMSs).
  2. Shut down the CSL and its components.

Appendixes

Glossary

active IMS   (1) In an RSR environment, an IMS that runs at an active site, performs production work, and is monitored by the *tracking IMS*. Contrast with tracking IMS. (2) In an XRF environment, an IMS that performs production work and is monitored by the alternate IMS. Contrast with *alternate IMS*. (3) If FDBR is used, the IMS that performs production work. The active IMS is monitored by a separate Fast Database Recovery IMS control region.

AIB mask   A mapping that the application program uses to interpret the AIB.

alternate IMS   In an XRF environment, the IMS that monitors the active IMS and takes over production work when the active IMS fails. Contrast with *active IMS*.

application interface block (AIB)

application control block (ACB)   A control block that is created by the ACBGEN utility from the output of DBDGEN and PSBGEN utilities and placed in the ACB library for use during online and DBB region type execution of IMS.

area   A subset of a DEDB that is defined as a VSAM ESDS data set. Each area in a DEDB consists of a root-addressable part, an independent-overflow part, and a sequential-dependent part.

back-end system   An IMS in an MSC network that accepts transactions from the front-end system, calls application programs for transaction processing, and routes replies back to the front-end system for response to the terminal. Contrast with *front-end system*.

basic checkpoint   A point in an application program where the work of the application is committed. Unlike with a symbolic checkpoint, you cannot restart application from a basic checkpoint.

checkpoint   See *synchronization point (sync point)*.

command code   The part of an SSA that tailors the call function, segment qualification, or setting of parentage to alter the results of a DL/I call.

control region   The z/OS main storage region that contains the IMS control program.

database description (DBD)   The collection of macro parameter statements that define the characteristics of a database, such as the database's organization and access method, the segments and fields in a database record, and the relationship between types of segments.

database record   In a database, a collection of segments that contains one occurrence of the root segment type and all of its dependents arranged in a hierarchical sequence. It may be smaller than, equal to, or larger than the access method logical record.

database resource adapter (DRA)   An interface to IMS DB full-function databases and DEDBs. The DRA can be used by a coordinator controller (CCTL) or a z/OS application program that uses the ODBA interface.

data sharing   The concurrent access of databases by two or more IMSs. The IMSs can be in one operating system image or in separate operating system images. They can share data at two levels: the database level and the block level.

dependent region   An address space in which IMS application programs run. Dependent regions are managed by the IMS control region. Dependent region types are MPR, BMP, IFP, JMP, and JBP.

dependent segment   In a database, a segment that relies on a higher level segment for its full hierarchical meaning. A child is a dependent segment of its parent. Contrast with *root segment*.

DL/I   The IMS data manipulation language, which is a common high-level interface between an application program and IMS.

dynamic terminal   A terminal that is created through the Extended Terminal Option (ETO). A dynamic terminal is not defined within the IMS system definition, and no control blocks for the terminal exist at IMS initialization time. Contrast with *static terminal*.

expedited message handler (EMH)   The IMS Fast Path facility that processes single-segment input and output messages. Fast Path messages that use the EMH bypass the normal message queuing and application scheduling and therefore these messages are processed faster than non-Fast Path messages.

extended restart   A restart, initiated by a DL/I call, that reestablishes database positioning and user-specified areas.

field   In an IMS database, a portion (as defined in the DBD) within a segment that is the smallest unit of the data that can be referred to. See also *sequence field*.

field-level sensitivity   A restriction on an application program that allows access to only specific fields instead of all of the fields in a segment.

free space element (FSE)   In a hierarchical direct database, the first 8 bytes of an area that is free space. The FSE describes the area of free space in a CI or block that is 8 or more bytes in length.

free space element anchor point (FSEAP)   In a hierarchical direct database, the first 4 bytes of a CI or block. The first 2byte field contains the offset, in bytes, to the first FSE in the CI or block. The second 2byte field identifies whether this block or CI contains a bit map.

front-end system   An IMS in an MSC network in which all terminals are connected, messages are routed to the proper back-end IMS, and all replies are routed to the terminals. Contrast with *back-end system*.

fuzzy image copy   An image copy of an online database. The database can be updated while the image copy is being taken and some, all, or none of the updates might appear in the image copy. Also called concurrent image copy.

image copy   (1) The process of creating a backup of a DBDS. (2) The backup data set created by the image copy process. See also *fuzzy image copy*.

IMSplex   One or more IMSs that work together as a unit. Typically these IMSs share resources, run in a Parallel Sysplex environment, and include a CSL.

indirect list data set (ILDS)   In a HALDB, an IMS system index data set. The ILDS is a repository for the indirect pointers used for PHDAM and PHIDAM databases. There is one ILDS per partition in PHDAM or PHIDAM databases.

indirect list entry (ILE)   In a HALDB, an entry in an indirect list data set.

indirect list entry key (ILK)   In a HALDB, a unique token that is assigned to a segment in PHDAM and PHIDAM databases when the segment is created. Eight bytes in length and stored in the prefix of the segment, the ILK uniquely identifies every segment in PHDAM and PHIDAM databases.

indirect pointer   In a HALDB, a pointer that is stored in the indirect list data set and that is used to eliminate the need to update pointers throughout other database records when a single partition is reorganized. Indirect pointers are stored in an indirect list data set.

logical database   A set of logical database record occurrences. It is composed of one or more physical databases; it represents hierarchical, structured relationships between data segments that can be different from the physical structure in which the segments were loaded. Contrast with *physical database*.

logical relationship   In a database, a user-defined path between two independent segments.

logical unit   An addressable resource such as an application program, a terminal, or a subsystem. For IMS, a logical unit is usually a terminal that logs onto IMS to do work.

master terminal   The IMS logical terminal that has complete control of IMS resources during online operations.

message   Data that is transmitted between any two terminals, application programs, or IMS systems. Each message has one or more segments.

message class   A class, assigned to a transaction code, that determines within which message region an application program is to process that transaction. See also *region class* and *transaction code*.

message queue   The data structure in which messages are queued before being processed by an application program or sent to a terminal. Local message queues are in IMS control regions and shared message queues are in coupling facility structures. See also *shared queues*.

online change   An IMS function that supports the adding, changing, or deleting of IMS resources such as transactions, database directories, program directories, DMBs, PSBs, and Fast Path routing codes without stopping the system to define them.

online log data set (OLDS)   A data set on direct access storage that contains the log records written by an online IMS system.

online reorganization   Database reorganization, which is available only for HALDBs and DEDBs, during which the database remains available for updates during the reorganization process.

partition   A subset of a HALDB that has the capacity of a non-HALDB database and that can be administered independently.

path call   A type of DL/I call that enables a hierarchical path of segments to be inserted or retrieved with one call.

PCB mask   A mapping in the application program that the application uses to interpret a PCB.

physical database   An ordered set of physical database records. Contrast with *logical database*.

program communication block (PCB)   (1) A component of a PSB that describes the application's view of a database or a message destination. (2) A control block that, during runtime, has status information from IMS about the application's current DL/I call. The application interprets the PCB through its PCB mask.

program isolation   An IMS facility that separates all the activity of an application program from any other active application program until that application program indicates, using a synchronization point, that the data it has modified or created is consistent and complete.

program specification block (PSB)   The control block that describes the databases and logical message destinations that are used by an application program. A PSB consists of one or more PCBs. See also *program communication block (PCB)*.

overflow area   In an HDAM or PHDAM database, the area in which IMS stores data when the root addressable area does not have enough space for a segment. Contrast with *root addressable area*.

qualified SSA   An SSA that contains, in addition to the segment name, one or more qualification statements. A qualified SSA describes the segment type and occurrence that is to be accessed.

RECON data set   A data set in which DBRC stores information about logging activity and events that might affect the recovery of databases.

region class   The class that IMS assigns to a message region that indicates the message classes that can be processed within the region. See also *message class*.

root addressable area   In an HDAM or PHDAM database, the primary storage area in HDAM and PHDAM databases. IMS always attempts to put new and updated segments in the root addressable area, and if there is not enough room, IMS puts the segment into the overflow area instead. Contrast with *overflow area.*

root anchor point (RAP)   In an HDAM database or DEDB, a pointer at the beginning of each block or CI that points to a root segment that belongs in that block and that chains the root segments that randomize to that CI or block.

root segment   The highest segment in the database hierarchy. The database is normally sequenced on the key field of this segment. All other segments depend upon the root segment and reference it as part of their complete identity. Contrast with *dependent segment.*

scratch pad area (SPA)   A work area that is used in conversational message processing to retain information from an application program across executions of the program.

secondary index   An index that is used to establish accessibility to a physical or logical database by a path different from the one provided by the database definition. It contains an index pointer segment type that is defined in a secondary index database.

segment   The unit of access for IMS. For IMS DB, a segment is the smallest amount of data that can be transferred by one IMS operation. For input terminal operations using IMS TM, a segment is defined by the particular terminal type and is obtained by an application program with one call.

segment search argument (SSA)   The portion of a DL/I call that identifies a segment or group of segments to be processed. Each SSA contains a segment name and, optionally, one or more command codes, and one or more qualification statements. Multiple SSAs may be required to identify the desired segment. See also *qualified SSA* and *unqualified SSA.*

sequence field   The field in a database segment that used to store segment occurrences in sequential ascending order. Also called a key field.

shared queue   A collection of data objects with the same name that reside on a coupling facility queue structure. Data objects on a shared queue are available to all CQS clients that have access to the structure. See also *message queue.*

sibling segments   Two or more occurrences of different segment types having a common parent segment occurrence. Contrast with *twin segments*.

single point of control (SPOC)   The control interface that sends commands to one or more members of an IMSplex and receives command responses.

static terminal   A terminal that is created through the IMS system definition process. Contrast with *dynamic terminal*.

symbolic checkpoint   A checkpoint in a batch, BMP, or JBP application that indicates to IMS that the program has reached a commit point and that establishes a place in the program from which the application can be restarted. See also *extended restart*.

synchronization point (sync point)   A point in time from which IMS or an application program can start over if a failure makes recovery necessary. The two types of synchronization points are system checkpoints, which are done by IMS itself, and application program checkpoints, which are done on behalf of individual application programs.

system definition   An IMS process that describes databases, application programs, terminals, and other resources to IMS.

system log data set (SLDS)   The permanent destination data set for IMS log records. The SLDS is usually on tape or MSS. In an IMS batch region, the SLDS is created at execution time. In an IMS online region, the SLDS is created by the Log Archive utility from the OLDS. Contrast with *online log data set (OLDS)* and *write-ahead data set (WADS)*.

tracking IMS   In an RSR environment, an IMS that tracks the activities of active IMSs to provide disaster recovery support. A tracking IMS is usually geographically remote from the active IMSs. contrast with *active IMS*.

transaction   (1) A single conversation iteration, from entering of an input message to receipt of one or more output messages in response. (2) A common way of referring to a transaction code.

transaction code   A 1- to 8-character alphanumeric code that invokes an IMS message processing program.

twin segments   In a database, all child segments of the same segment type that have a particular instance of the same parent segment type. Root segments are also considered twins to each other. Contrast with *sibling segments*.

type-1 command   A command, generally preceded by a leading slash character, that can be entered from any valid IMS command source. Contrast with *type-2 command*.

type-2 command   A command that is entered only through the OM API. Type-2 commands are more flexible and can have a broader scope than type-1 commands. Contrast with *type-1 command*.

unqualified SSA   An SSA that contains only one segment name. Contrast with *qualified SSA*.

write-ahead data set (WADS)   A data set that contains log records that reflect completed operations and are not yet written to an OLDS. Contrast with *online log data set* and *system log data set*.

Acronyms and Abbreviations Used in This Book

ACB application control block

ADS area data set

AGN Application Group Name

AIB application interface block

AO automated operator

AOI automated operator interface

AOP automated operator program

API application programming interface

APPC Advanced Program-to-Program Communication

ARM Automatic Restart Manager

BMP Batch Message Processing

BPE Base Primitive Environment

CA control area or change accumulation

CCTL coordinator controller

CFRM Coupling Facility Resource Manager

CI control interval

CPC central processing complex

CQS Common Queue Server

CRC command recognition character

CSL Common Service Layer

CTC channel-to-channel

DASD direct access storage device

DBCTL Database Control

DBD database description

DBMS database management system

DBRC   Database Recovery Control

DC   data communication

DCB   database control block

DCCTL   Data Communications Control

DDEP   direct dependent

DEDB   Data Entry Database

DIF   device input format

DL/I   Data Language/I

DLISAS   DL/I Separate Address Space

DMB   database management block

DOF   device output format

DRA   database resource adapter

EJB   Enterprise JavaBean

EMH   Expedited Message Handler

EOD   end of data

EOM   end of message

EOS   end of segment

ESAF   External Subsystem Attach Facility

ESCA   extended system control area

ESDS   entry-sequenced data set

ETO   Extended Terminal Option

FDBR   Fast Database Recovery

FSE   free space element

FSEAP   free space element anchor point

GSAM   Generalized Sequential Access Method

HALDB   High Availability Large Database

HDAM   Hierarchical Direct Access Method

HIDAM   Hierarchical Indexed Direct Access Method

HISAM   Hierarchical Indexed Sequential Access Method

HSAM   Hierarchical Sequential Access Method

HSSP   high speed sequential processing

ICS   Information Control System

IFP   IMS Fast Path

ILDS   indirect link data set

ILE   indirect list entry

ILK   indirect list entry key

ILS   isolated log sender

IMS   Information Management System

IOVF   independent overflow

IRLM   internal resource lock manager

ISC   Intersystem Communications

ISPF   Interactive System Productivity Facility

IVP   installation verification program

JBP   Java Batch Processing

JCL   job control language

JMP   Java Message Processing

KBLA   Knowledge-Based Log Analysis

KSDS   key-sequenced data set

LBG   load balancing group

LPAR   logical partition

LTERM   logical terminal

LU   logical unit

MADS   multiple area data set

MFS   Message Format Service

MIF   message input format

MNPS   multinode persistent sessions

MOF   message output format

MPP   message processing program

MPR   Message Processing Region

MSC   Multiple Systems Communication

MSDB   Main Storage Database

MSS   mass storage system

MTO   master terminal operator

NCP   Network Communications Program

ODBA   Open Database Access

OLDS   online log data set

OLR   Online Reorganization

OM   Operations Manager

OSAM   Overflow Sequential Access Method

OTMA   Open Transaction Manager Access

PCB   program communication block

PCF   physical child forward

PDS   partitioned data set

PDS/E   partitioned data set/extended

PHDAM   Partitioned Hierarchical Direct Access Method

PHIDAM   Partitioned Hierarchical Indexed Direct Access Method

PI   program isolation

PSB   program specification block

PTB   physical twin back

PTERM   physical terminal

PTF   physical twin forward

RACF   Resource Access Control Facility

RAP   root anchor point

RAS   resource access security

RBA   relative byte area

RLDS   recovery log data set

RM   Resource Manager

RNR   Rapid Network Reconnect

RRS   Resource Recovery Services

RRSAF   Resource Recovery Services attachment facility

RSR   Remote Site Recovery

RTT   resource translation table

SAF   System Authorization Facility

SAS   separate address space

SB   sequential buffering

SCA   system control area

SCI   Structured Call Interface

SDEP   sequential dependent

SHISAM   Simple Hierarchical Indexed Sequential Access Method

SHSAM   Simple Hierarchical Sequential Access Method

SLDS   system log data set

SMP/E   System Modification Program/ Extended

SNA   Systems Network Architecture

SNPS   single-node persistent session

SPA   scratch pad area

SPOC   single point of control

SRDS   structure recovery data set

SSA   segment search argument

SVC   supervisor call

TCO   time-controlled operations

TCP/IP   Transmission Control Protocol/ Internet Protocol

TM   Transaction Manager

TSO   Time Sharing Option

UCF   Utility Control Facility

UDB   Universal Database

UDF   user-defined function

UOR   unit of recovery

UOW   unit of work

VGR   VTAM Generic Resources

VLF   Virtual Lookaside Facility

VSAM   virtual storage access method

VSO   Virtual Storage Option

VTAM   Virtual Telecommunications Access Method

WADS   write-ahead data set

WFI   wait for input

WLM   Workload Manager

XCF   cross-system coupling facility

XES   cross-system extended services

XML   Extensible Markup Language

XRF   Extended Recovery Facility

Notices

This information was developed for products and services offered in the U.S.A. IBM may not offer the products, services, or features discussed in this document in other countries. Consult your local IBM representative for information on the products and services currently available in your area. Any reference to an IBM product, program, or service is not intended to state or imply that only that IBM product, program, or service may be used. Any functionally equivalent product, program, or service that does not infringe any IBM intellectual property right may be used instead. However, it is the user's responsibility to evaluate and verify the operation of any non-IBM product, program, or service.

IBM may have patents or pending patent applications covering subject matter described in this document. The furnishing of this document does not give you any license to these patents. You can send license inquiries, in writing, to:

IBM Director of Licensing
IBM Corporation
North Castle Drive
Armonk, NY 10504-1785
U.S.A.

For license inquiries regarding double-byte (DBCS) information, contact the IBM Intellectual Property Department in your country or send inquiries, in writing, to:

IBM World Trade Asia Corporation
Licensing
2-31 Roppongi 3-chome, Minato-ku
Tokyo 106, Japan

The following paragraph does not apply to the United Kingdom or any other country where such provisions are inconsistent with local law: INTERNATIONAL BUSINESS MACHINES CORPORATION PROVIDES THIS PUBLICATION "AS IS" WITHOUT WARRANTY OF ANY KIND, EITHER EXPRESS OR IMPLIED, INCLUDING, BUT NOT LIMITED TO, THE IMPLIED WARRANTIES OF NON-INFRINGEMENT, MERCHANT-ABILITY OR FITNESS FOR A PARTICULAR PURPOSE. Some states do not allow disclaimer of express or implied warranties in certain transactions, therefore, this statement may not apply to you.

This information could include technical inaccuracies or typographical errors. Changes are periodically made to the information herein; these changes will be incorporated in new editions of the publication. IBM may make improvements and/or changes in the product(s) and/or the program(s) described in this publication at any time without notice.

Any references in this information to non-IBM Web sites are provided for convenience only and do not in any manner serve as an endorsement of those Web sites. The materials at those Web sites are not part of the materials for this IBM product and use of those Web sites is at your own risk.

IBM may use or distribute any of the information you supply in any way it believes appropriate without incurring any obligation to you.

Licensees of this program who wish to have information about it for the purpose of enabling: (i) the exchange of information between independently created programs and other programs (including this one) and (ii) the mutual use of the information which has been exchanged, should contact:

> IBM Corporation
> J46A/G4
> 555 Bailey Avenue
> San Jose, CA 95141-1003
> U.S.A.

Such information may be available, subject to appropriate terms and conditions, including in some cases, payment of a fee.

The licensed program described in this information and all licensed material available for it are provided by IBM under terms of the IBM Customer Agreement, IBM International Program License Agreement, or any equivalent agreement between us.

Any performance data contained herein was determined in a controlled environment. Therefore, the results obtained in other operating environments may vary significantly. Some measurements may have been made on development-level systems and there is no guarantee that these measurements will be the same on generally available systems. Furthermore, some measurement may have been estimated through extrapolation. Actual results may vary. Users of this document should verify the applicable data for their specific environment.

Information concerning non-IBM products was obtained from the suppliers of those products, their published announcements or other publicly available sources. IBM has not tested those products and cannot confirm the accuracy of performance, compatibility or any other claims related to non-IBM products. Questions on the capabilities of non-IBM products should be addressed to the suppliers of those products.

All statements regarding IBM's future direction or intent are subject to change or withdrawal without notice, and represent goals and objectives only.

This information is for planning purposes only. The information herein is subject to change before the products described become available.

This information contains examples of data and reports used in daily business operations. To illustrate them as completely as possible, the examples include the names of individuals, companies, brands, and products. All of these names are fictitious and any similarity to the names and addresses used by an actual business enterprise is entirely coincidental.

COPYRIGHT LICENSE:

This information contains sample application programs in source language, which illustrates programming techniques on various operating platforms. You may copy, modify, and distribute these sample programs in any form without payment to IBM, for the purposes of developing, using, marketing or distributing application programs conforming to the application programming interface for the operating platform for which the sample programs are written. These examples have not been thoroughly tested under all conditions. IBM, therefore, cannot guarantee or imply reliability, serviceability, or function of these programs. You may copy, modify, and distribute these sample programs in any form without payment to IBM for the purposes of developing, using, marketing, or distributing application programs conforming to IBM's application programming interfaces.

Each copy or any portion of these sample programs or any derivative work, must include a copyright notice as follows:

© (your company name) (year). Portions of this code are derived from IBM Corp. Sample Programs. © Copyright IBM Corp. _enter the year or years_. All rights reserved.

TRADEMARKS

The following terms are trademarks of the IBM Corporation in the United States or other countries or both:

AIX	OS/2
CICS	OS/390
DataPropagator	Parallel Sysplex
DB2	RACF
DB2 Universal Database	S/390
DFSMSdfp	SAA
DFSMSdss	SecureWay
DFSMS	System/360
DFSORT	Tivoli Netview
IBM	VisualAge
IMS	VSE/ESA
IMS/ESA	VTAM
iSeries	WebSphere
GDDM	WebSphere MQ
Language Environment	z/OS
MVS	zSeries

Java and all Java-based trademarks and logos are trademarks of Sun Microsystems, Inc., in the United States, other countries, or both.

Other company, product, and service names may be the trademarks or service marks of others.

PRODUCT NAMES

In this book, the licensed program "DB2 Universal Database for z/OS" is referred to as "DB2."

Bibliography

This bibliography lists all of the references quoted in this book, including the IMS Version 9 library. For a list of links to the z/OS documentation, the IBM Redbooks, or the IMS library, go to www.ibm.com/ims and click on the "Library" link in the navigation pane on the left side of the page.

- *DB2 UDB for z/OS Application Programming and SQL Guide*, SC18-7415
- *DB2 UDB for z/OS Installation Guide*, GC18-7418
- *DFSMS/MVS V1R5 DFSMSdss Storage Administration Guide*, SC26-4930
- *DFSMS/MVS V1R5 DFSMSdss Storage Administration Reference*, SC26-4929
- *Enterprise COBOL for z/OS and OS/390: Programming Guide*, SC27-1412
- *IBM IMS Workload Router for z/OS User's Guide*, SC26-8945
- *Blackman, Kenneth. 1998. "Technical Note — IMS celebrates thirty years as an IBM product" in IBM Systems Journal, Volume 37, Number 4*, G321-5693
- *IMS Fast Path Solutions Guide*, SG24-4301
- *IMS in the Parallel Sysplex: Volume I: Reviewing the IMSplex Technology*, SG24-6908
- *IMS in the Parallel Sysplex: Volume II: Planning the IMSplex*, SG24-6928
- *IMS in the Parallel Sysplex: Volume III: IMSplex Implementation and Operations*, SG24-6929
- *IMS Connect Guide and Reference*, SC18-7260
- *IMS Fast Path Solutions Guide*, SG24-4301
- *IMS Version 7 Performance Monitoring and Tuning Update*, SG24-6404
- *IMS Queue Control Facility for z/OS*, SC26-9685
- *IMS V6 Security Guide*, SG24-5363
- *IMS Version 7 Release Planning Guide*, GC26-9437

- *IMS Version 8 Release Planning Guide*, GC27-1305
- *SMP/E V3R2.0 for z/OS and OS/390 User's Guide*, SA22-7773
- *The Complete IMS HALDB Guide All You Need to Know to Manage HALDBs*, SG24-6945
- *z/OS V1R4.0 MVS Diagnosis: Tools and Service Aids*, GA22-7589
- *z/OS MVS Programming: Writing Transaction Programs for APPC/MVS*, SA227621
- *z/OS MVS Setting Up a Sysplex*, SA22-7625
- *z/OS MVS System Commands*, SA22-7627
- *z/OS V1R4.0 z/OS Communications Server SNA Network Implementation Guide*, SC31-8777
- *z/OS V1R4 Security Server RACF Security Administrator's Guide*, SA22-7683

IMS VERSION 9 LIBRARY

Title	Acronym	Order number
IMS Version 9: Administration Guide: Database Manager	ADB	SC18-7806
IMS Version 9: Administration Guide: System	AS	SC18-7807
IMS Version 9: Administration Guide: Transaction Manager	ATM	SC18-7808
IMS Version 9: Application Programming: Database Manager	APDB	SC18-7809
IMS Version 9: Application Programming: Design Guide	APDG	SC18-7810
IMS Version 9: Application Programming: EXEC DLI Commands for CICS and IMS	APCICS	SC18-7811
IMS Version 9: Application Programming: Transaction Manager	APTM	SC18-7812
IMS Version 9: Base Primitive Environment Guide and Reference	BPE	SC18-7813
IMS Version 9: Command Reference	CR	SC18-7814
IMS Version 9: Common Queue Server Guide and Reference	CQS	SC18-7815
IMS Version 9: Common Service Layer Guide and Reference	CSL	SC18-7816
IMS Version 9: Customization Guide	CG	SC18-7817
IMS Version 9: Database Recovery Control (DBRC) Guide and Reference	DBRC	SC18-7818
IMS Version 9: Diagnosis Guide and Reference	DGR	LY37-3203
IMS Version 9: Failure Analysis Structure Tables (FAST) for Dump Analysis	FAST	LY37-3204
IMS Version 9: IMS Connect Guide and Reference	CT	SC18-9287
IMS Version 9: IMS Java Guide and Reference	JGR	SC18-7821

Title	Acronym	Order number
IMS Version 9: Installation Volume 1: Installation Verification	IIV	GC18-7822
IMS Version 9: Installation Volume 2: System Definition and Tailoring	ISDT	GC18-7823
IMS Version 9: Master Index and Glossary	MIG	SC18-7826
IMS Version 9: Messages and Codes, Volume 1	MC1	GC18-7827
IMS Version 9: Messages and Codes, Volume 2	MC2	GC18-7828
IMS Version 9: Open Transaction Manager Access Guide and Reference	OTMA	SC18-7829
IMS Version 9: Operations Guide	OG	SC18-7830
IMS Version 9: Release Planning Guide	RPG	GC17-7831
IMS Version 9: Summary of Operator Commands	SOC	SC18-7832
IMS Version 9: Utilities Reference: Database and Transaction Manager	URDBTM	SC18-7833
IMS Version 9: Utilities Reference: System	URS	SC18-7834

SUPPLEMENTARY PUBLICATIONS

Title	Order number
IMS Connector for Java 2.2.2 and 9.1.0.1 Online Documentation for WebSphere Studio Application Developer Integration Edition 5.1.1	SC09-7869
IMS Version 9 Fact Sheet	GC18-7697
IMS Version 9: Licensed Program Specifications	GC18-7825

PUBLICATION COLLECTIONS

Title	Format	Order number
IMS Version 9 Softcopy Library	CD	LK3T-7213
IMS Favorites	CD	LK3T-7144
Licensed Bill of Forms (LBOF): IMS Version 9 Hardcopy and Softcopy Library	Hardcopy and CD	LBOF-7789
Unlicensed Bill of Forms (SBOF): IMS Version 9 Unlicensed Hardcopy Library	Hardcopy	SBOF-7790
OS/390 Collection	CD	SK2T-6700
z/OS Software Products Collection	CD	SK3T-4270
z/OS and Software Products DVD Collection	DVD	SK3T-4271

INDEX

M

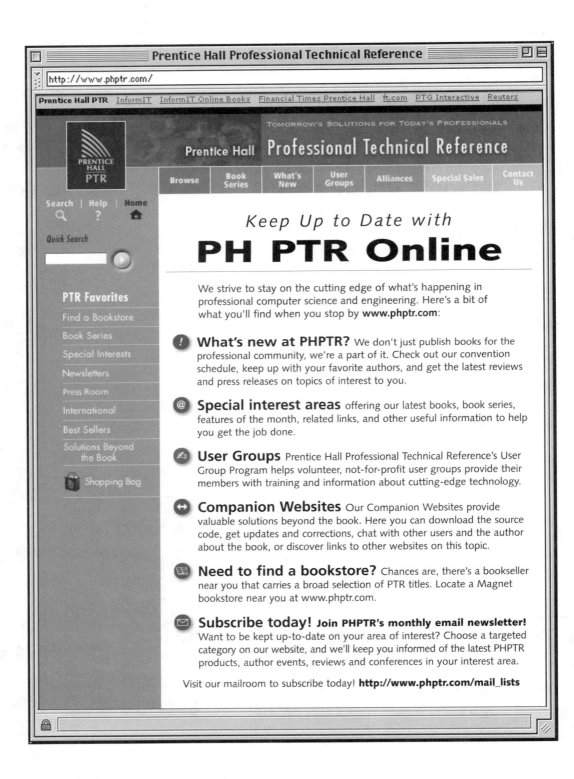